The Most Costly Journey
El Viaje Más Caro

THE MOST COSTLY

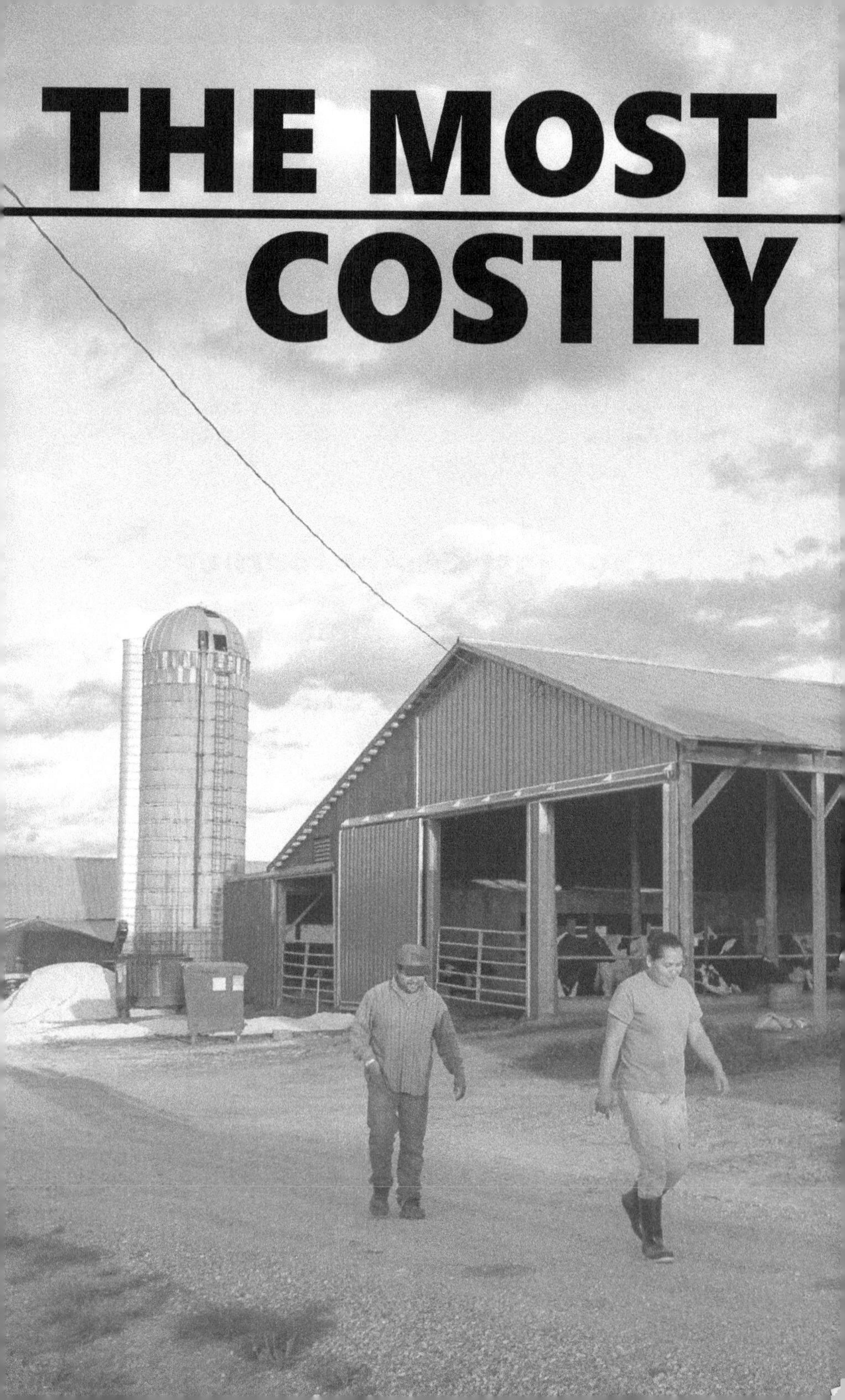

El Viaje Más Caro

JOURNEY

Stories of Migrant Farmworkers in Vermont, Drawn by New England Cartoonists

Edited by
Marek Bennett
Julia Grand Doucet
Teresa Mares
Andy Kolovos

Open Door Clinic
Vermont Folklife Center
UVM Extension Bridges to Health
UVM Anthropology
Marek Bennett's Comics Workshop

The Most Costly Journey: Stories of Migrant Farmworkers in Vermont,
Drawn by New England Cartoonists
Edited by
Marek Bennett, Julia Grand Doucet, Teresa Mares, Andy Kolovos
© 2021 by *El Viaje Más Caro*
English Language Edition
ISBN: 978-0-916718-00-8
LCCN: 2021932606

All stories © the respective storytellers: Ana, Ana Teresa, Bob,
Carlos, Carlos, la familia Cruz, Daniel, Delmar, Gregorio, Guadalupe, El
migrante de Hidalgo, Jesús, José, Juana, Lara, Olivia, Paco, Pablo,
Piero, Ponciano, Saul, Rubén

All artwork © the respective artists: Marek Bennett, Angela Boyle,
John Carvajal, Glynnis Fawkes, Iona Fox, Greg Giordano, Kane Lynch,
Kevin Kite, Shashwat Mishra, Michelle Sayles, Michael Tonn, Ezra
Veitch, Rick Veitch, Tillie Walden, Teppi Zuppo

All text © the respective authors: Julia Alvarez, Stephen R. Bissette,
Julia Grand Doucet, Andy Kolovos, Teresa Mares

These stories first appeared as mini-comics published by the *El Viaje*
Más Caro project at Open Door Clinic, Middlebury, VT (2015-2018).

Title spread photo © Caleb Kenna
www.CalebKenna.com

Book design & production by
Marek Bennett's COMICS WORKSHOP
www.MarekBennett.com

CONTENTS:

FOREWORD by Julia Alvarez .... *v*
PREFACE by Julia Grand Doucet ....*ix*
INTRODUCTION by Stephen R. Bissette ..... *xv*

A New Kind of Work 1
The Story of Delmar
Art by Tillie Walden

Painful to Remember 11
The Story of José
Art by Marek Bennett

It's Worth it 21
Gregorio's Story
Art by Kevin Kite

**The Most Important Love of
Every Woman Should Be Herself** 31
The Story of Guadalupe
Art by Iona Fox

Far From My Family 41
The Story of Carlos
Art by Kane Lynch

Suffering to Come Here 51
The Story of Rubén
Art by Teppi Zuppo

ii

Algo Adentro / Something Inside **61**
The Story of the Migrant of Hidalgo
Art by Marek Bennett

In Your Hands **85**
The Story of Jesús
Art by John Carvajal

You Will Be Accepted **95**
The Story of Daniel
Art by Teppi Zuppo

A Heart Split in Two **105**
The Story of Juana
Art by Michael Tonn

The Best Thing **113**
The Story of the Cruz Family
Art by Angela Boyle

**One Suffers to Provide
for the Family** **121**
Pablo's Story
Art by Rick Veitch (A Eureka Comics Production)

It Wasn't Our Plan **129**
The Story of Ana
Art by Glynnis Fawkes

Now That I Have My License 137
Reflections on Driving
Art by Marek Bennett

**The Two of Us Together
(Mexican American)** 151
The Story of Felix & Alejandro
Art by Greg Giordano

Language Is Power 161
The Story of Carlos & Bob
Art by Ezra Veitch

How Do You Explain This? 169
The Story of Ana Teresa
Art by Shashwat Mishra

School of Life 181
The Story of Ponciano
Art by Michelle Sayles

What I've Planted Here 191
The Story of Lara
Art by Tillie Walden

AFTERWORD 201
by Teresa Mares & Andy Kolovos

CREDITS 221

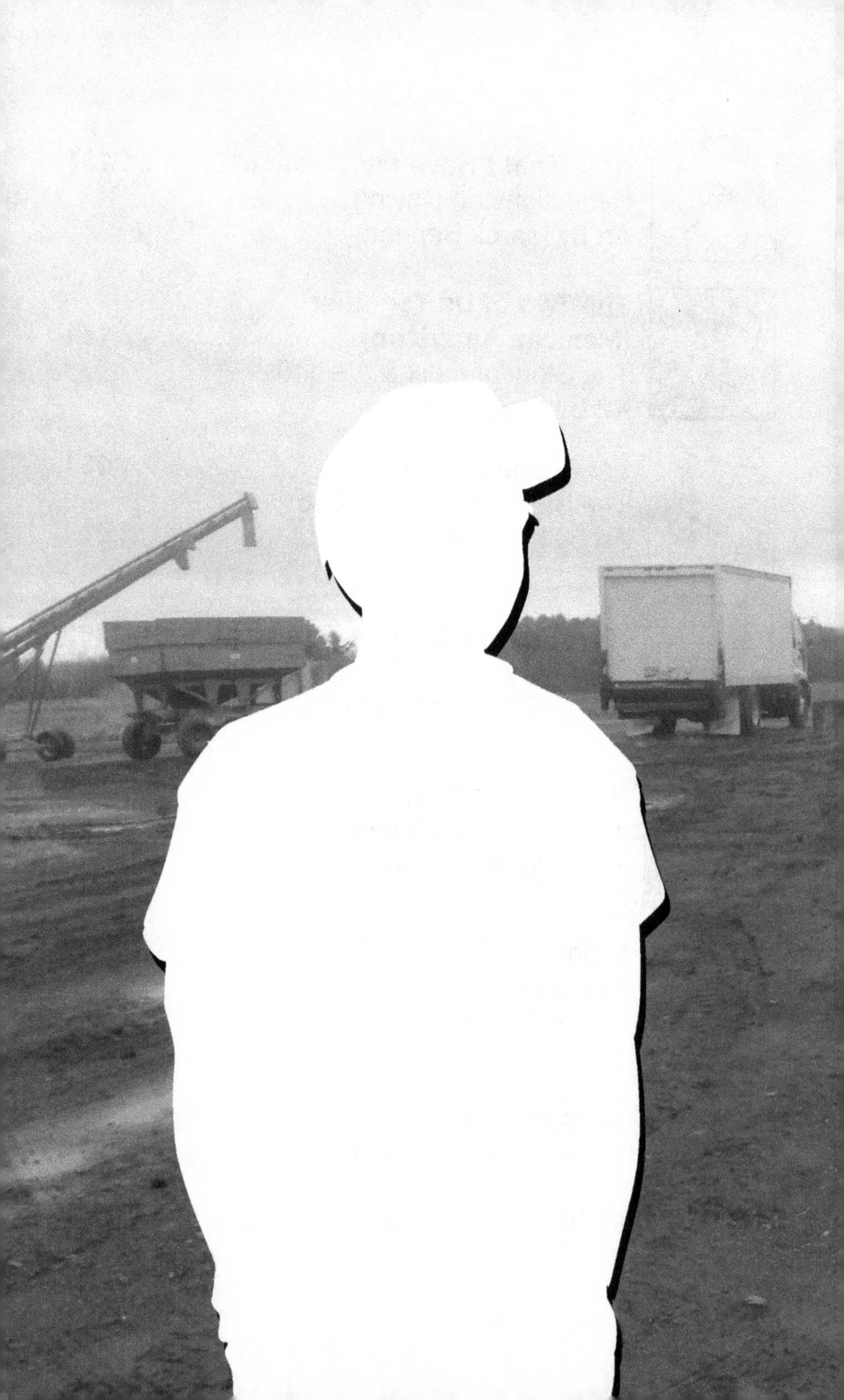

FOREWORD

by Julia Alvarez

The journey of those forced to leave a homeland is always a costly one. They leave behind not just a place but a family, a culture, a native language, traditions that help each generation navigate its way from past to future. The toll is so huge that it's a wonder anyone would undertake such a journey. But necessity seldom allows the migrant the privilege of choice. There is only one option: survival for oneself and the loved ones left behind.

Those lucky enough not to have to undertake such journeys have a responsibility towards these new arrivals. As our master storyteller Toni Morrison reminds us, "The function of freedom is to free someone else." There are many ways to welcome and help. We can support programs that provide social services, such as the Open Door Clinic, Bridges to Health, Migrant Justice, among others. We can volunteer our time and resources. We can advocate for reforms that humanize our immigration laws, elect candidates who uphold the foundational tenets of this nation, remembering that, even if not within individual memory, our predecessors in this nation of immigrants once made that costly journey, too.

But this extension of a helping hand, while effective and necessary, can feel disempowering, a confirmation of the status of needy outsider. Deep within the migrant community exists its own powerful resource: storytelling. A story can cross any boundary, including that often most heavily-guarded boundary, between self and other, us and them. It is portable, easy to carry across deserts and oceans, languages, cultures. To tap this resource means that the most healing and lasting balm is coming from the community itself, an empowering and self-affirming circle. This is something no aid or advocacy program or person can provide: a way of making meaning, of connecting to each other. Those who have felt isolated, unseen, and discounted suddenly find fellow travelers and guides to help navigate the dangers – and also the joys – that lie ahead.

Reading the stories collected in *El Viaje Más Caro/The Most Costly Journey*, we cannot help but marvel at the perils and challenges these fellow Americans (who share the hemisphere and name with us) have endured to come here to help us with the work that otherwise would not get done. Who else would milk our cows, grow our food, process it, cook and serve it? Who would feed and bathe our viejitos in nursing homes and hospitals, look after our niñitos in day care centers and preschools? Who would clean and build our houses, mow our lawns, and within a generation or two, with access to education, serve as our doctors, nurses, teachers, CEOs, senators and representatives? This is how America renews itself. Courage, endurance, resilience, compassion flow from these stories into our hearts.

What is especially gratifying about these stories is their collaborative nature. New England cartoonists have teamed up with storytellers from the migrant community, U.S. citizens joining together with new arrivals. This is what America looks like and sounds like when we work together.

The first Americans were themselves travelers and migrants. In *Songlines*, Bruce Chatwin tells of the original tribes on the northwest coast who lived half on the islands and half on the mainland. . . . They would travel over the sea and navigate their canoes up the current from California to the Bering Strait, which they called Klin Otto. The navigators were priestesses. The words of this old woman represent a tradition about 15,000 years old.

*Everythin' we ever knew about the movement of the sea
was preserved in the verses of a song. For thousands of
years, we went where we wanted and came home safe,
because of the song. On clear nights we had the stars to
guide us, and in the fog, we had the streams and the
creeks of the sea, the streams and creeks that flow into
and become Klin Otto.*

*There was a song for goin' to China and a song for
goin' to Japan, a song for the big island and a song for
the smaller one. All she had to know was the song and
she knew where she was. To get back, she just sang the
song in reverse.*

Fifteen-thousand years later, this ancient wisdom still holds true: we need our stories to ensure our survival, not just as a nation, but as a species. We need narratives to help us navigate our way home to the circle of our shared humanity.

That is the costly and critical journey we are all embarked on.

– Julia Alvarez
2020

Julia Alvarez is a storyteller whose family made the costly journey to Nueva York in 1960. She went on to attend college and graduate school, becoming a teacher and author of many books, including the novels, *Return to Sender* and *How the García Girls Lost Their Accents*, and the national bestseller, *Afterlife*. In 2013 President Obama awarded her the National Medal of Arts, acknowledging that our storytellers are national heroes whose contributions are vital to the health and happiness of this country.

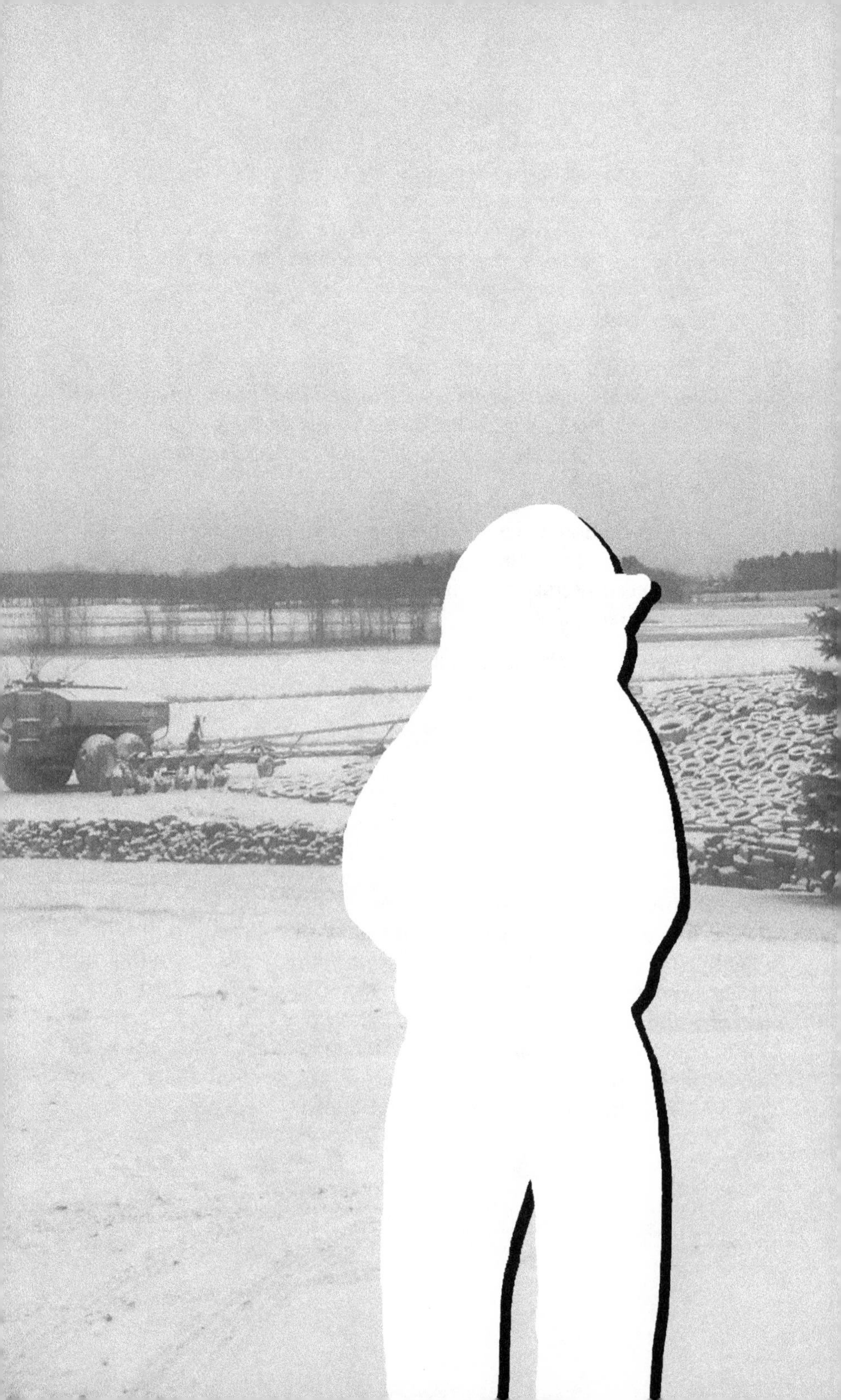

PREFACE

by Julia Grand Doucet

"La vida no es la que uno vivió, sino la que uno recuerda, y cómo la recuerda para contarla."

"Life isn't what one has lived, but what one remembers, and how one remembers it in order to retell it."

-Gabriel Garcia Marquez

I first met José Luis in 2017 when he came for an appointment at the Open Door Clinic in Middlebury, Vermont. As a free health clinic that serves uninsured adults, it is not uncommon to have Spanish speaking immigrant farmworkers as patients. In fact, half of all the patients we see are Latinx agricultural workers who come from the southern states of Mexico or northern Central America to work in local dairies.

Before he came to Vermont, José Luis had never left his small village in the mountains in Chiapas, Mexico. As time went on he found it increasingly difficult to feed his four children and pay for their books and uniforms at school. He began to consider his options. His cousin had recently left Mexico and found work on a dairy farm in Vermont, sending home money that allowed his family to build a house, acquire additional land to expand their coffee farm, and purchase a truck to transport their crops to market. José Luis thought about all the opportunities his family could have if he joined his cousin. He decided the time might be right to migrate to the United States.

The initial decision to come to the United States is often no decision at all, but rather a necessity forced upon able-bodied men trying to survive where there are very few opportunities to do so. The southern states of Mexico from which these men come are generally rural and impoverished. Faced with limited economic mobility or opportunities, many boys abandon education after primary school to work on subsistence plots of land with their fathers, uncles, and cousins. School both costs money and leads to loss of income due to fewer bodies working in the fields. The lure of stable employment and good wages in the US is tempting, despite the tremendous risk involved in the journey.

By the time José Luis reached our clinic, he had a host of physical complaints including many months of nonspecific abdominal pain, stomach cramping, and occasional bloating. His head hurt. His bones hurt. He was tired but unable to sleep. He had little appetite and had lost weight. After many appointments, diagnostic imaging and lab tests, everything came back normal. We could find no medical explanation for his symptoms.

José Luis was not alone. He was one of many of our farmworker patients who presented with physical symptoms that could not be diagnosed as somatic illnesses or injuries. There was Jesús who had left arm numbness radiating to his fingers. His left leg had "hormigueo" a tingling/burning sensation. He had diminished sensation and weakness in all his limbs and extremities. Pedro had debilitating headaches that would strike with no apparent warning or reason. Estefan experienced periodic hot flashes, sweats, and heart palpitations. Sometimes his chest and back clenched up and he could not breathe. Each of these patients went through countless tests and months of appointments with medical providers and specialists. Ultimately, not one of them was diagnosed with a medical disorder. We were left to conclude that their physical symptoms were manifestations of chronic stress and anxiety. They all suffered from psychosomatic illnesses stemming from their separation from family, patria, language, and culture. Stripped of all things familiar and comforting, and thrust into the cold, dark, rural countryside of Vermont, they were overwhelmed with a suffering they could not name or confront.

As a registered nurse working directly with these men, I was at a loss as to how to help. Mental health clinicians in our state are overburdened and have long wait lists. They are generally not bilingual or bicultural, and care is expensive. For these patients who are most often from rural, impoverished areas in southern Mexico, mental health counseling is not culturally familiar or recognized. The care they might seek at home, the treatment from curanderos (traditional healers) and priests, herbalists or hueseros (bone setters), is not available here.

I reached out to Ximena Mejia, Counseling Director at Middlebury College. She was born in Ecuador and completed her doctorate in Florida where she worked with Mexican agricultural workers. She also worked as the director of the Cross Cultural Center at Stetson University and had expertise in immigrant mental health. Ximena provided clinc staff with insight into working with the Latino farmworker population and shared a "fotonovela" project around domestic abuse that she had been involved in. At the end of our initial meeting she commented, "There is a lot of power in sharing one's story". That struck me. Could simply bearing witness to someone's truth and experience be the key that allowed us as clinicians to help? Would sharing and hearing other workers' stories help our patients feel less alone?

Thirty-eight percent of the Latin American migrant workers in Vermont have less than an eighth-grade level of education, and even those with more education are often uncomfortable reading blocks of text. Almost ten percent of the population are indigenous language speakers whose second language is Spanish. How could we collect stories from everyone who needed support? How might we share them with others? The challenges were daunting.

Later that week I serendipitously heard a piece on our local public radio station about the Center for Cartoon Studies (CCS), a school dedicated to teaching cartooning located right here in Vermont; I had no idea such a place existed, especially in such close proximity. The reporter spoke about the projects CCS students did and their involvement in the community. I realized that using graphic art to illustrate the workers' words was a perfect solution.

Comics are a culturally familiar medium in Mexico that historically has been used to communicate information to low-literacy people, and to address everything from entertainment to politics. I reached out to CCS in search of an artist interested in taking on the project. Among the many responses, the work of Tillie Walden stuck out. Her ability to evoke emotion was evident in the samples of work she sent.

We started with one story collected by Teresa Mares from the UVM Department of Anthropology that Tillie adapted into a comic. It was a simple tale of leaving home and finding new work, but the themes of isolation, cultural differences, and employment in a new country, were powerful.

Working with Teresa, my colleague Naomi Wolcott-MacCausland of UVM Extension's Bridges to Health program, and bilingual interns from UVM and Middlebury College, we began to collect stories from workers across the state. We sought out stories that encompassed the common themes we saw reflected in the population: traumatic journeys, family separation, community alienation, and as importantly, the positive and negative coping skills used to navigate these challenges. With each telling of each story, we noticed a change in the storyteller. A sense of relief and of letting go accompanied their revelations. For some, it was the first time that they had given words to their experiences.

Maya Angelou once said, "There is no greater agony than bearing an untold story inside of you." This project provided an outlet for workers to begin processing their experience, understand their emotions, and ultimately to gain acceptance. Being able to bear witness to someone's story is both a humbling and deeply touching experience. It is incredibly powerful to accompany someone on their path to catharsis and healing.

Now, more than ever, it is vitally important that we challenge ourselves to understand others who are different from us, that we listen to their experiences, and begin to build compassion both locally and globally. In an era of hatred, anger, and dehumanization towards the "other," taking a moment to truly hear someone's story can open doors toward greater unity and acceptance. The more one can understand another's struggles, the easier it is to resist the hurtful rhetoric flung by those in power towards immigrants. These stories are individual voices about individual experiences but they speak to the broader experience of what it means to be an immigrant, feel like an outsider, and overcome adversity.

With the rise of neo-nationalism worldwide, countries continue to turn inward and withdraw from international engagement, even as war, violence and political instability drive millions to seek safety and refuge outside their own borders. In our own country, the voices of Brown, Black, Indigenous and white people rise in anger at the white supremacy and injustice underlying our society. We must pause and consider who we are as a country, who we want to be, and the values we wish to reflect. We must make choices daily to work towards and manifest that vision together. Let us listen to the rich diversity of voices, be heard in all we have to say, and incorporate everyone in our national conversation.

– Julia Grand Doucet
2021

Julia Grand Doucet (RN) is the outreach nurse at the Open Door Clinic, and a founding member of the *El Viaje* project.

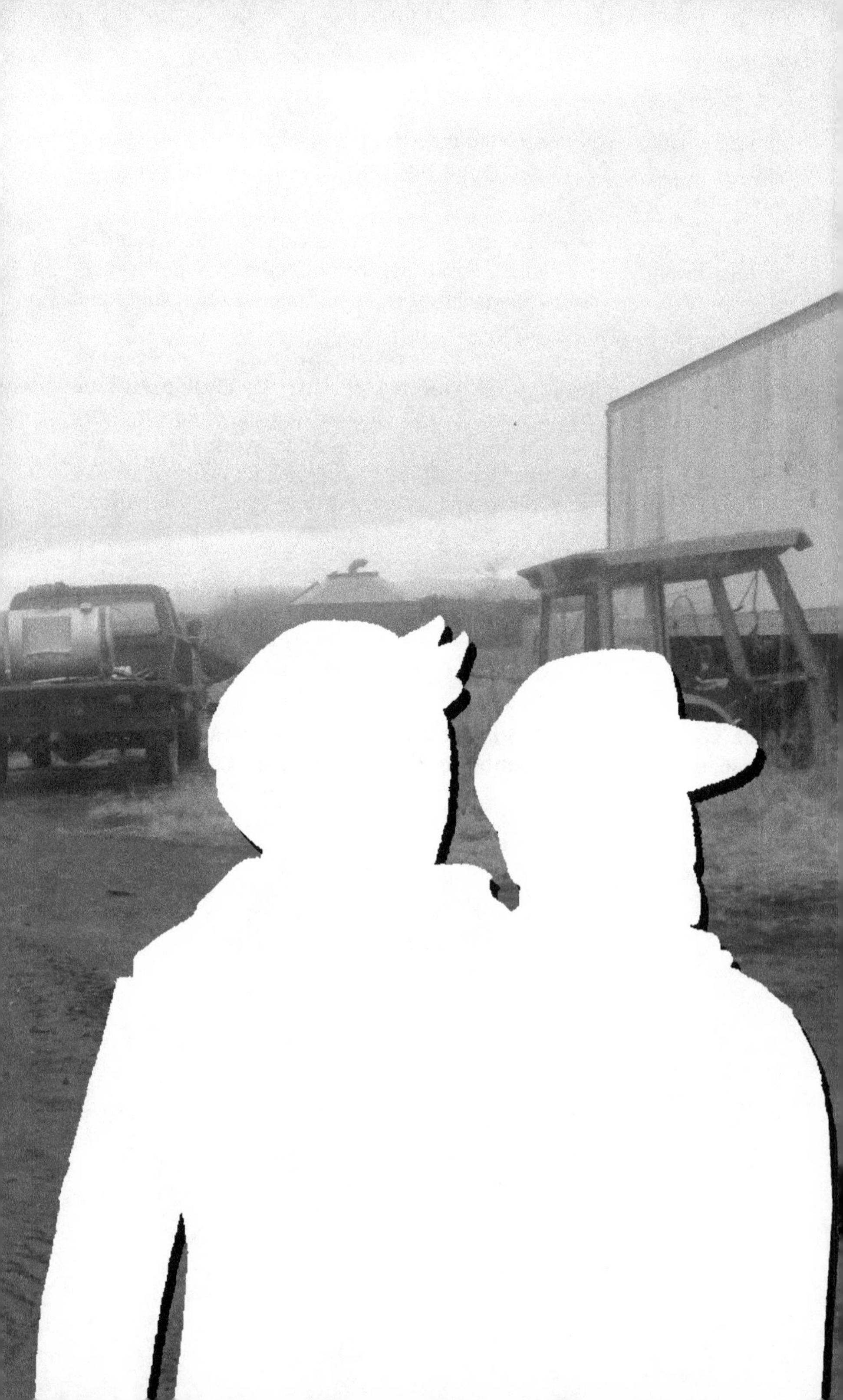

INTRODUCTION:
Intimate Spaces

Telling Tales in Little Boxes,
From *Algo Adentro* to *The Two of Us Together*

Stephen R. Bissette

You hold in your hands a unique book, a compilation of personal accounts of the lives and times of 21st century migrant workers working (or trying to work) here in America.

This is a singular anthology and undertaking in a number of ways.

On the one hand, this anthology offers first-person accounts of the trials and tribulations of migrant and immigrant workers. These provide snapshots—panels are windows, into their lives—of these workers and their families, their hopes, dreams, and real-world experiences.

On the other hand, this anthology strives to make the invisible visible—but visible on *their own terms*. Visible in ways they wish to be visible, though they've learned by hard experience that being visible at all is in and of itself a risk, and the dangers of being visible are all too immediate and real.

In our own shared day-to-day lives, workers such as these remain perversely invisible, even as the political theater of our times seems to force them time and time again into the spotlight. These individuals are the invisible rendered all-too-visible, against their wishes: they are the migrants and immigrants we are told are a threat to our nation, ourselves, our livelihoods and our loved ones. And yet they are everywhere, working in farms and fields, nurturing and harvesting our food, cleaning rooms homes, public venues, restaurants, businesses, local inns and hotels. They are everywhere, and nowhere, working harder than most Americans ever do or ever will or ever would, and yet, we rarely or never *see* their lives. We surely rarely, if ever, *hear* their stories.

Day in, day out, vocal politicians and pundits treat these individuals only as an abstraction to be used, abused, misnamed, mislabeled, misrepresented, tagged, vilified, demonized, rendered "Other" instead of recognized as fellow human beings—while never allowing them to actually be seen at all.

And so, these panels, these pages are presented here for you, so that—aided by cartoonists who put their stories down in narrative illustrated form, as comics—you *can* see them, for a few pages. You can *hear* them, via these accounts of their own lives and times. Thus, *Algo Adentro*—something inside—can be externalized in a form that you can experience, read, steep yourself in.

To tell the stories of these individuals, yes, it was necessary to collaboratively work with cartoonists to bring them to these pages.

Some may have issues with this, in this age of concern over cultural appropriation, cultural authenticity, and above all the legitimacy and permissions of who has the right to tell, or participate in the telling of, stories that are not one's own heritage or experience.

The fact of the matter is there are utterly pragmatic reasons for the collaborative format: those storytellers who cannot draw *ipso facto* cannot draw their own comics stories. As underground comix master Harvey Pekar once said about the artists who drew his stories, "They make them look more like what I want them to look like, the way I would picture them if I could draw."

Seeking to bridge that gap, this present-day partnership of *El Viaje Más Caro—The Most Costly Journey* builds upon the same creative collaborative spirit Pekar initiated and nurtured in the 1970s and 80s. In the words of the project partners, this "collaboration between migrant storytellers and New England cartoonists" aims to unite those who lived these stories with those who have the 'chops' to draw these stories, to illustrate and hopefully amplify the experiences-lived into experiences-shared. In a span of almost twenty self-standing mini-comics published between December 2016 to December 2017, a procession of migrant storytellers tell some of their stories, but just "some."

There is always much, much more untold, but the telling must begin somewhere, sometime, and this is where Delmar, the Cruz Family, Juana, Pablo, José, Ponciano, Rubén, Lara, Jesús, Gregorio, Ana, Carlos, Bob, Daniel, Ana, Alejandro, Felix, and others have chosen to share some of their stories.

The project partners include the Open Door Clinic, the Vermont Folklife Center, Marek Bennett's Comics Workshop, and the University of Vermont Extension and UVM Department of Anthropology. Under the umbrella of their sponsorship, it's taken the work of many to bring these stories to the page, and while I could go on and on about each of those involved, simply citing them by name is all that our space herein presently allows.

The active hands-on—as in inky hands, at the drawing board—partners embody another kind of diversity, a diversity of ages and experience bringing vibrant pen, brush, and ink life to the stories featured here. Some of the artists did their work digitally, some worked traditionally (i.e., real pencils on real paper rendered with real ink, real pen, real brushes, etc.). All took a break from telling their own stories (fiction and non-fiction) in order to lend their time and talents to the telling of *these* stories.

Of the artists, Rick Veitch (illuminating Pablo's story, "One Suffers to Provide for the Family," December 2016), Marek Bennett ("Algo Adentro/Something Inside," "Painful to Remember," "Now That I Have My License"), and Glynnis Fawkes ("It Wasn't Our Plan") are the most experienced of the creative partners who dove into the fray, with Rick Veitch's career in fact dating back to the 1960s and '70s underground comix movement Harvey Pekar emerged from (all of this being a very polite way to say "these are the eldest and wisest of the artistic contributors"). Rick's oldest son Ezra Veitch is among the younger artists contributing to this effort (with "Language is Power"), joined by the likes of Angela Boyle ("The Best Thing"), Michael Tonn ("A Heart Split in Two"), Iona Fox ("The Most Important Love of Every Woman Should Be Herself"), Michelle Sayles ("The School of Life"), Teppi Zuppo ("Suffering to Come Here," "You Will Be Accepted"), John Carvajal ("In Your Hands"), Kevin Kite ("It's Worth It"), Shashwat Mishra ("How Do You Explain This?"), Kane Lynch ("Far From My Family"), Greg Giordano ("The Two of Us Together), and the already-prolific graphic novelist Tillie Walden ("A New Kind of Work," "What I've Planted Here"). Actually, Ezra and Greg are among the *oldest* of the younger artists, it must be said, but *everyone* brought their best work to their respective tables, which is self-evident in the work itself.

I hasten to add that none of these talented artists worked alone. A small army of diligent partners also laid the groundwork (collecting the stories, recording, translating, etc.) for the cartoonists, and saw to the production and polish necessary for final presentation (i.e., proofreading, book design, etc.). Some of the artists named above lent their time and talents to this part of the labor, too (Marek Bennett prominent among them). Among those who did the foundational and followup tasks were Teresa Mares, Julia Grand Doucet, Susan Stone, Juan Meza, Ammy Martinez, Sara Stowell, Roberto Veguez, Ainaka Luna, Estafania Puerta, Chris Kokubo, Cooper Couch, Diego Galan Donlo, Naomi Wolcott-MacCausland, Alissa Gamberg, Magnolia O., Jessie Mazar, Marito Canedo, Nathan Shepard, Marie Vasitis, Josh Lanney, Luis Q. P., Raul Terrones, C. Alice Rodriguez, Dana Bronstein, Olivia Raggio, William Woodcock, Jr., Sebastian Castro, and others. Some chose to work uncredited, or as part of their ongoing efforts with the sponsoring project partners (I know, for instance, that Andy Kolovos, Michelle Ollie, and James Sturm are among that number).

Finally, it must be noted that the stories shared in these pages predate much of the recent under-reported oppressive activities of government agencies making the lives of migrant and immigrant workers and families even more difficult. It's sad to note that the stories herein are already artifacts of a different time and place in American history; without a doubt, this compilation cannot be in any way truly representative, much less definitive, especially given the radical changes to government policies since January 2017.

There will always be more stories to tell—stories that *must* be told. And there will always be, come what may, storytellers brave enough to tell them.

Turn the page, and let the storytellers begin...

– Stephen R. Bissette
Mountains of Madness, VT, 2021

Stephen R. Bissette, a pioneer graduate of the Joe Kubert School, was an instructor at the Center for Cartoon Studies from 2005-2020. He is renowned for his work on *Swamp Thing*, *Taboo* (launching *From Hell* and *Lost Girls*), '1963,' *S.R. Bissette's Tyrant*®, co-creating John Constantine, and creating the world's second '24-Hour Comic' (invented by Scott McCloud for Bissette).

*Dedicado
a los narradores
y narradoras,
y a sus familias...*

**Dedicated
to the storytellers,
and to their families...**

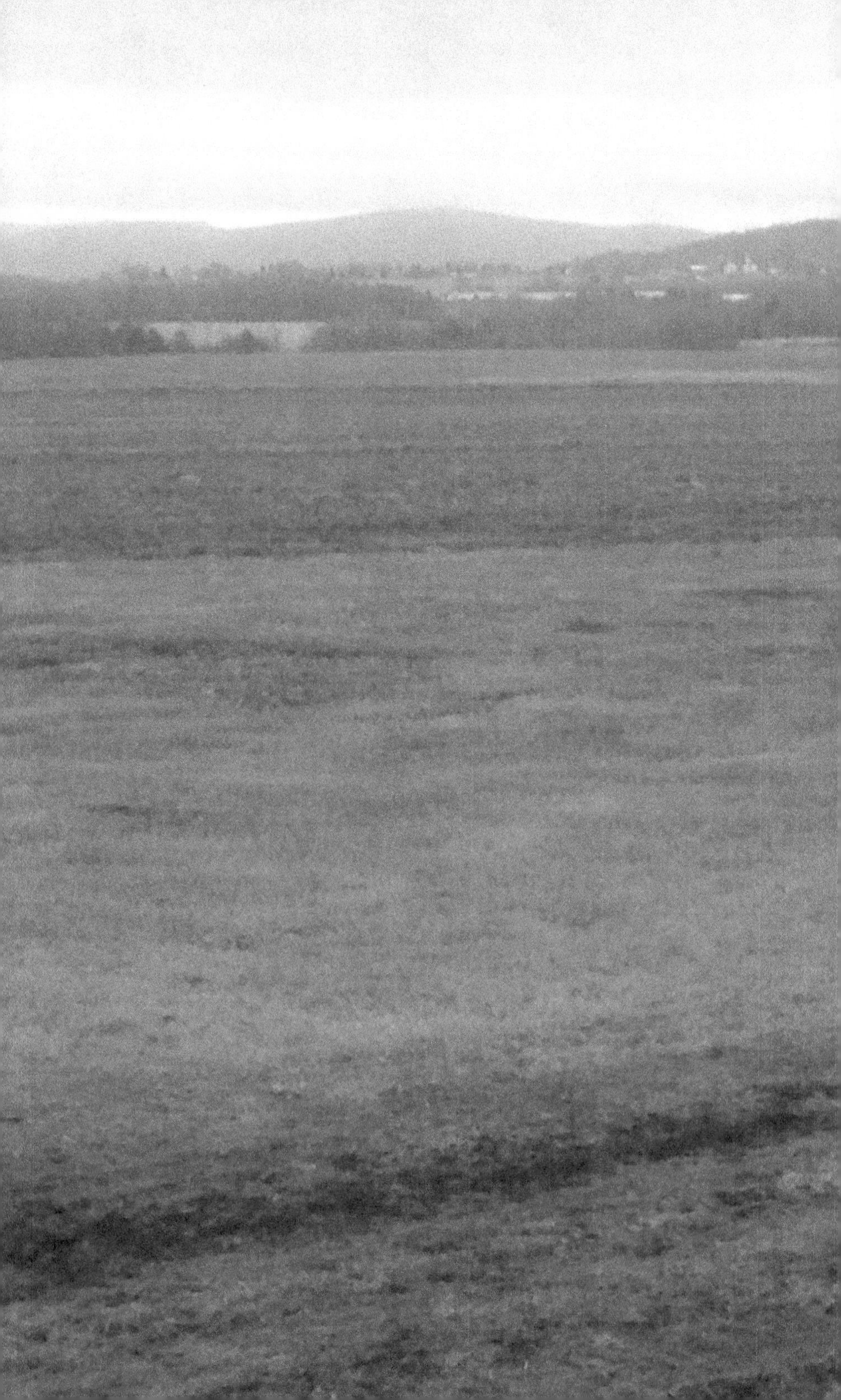

"EL VIAJE MAS CARO" / "THE MOST COSTLY JOURNEY" presents:

A NEW KIND OF WORK

*The Story of Delmar
Art by Tillie Walden*

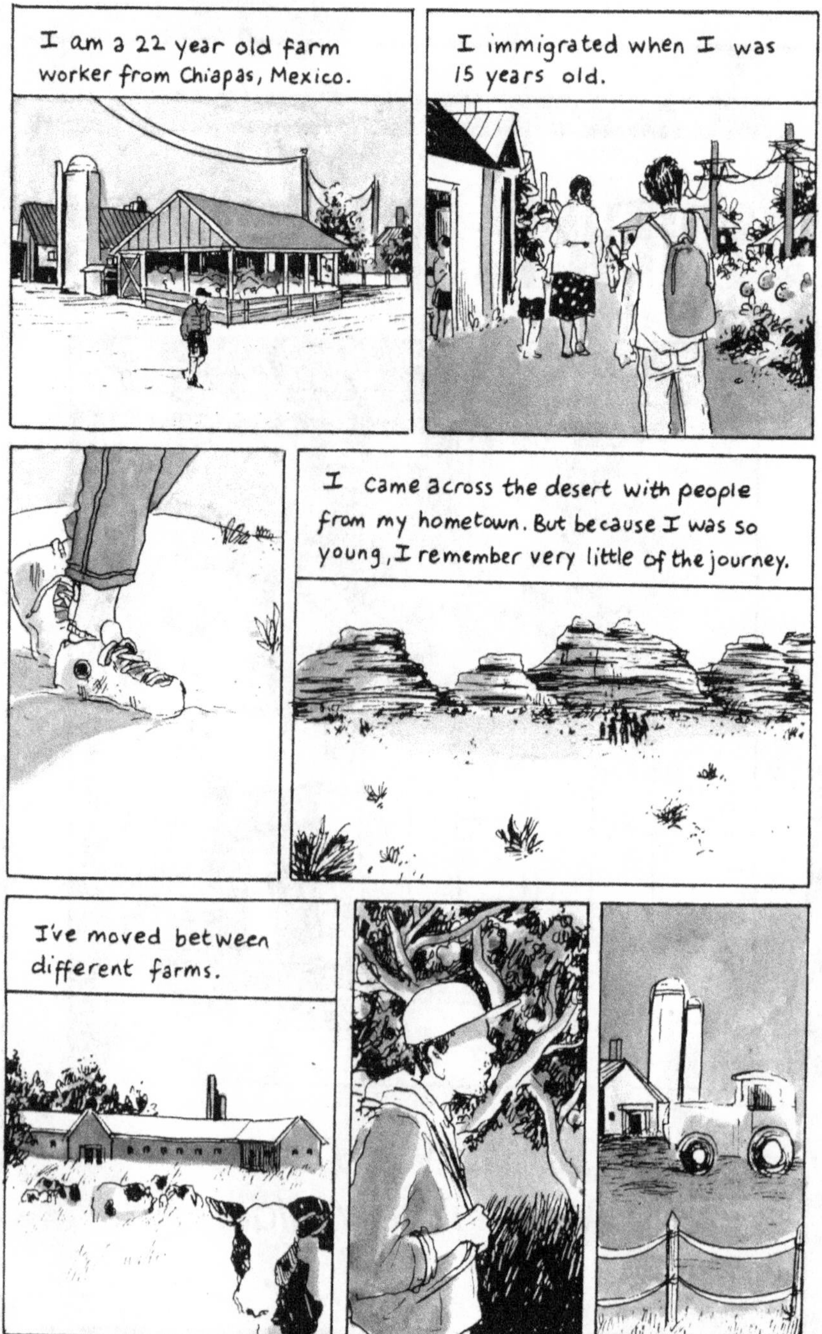
I am a 22 year old farm worker from Chiapas, Mexico.
I immigrated when I was 15 years old.
I came across the desert with people from my hometown. But because I was so young, I remember very little of the journey.
I've moved between different farms.

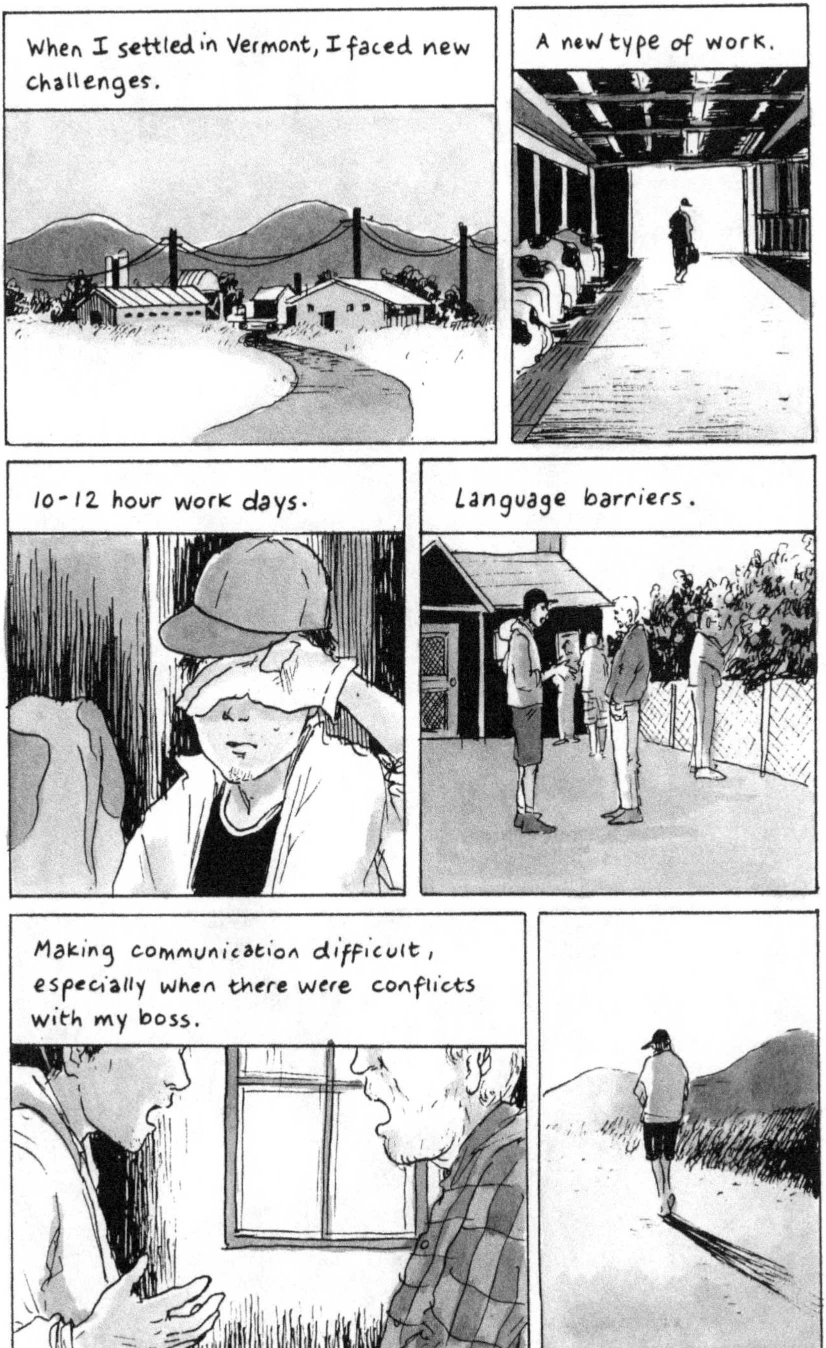
When I settled in Vermont, I faced new challenges.
A new type of work.
10-12 hour work days.
Language barriers.
Making communication difficult, especially when there were conflicts with my boss.

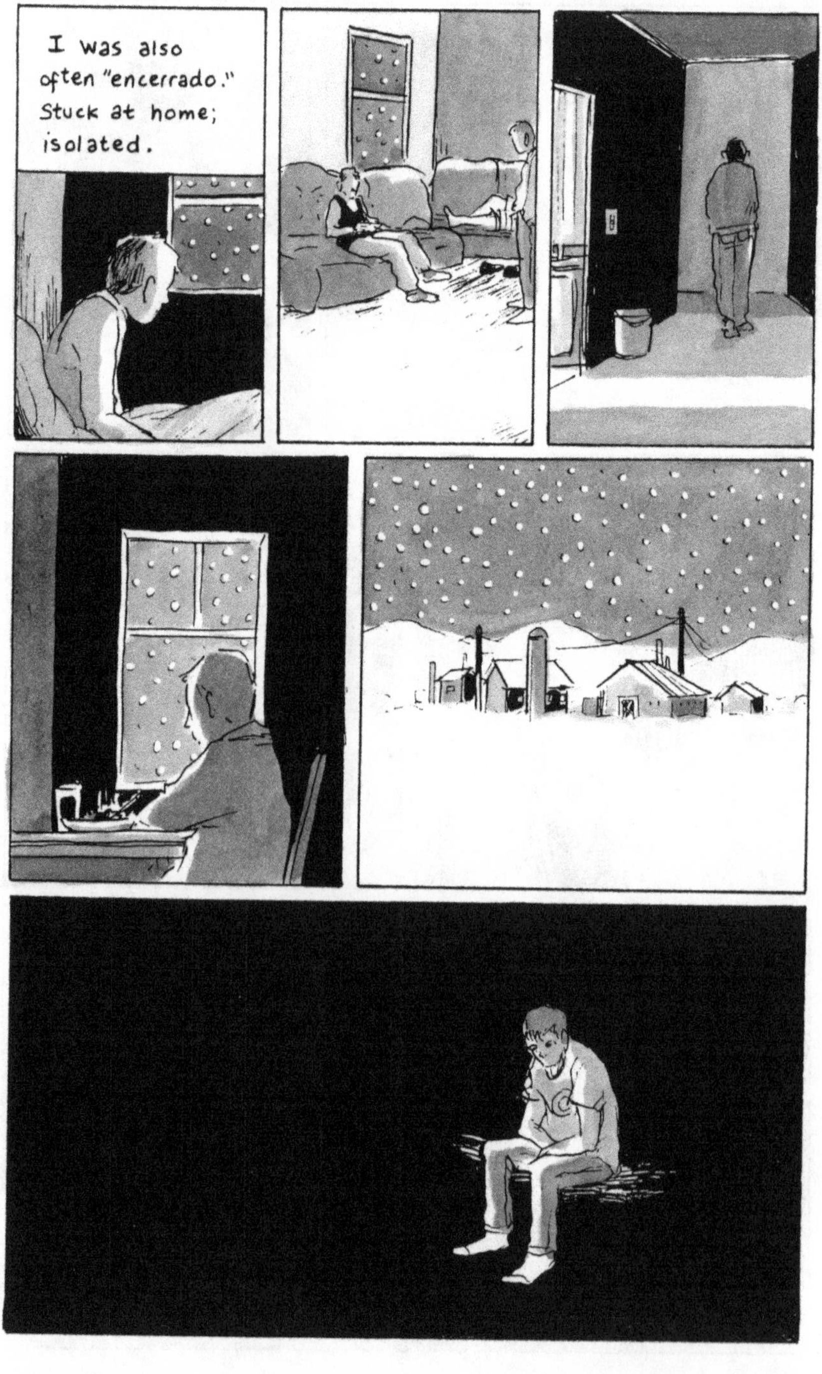
I was also often "encerrado." Stuck at home; isolated.

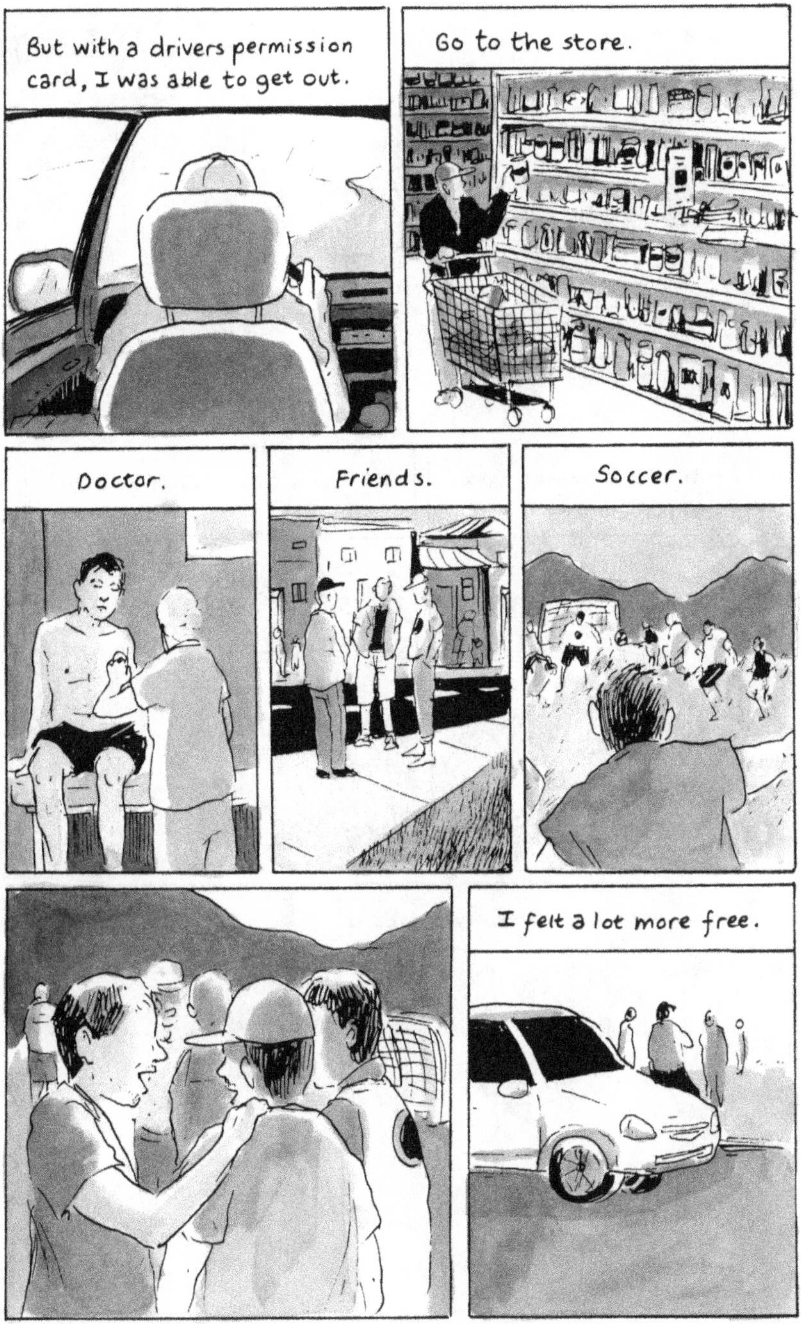
But with a drivers permission card, I was able to get out.
Go to the store.
Doctor.
Friends.
Soccer.
I felt a lot more free.

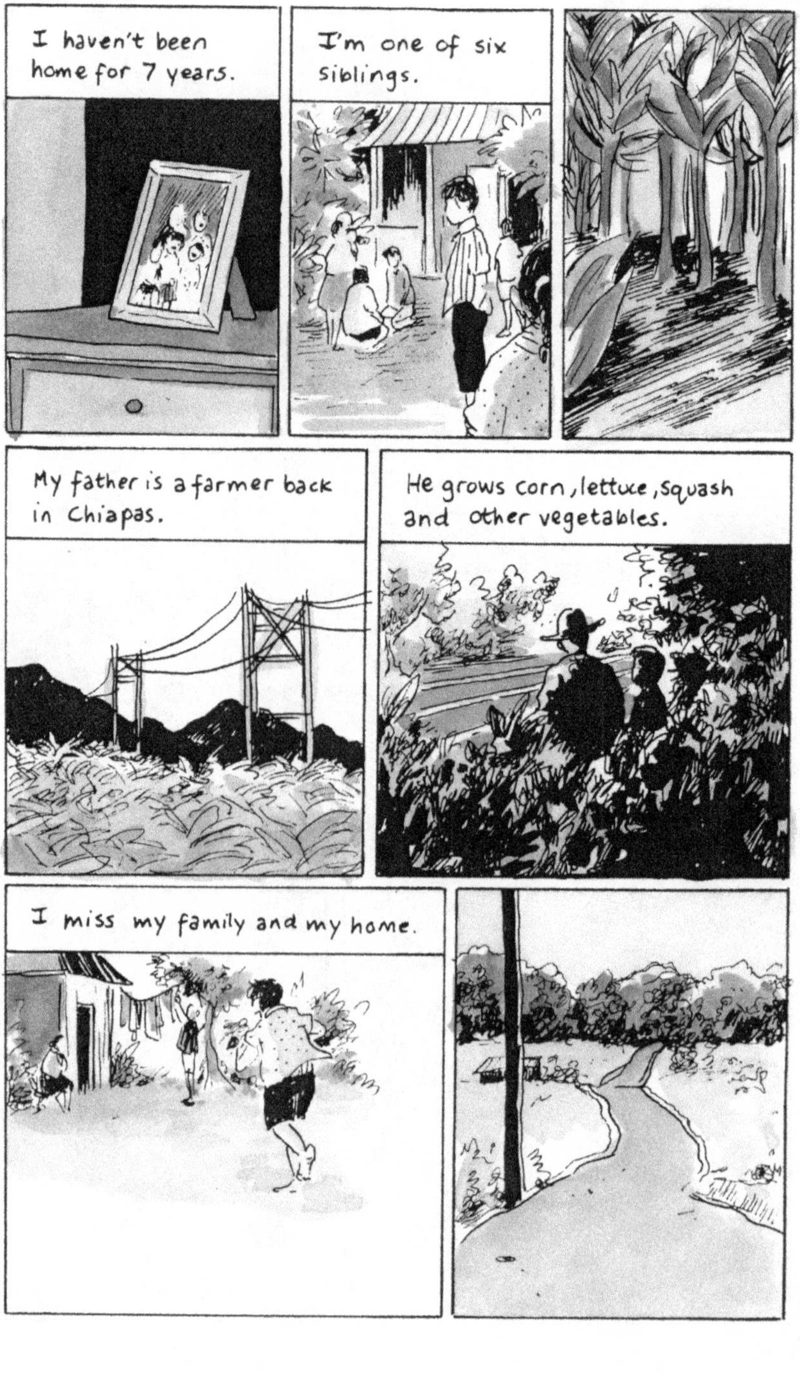
I haven't been home for 7 years.
I'm one of six siblings.
My father is a farmer back in Chiapas.
He grows corn, lettuce, squash and other vegetables.
I miss my family and my home.

I miss the food.

Especially my mother's handmade tortillas.

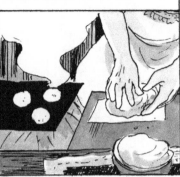

But at least the countryside of Vermont reminds me of the land back in Chiapas.

In the future, I want a wife and three kids.

I plan to one day leave Vermont and return to Chiapas

and raise sheep on my family's land.

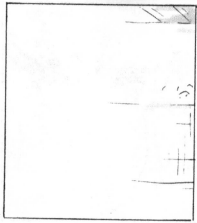

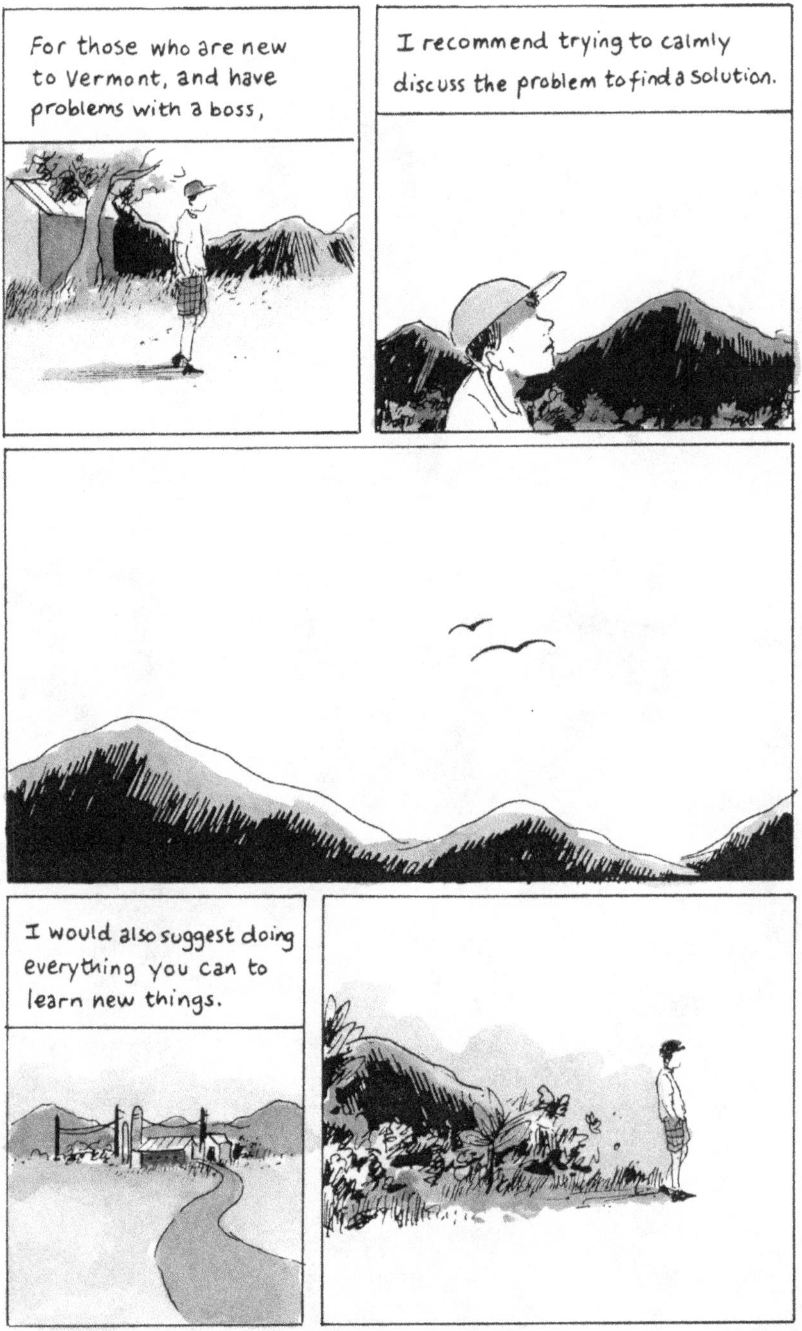
For those who are new to Vermont, and have problems with a boss,
I recommend trying to calmly discuss the problem to find a solution.
I would also suggest doing everything you can to learn new things.

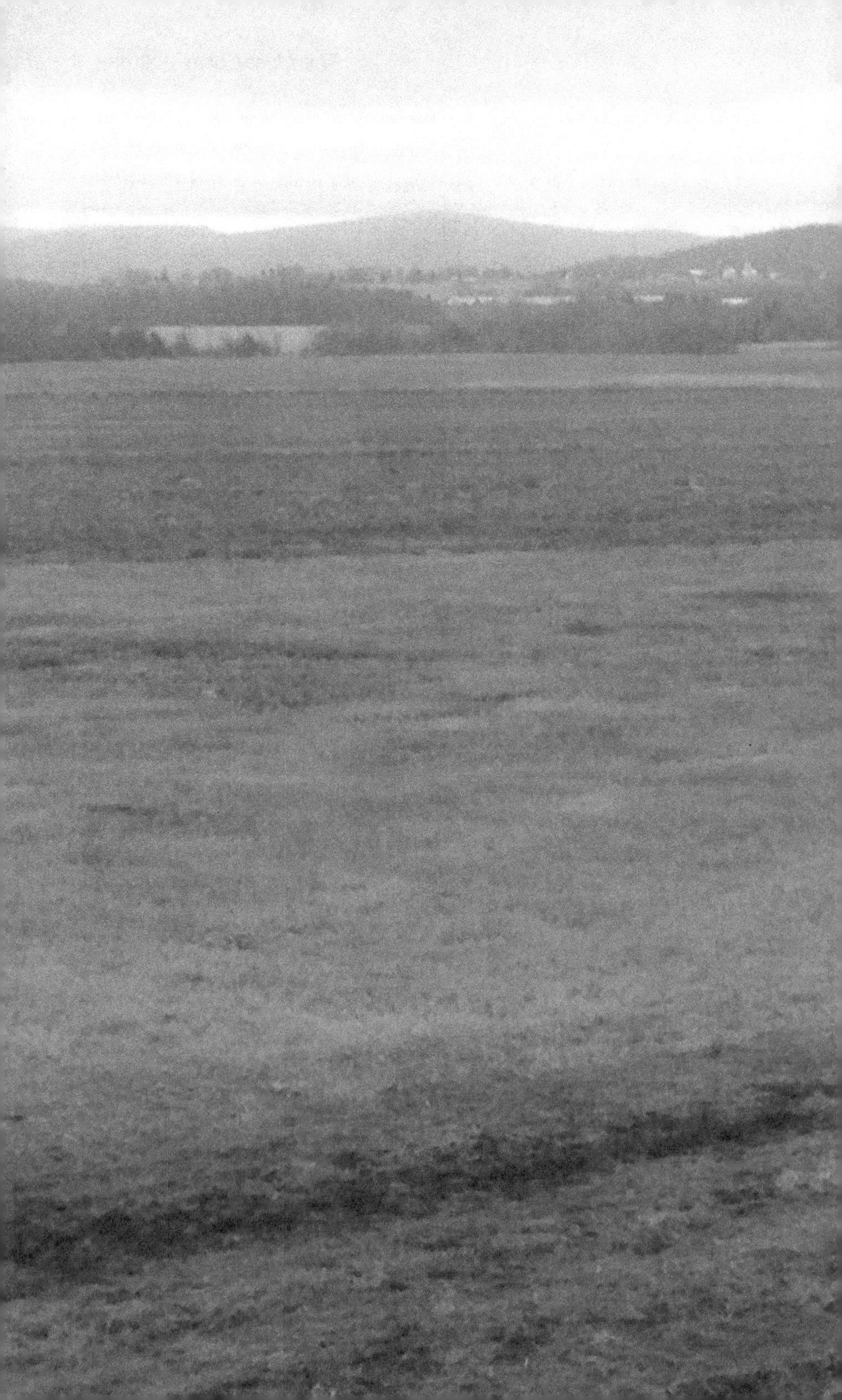

"EL VIAJE MAS CARO" / "THE MOST COSTLY JOURNEY" *presents:*

PAINFUL TO REMEMBER

One Immigrant's Quest to Find Work and Dignity in the USA

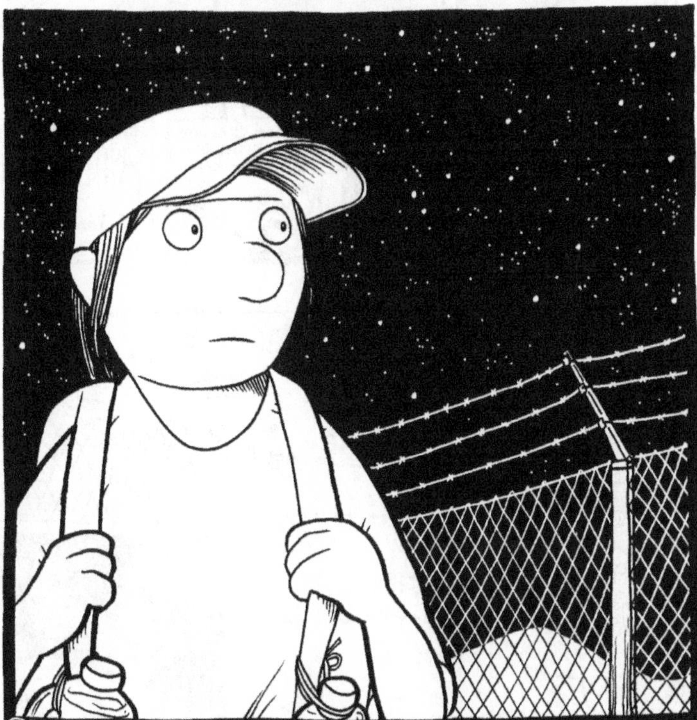
©MMXV www.MarekBennett.com

The Story of José
Art by Marek Bennett

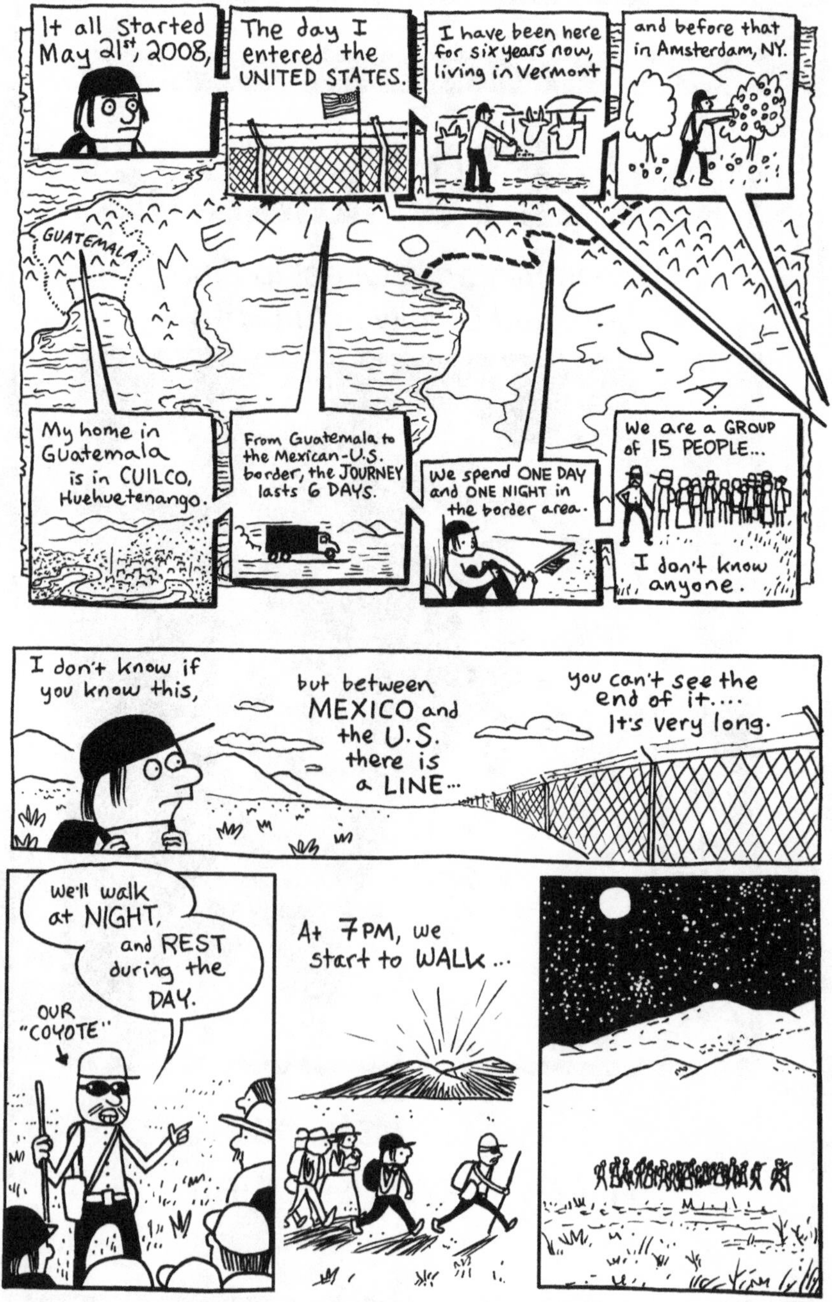
It all Started May 21st, 2008,
The day I entered the UNITED STATES.
I have been here for six years now, living in Vermont
and before that in Amsterdam, NY.
GUATEMALA
MEXICO
U.S.A.
My home in Guatemala is in CUILCO, Huehuetenango.
From Guatemala to the Mexican-U.S. border, the JOURNEY lasts 6 DAYS.
We spend ONE DAY and ONE NIGHT in the border area.
We are a GROUP of 15 PEOPLE...
I don't know anyone.
I don't know if you know this,
but between MEXICO and the U.S. there is a LINE...
you can't see the end of it....
It's very long.
We'll walk at NIGHT, and REST during the DAY.
OUR "COYOTE"
At 7PM, we start to WALK...

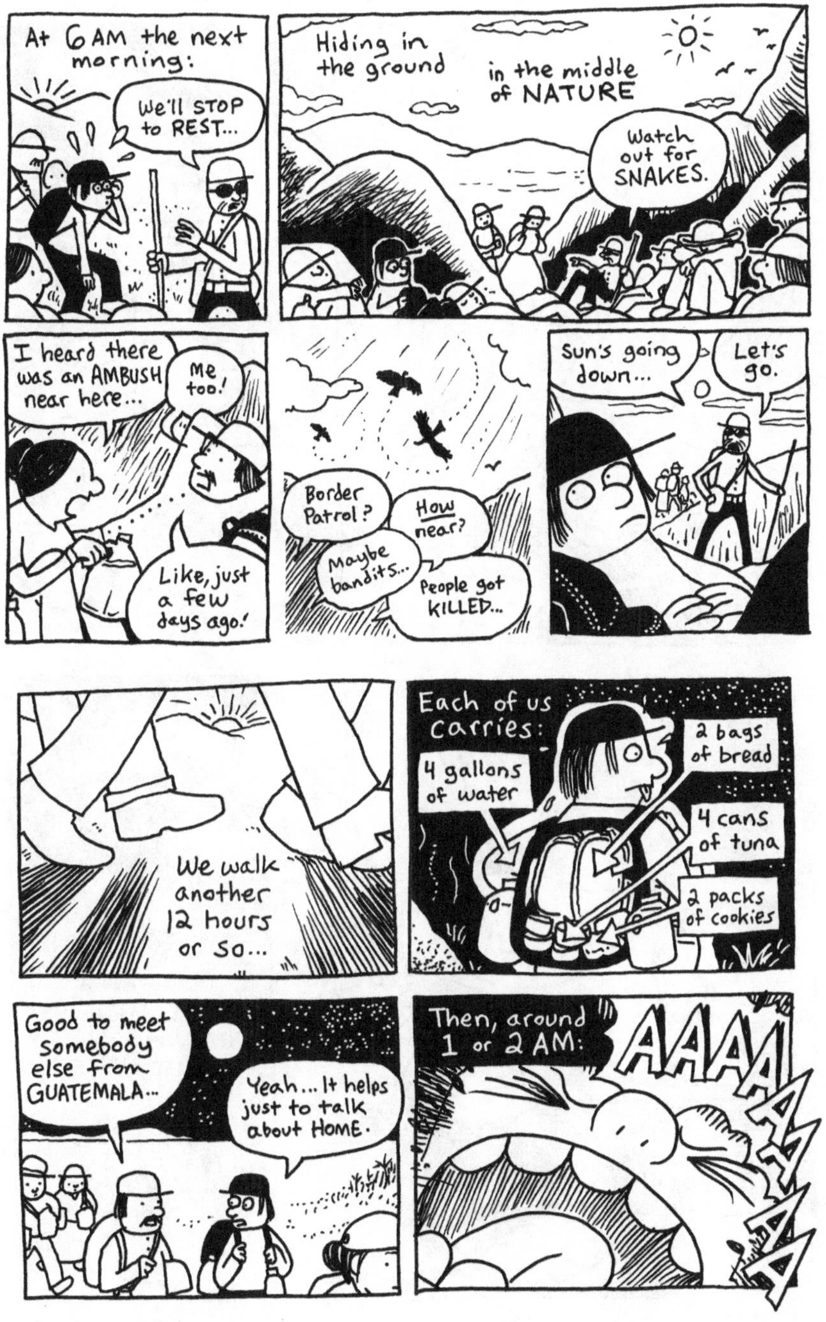
At 6 AM the next morning:
We'll STOP to REST...
Hiding in the ground
in the middle of NATURE
Watch out for SNAKES.
I heard there was an AMBUSH near here...
Me too!
Like, just a few days ago!
Border Patrol?
How near?
Maybe bandits...
People got KILLED...
Sun's going down...
Let's go.
We walk another 12 hours or so...
Each of us carries:
4 gallons of water
2 bags of bread
4 cans of tuna
2 packs of cookies
Good to meet somebody else from GUATEMALA...
Yeah... It helps just to talk about HOME.
Then, around 1 or 2 AM:
AAAAAAAAA

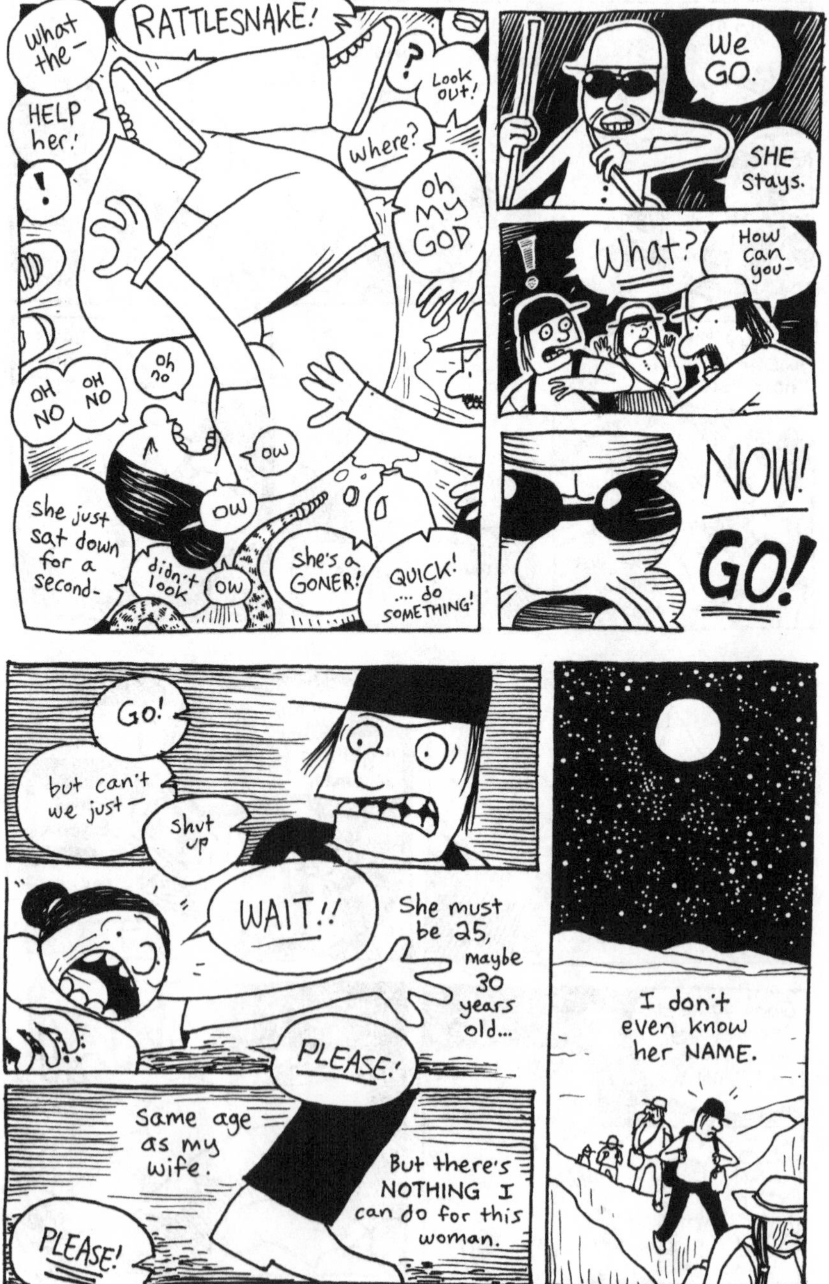
what the—
RATTLESNAKE!
?
Look out!
HELP her!
where?
!
oh my GOD
oh no
OH NO
OH NO
ow
OW
she just sat down for a second—
didn't look
OW
she's a GONER!
QUICK! ... do SOMETHING!
We GO.
SHE stays.
!
What?
How can you—
NOW!
GO!
Go!
but can't we just—
shut up
WAIT!!
She must be 25, maybe 30 years old...
PLEASE!
Same age as my wife.
But there's NOTHING I can do for this woman.
PLEASE!
I don't even know her NAME.

7 AM: We stop to rest again.
3PM:
Time...
Hey, C'mon!
we're going ...
Hey?
What NOW?
...Another RATTLESNAKE?
Oh—
see the FOAM?
Spider got him.
Christ, I said be careful...
He was my COMPATRIOT, all the way from GUATEMALA...
but I don't know his name, either.
On my knees
he has his last breath.
All right, take what you want of his things and let's GO.

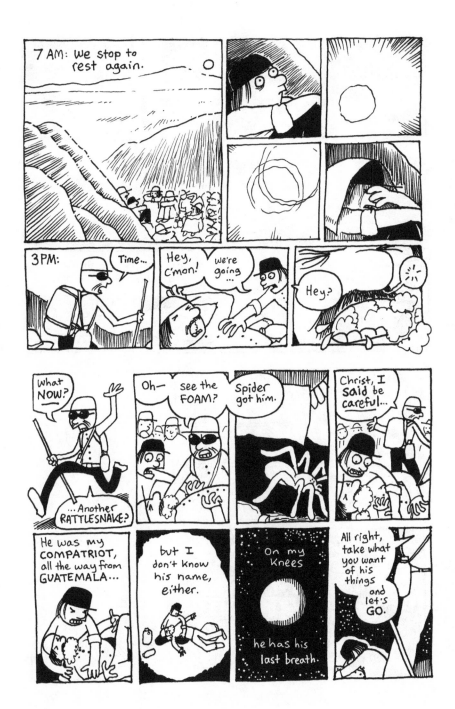

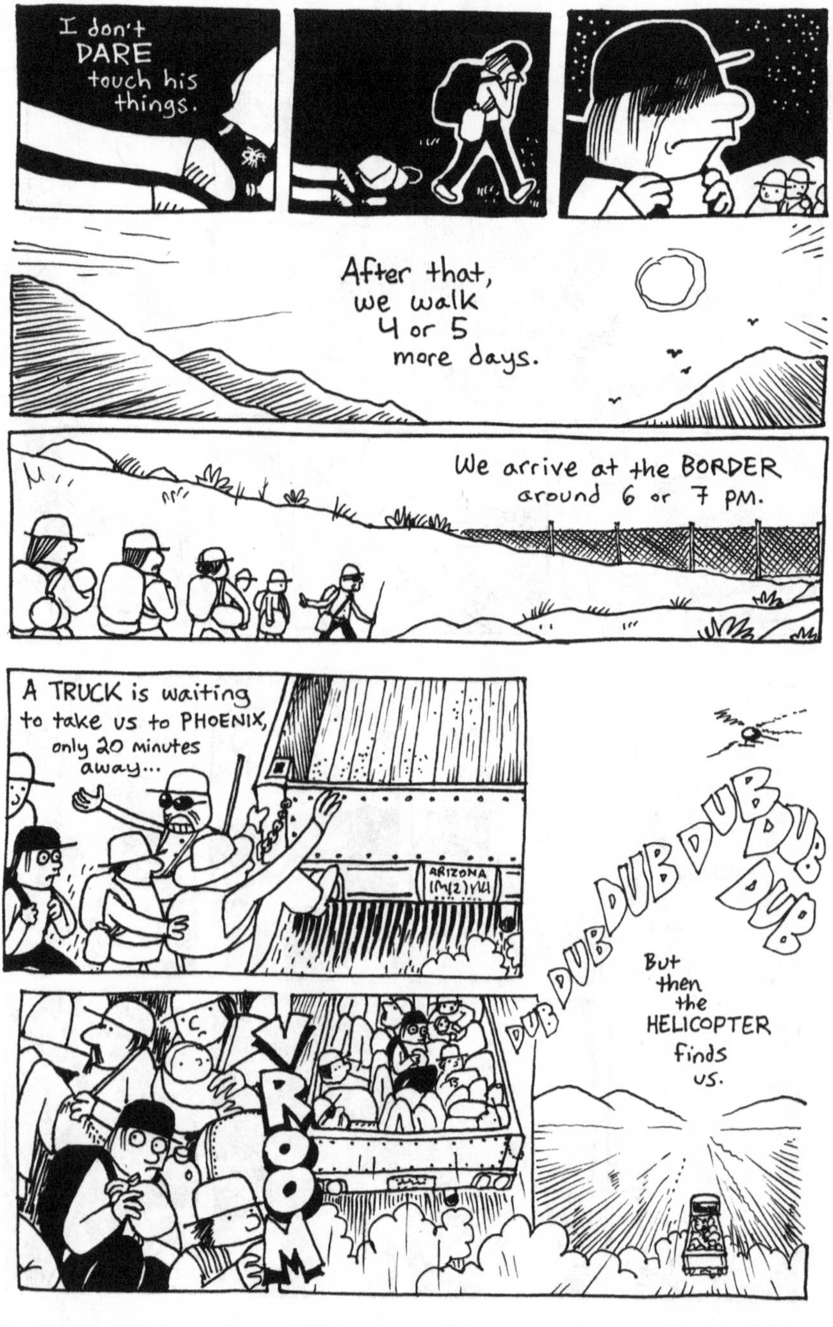
I don't DARE touch his things.
After that, we walk 4 or 5 more days.
We arrive at the BORDER around 6 or 7 PM.
A TRUCK is waiting to take us to PHOENIX, only 20 minutes away...
ARIZONA
VROOM
DUB DUB DUB DUB DUB DUB DUB
But then the HELICOPTER finds us.

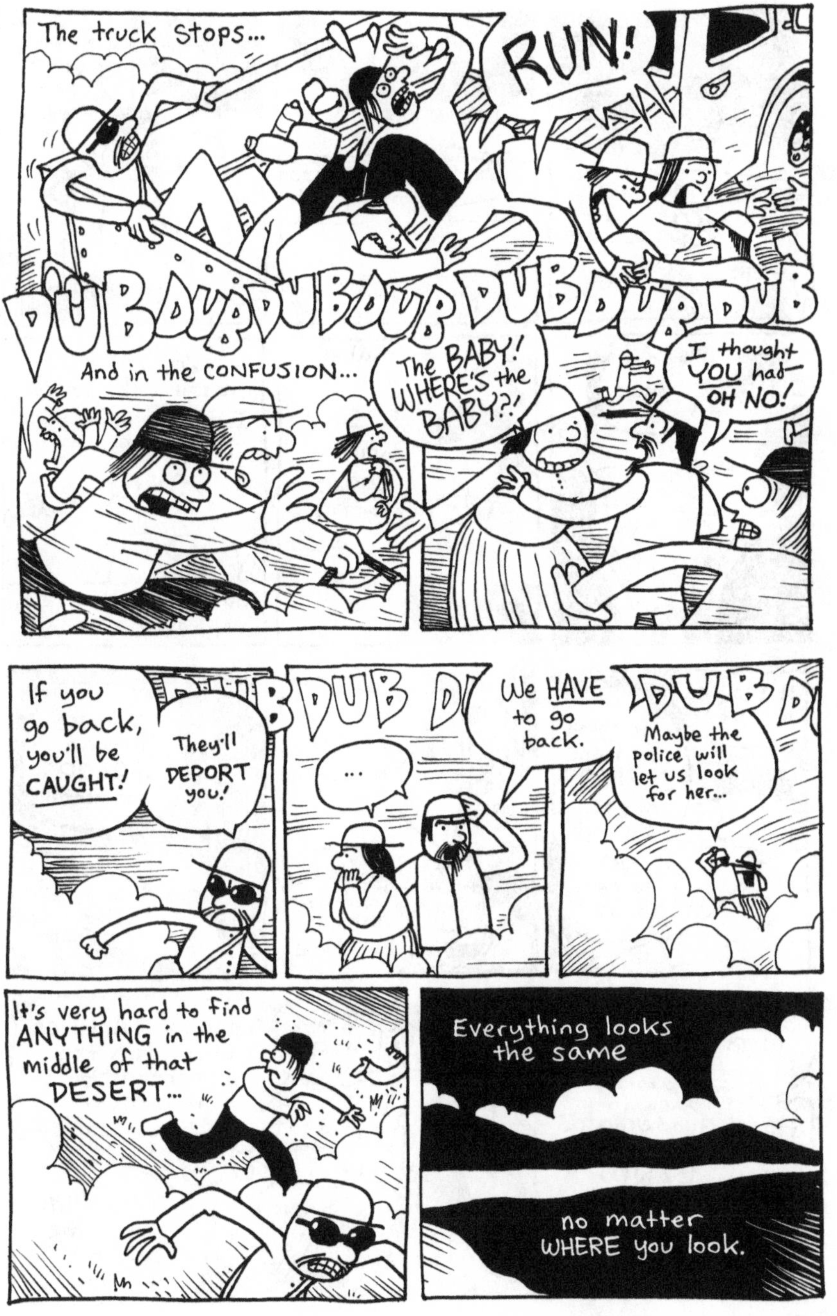
The truck stops...
RUN!
DUB DUB DUB DUB DUB DUB DUB
And in the CONFUSION...
The BABY! WHERE'S the BABY?!
I thought YOU had— OH NO!
If you go back, you'll be CAUGHT!
They'll DEPORT you!
DUB DUB
...
We HAVE to go back.
DUB
Maybe the police will let us look for her...
It's very hard to find ANYTHING in the middle of that DESERT...
Everything looks the same
no matter WHERE you look.

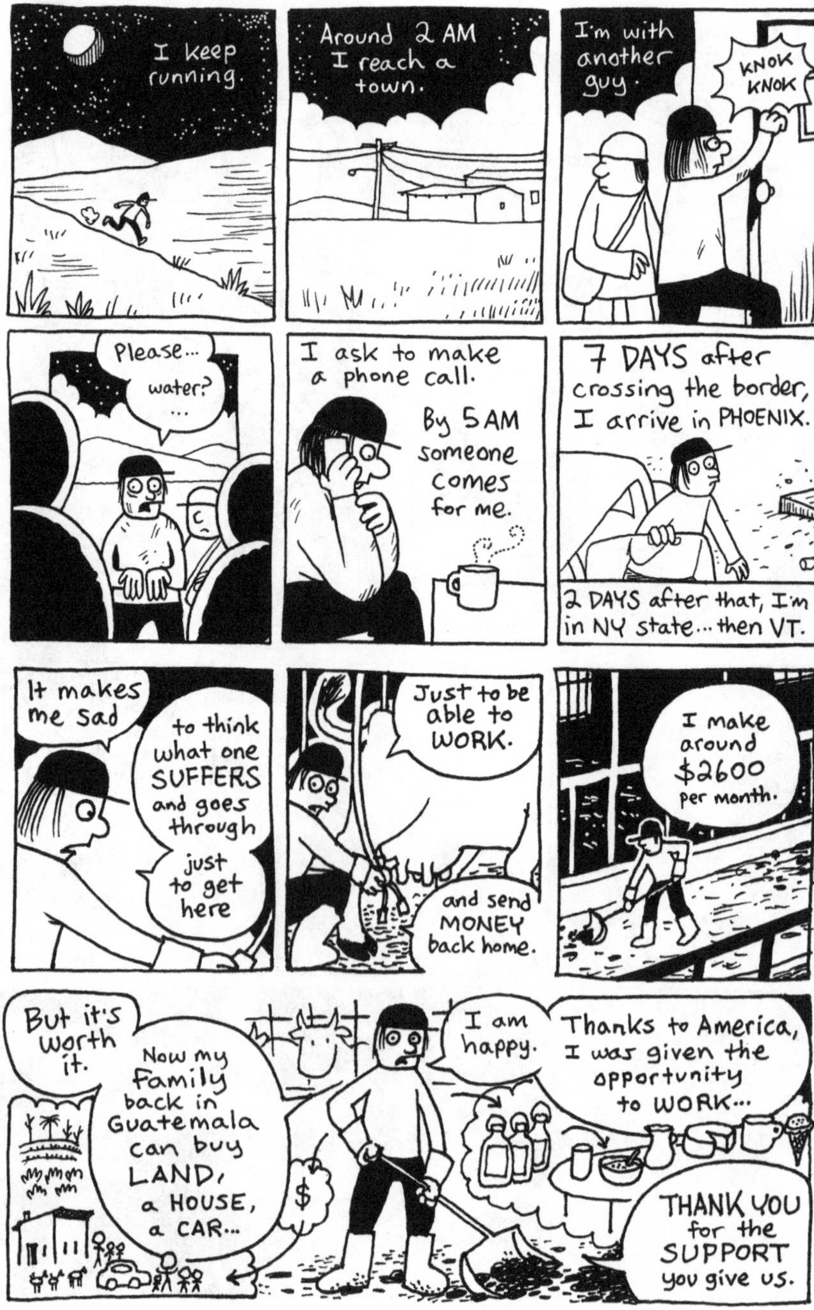
I keep running.
Around 2 AM I reach a town.
I'm with another guy.
KNOK KNOK
Please... water? ...
I ask to make a phone call.
By 5 AM someone comes for me.
7 DAYS after crossing the border, I arrive in PHOENIX.
2 DAYS after that, I'm in NY state... then VT.
It makes me sad
to think what one SUFFERS and goes through
just to get here
Just to be able to WORK.
and send MONEY back home.
I make around $2600 per month.
But it's worth it.
Now my Family back in Guatemala can buy LAND, a HOUSE, a CAR...
$
I am happy.
Thanks to America, I was given the opportunity to WORK...
THANK YOU for the SUPPORT you give us.

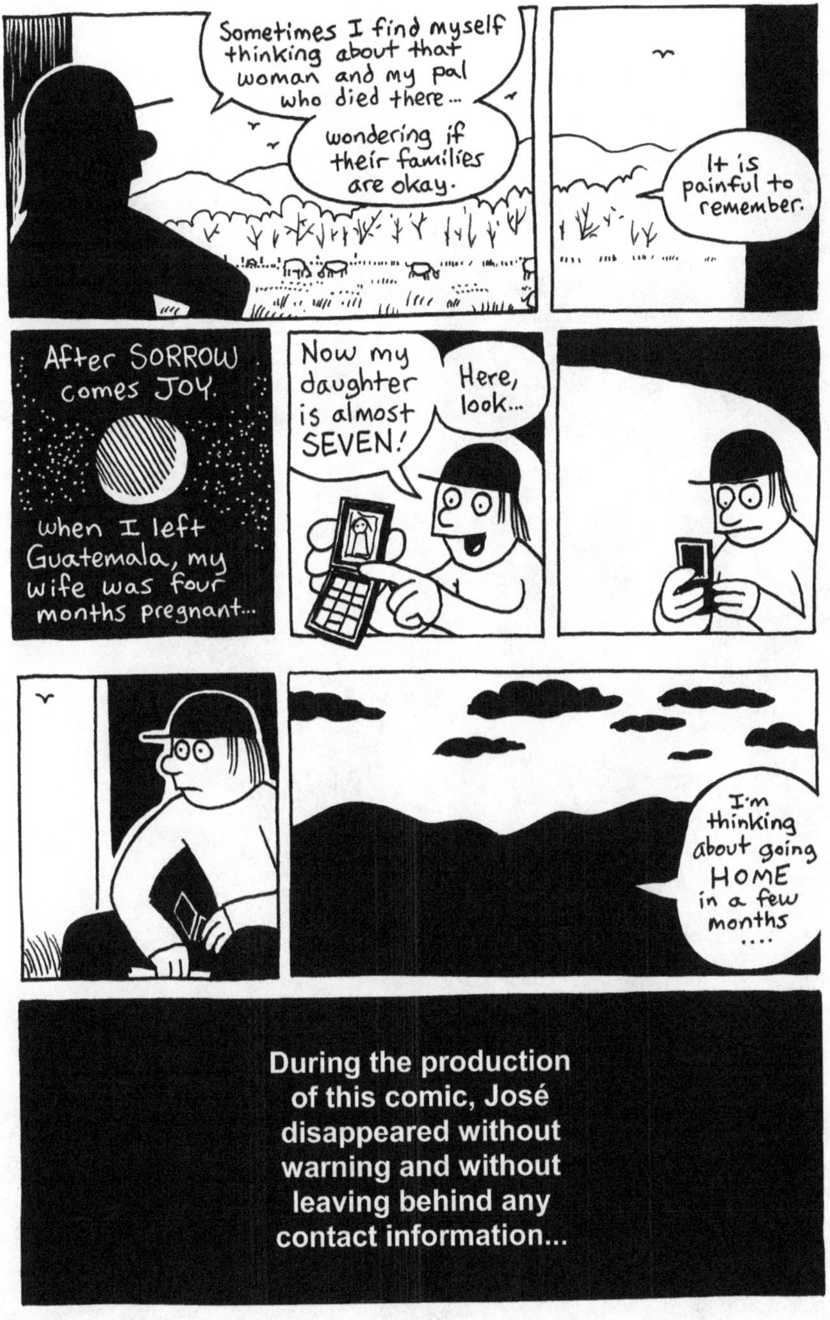
Sometimes I find myself thinking about that woman and my pal who died there...
wondering if their families are okay.
It is painful to remember.
After SORROW comes JOY.
when I left Guatemala, my wife was four months pregnant...
Now my daughter is almost SEVEN!
Here, look...
I'm thinking about going HOME in a few months ....

During the production of this comic, José disappeared without warning and without leaving behind any contact information...

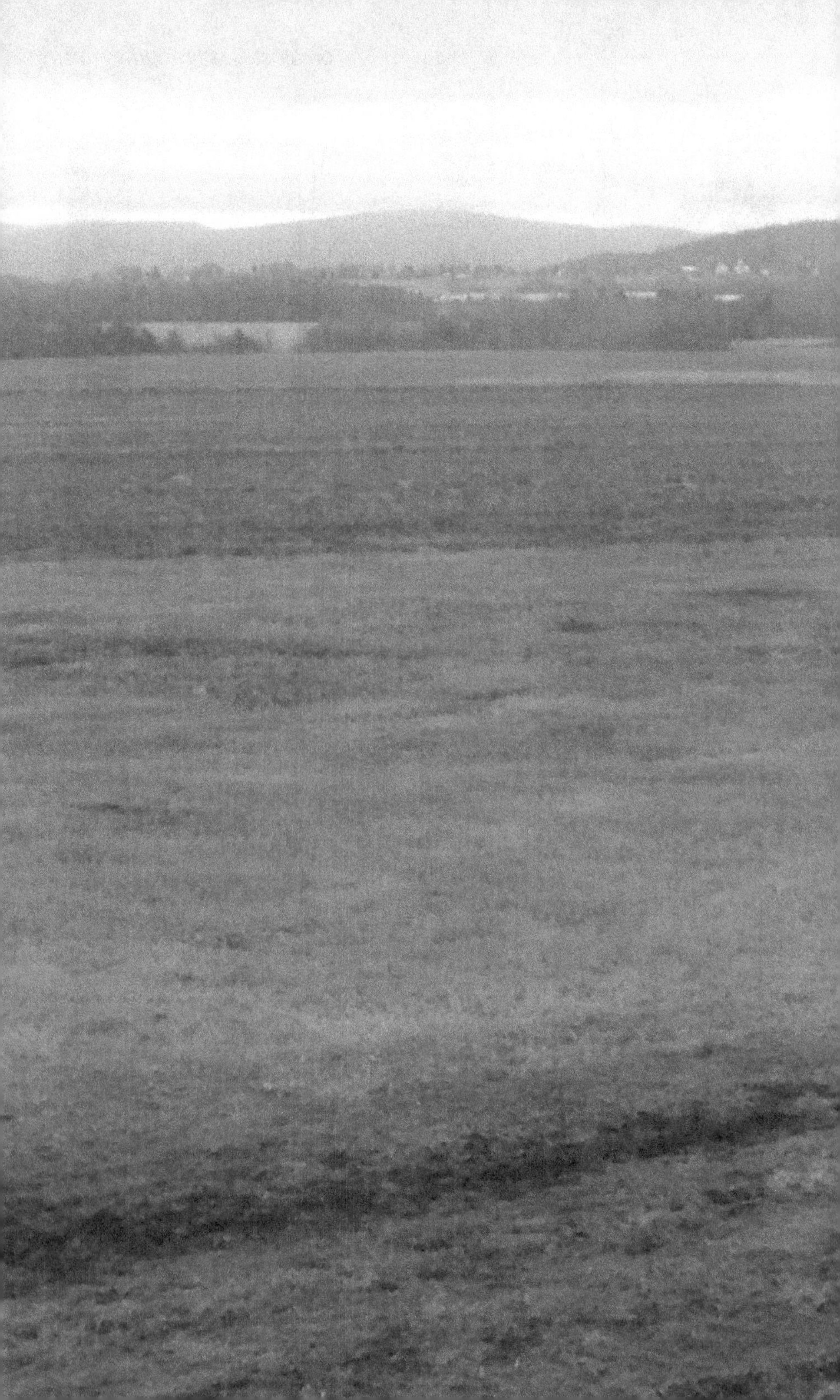

"EL VIAJE MAS CARO" / "THE MOST COSTLY JOURNEY" *presents:*

IT'S WORTH IT

Gregorio's Story
Art by Kevin Kite

I SACRIFICED MY YOUTH COMING TO VERMONT.

ON THE FARM, I WORK ELEVEN HOURS A DAY, SIX DAYS A WEEK.

OFF THE FARM, PEOPLE DON'T UNDERSTAND ME BECAUSE I DON'T SPEAK ENGLISH WELL.

I'M SORRY. WHAT DID YOU SAY?

I DIDN'T WANT TO LEAVE MEXICO, BUT I WAS SEARCHING FOR BETTER OPPORTUNITIES FOR MY FAMILY.

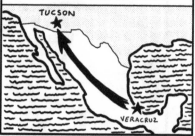

TUCSON

VERACRUZ

MY FATHER WAS WORKING IN A RESTAURANT IN TENNESSEE. WE TALKED ABOUT MY COMING.

LIFE IS HARD HERE, BUT THE MONEY'S GOOD. YOUR UNCLE'S COMING. YOU COULD COME WITH HIM. IT'S UP TO YOU.

I'D DO ANYTHING FOR MY FAMILY.

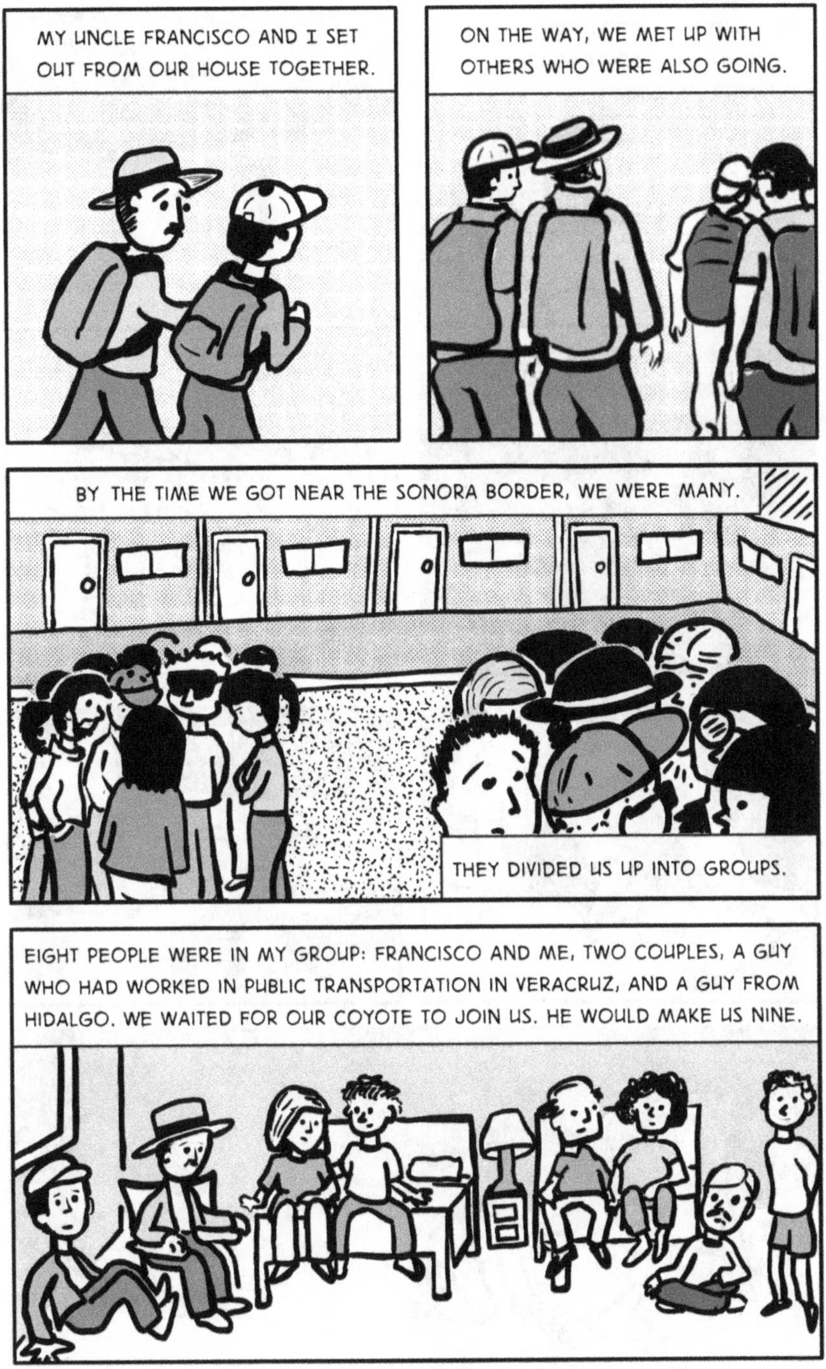
MY UNCLE FRANCISCO AND I SET OUT FROM OUR HOUSE TOGETHER.
ON THE WAY, WE MET UP WITH OTHERS WHO WERE ALSO GOING.
BY THE TIME WE GOT NEAR THE SONORA BORDER, WE WERE MANY.
THEY DIVIDED US UP INTO GROUPS.
EIGHT PEOPLE WERE IN MY GROUP: FRANCISCO AND ME, TWO COUPLES, A GUY WHO HAD WORKED IN PUBLIC TRANSPORTATION IN VERACRUZ, AND A GUY FROM HIDALGO. WE WAITED FOR OUR COYOTE TO JOIN US. HE WOULD MAKE US NINE.

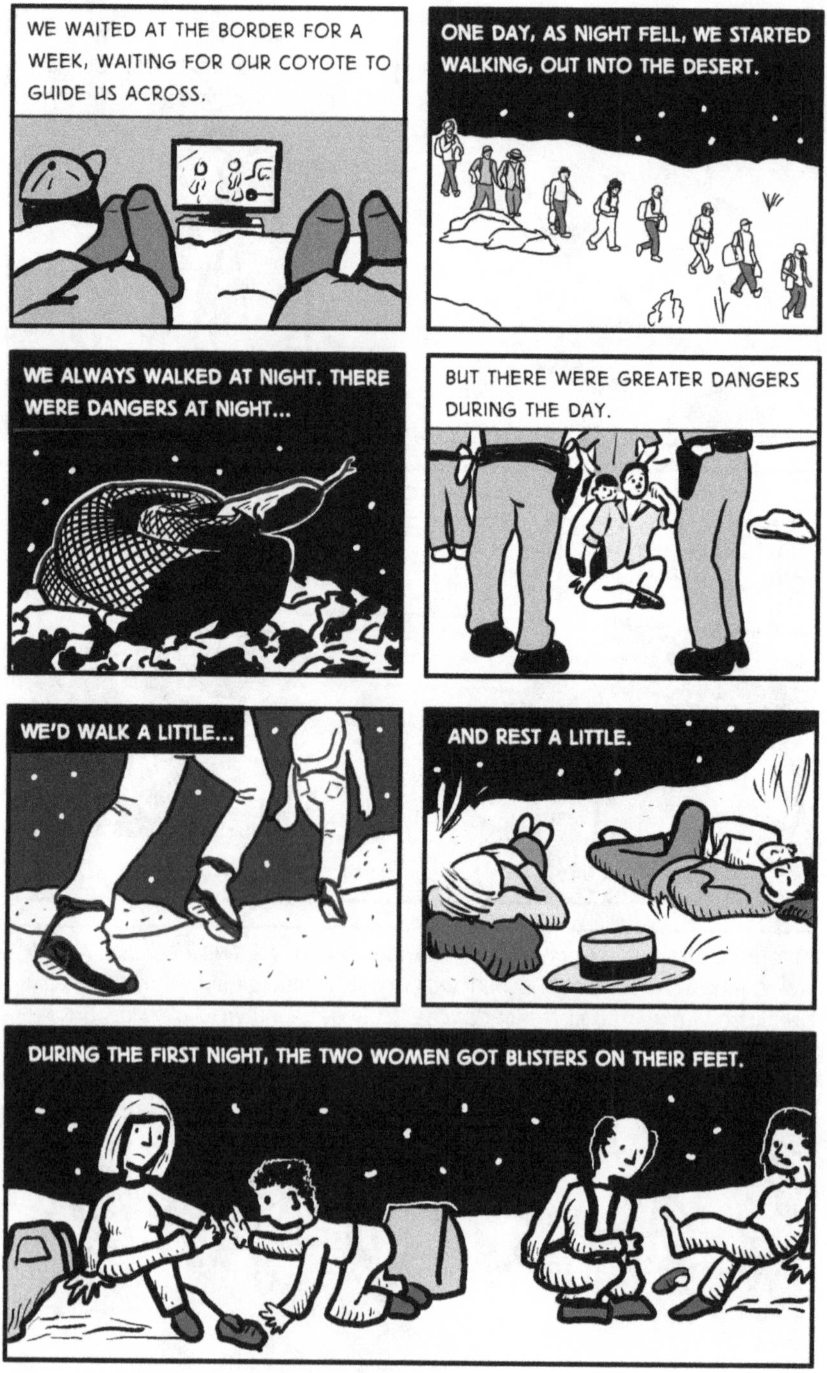
WE WAITED AT THE BORDER FOR A WEEK, WAITING FOR OUR COYOTE TO GUIDE US ACROSS.
ONE DAY, AS NIGHT FELL, WE STARTED WALKING, OUT INTO THE DESERT.
WE ALWAYS WALKED AT NIGHT. THERE WERE DANGERS AT NIGHT...
BUT THERE WERE GREATER DANGERS DURING THE DAY.
WE'D WALK A LITTLE...
AND REST A LITTLE.
DURING THE FIRST NIGHT, THE TWO WOMEN GOT BLISTERS ON THEIR FEET.

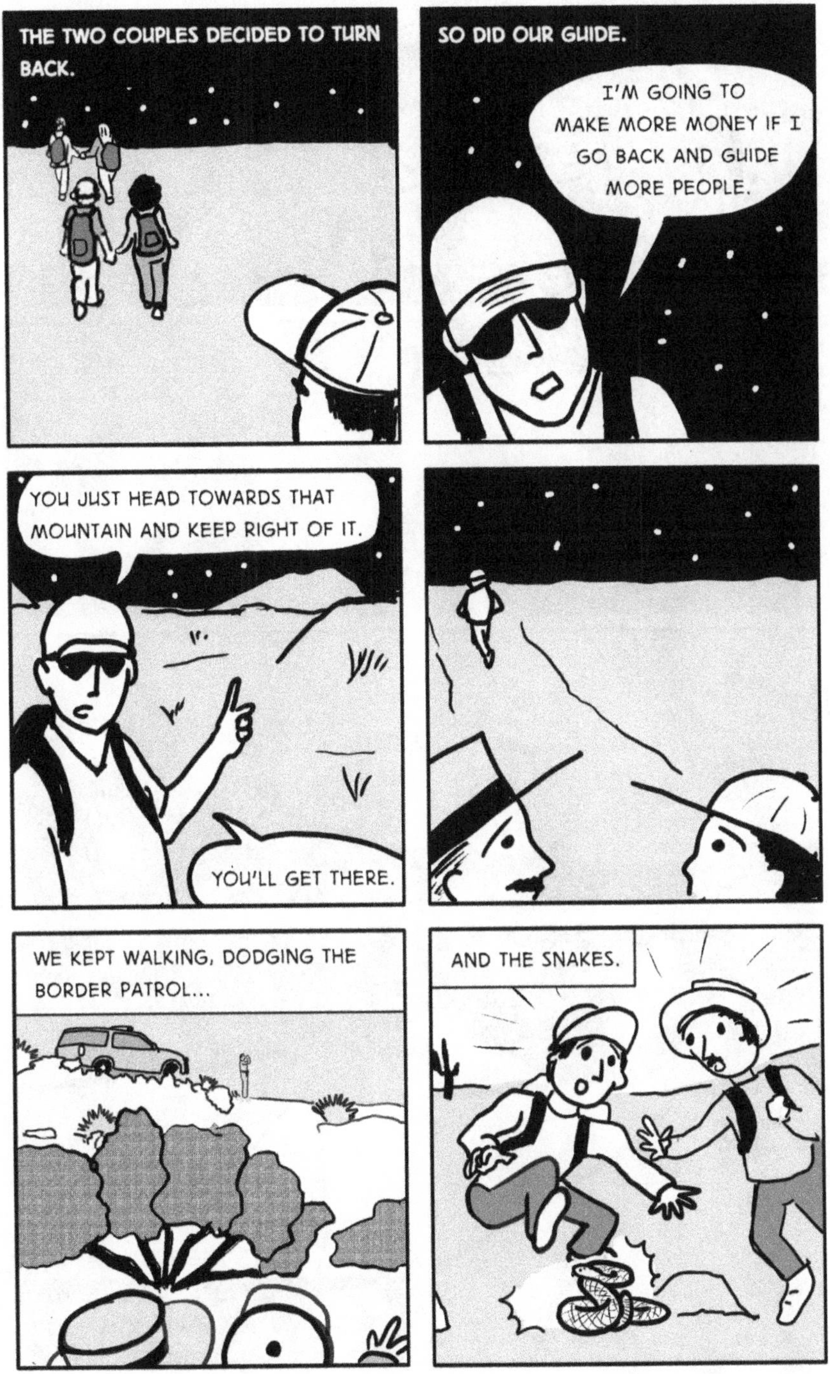
THE TWO COUPLES DECIDED TO TURN BACK.
SO DID OUR GUIDE.
I'M GOING TO MAKE MORE MONEY IF I GO BACK AND GUIDE MORE PEOPLE.
YOU JUST HEAD TOWARDS THAT MOUNTAIN AND KEEP RIGHT OF IT.
YOU'LL GET THERE.
WE KEPT WALKING, DODGING THE BORDER PATROL...
AND THE SNAKES.

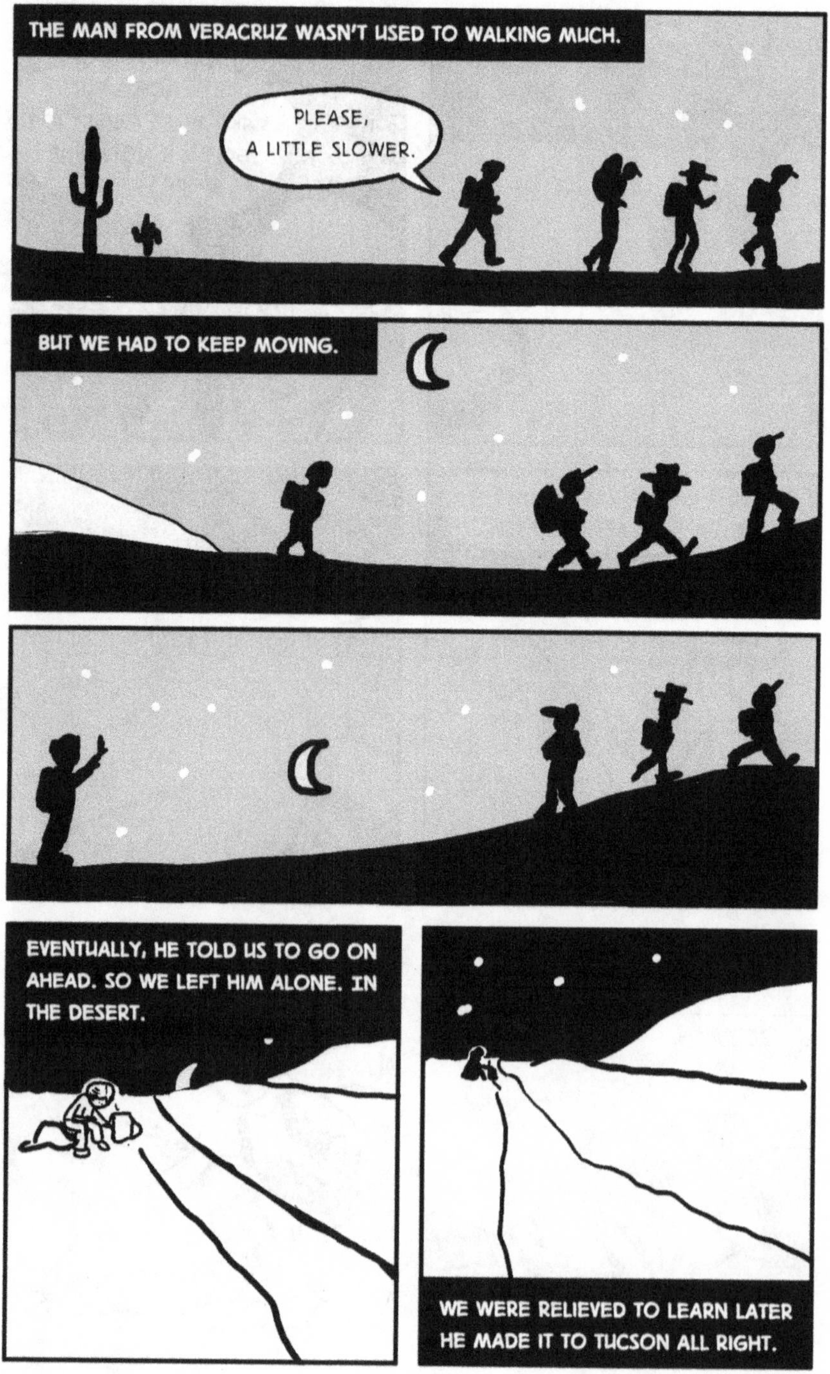
THE MAN FROM VERACRUZ WASN'T USED TO WALKING MUCH.
PLEASE, A LITTLE SLOWER.
BUT WE HAD TO KEEP MOVING.
EVENTUALLY, HE TOLD US TO GO ON AHEAD. SO WE LEFT HIM ALONE. IN THE DESERT.
WE WERE RELIEVED TO LEARN LATER HE MADE IT TO TUCSON ALL RIGHT.

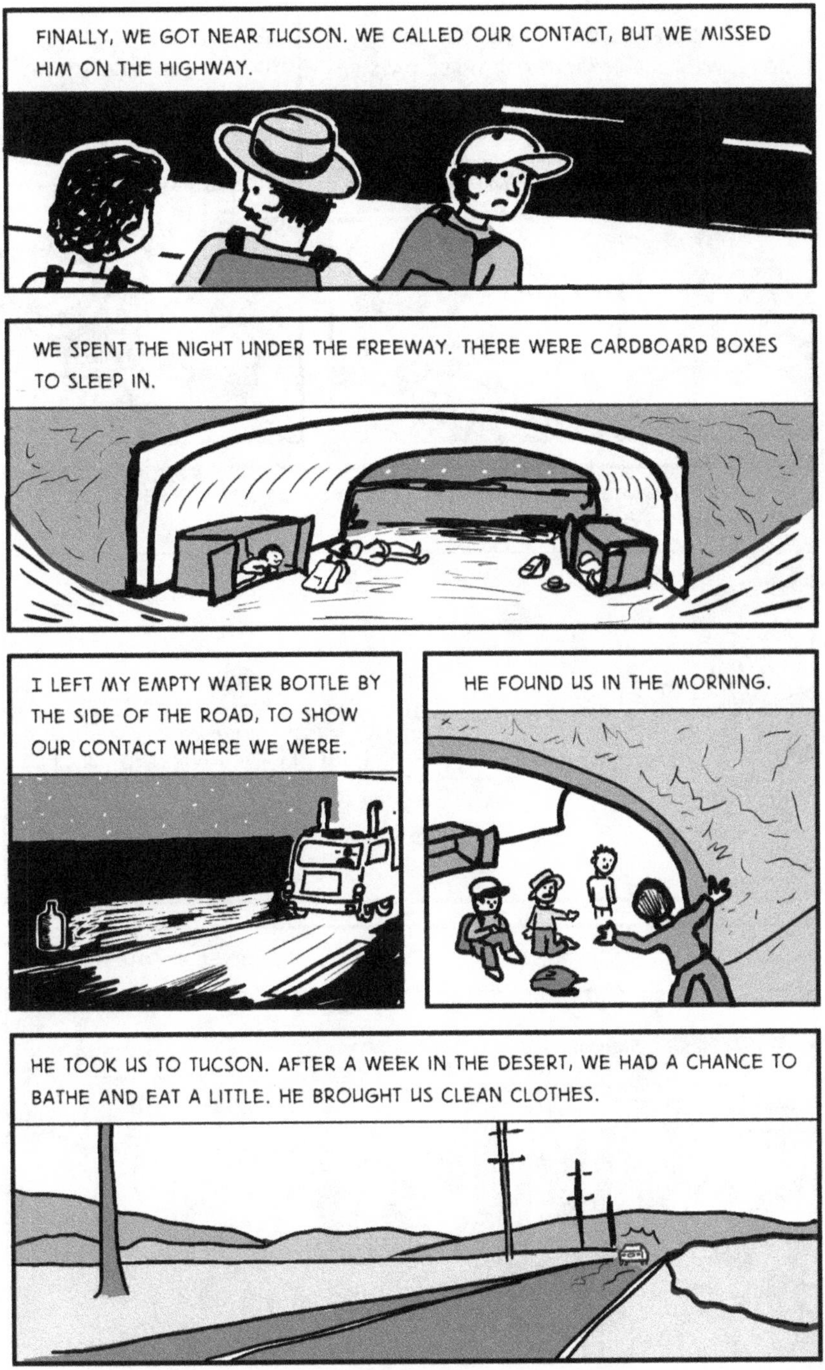
FINALLY, WE GOT NEAR TUCSON. WE CALLED OUR CONTACT, BUT WE MISSED HIM ON THE HIGHWAY.
WE SPENT THE NIGHT UNDER THE FREEWAY. THERE WERE CARDBOARD BOXES TO SLEEP IN.
I LEFT MY EMPTY WATER BOTTLE BY THE SIDE OF THE ROAD, TO SHOW OUR CONTACT WHERE WE WERE.
HE FOUND US IN THE MORNING.
HE TOOK US TO TUCSON. AFTER A WEEK IN THE DESERT, WE HAD A CHANCE TO BATHE AND EAT A LITTLE. HE BROUGHT US CLEAN CLOTHES.

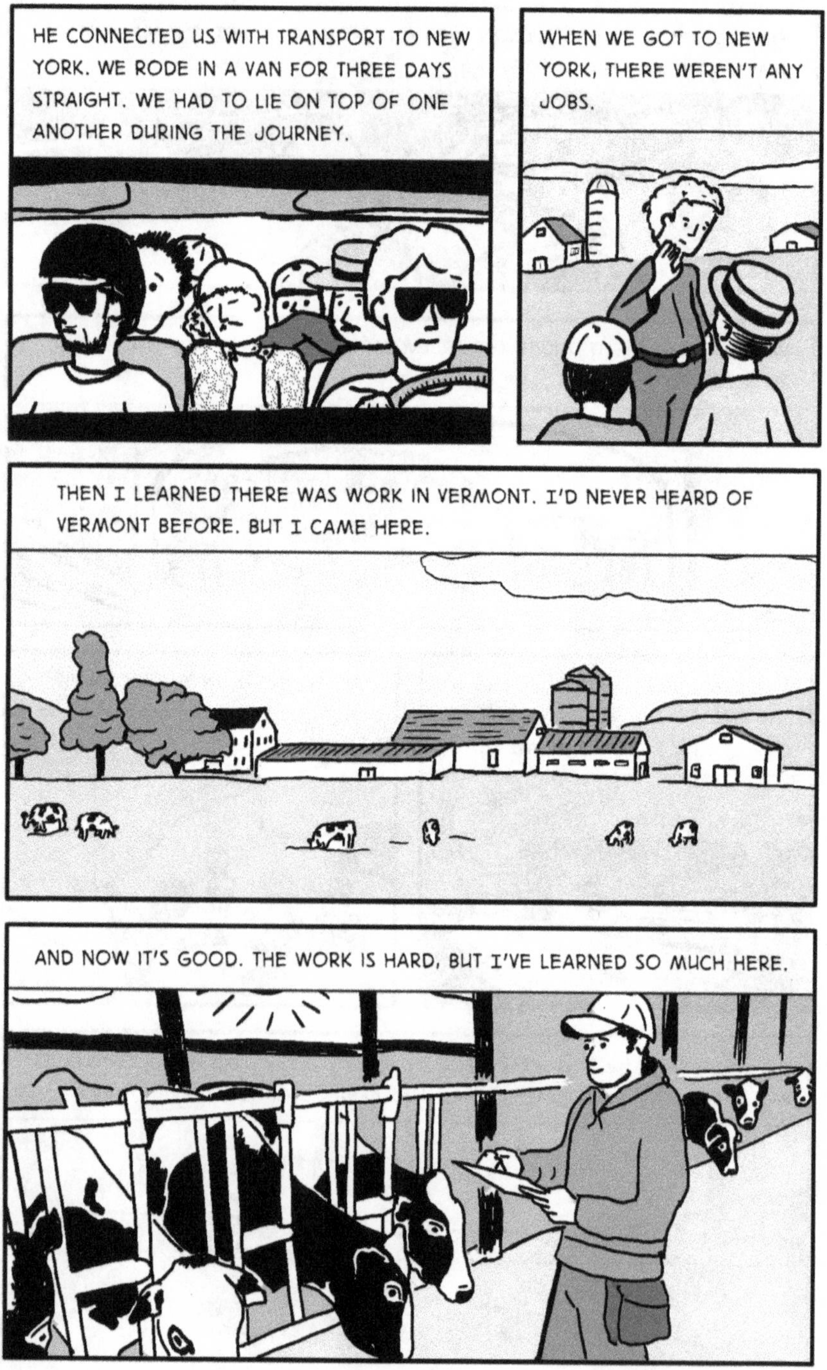
HE CONNECTED US WITH TRANSPORT TO NEW YORK. WE RODE IN A VAN FOR THREE DAYS STRAIGHT. WE HAD TO LIE ON TOP OF ONE ANOTHER DURING THE JOURNEY.
WHEN WE GOT TO NEW YORK, THERE WEREN'T ANY JOBS.
THEN I LEARNED THERE WAS WORK IN VERMONT. I'D NEVER HEARD OF VERMONT BEFORE. BUT I CAME HERE.
AND NOW IT'S GOOD. THE WORK IS HARD, BUT I'VE LEARNED SO MUCH HERE.

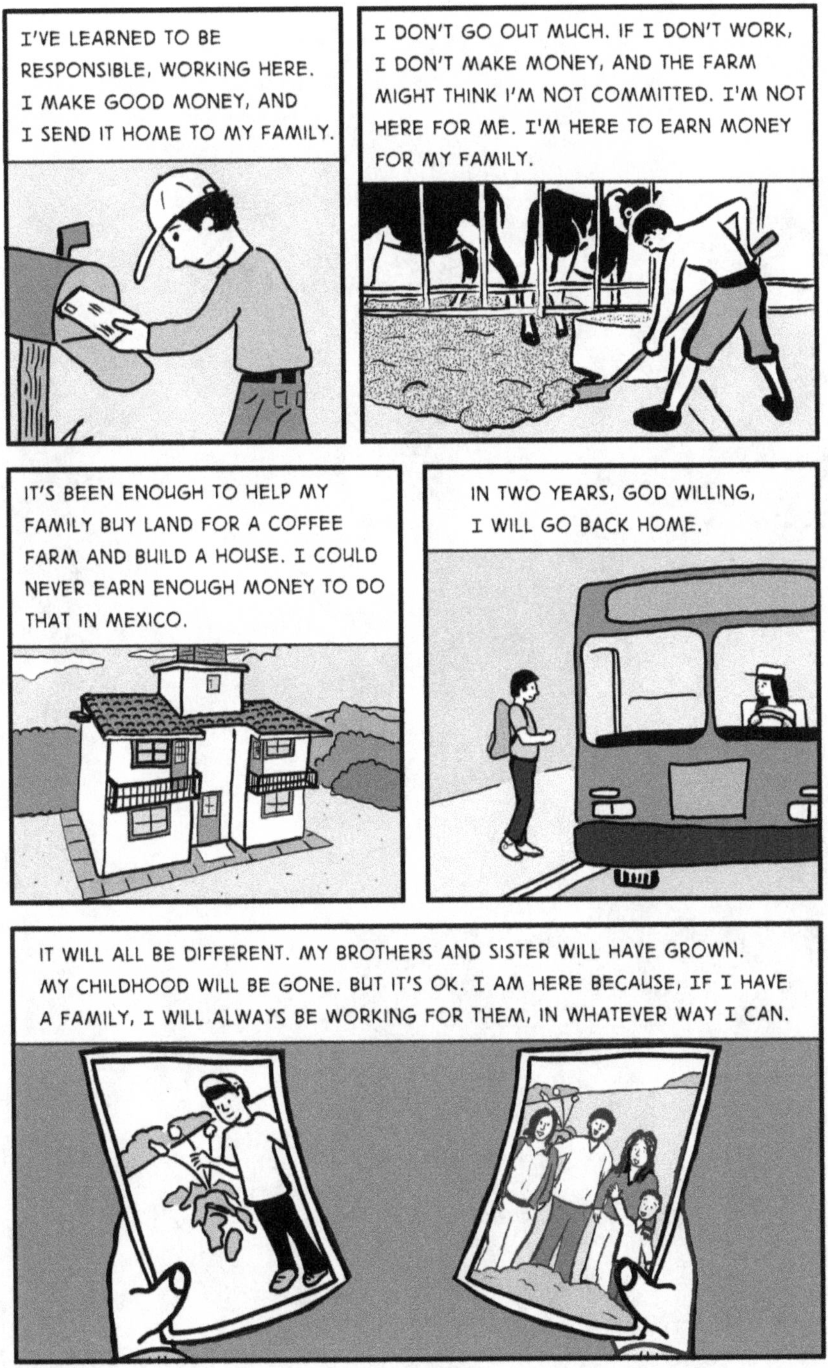
I'VE LEARNED TO BE RESPONSIBLE, WORKING HERE. I MAKE GOOD MONEY, AND I SEND IT HOME TO MY FAMILY.
I DON'T GO OUT MUCH. IF I DON'T WORK, I DON'T MAKE MONEY, AND THE FARM MIGHT THINK I'M NOT COMMITTED. I'M NOT HERE FOR ME. I'M HERE TO EARN MONEY FOR MY FAMILY.
IT'S BEEN ENOUGH TO HELP MY FAMILY BUY LAND FOR A COFFEE FARM AND BUILD A HOUSE. I COULD NEVER EARN ENOUGH MONEY TO DO THAT IN MEXICO.
IN TWO YEARS, GOD WILLING, I WILL GO BACK HOME.
IT WILL ALL BE DIFFERENT. MY BROTHERS AND SISTER WILL HAVE GROWN. MY CHILDHOOD WILL BE GONE. BUT IT'S OK. I AM HERE BECAUSE, IF I HAVE A FAMILY, I WILL ALWAYS BE WORKING FOR THEM, IN WHATEVER WAY I CAN.

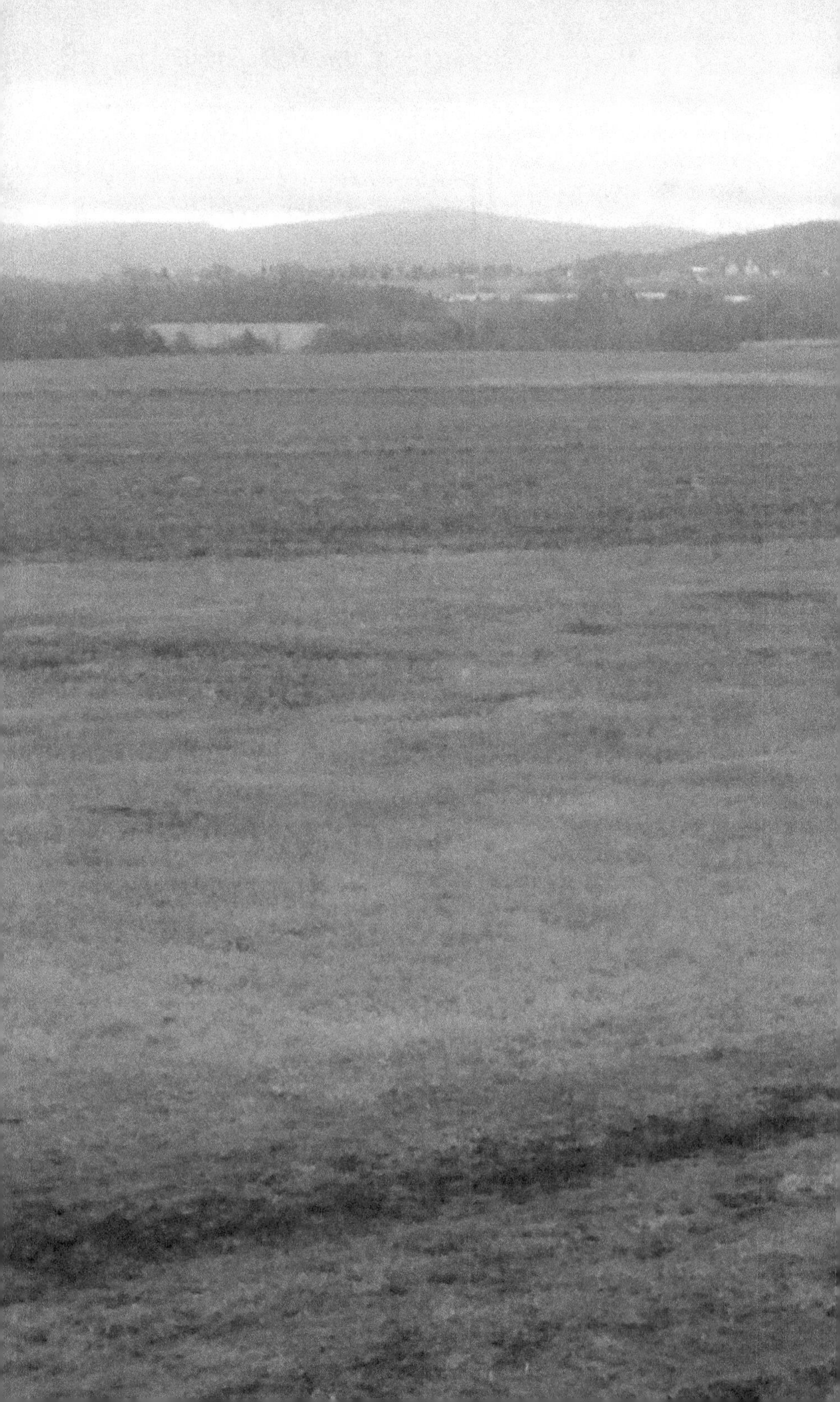

"EL VIAJE MAS CARO" / "THE MOST COSTLY JOURNEY" *presents:*

"THE MOST IMPORTANT LOVE OF EVERY WOMAN SHOULD BE HERSELF"

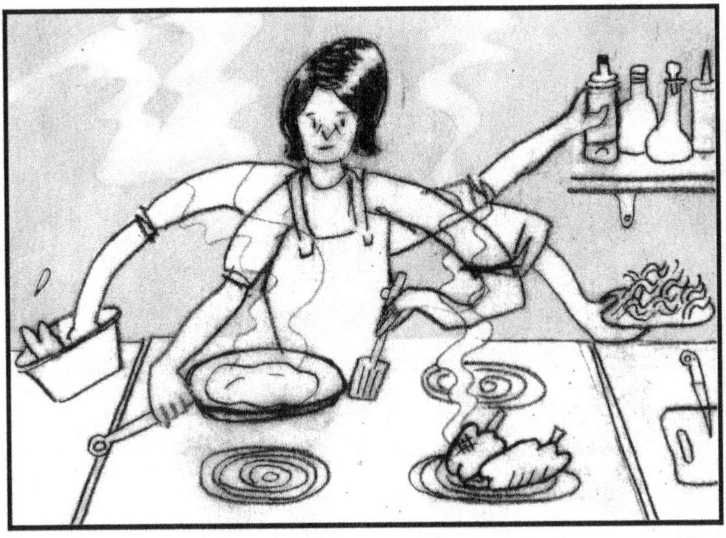

The Story of Guadalupe
Art by Iona Fox

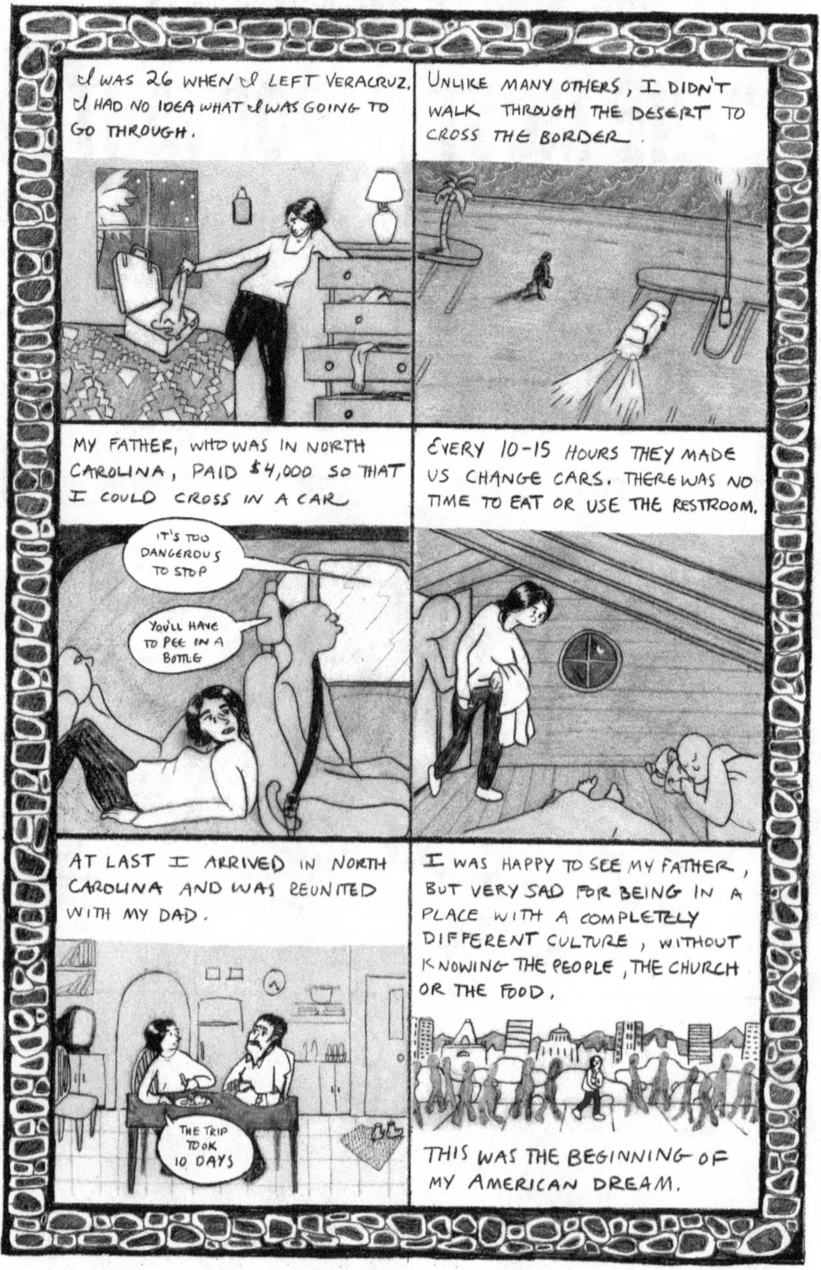
I WAS 26 WHEN I LEFT VERACRUZ. I HAD NO IDEA WHAT I WAS GOING TO GO THROUGH.
UNLIKE MANY OTHERS, I DIDN'T WALK THROUGH THE DESERT TO CROSS THE BORDER.
MY FATHER, WHO WAS IN NORTH CAROLINA, PAID $4,000 SO THAT I COULD CROSS IN A CAR
IT'S TOO DANGEROUS TO STOP
YOU'LL HAVE TO PEE IN A BOTTLE
EVERY 10-15 HOURS THEY MADE US CHANGE CARS. THERE WAS NO TIME TO EAT OR USE THE RESTROOM.
AT LAST I ARRIVED IN NORTH CAROLINA AND WAS REUNITED WITH MY DAD.
THE TRIP TOOK 10 DAYS
I WAS HAPPY TO SEE MY FATHER, BUT VERY SAD FOR BEING IN A PLACE WITH A COMPLETELY DIFFERENT CULTURE, WITHOUT KNOWING THE PEOPLE, THE CHURCH OR THE FOOD.
THIS WAS THE BEGINNING OF MY AMERICAN DREAM.

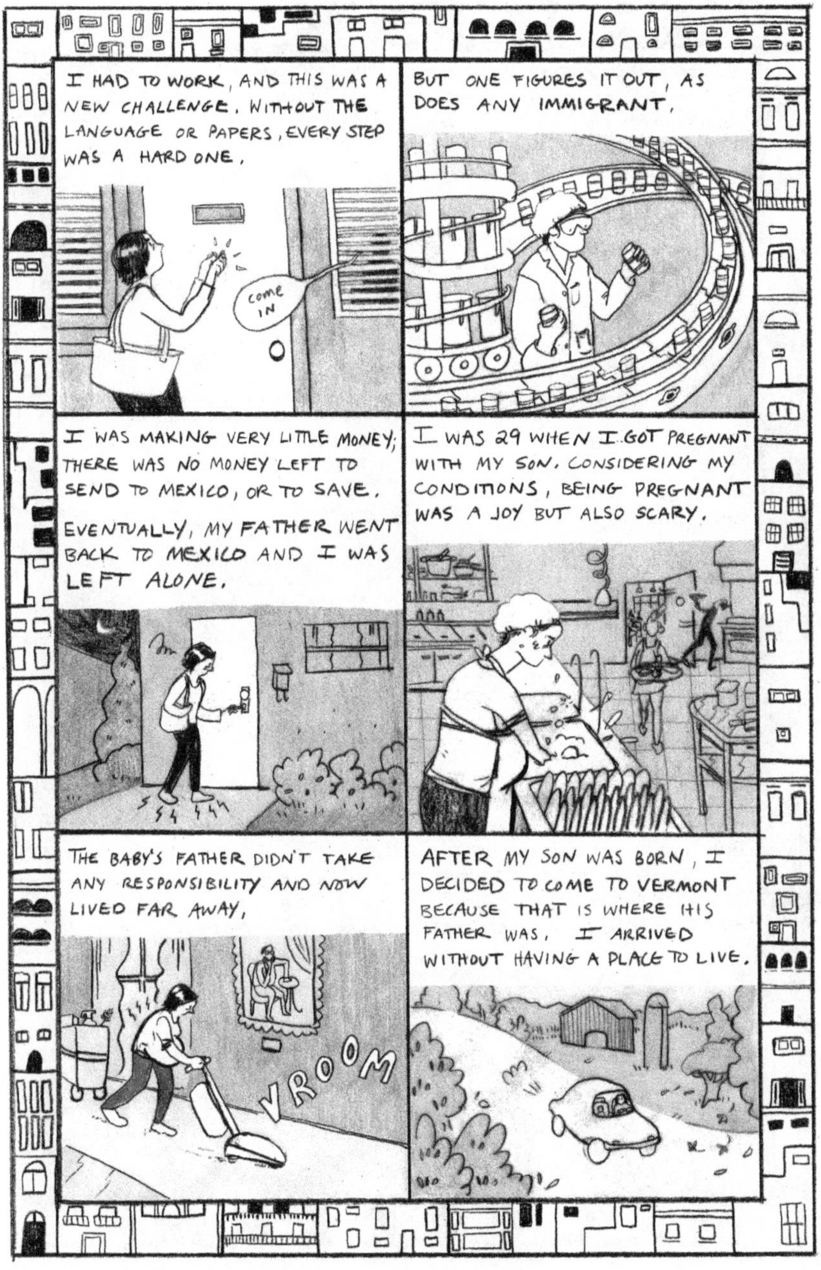
I HAD TO WORK, AND THIS WAS A NEW CHALLENGE. WITHOUT THE LANGUAGE OR PAPERS, EVERY STEP WAS A HARD ONE.
COME IN
BUT ONE FIGURES IT OUT, AS DOES ANY IMMIGRANT.
I WAS MAKING VERY LITTLE MONEY; THERE WAS NO MONEY LEFT TO SEND TO MEXICO, OR TO SAVE.
EVENTUALLY, MY FATHER WENT BACK TO MEXICO AND I WAS LEFT ALONE.
I WAS 29 WHEN I GOT PREGNANT WITH MY SON. CONSIDERING MY CONDITIONS, BEING PREGNANT WAS A JOY BUT ALSO SCARY.
THE BABY'S FATHER DIDN'T TAKE ANY RESPONSIBILITY AND NOW LIVED FAR AWAY,
VROOM
AFTER MY SON WAS BORN, I DECIDED TO COME TO VERMONT BECAUSE THAT IS WHERE HIS FATHER WAS. I ARRIVED WITHOUT HAVING A PLACE TO LIVE.

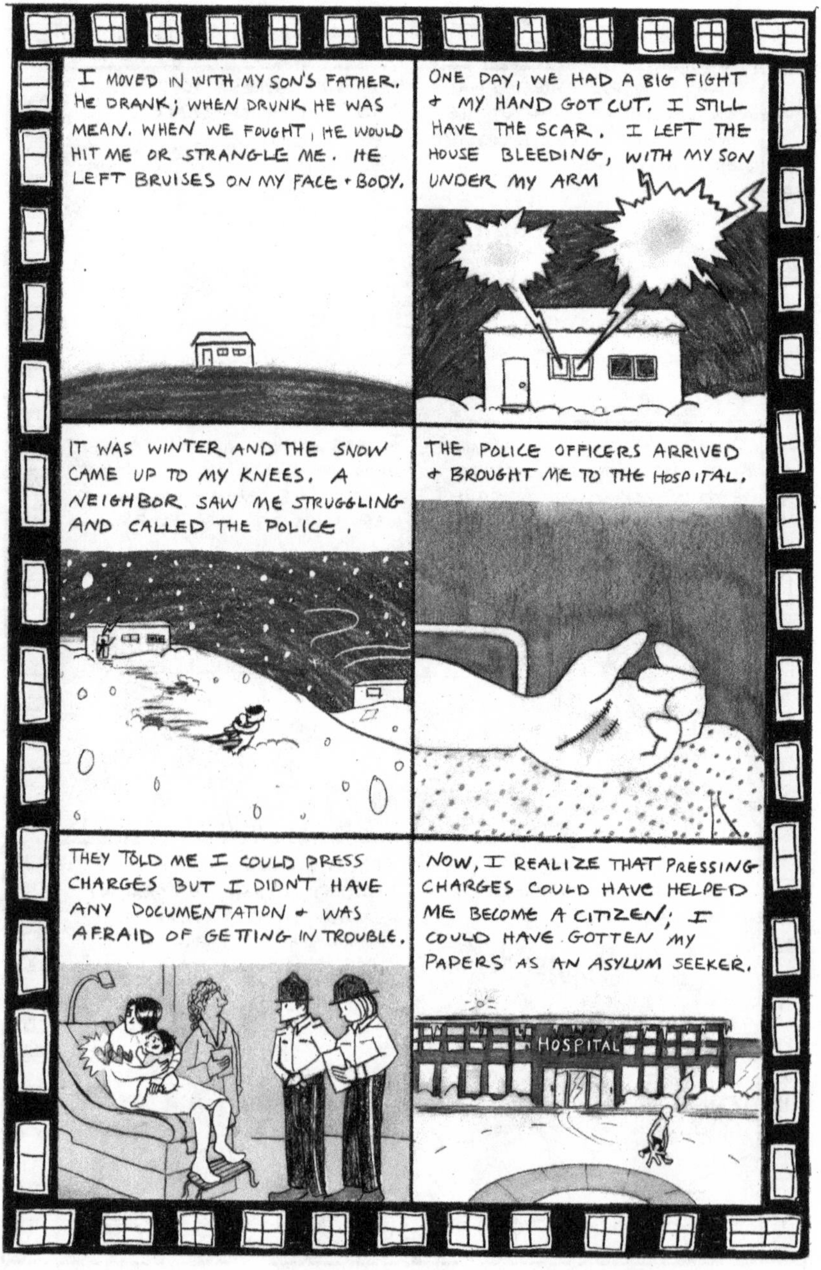
I MOVED IN WITH MY SON'S FATHER. HE DRANK; WHEN DRUNK HE WAS MEAN. WHEN WE FOUGHT, HE WOULD HIT ME OR STRANGLE ME. HE LEFT BRUISES ON MY FACE + BODY.
ONE DAY, WE HAD A BIG FIGHT + MY HAND GOT CUT. I STILL HAVE THE SCAR. I LEFT THE HOUSE BLEEDING, WITH MY SON UNDER MY ARM
IT WAS WINTER AND THE SNOW CAME UP TO MY KNEES. A NEIGHBOR SAW ME STRUGGLING AND CALLED THE POLICE.
THE POLICE OFFICERS ARRIVED + BROUGHT ME TO THE HOSPITAL.
THEY TOLD ME I COULD PRESS CHARGES BUT I DIDN'T HAVE ANY DOCUMENTATION + WAS AFRAID OF GETTING IN TROUBLE.
NOW, I REALIZE THAT PRESSING CHARGES COULD HAVE HELPED ME BECOME A CITIZEN; I COULD HAVE GOTTEN MY PAPERS AS AN ASYLUM SEEKER.
HOSPITAL

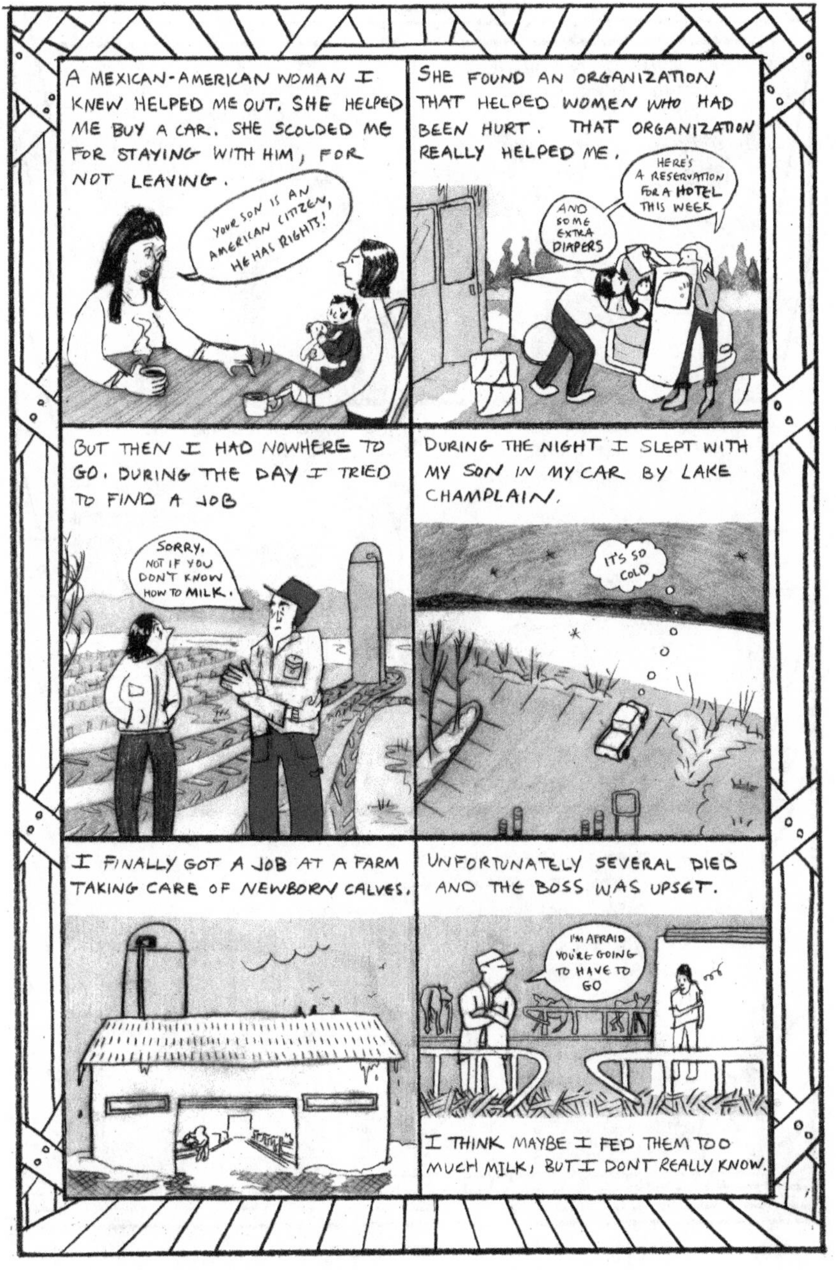
A MEXICAN-AMERICAN WOMAN I KNEW HELPED ME OUT. SHE HELPED ME BUY A CAR. SHE SCOLDED ME FOR STAYING WITH HIM, FOR NOT LEAVING.
YOUR SON IS AN AMERICAN CITIZEN, HE HAS RIGHTS!
SHE FOUND AN ORGANIZATION THAT HELPED WOMEN WHO HAD BEEN HURT. THAT ORGANIZATION REALLY HELPED ME.
HERE'S A RESERVATION FOR A HOTEL THIS WEEK
AND SOME EXTRA DIAPERS
BUT THEN I HAD NOWHERE TO GO. DURING THE DAY I TRIED TO FIND A JOB
SORRY. NOT IF YOU DON'T KNOW HOW TO MILK.
DURING THE NIGHT I SLEPT WITH MY SON IN MY CAR BY LAKE CHAMPLAIN.
IT'S SO COLD
I FINALLY GOT A JOB AT A FARM TAKING CARE OF NEWBORN CALVES.
UNFORTUNATELY SEVERAL DIED AND THE BOSS WAS UPSET.
I'M AFRAID YOU'RE GOING TO HAVE TO GO
I THINK MAYBE I FED THEM TOO MUCH MILK, BUT I DONT REALLY KNOW.

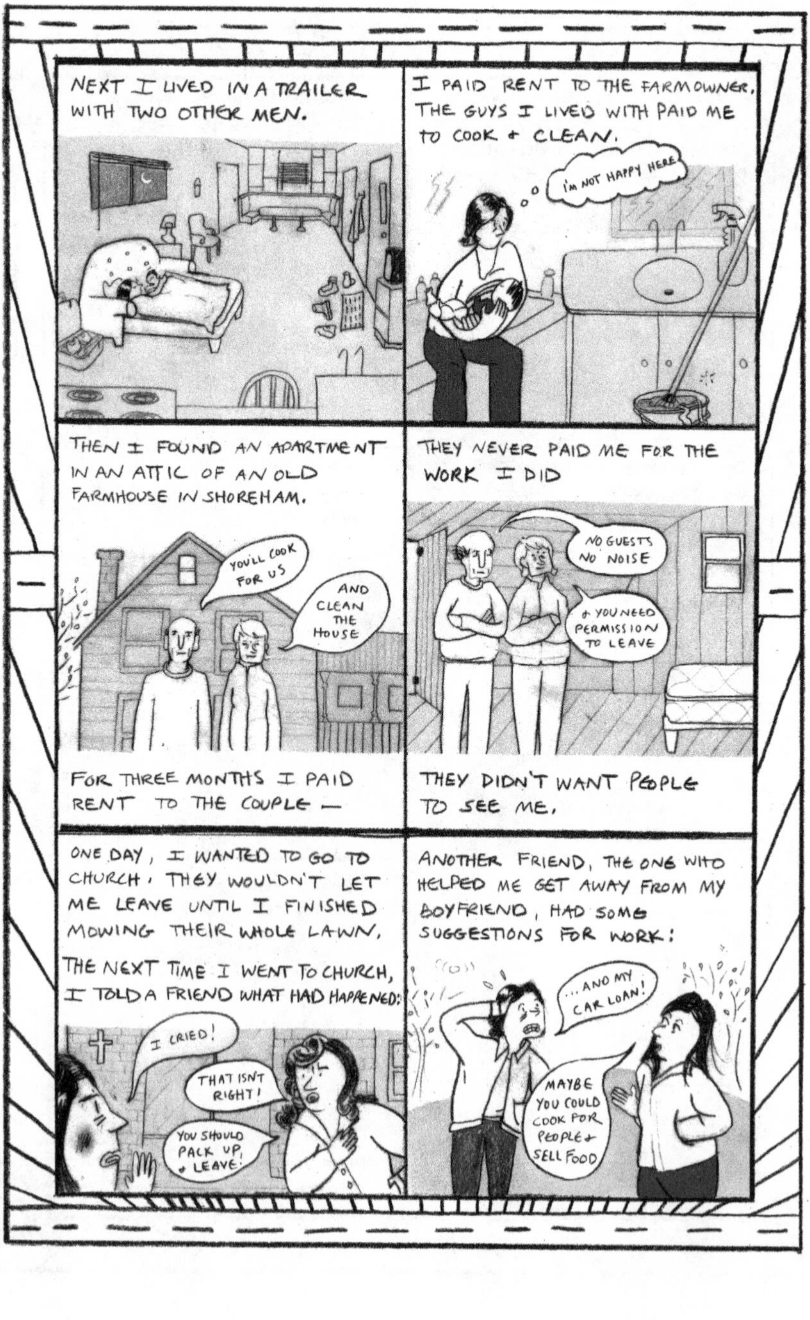
NEXT I LIVED IN A TRAILER WITH TWO OTHER MEN.
I PAID RENT TO THE FARMOWNER. THE GUYS I LIVED WITH PAID ME TO COOK + CLEAN.
I'M NOT HAPPY HERE
THEN I FOUND AN APARTMENT IN AN ATTIC OF AN OLD FARMHOUSE IN SHOREHAM.
YOU'LL COOK FOR US
AND CLEAN THE HOUSE
FOR THREE MONTHS I PAID RENT TO THE COUPLE —
THEY NEVER PAID ME FOR THE WORK I DID
NO GUESTS NO NOISE
+ YOU NEED PERMISSION TO LEAVE
THEY DIDN'T WANT PEOPLE TO SEE ME.
ONE DAY, I WANTED TO GO TO CHURCH. THEY WOULDN'T LET ME LEAVE UNTIL I FINISHED MOWING THEIR WHOLE LAWN.
THE NEXT TIME I WENT TO CHURCH, I TOLD A FRIEND WHAT HAD HAPPENED:
I CRIED!
THAT ISN'T RIGHT!
YOU SHOULD PACK UP + LEAVE!
ANOTHER FRIEND, THE ONE WHO HELPED ME GET AWAY FROM MY BOYFRIEND, HAD SOME SUGGESTIONS FOR WORK:
...AND MY CAR LOAN!
MAYBE YOU COULD COOK FOR PEOPLE + SELL FOOD

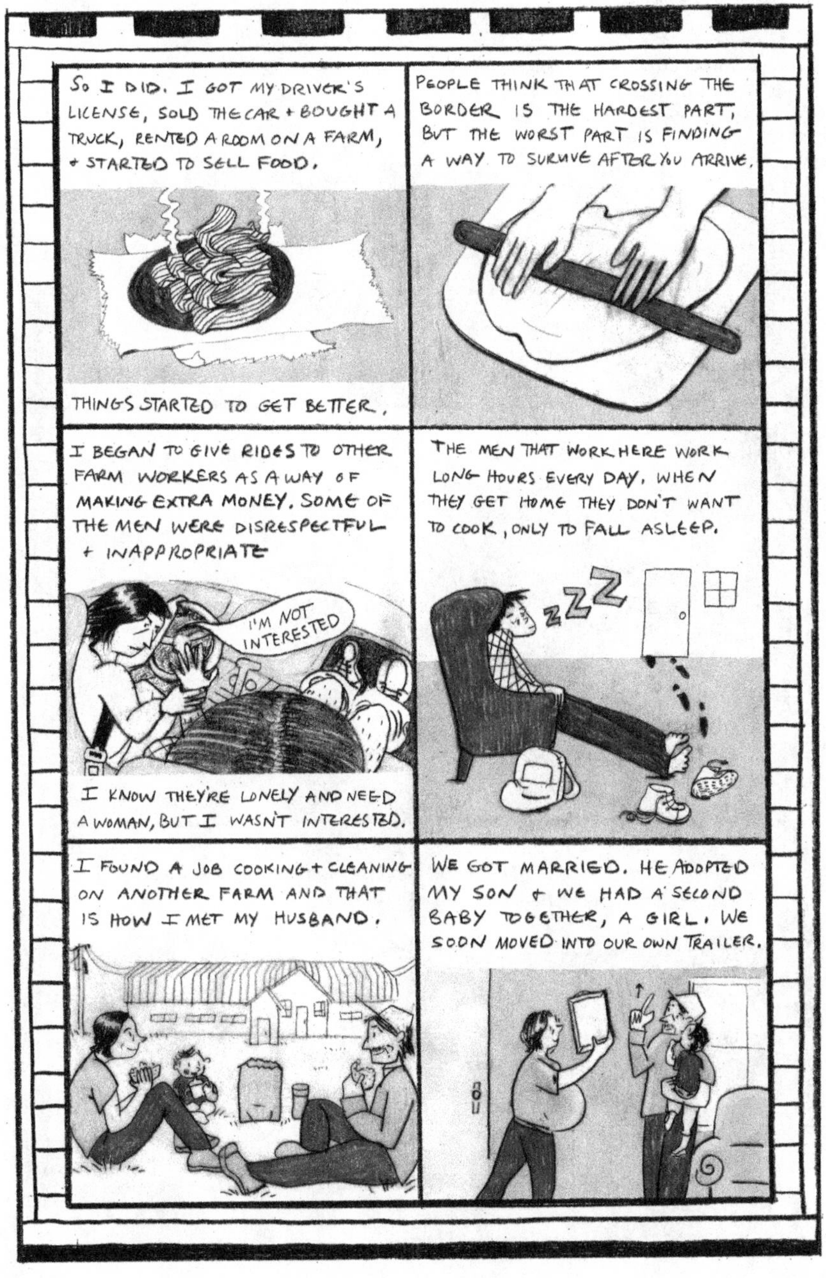
SO I DID. I GOT MY DRIVER'S LICENSE, SOLD THE CAR + BOUGHT A TRUCK, RENTED A ROOM ON A FARM, + STARTED TO SELL FOOD.
THINGS STARTED TO GET BETTER.
PEOPLE THINK THAT CROSSING THE BORDER IS THE HARDEST PART, BUT THE WORST PART IS FINDING A WAY TO SURVIVE AFTER YOU ARRIVE.
I BEGAN TO GIVE RIDES TO OTHER FARM WORKERS AS A WAY OF MAKING EXTRA MONEY. SOME OF THE MEN WERE DISRESPECTFUL + INAPPROPRIATE
I'M NOT INTERESTED
I KNOW THEY'RE LONELY AND NEED A WOMAN, BUT I WASN'T INTERESTED.
THE MEN THAT WORK HERE WORK LONG HOURS EVERY DAY. WHEN THEY GET HOME THEY DON'T WANT TO COOK, ONLY TO FALL ASLEEP.
ZZZ
I FOUND A JOB COOKING + CLEANING ON ANOTHER FARM AND THAT IS HOW I MET MY HUSBAND.
WE GOT MARRIED. HE ADOPTED MY SON + WE HAD A SECOND BABY TOGETHER, A GIRL. WE SOON MOVED INTO OUR OWN TRAILER.

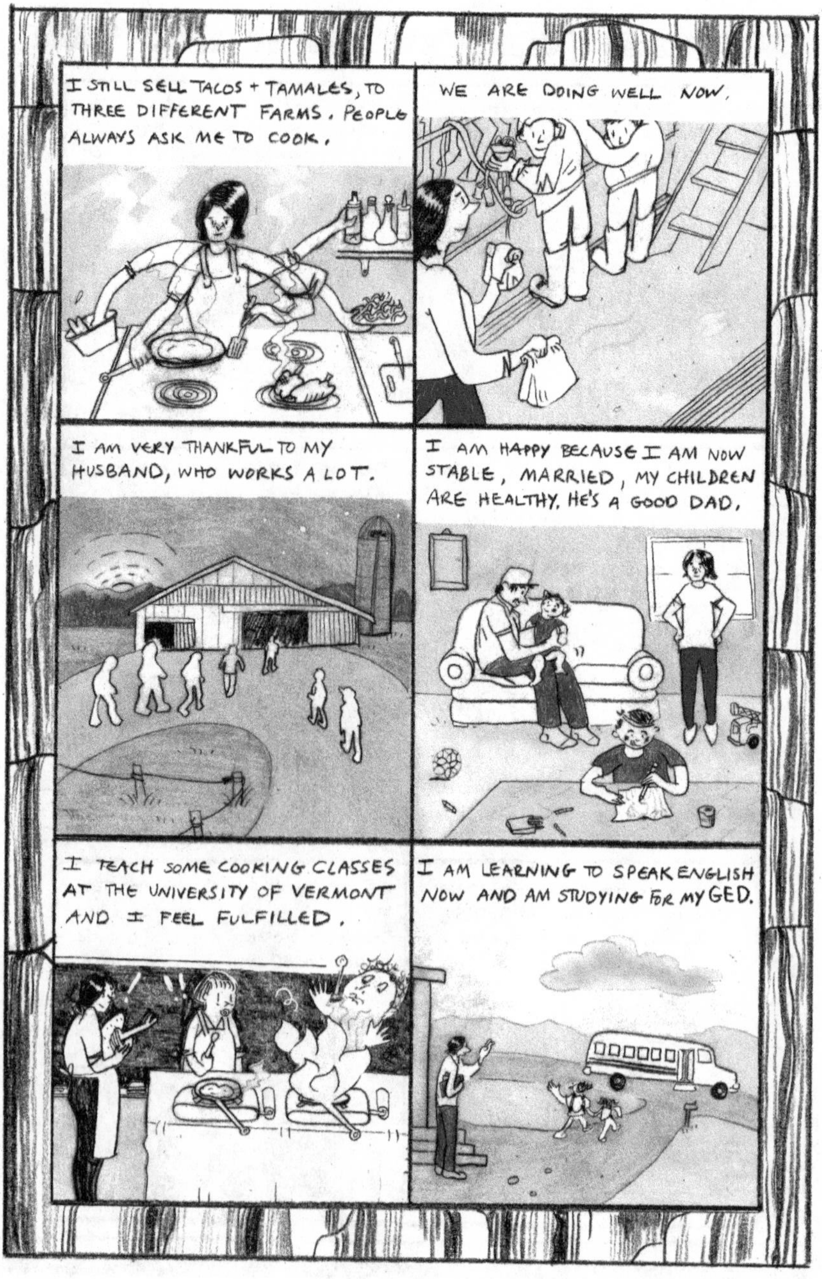
I STILL SELL TACOS + TAMALES, TO THREE DIFFERENT FARMS. PEOPLE ALWAYS ASK ME TO COOK.
WE ARE DOING WELL NOW.
I AM VERY THANKFUL TO MY HUSBAND, WHO WORKS A LOT.
I AM HAPPY BECAUSE I AM NOW STABLE, MARRIED, MY CHILDREN ARE HEALTHY. HE'S A GOOD DAD.
I TEACH SOME COOKING CLASSES AT THE UNIVERSITY OF VERMONT AND I FEEL FULFILLED.
I AM LEARNING TO SPEAK ENGLISH NOW AND AM STUDYING FOR MY GED.

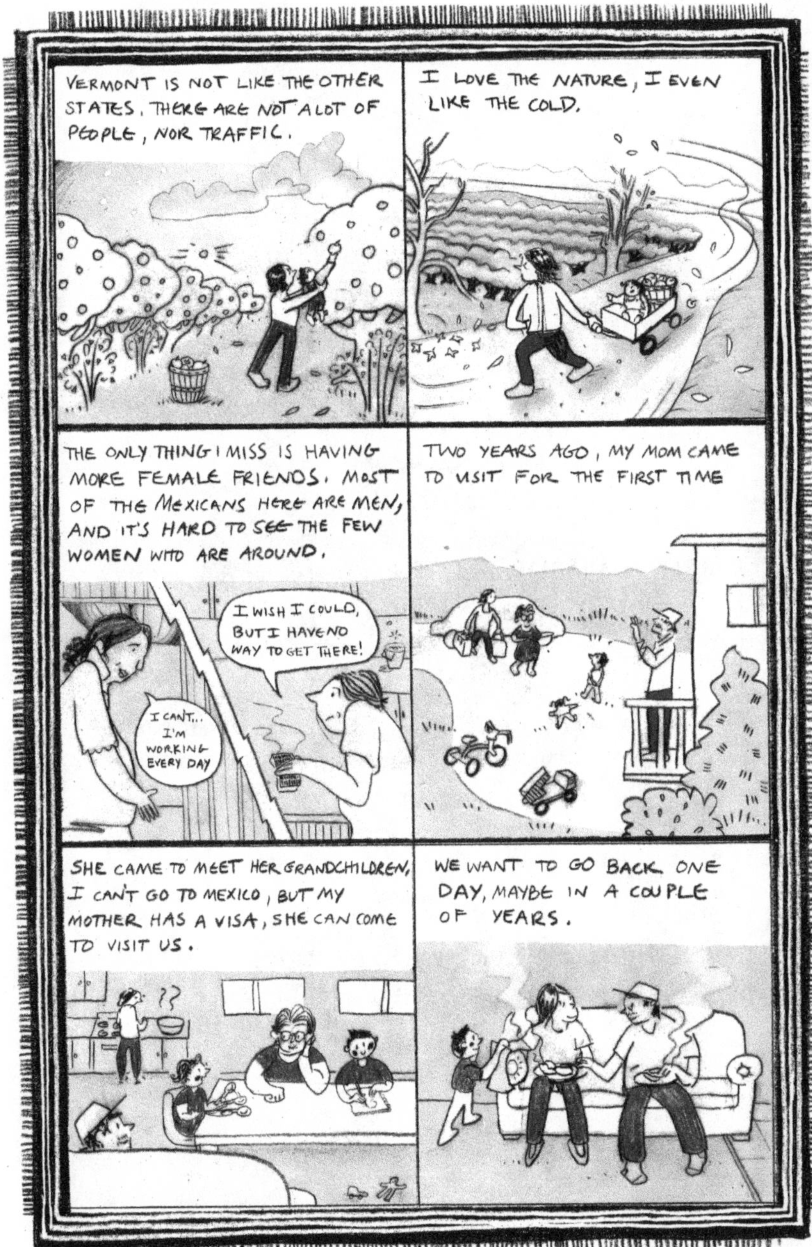
VERMONT IS NOT LIKE THE OTHER STATES. THERE ARE NOT A LOT OF PEOPLE, NOR TRAFFIC.
I LOVE THE NATURE, I EVEN LIKE THE COLD.
THE ONLY THING I MISS IS HAVING MORE FEMALE FRIENDS. MOST OF THE MEXICANS HERE ARE MEN, AND IT'S HARD TO SEE THE FEW WOMEN WHO ARE AROUND.
I WISH I COULD, BUT I HAVE NO WAY TO GET THERE!
I CAN'T... I'M WORKING EVERY DAY
TWO YEARS AGO, MY MOM CAME TO VISIT FOR THE FIRST TIME
SHE CAME TO MEET HER GRANDCHILDREN, I CAN'T GO TO MEXICO, BUT MY MOTHER HAS A VISA, SHE CAN COME TO VISIT US.
??
WE WANT TO GO BACK ONE DAY, MAYBE IN A COUPLE OF YEARS.

I THANK GOD FOR ALL THE CHALLENGES HE
PUT IN MY WAY. WITHOUT THEM, I WOULDN'T
HAVE GOTTEN TO WHERE I AM TODAY.

I WOULD LIKE MY STORY TO HELP OTHER WOMEN.
IT DOESN'T MATTER ALL THE OBSTACLES THAT ONE
FACES IN LIFE. THERE IS ALWAYS LIGHT AT
THE END OF THE TUNNEL.

IF YOU OR SOMEONE YOU KNOW IS BEING HURT,
WHETHER OR NOT YOU ARE DOCUMENTED,
PLEASE CALL WomenSAFE AT 1-800-388-4205.
SE HABLA ESPAÑOL.

"EL VIAJE MAS CARO" / "THE MOST COSTLY JOURNEY" presents:

FAR FROM MY FAMILY

The Story of Carlos
Art by Kane Lynch

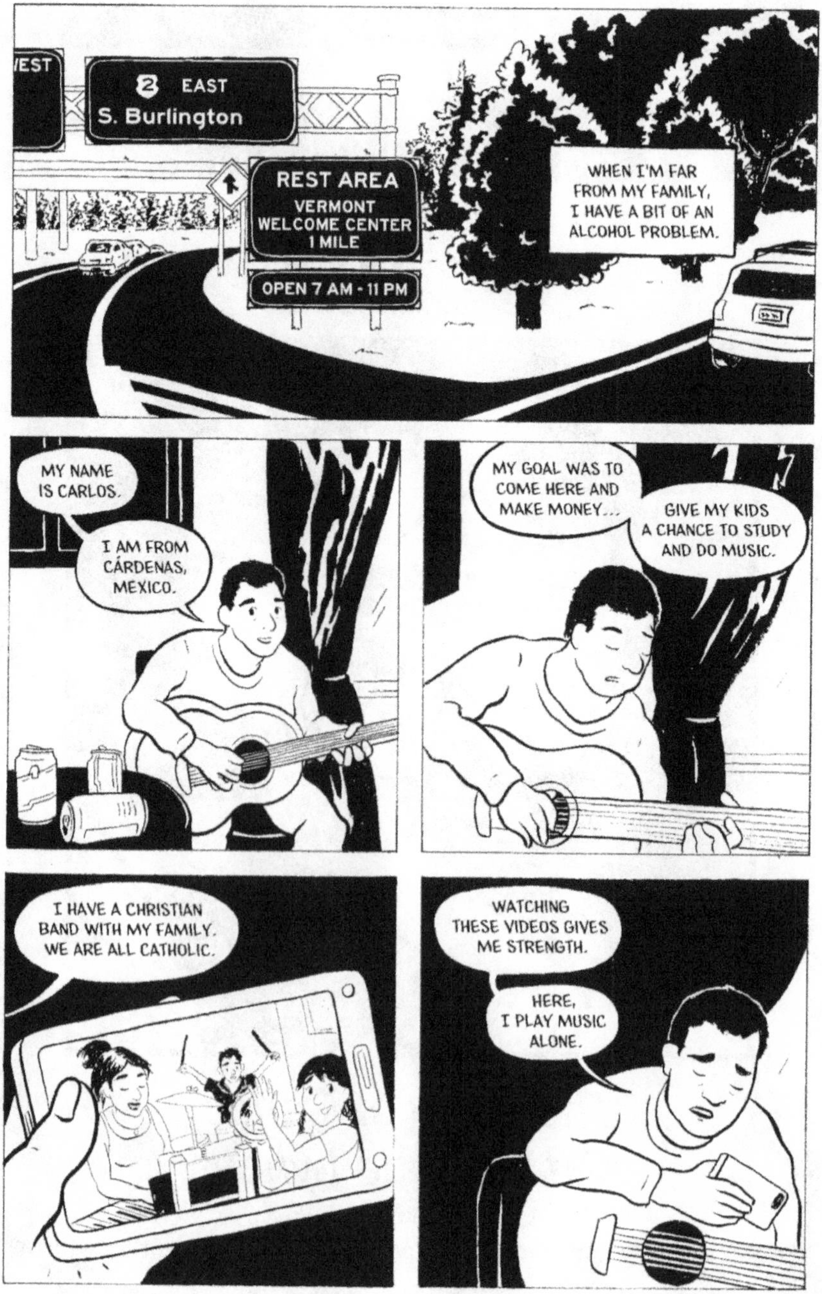
WEST
2 EAST
S. Burlington
REST AREA
VERMONT
WELCOME CENTER
1 MILE
OPEN 7 AM - 11 PM
WHEN I'M FAR FROM MY FAMILY, I HAVE A BIT OF AN ALCOHOL PROBLEM.
MY NAME IS CARLOS.
I AM FROM CÁRDENAS, MEXICO.
MY GOAL WAS TO COME HERE AND MAKE MONEY...
GIVE MY KIDS A CHANCE TO STUDY AND DO MUSIC.
I HAVE A CHRISTIAN BAND WITH MY FAMILY. WE ARE ALL CATHOLIC.
WATCHING THESE VIDEOS GIVES ME STRENGTH.
HERE, I PLAY MUSIC ALONE.

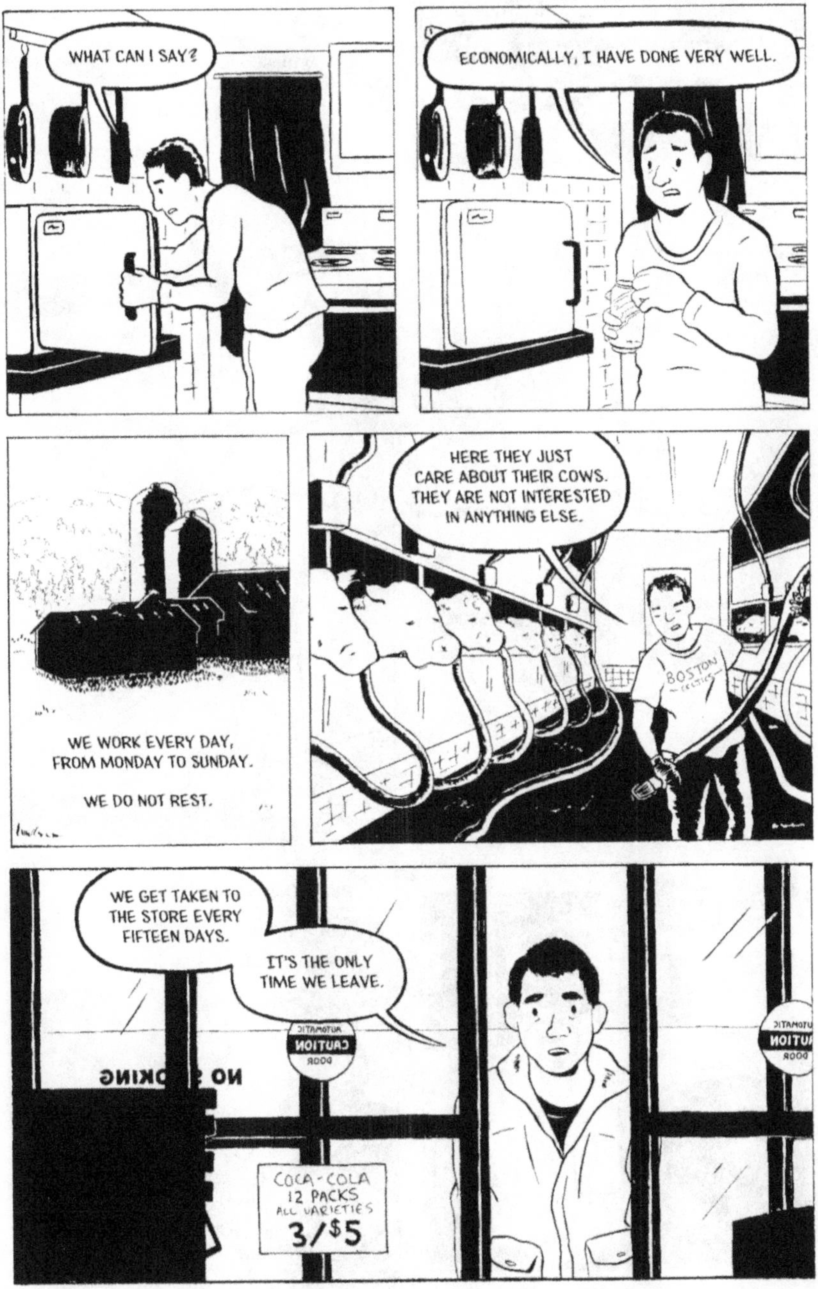
WHAT CAN I SAY?
ECONOMICALLY, I HAVE DONE VERY WELL.
WE WORK EVERY DAY, FROM MONDAY TO SUNDAY.
WE DO NOT REST.
HERE THEY JUST CARE ABOUT THEIR COWS. THEY ARE NOT INTERESTED IN ANYTHING ELSE.
BOSTON CELTICS
WE GET TAKEN TO THE STORE EVERY FIFTEEN DAYS.
IT'S THE ONLY TIME WE LEAVE.
AUTOMATIC CAUTION DOOR
NO SMOKING
COCA-COLA 12 PACKS ALL VARIETIES 3/$5

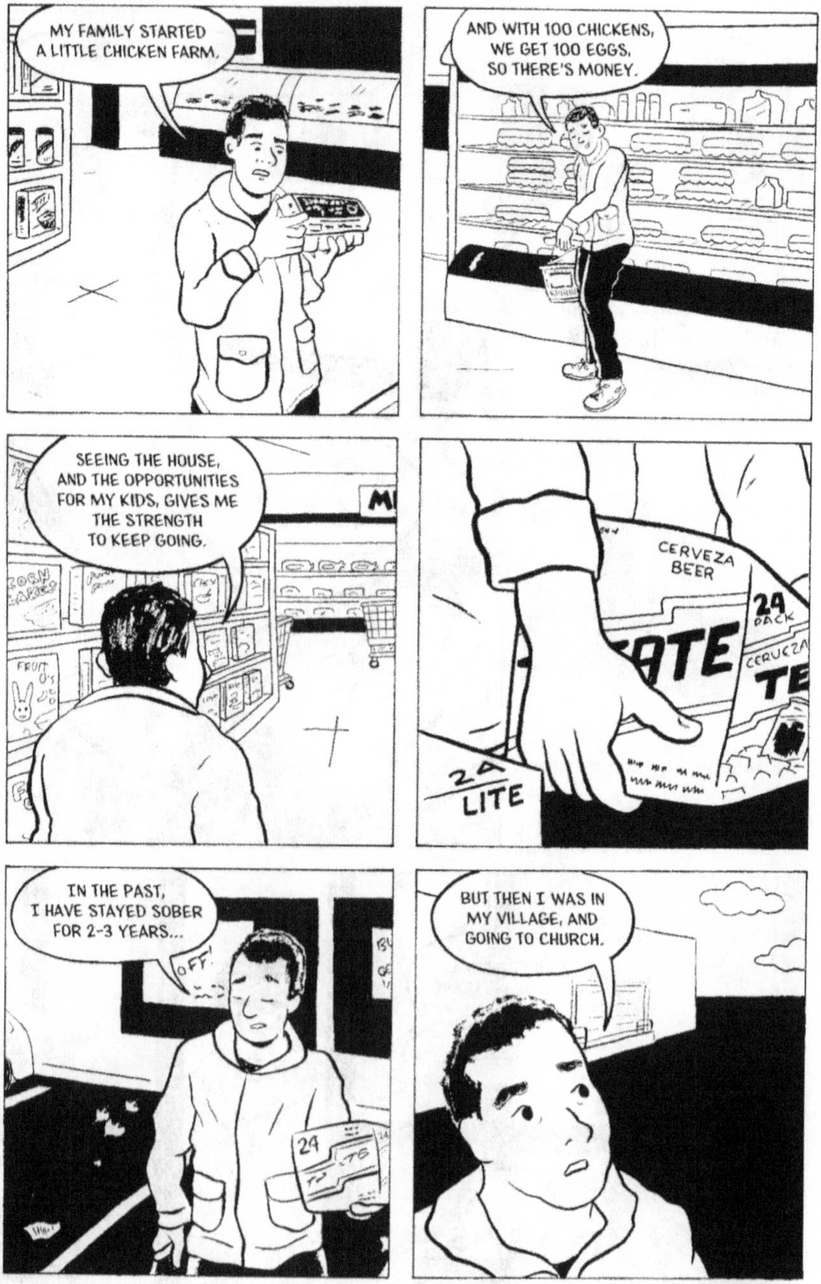
MY FAMILY STARTED A LITTLE CHICKEN FARM.
AND WITH 100 CHICKENS, WE GET 100 EGGS, SO THERE'S MONEY.
SEEING THE HOUSE, AND THE OPPORTUNITIES FOR MY KIDS, GIVES ME THE STRENGTH TO KEEP GOING.
CORN FLAKES
FRUIT O'S
CERVEZA BEER
24 PACK
24 LITE
IN THE PAST, I HAVE STAYED SOBER FOR 2-3 YEARS...
OFF!
24
BUT THEN I WAS IN MY VILLAGE, AND GOING TO CHURCH.

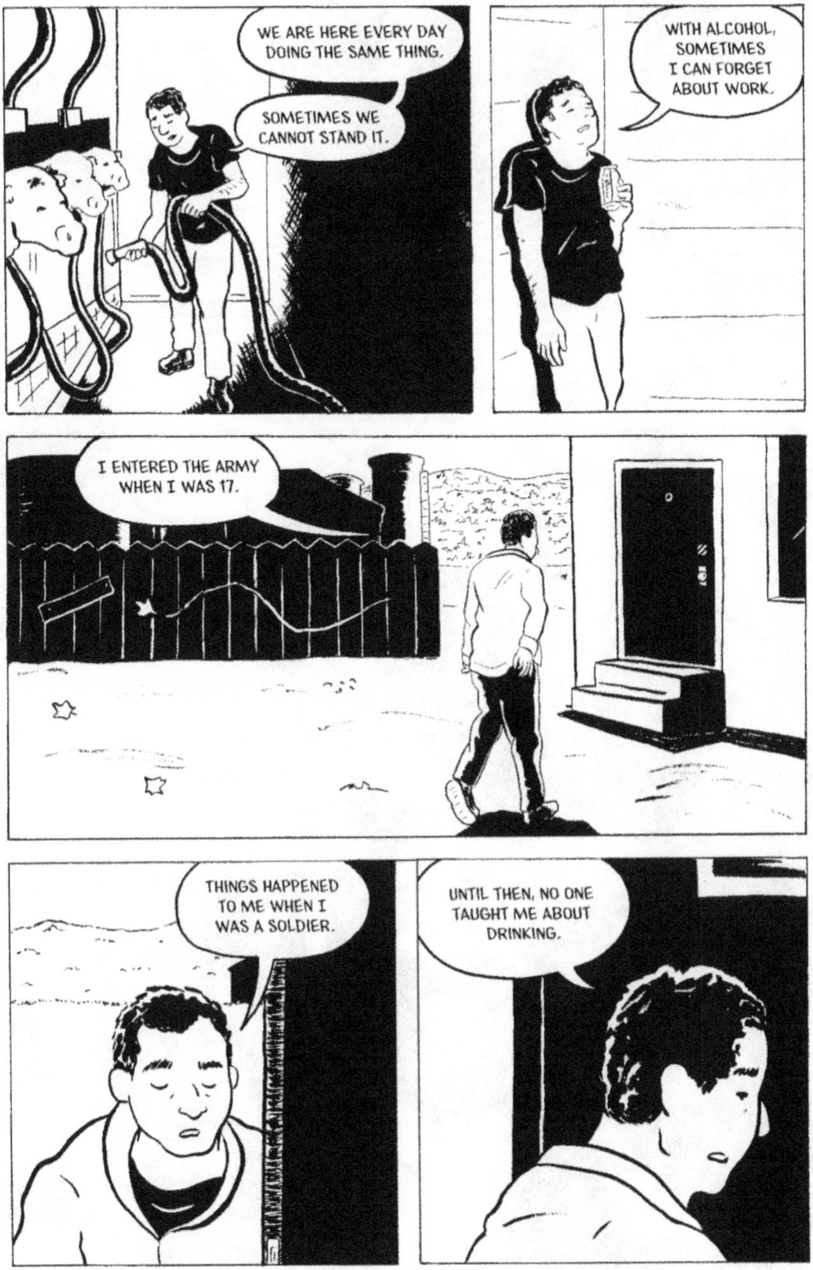
WE ARE HERE EVERY DAY DOING THE SAME THING.
SOMETIMES WE CANNOT STAND IT.
WITH ALCOHOL, SOMETIMES I CAN FORGET ABOUT WORK.
I ENTERED THE ARMY WHEN I WAS 17.
THINGS HAPPENED TO ME WHEN I WAS A SOLDIER.
UNTIL THEN, NO ONE TAUGHT ME ABOUT DRINKING.

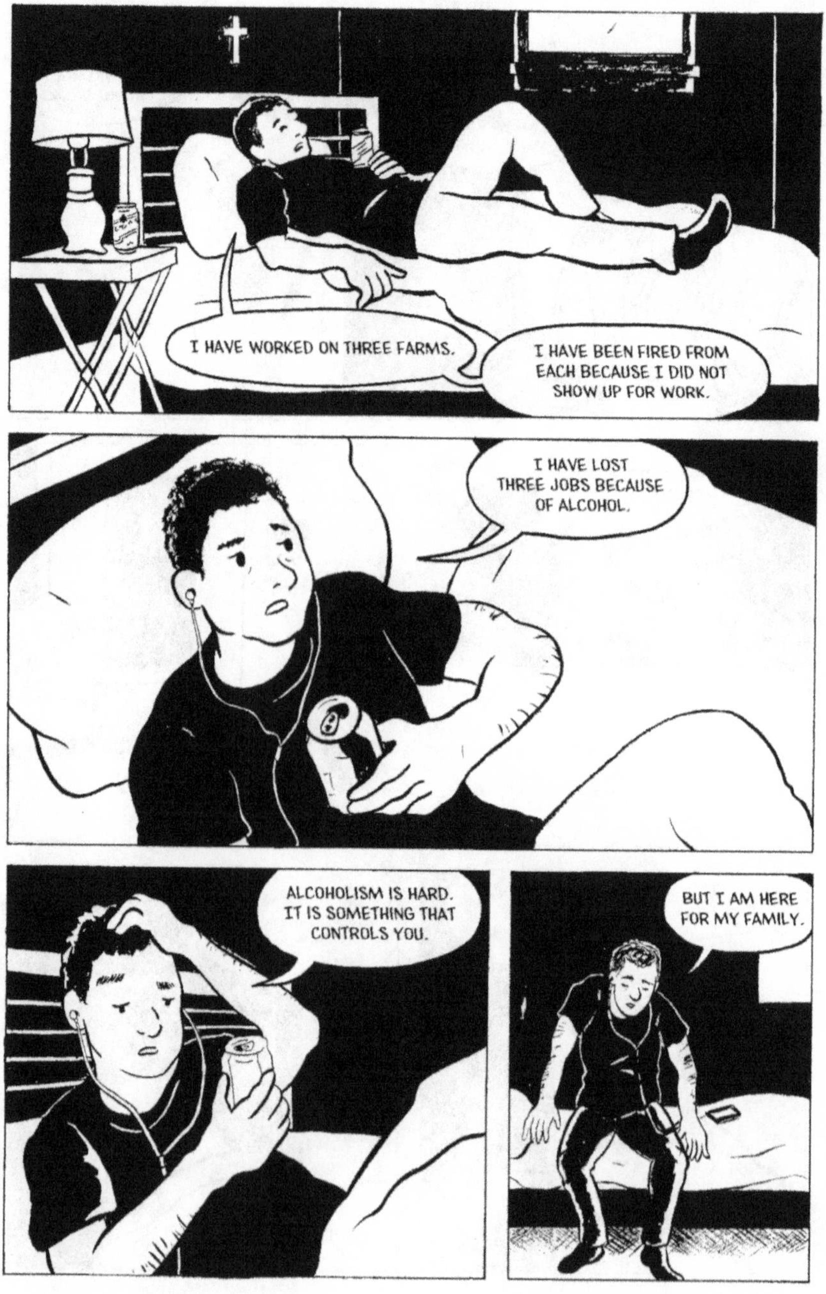
I HAVE WORKED ON THREE FARMS.
I HAVE BEEN FIRED FROM EACH BECAUSE I DID NOT SHOW UP FOR WORK.
I HAVE LOST THREE JOBS BECAUSE OF ALCOHOL.
ALCOHOLISM IS HARD. IT IS SOMETHING THAT CONTROLS YOU.
BUT I AM HERE FOR MY FAMILY.

I WAS THINKING ABOUT GOING HOME BUT I CUT MY HAND VERY BADLY.

THE TRUTH IS, I DON'T EVEN KNOW WHAT HAPPENED.

I WAS TOO DRUNK.

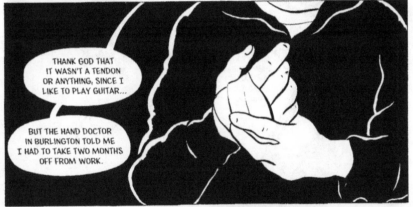

THANK GOD THAT IT WASN'T A TENDON OR ANYTHING, SINCE I LIKE TO PLAY GUITAR...

BUT THE HAND DOCTOR IN BURLINGTON TOLD ME I HAD TO TAKE TWO MONTHS OFF FROM WORK.

Mis Quince Años

I MISSED MY DAUGHTER'S QUINCEAÑERA.

I'M MISSING A LOT OF GREAT MOMENTS IN MY FAMILY.

BUT WE ALL HAVE TO BE UNITED TO MAKE THIS WORK.

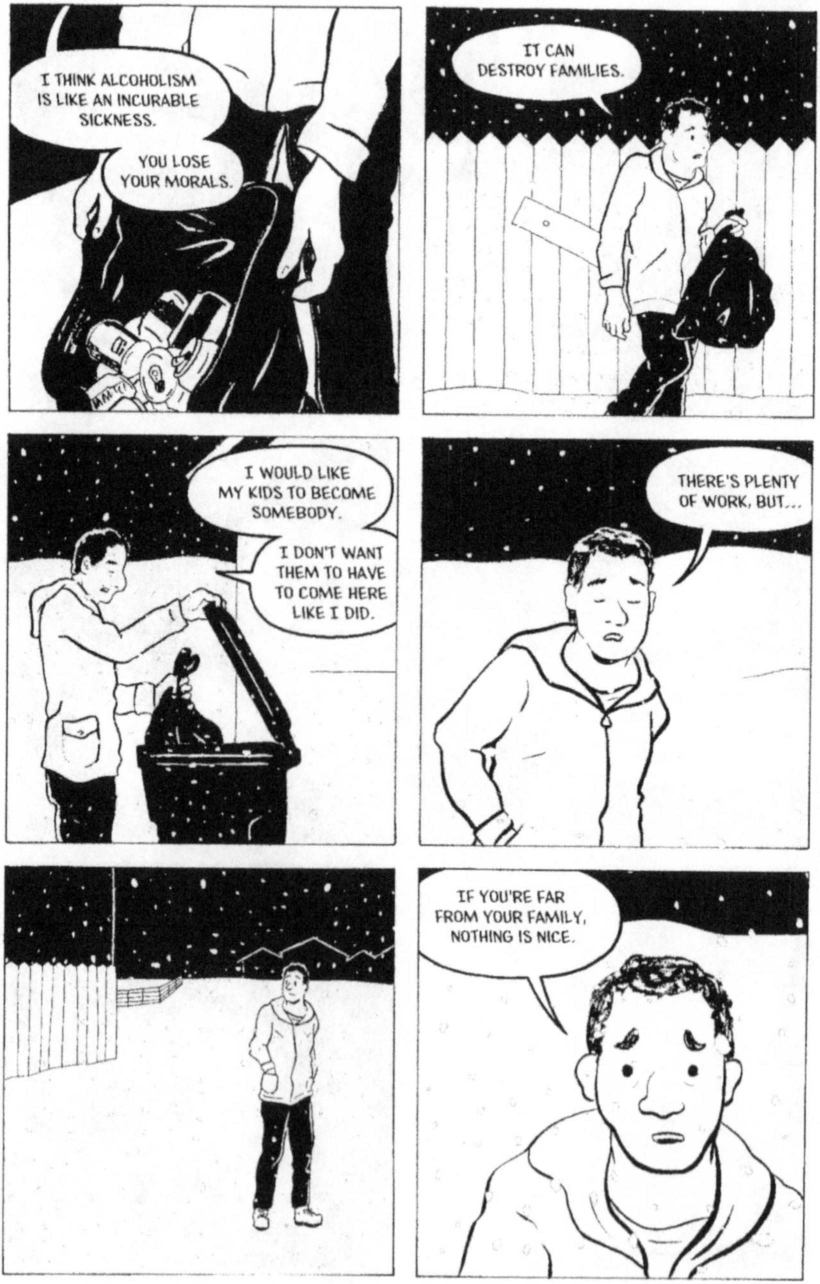
I THINK ALCOHOLISM IS LIKE AN INCURABLE SICKNESS.
YOU LOSE YOUR MORALS.
IT CAN DESTROY FAMILIES.
I WOULD LIKE MY KIDS TO BECOME SOMEBODY.
I DON'T WANT THEM TO HAVE TO COME HERE LIKE I DID.
THERE'S PLENTY OF WORK, BUT...
IF YOU'RE FAR FROM YOUR FAMILY, NOTHING IS NICE.

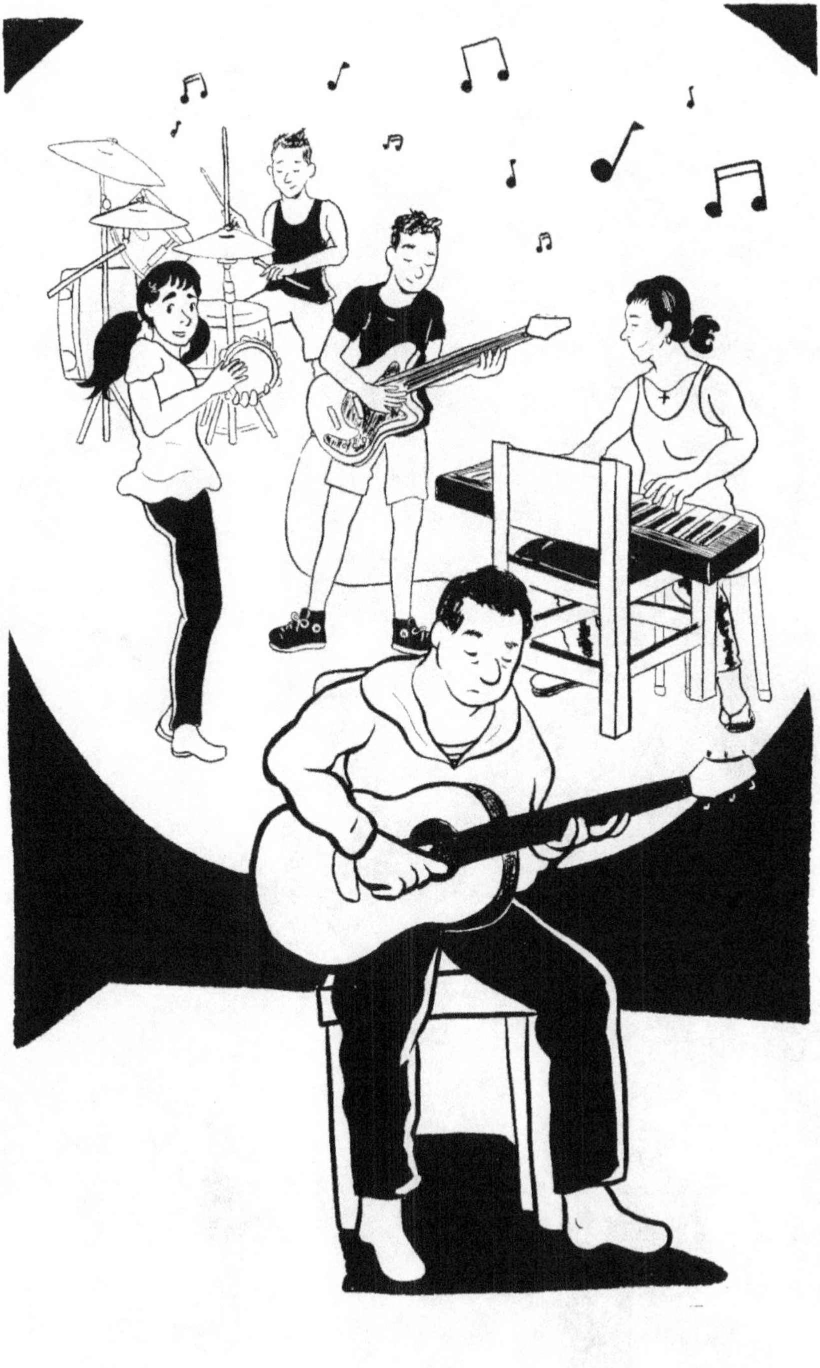

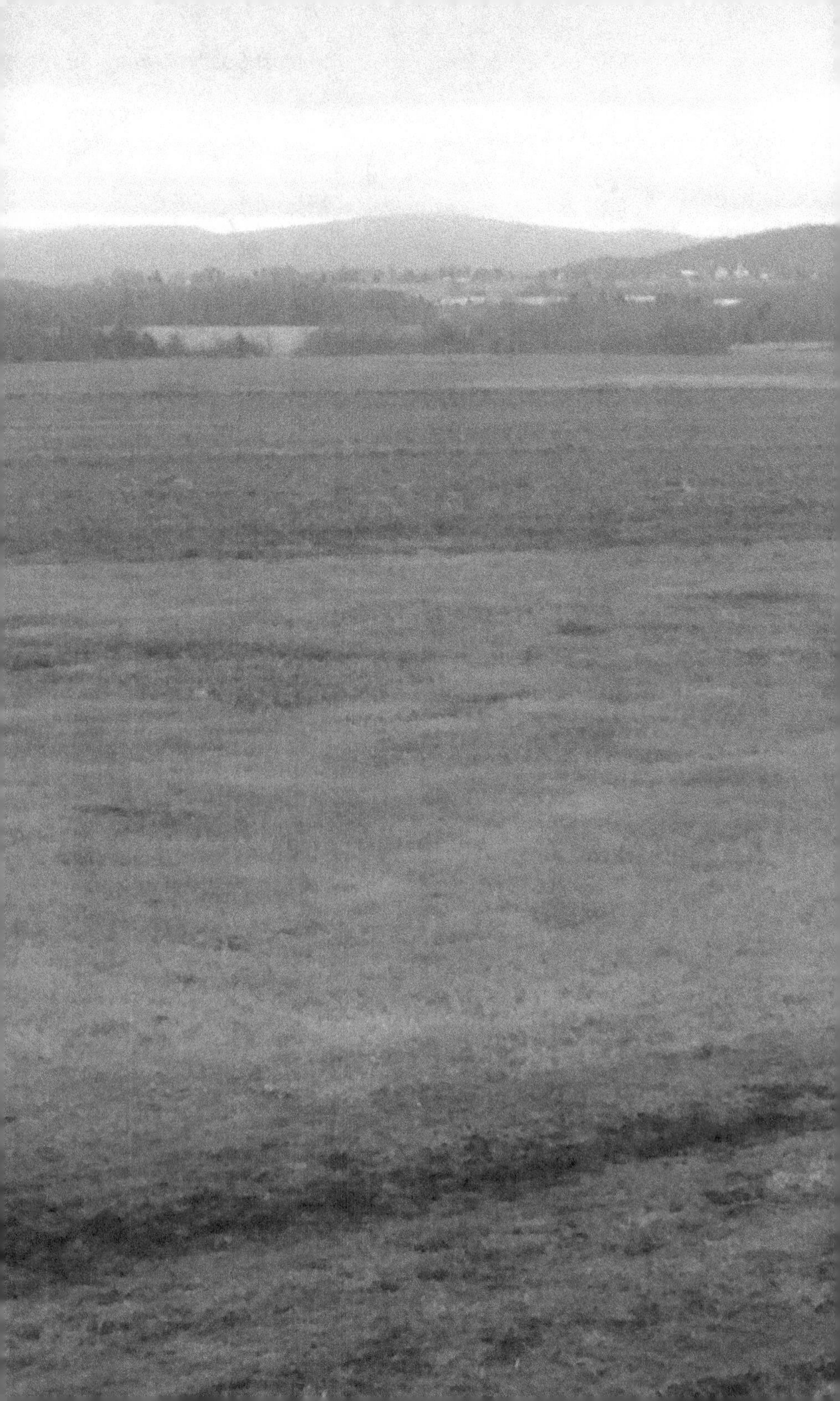

"EL VIAJE MAS CARO" / "THE MOST COSTLY JOURNEY" presents:

SUFFERING TO COME HERE

The Story of Rubén
Art by Teppi Zuppo

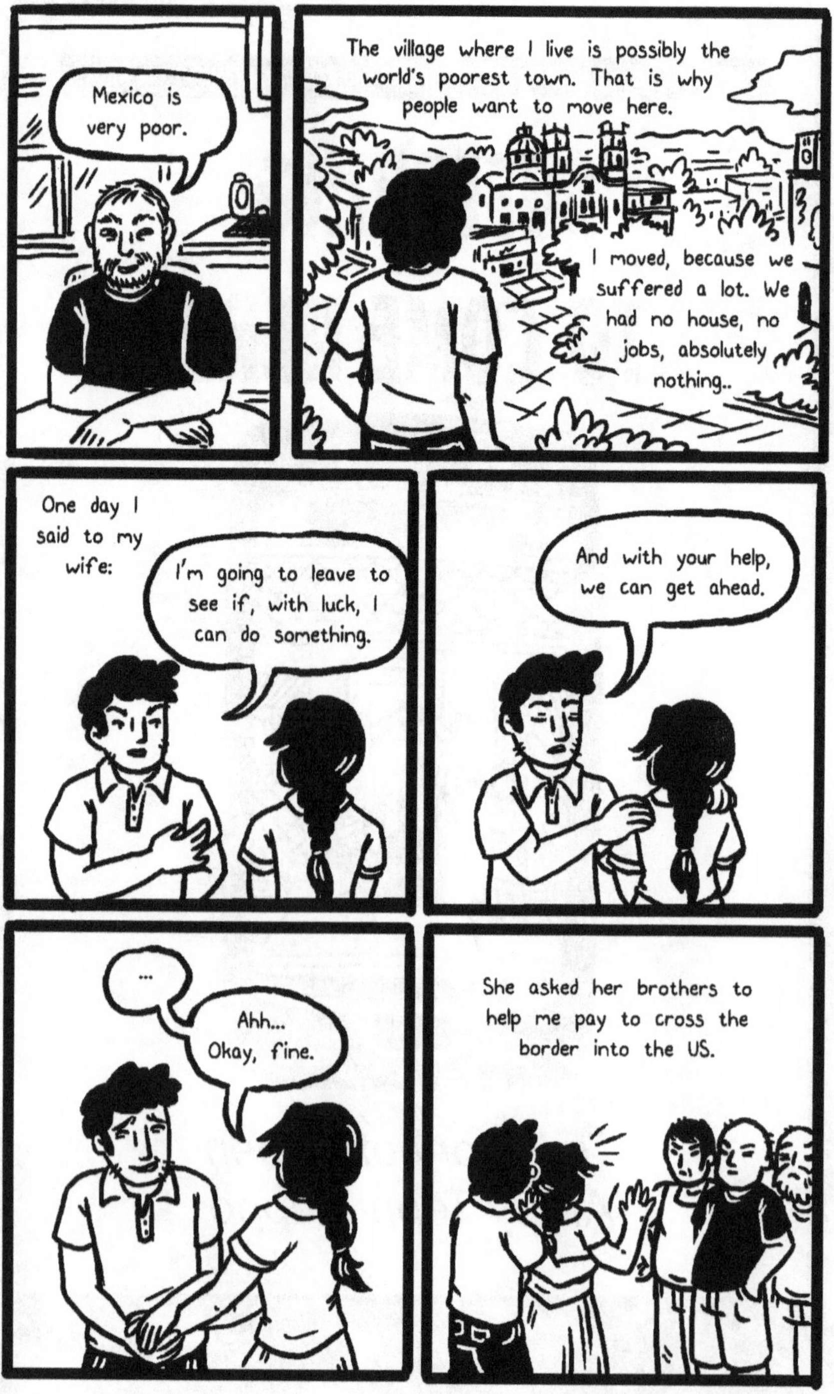
Mexico is very poor.
The village where I live is possibly the world's poorest town. That is why people want to move here.
I moved, because we suffered a lot. We had no house, no jobs, absolutely nothing..
One day I said to my wife:
I'm going to leave to see if, with luck, I can do something.
And with your help, we can get ahead.
...
Ahh... Okay, fine.
She asked her brothers to help me pay to cross the border into the US.

That first time crossing was very sad because I was kidnapped.

The same coyotes, as we call them, that got us to the border held me hostage for about ten days.

We had already crossed the desert, and the desert for us is very hard.

I got lost, separated from the group I was with.

After seven days alone, I joined others that were crossing.

Eventually, the original coyotes found me and kidnapped me.

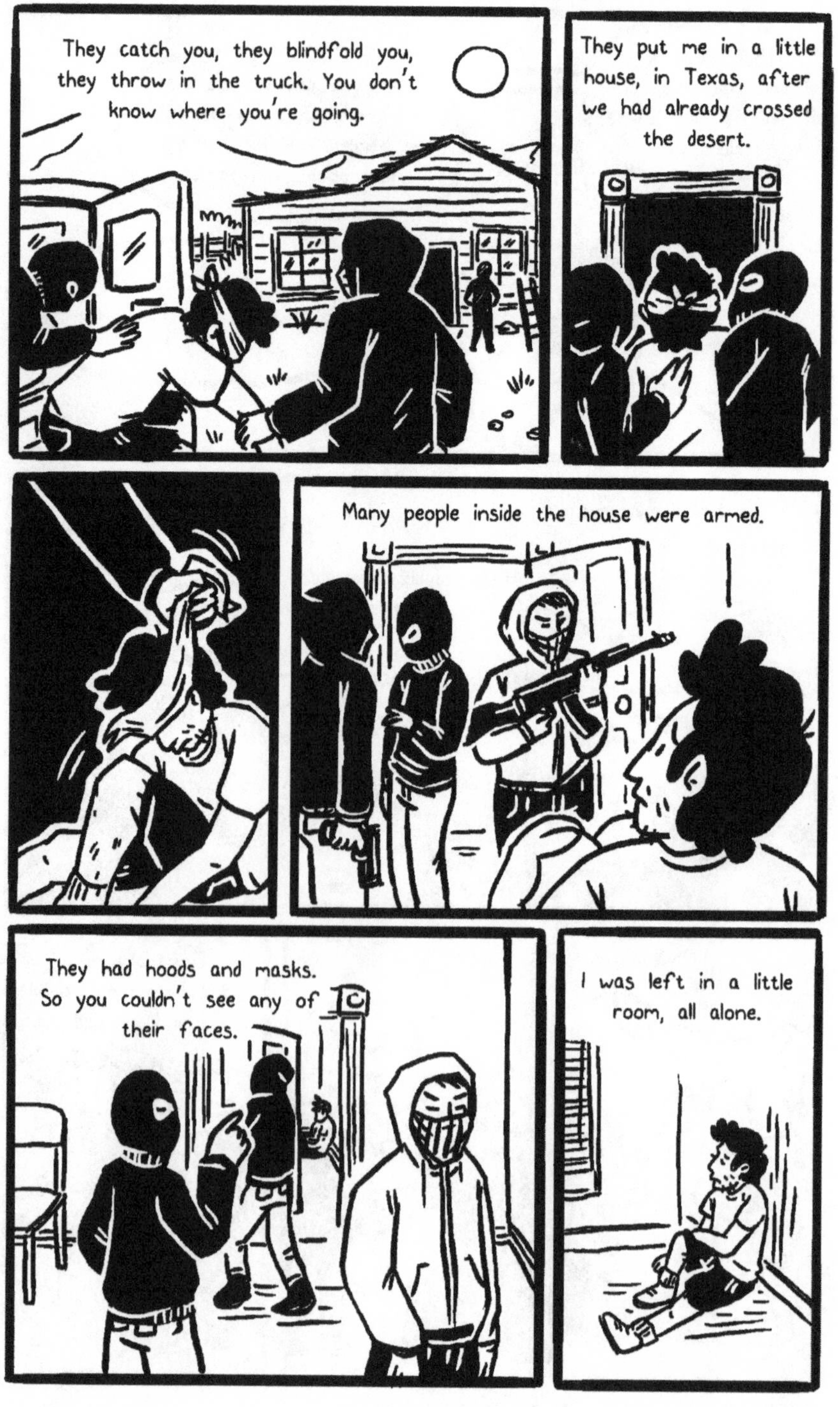
They catch you, they blindfold you, they throw in the truck. You don't know where you're going.
They put me in a little house, in Texas, after we had already crossed the desert.
Many people inside the house were armed.
They had hoods and masks. So you couldn't see any of their faces.
I was left in a little room, all alone.

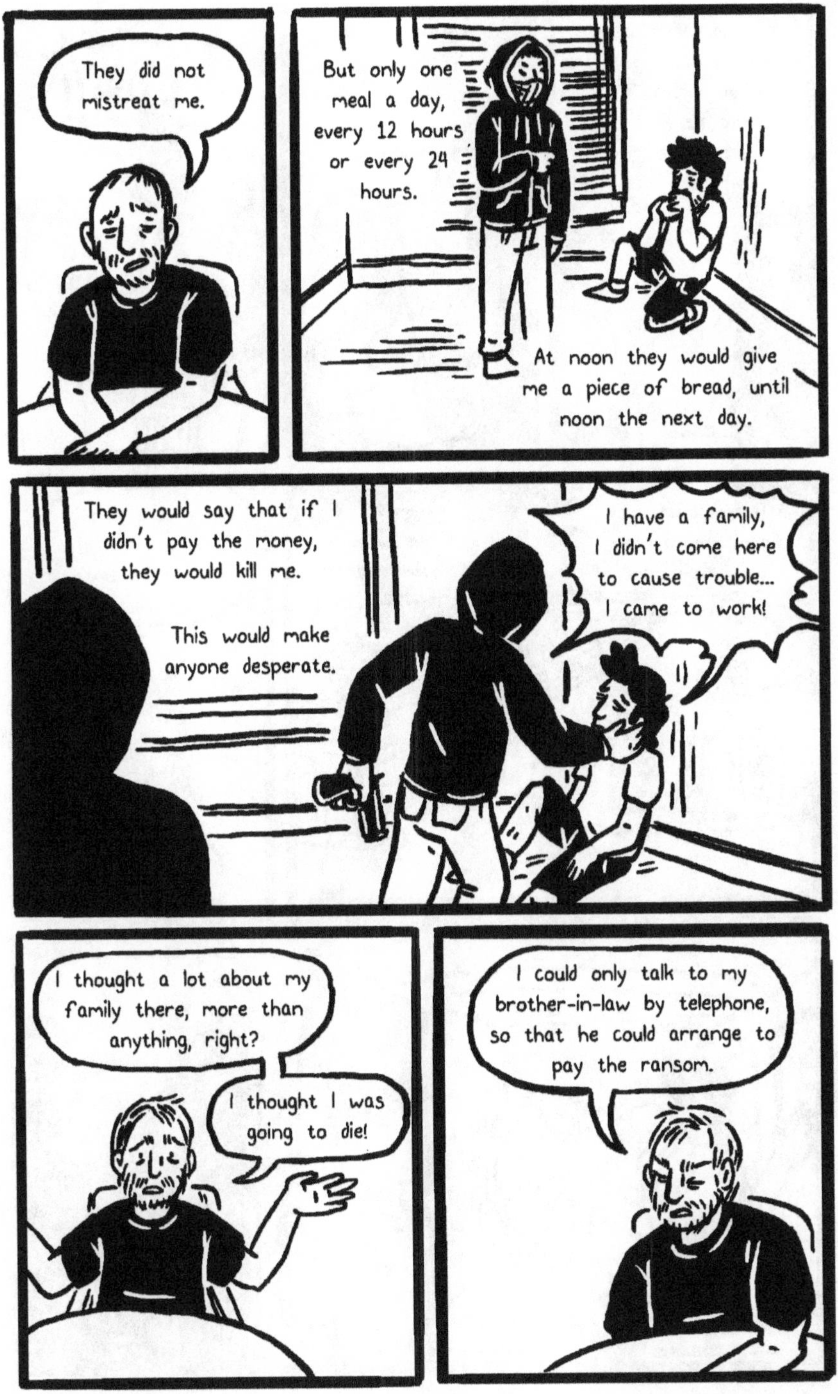
They did not mistreat me.
But only one meal a day, every 12 hours or every 24 hours.
At noon they would give me a piece of bread, until noon the next day.
They would say that if I didn't pay the money, they would kill me.
This would make anyone desperate.
I have a family, I didn't come here to cause trouble... I came to work!
I thought a lot about my family there, more than anything, right?
I thought I was going to die!
I could only talk to my brother-in-law by telephone, so that he could arrange to pay the ransom.

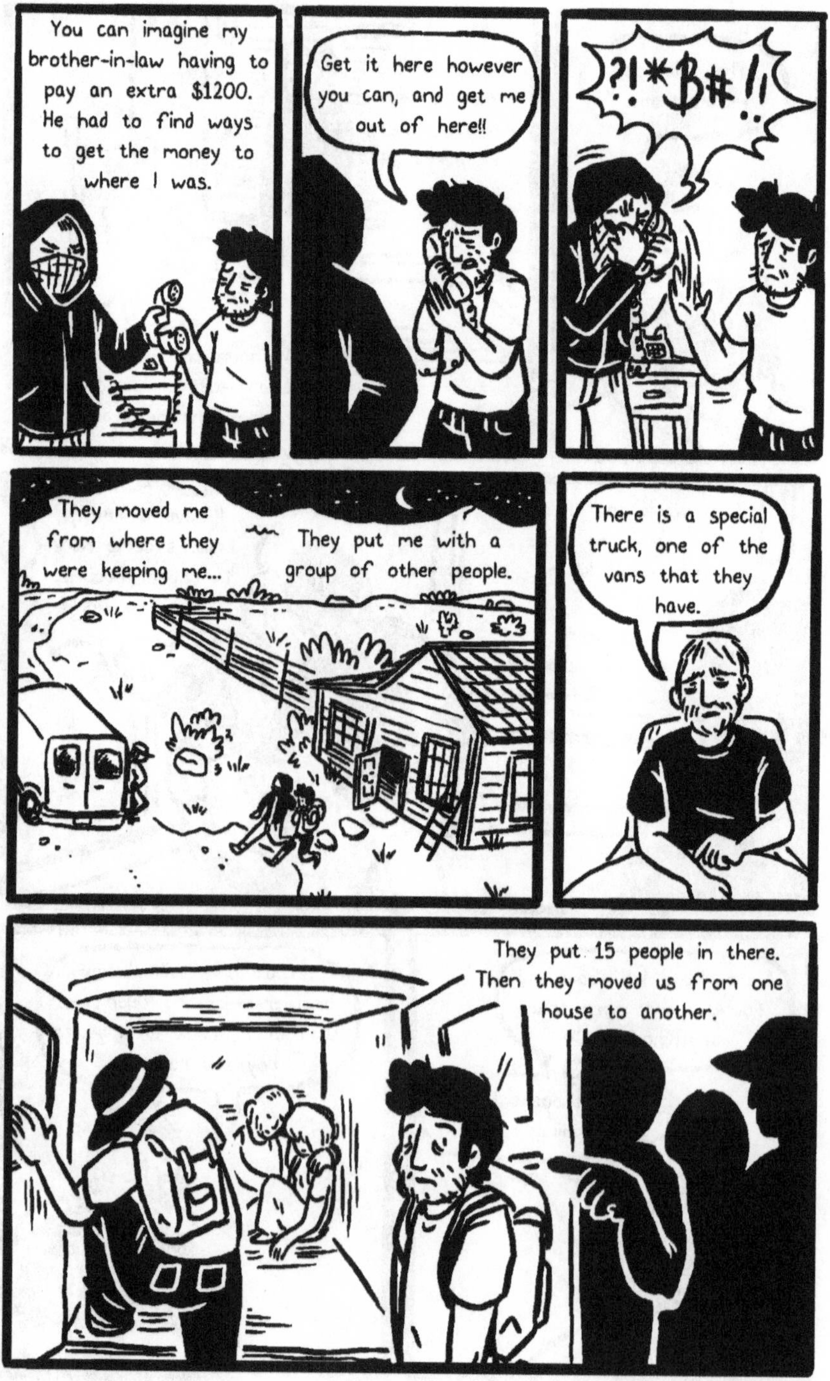

You can imagine my brother-in-law having to pay an extra $1200. He had to find ways to get the money to where I was.
Get it here however you can, and get me out of here!!
?!*$#!!
They moved me from where they were keeping me...
They put me with a group of other people.
There is a special truck, one of the vans that they have.
They put 15 people in there. Then they moved us from one house to another.

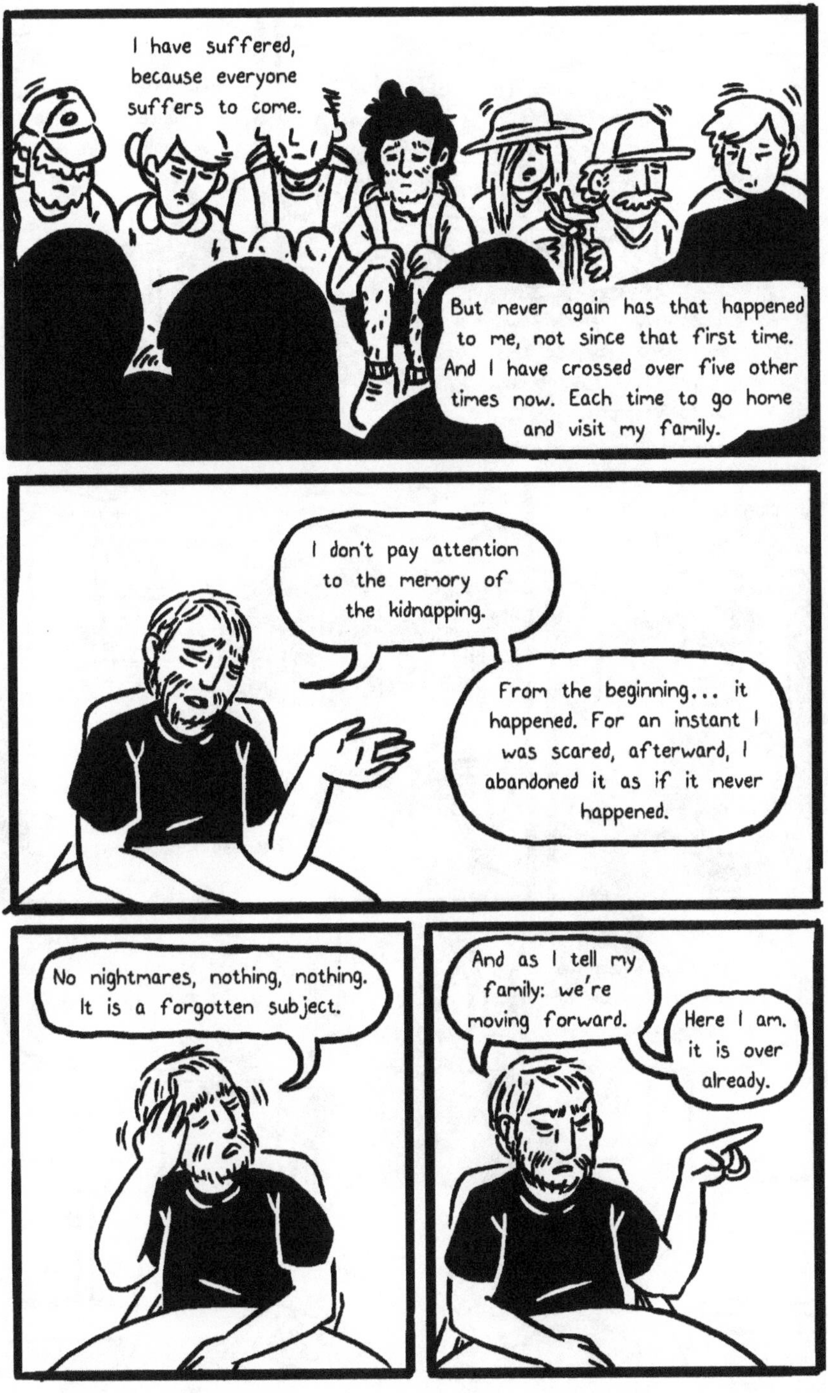
I have suffered, because everyone suffers to come.
But never again has that happened to me, not since that first time. And I have crossed over five other times now. Each time to go home and visit my family.
I don't pay attention to the memory of the kidnapping.
From the beginning... it happened. For an instant I was scared, afterward, I abandoned it as if it never happened.
No nightmares, nothing, nothing. It is a forgotten subject.
And as I tell my family: we're moving forward.
Here I am. it is over already.

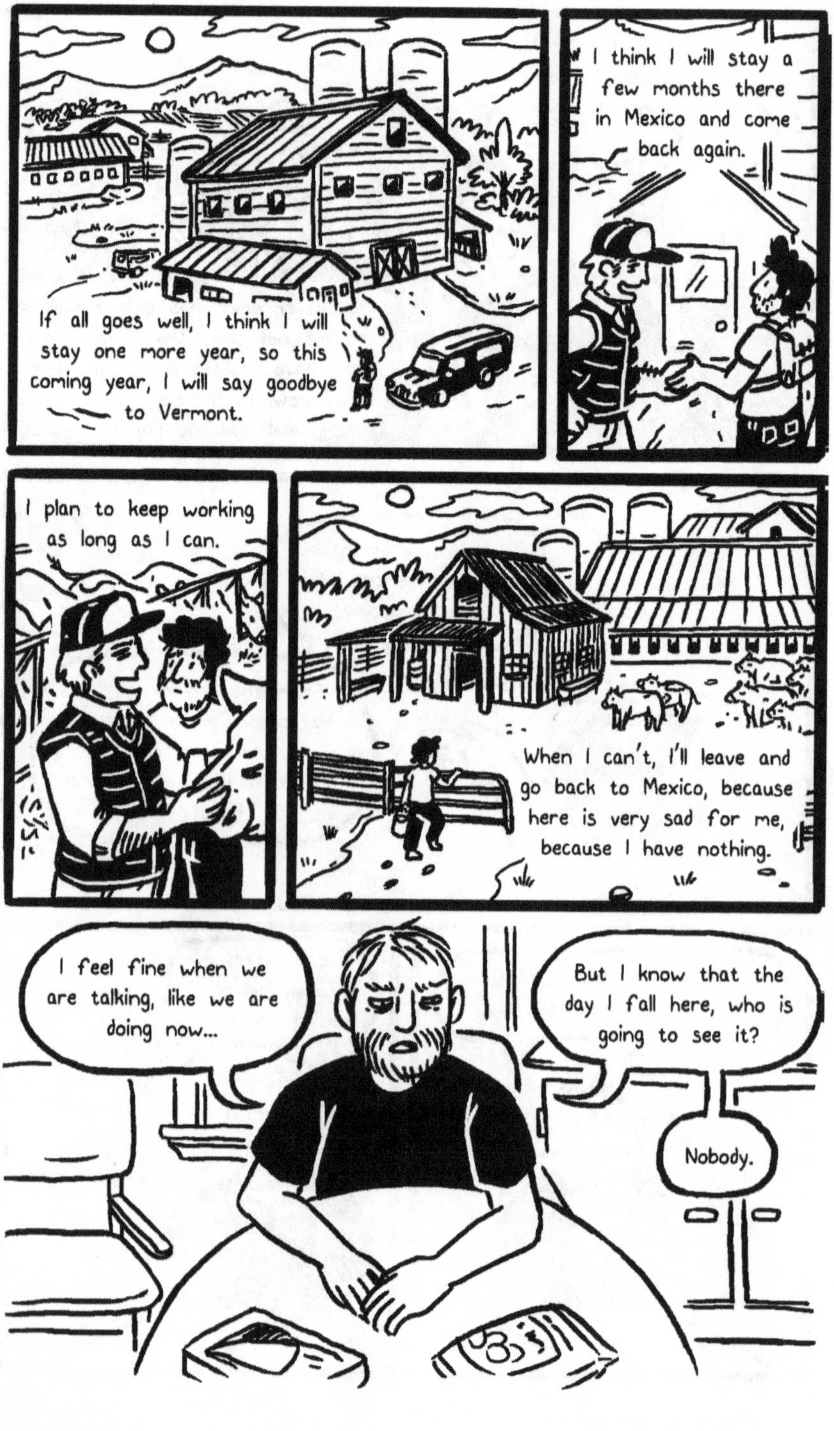

If all goes well, I think I will stay one more year, so this coming year, I will say goodbye to Vermont.
I think I will stay a few months there in Mexico and come back again.
I plan to keep working as long as I can.
When I can't, I'll leave and go back to Mexico, because here is very sad for me, because I have nothing.
I feel fine when we are talking, like we are doing now...
But I know that the day I fall here, who is going to see it?
Nobody.

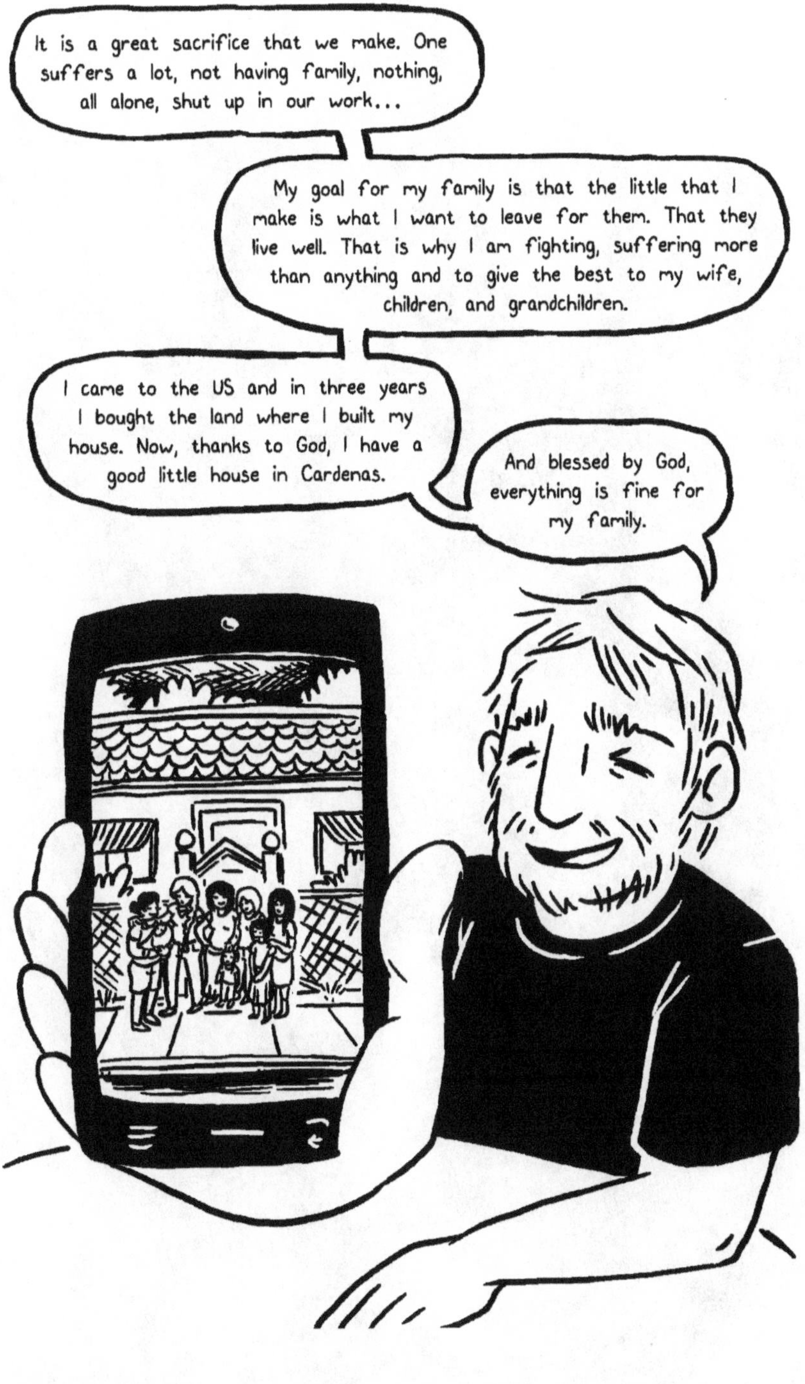
It is a great sacrifice that we make. One suffers a lot, not having family, nothing, all alone, shut up in our work...
My goal for my family is that the little that I make is what I want to leave for them. That they live well. That is why I am fighting, suffering more than anything and to give the best to my wife, children, and grandchildren.
I came to the US and in three years I bought the land where I built my house. Now, thanks to God, I have a good little house in Cardenas.
And blessed by God, everything is fine for my family.

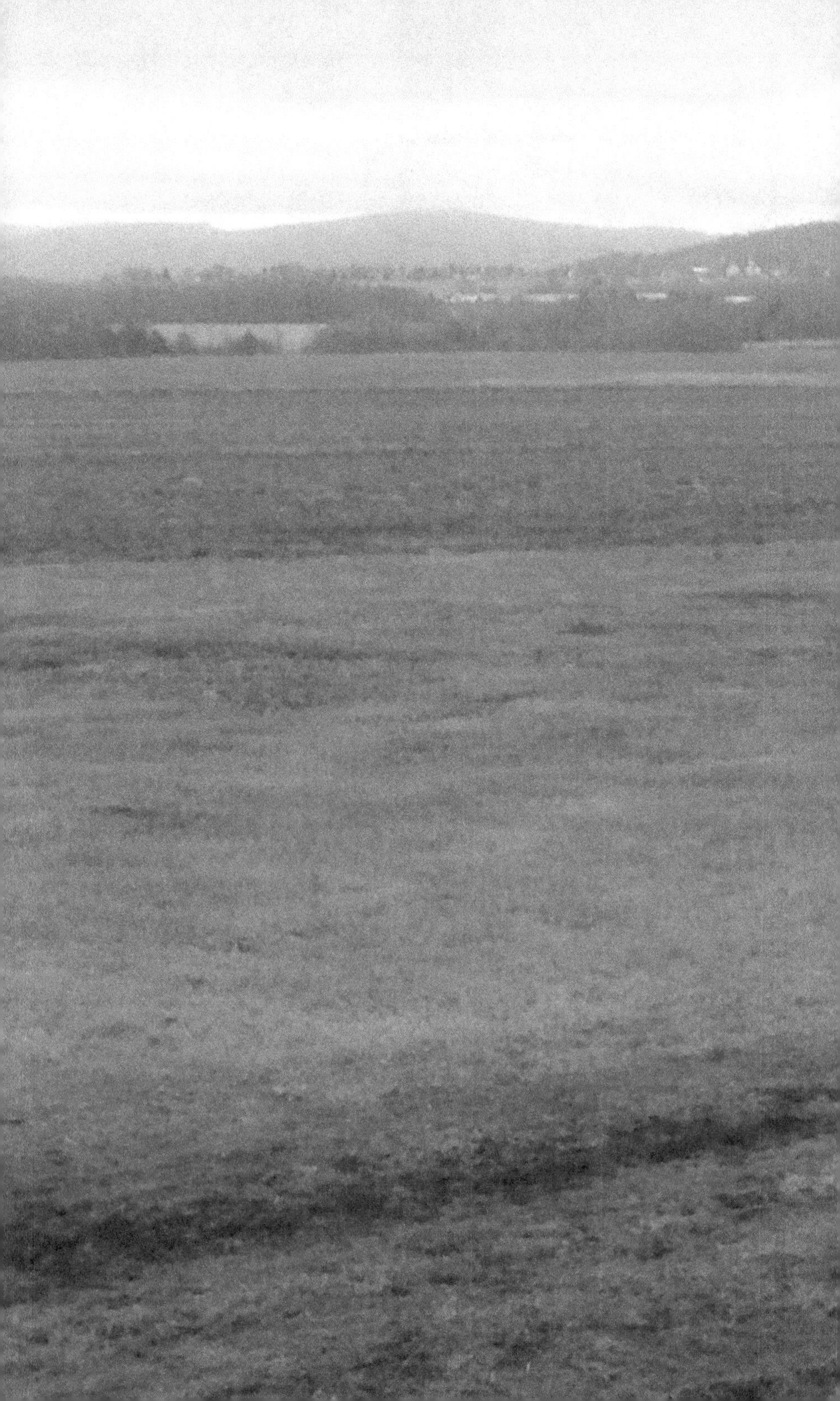

"EL VIAJE MÁS CARO" / *"THE MOST COSTLY JOURNEY"*

ALGO ADENTRO

- SOMETHING INSIDE -

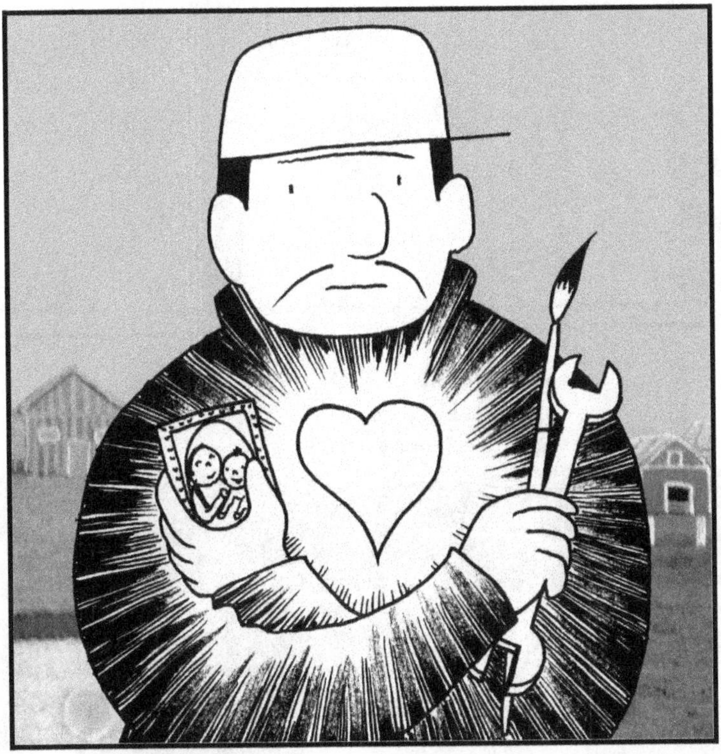

Historia y pintura por: *Story & paintings by:* **El migrante de Hidalgo**

Historieta por: *Comics by:* **Marek Bennett**

We all want to go back.

At least to visit the family...

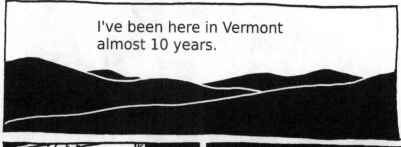

I've been here in Vermont almost 10 years.

To be here, with my family on the other side,

It's frustrating.

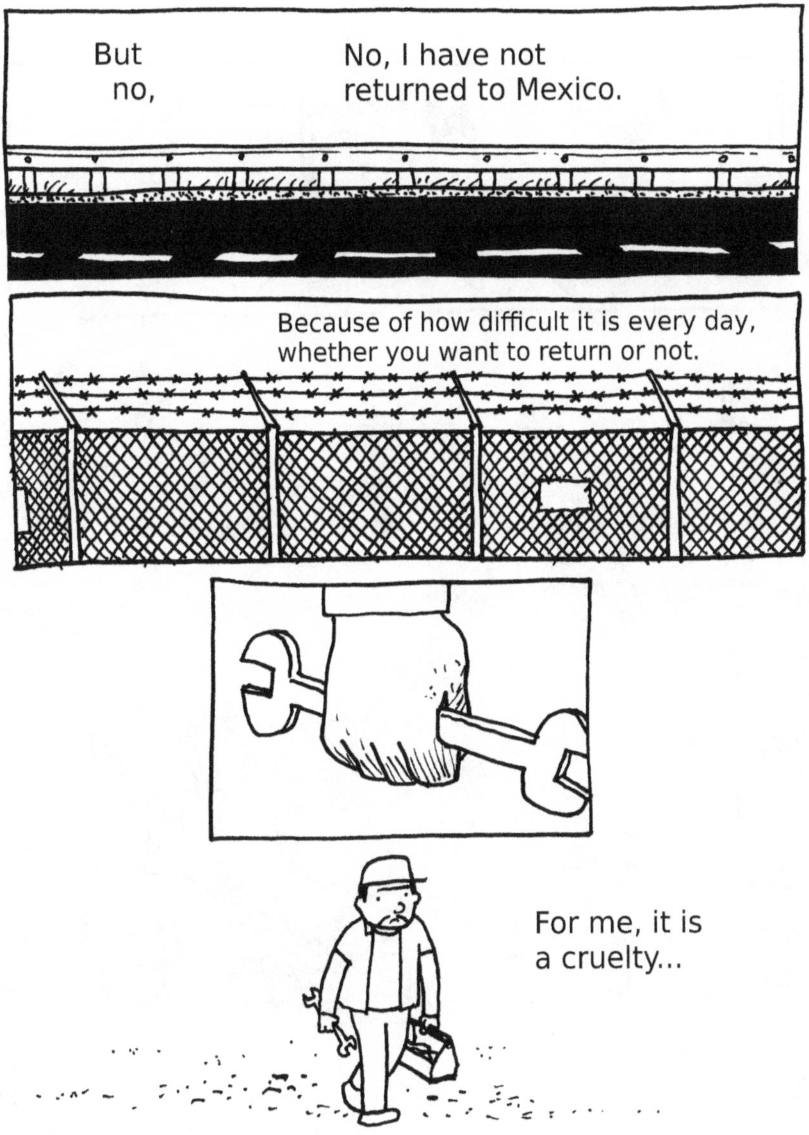
But
no,
No, I have not
returned to Mexico.
Because of how difficult it is every day,
whether you want to return or not.
For me, it is
a cruelty...

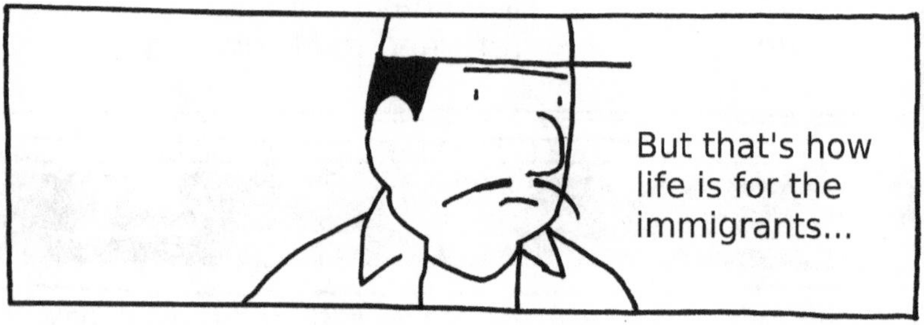
But that's how
life is for the
immigrants...

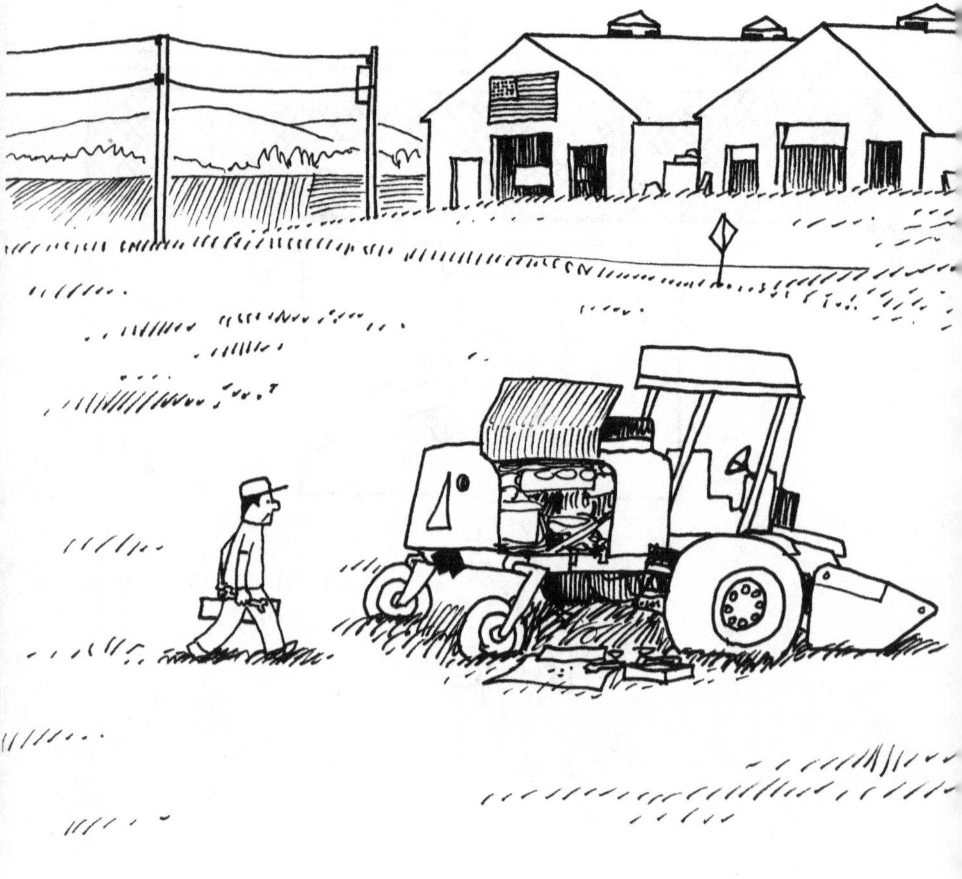

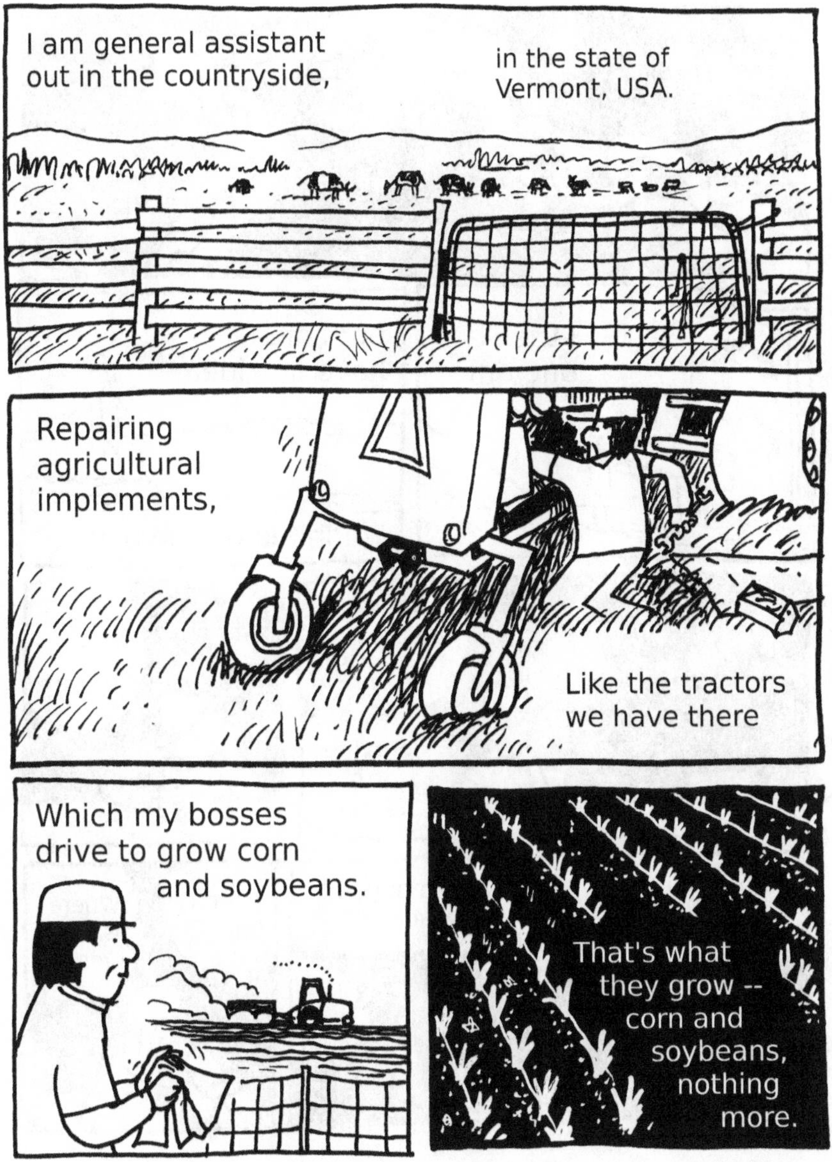
I am general assistant out in the countryside,
in the state of Vermont, USA.
Repairing agricultural implements,
Like the tractors we have there
Which my bosses drive to grow corn and soybeans.
That's what they grow -- corn and soybeans, nothing more.

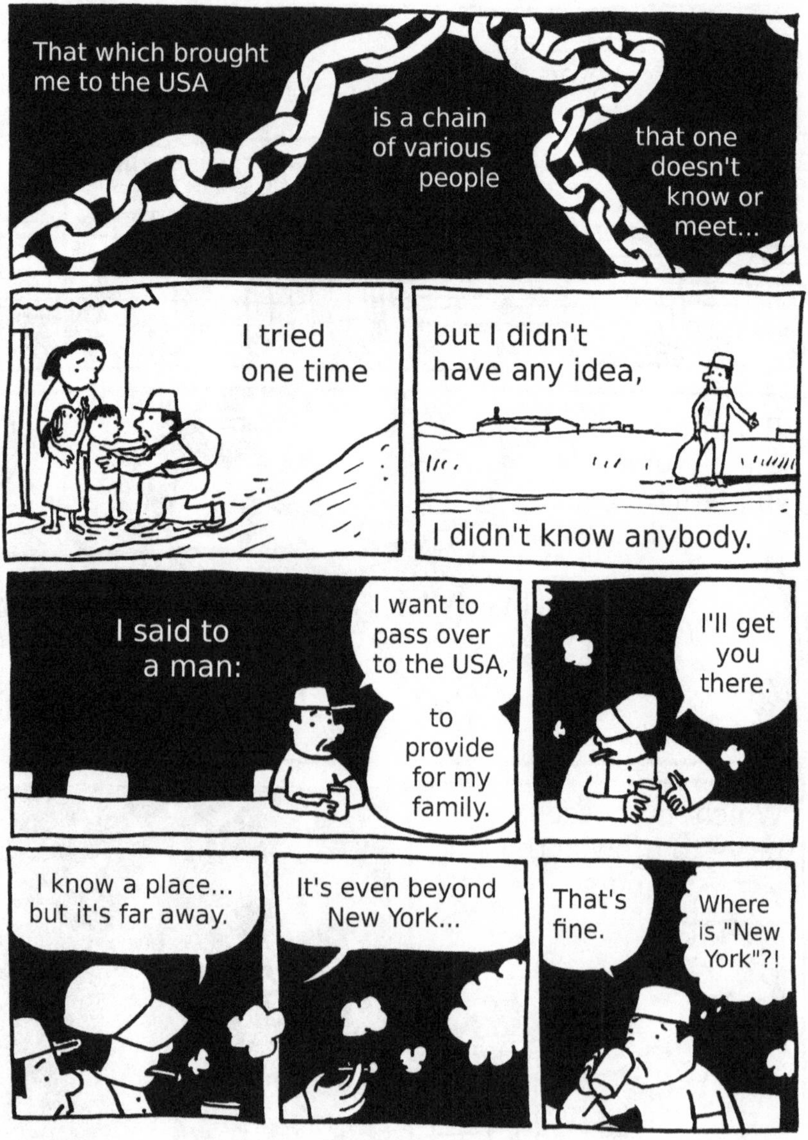
That which brought me to the USA
is a chain of various people
that one doesn't know or meet...
I tried one time
but I didn't have any idea,
I didn't know anybody.
I said to a man:
I want to pass over to the USA,
to provide for my family.
I'll get you there.
I know a place... but it's far away.
It's even beyond New York...
That's fine.
Where is "New York"?!

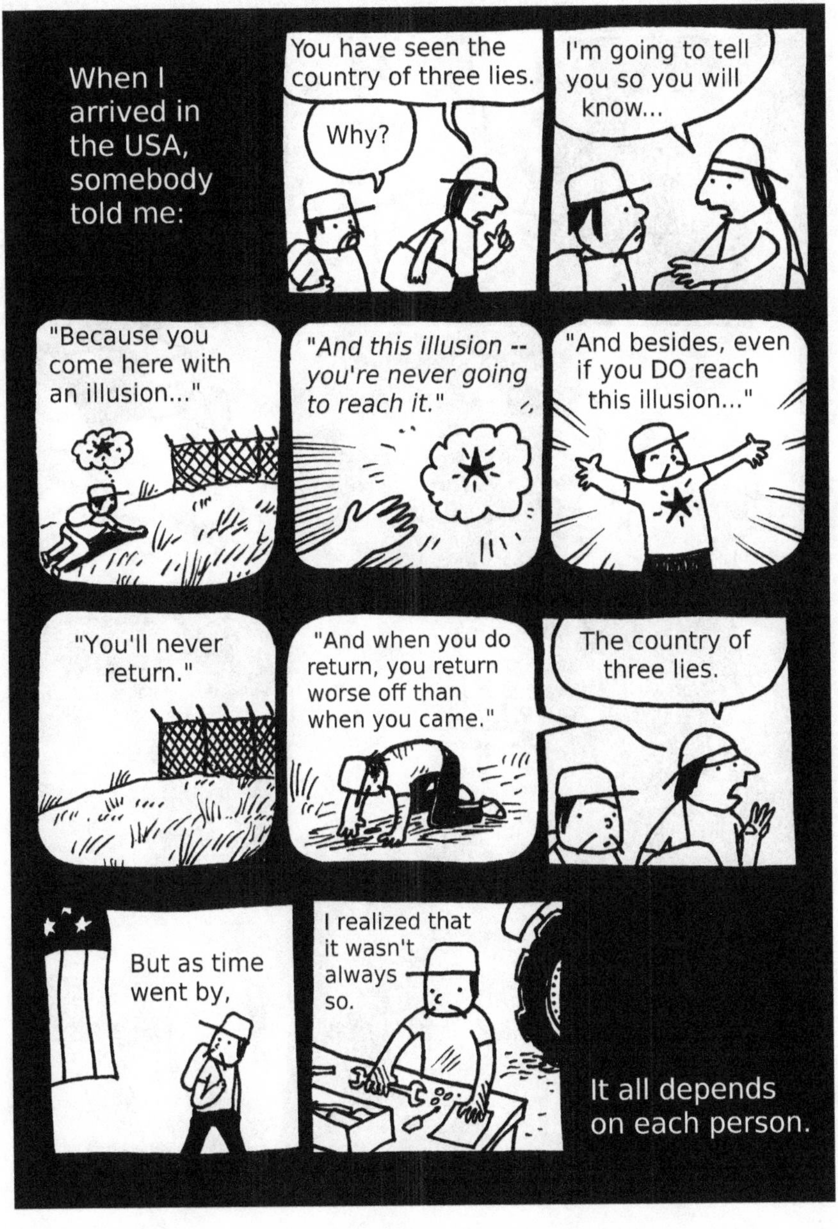
When I arrived in the USA, somebody told me:
You have seen the country of three lies.
Why?
I'm going to tell you so you will know...
"Because you come here with an illusion..."
"And this illusion -- you're never going to reach it."
"And besides, even if you DO reach this illusion..."
"You'll never return."
"And when you do return, you return worse off than when you came."
The country of three lies.
But as time went by,
I realized that it wasn't always so.
It all depends on each person.

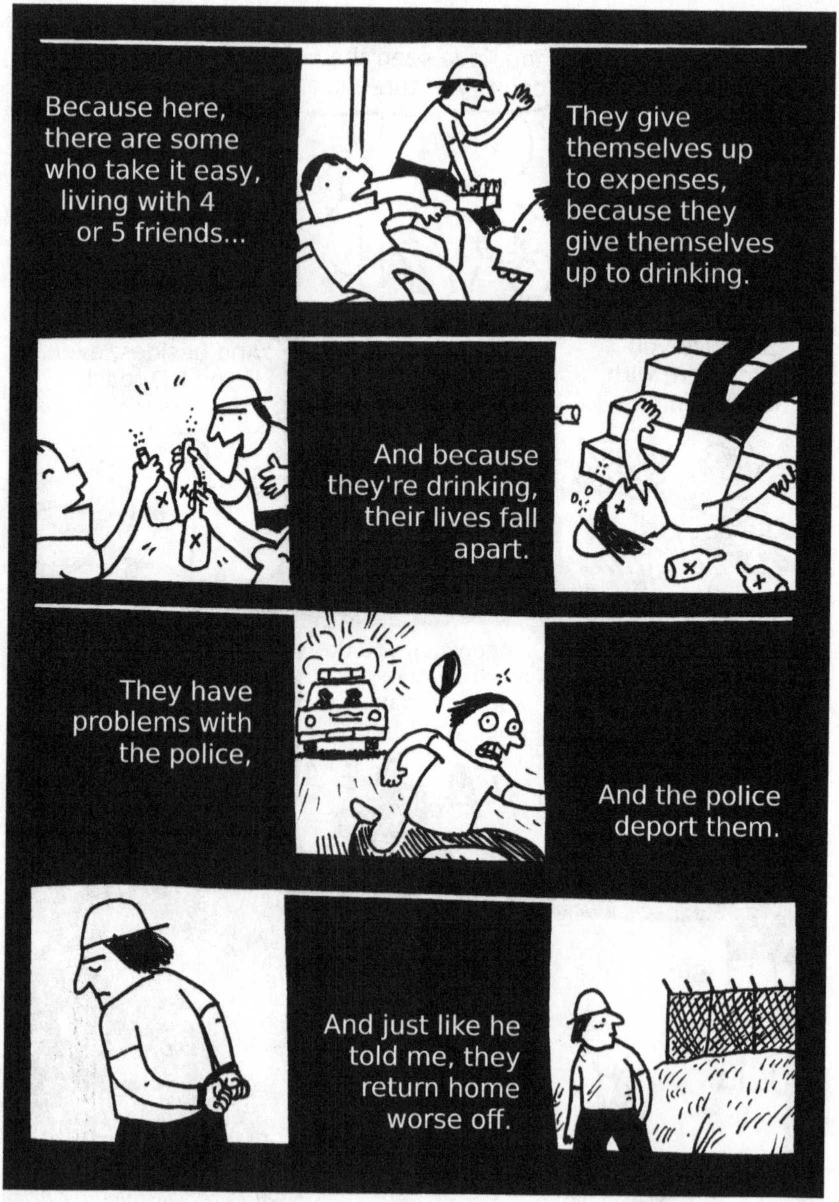
Because here, there are some who take it easy, living with 4 or 5 friends...
They give themselves up to expenses, because they give themselves up to drinking.
And because they're drinking, their lives fall apart.
They have problems with the police,
And the police deport them.
And just like he told me, they return home worse off.

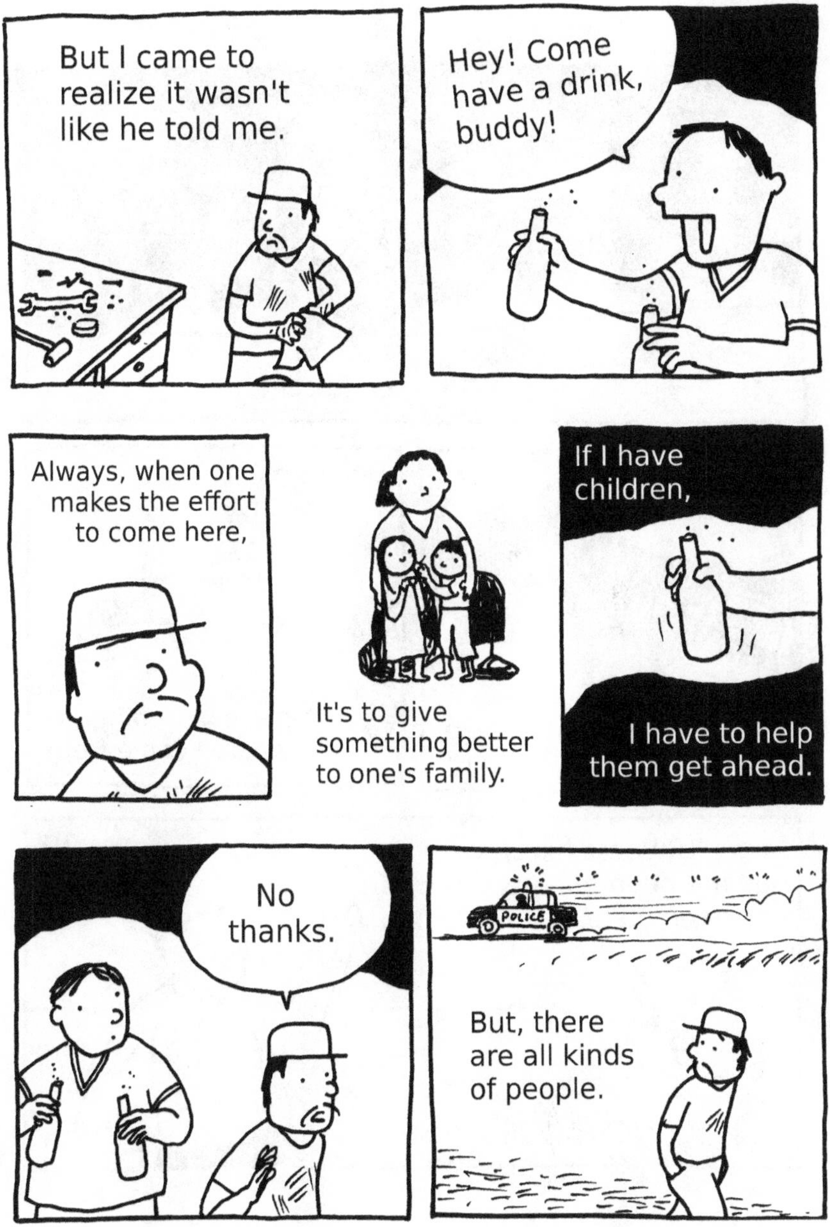
But I came to realize it wasn't like he told me.
Hey! Come have a drink, buddy!
Always, when one makes the effort to come here,
It's to give something better to one's family.
If I have children,
I have to help them get ahead.
No thanks.
POLICE
But, there are all kinds of people.

When I arrived here in Vermont, I arrived in November — a season of snow, everything white.

In Mexico, there was nothing like this!

I'm going to work HERE?!

It's snow everywhere, nooooo?!

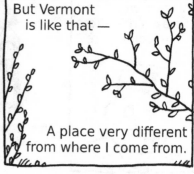

But Vermont is like that —

A place very different from where I come from.

In my 10 years here, there has not been one person who has been disrespectful to me.

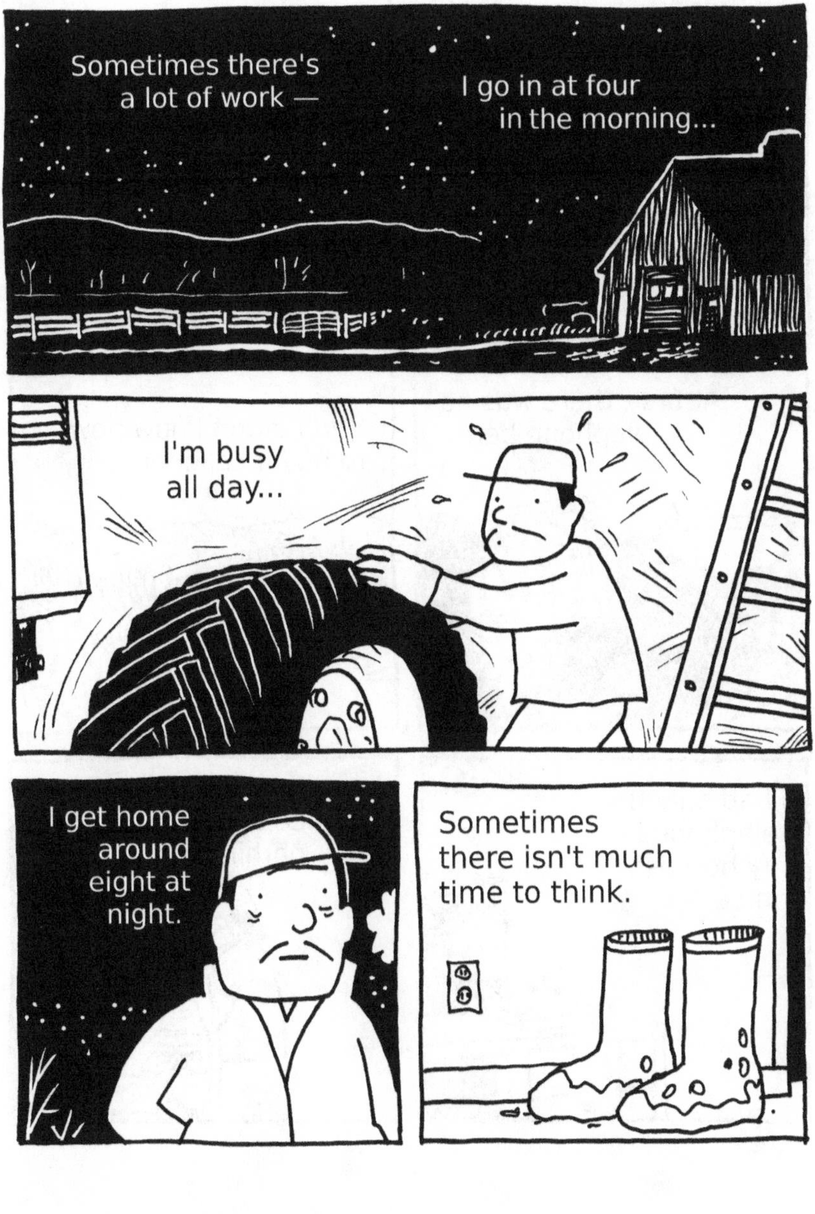
Sometimes there's a lot of work —
I go in at four in the morning...
I'm busy all day...
I get home around eight at night.
Sometimes there isn't much time to think.

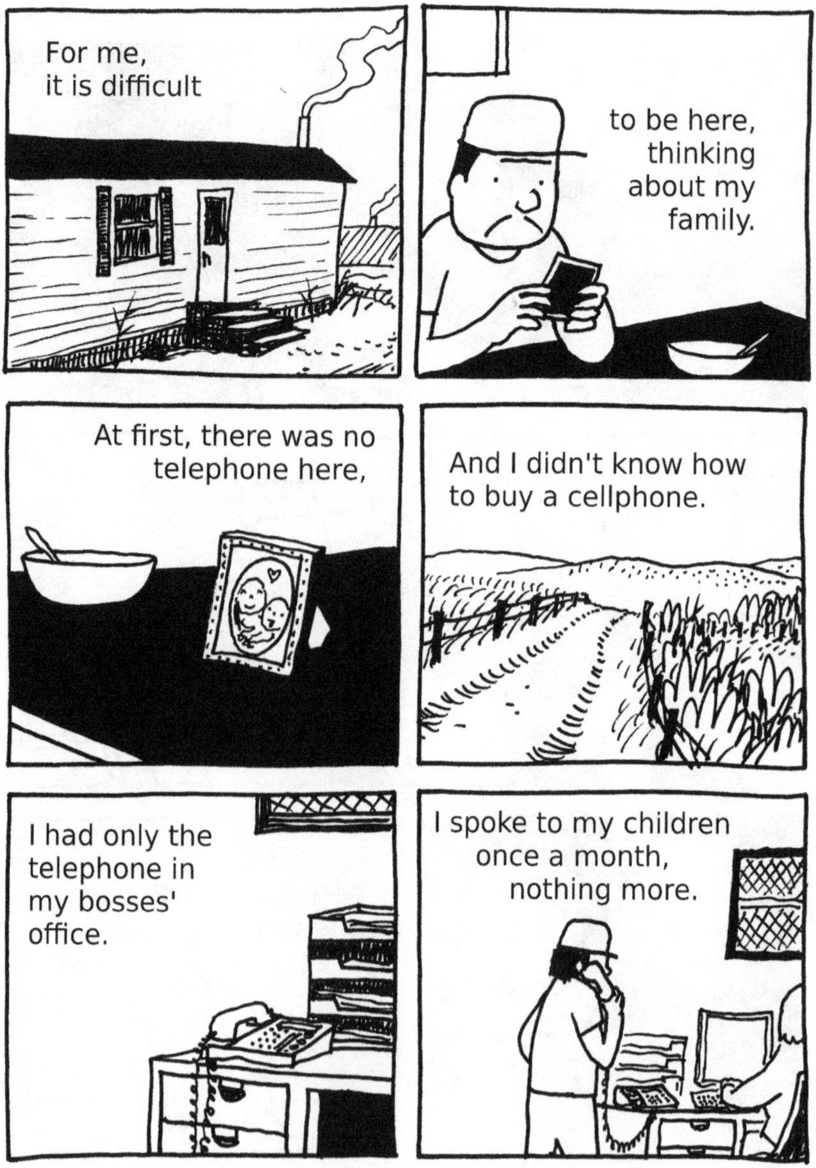
For me,
it is difficult
to be here,
thinking
about my
family.
At first, there was no
telephone here,
And I didn't know how
to buy a cellphone.
I had only the
telephone in
my bosses'
office.
I spoke to my children
once a month,
nothing more.

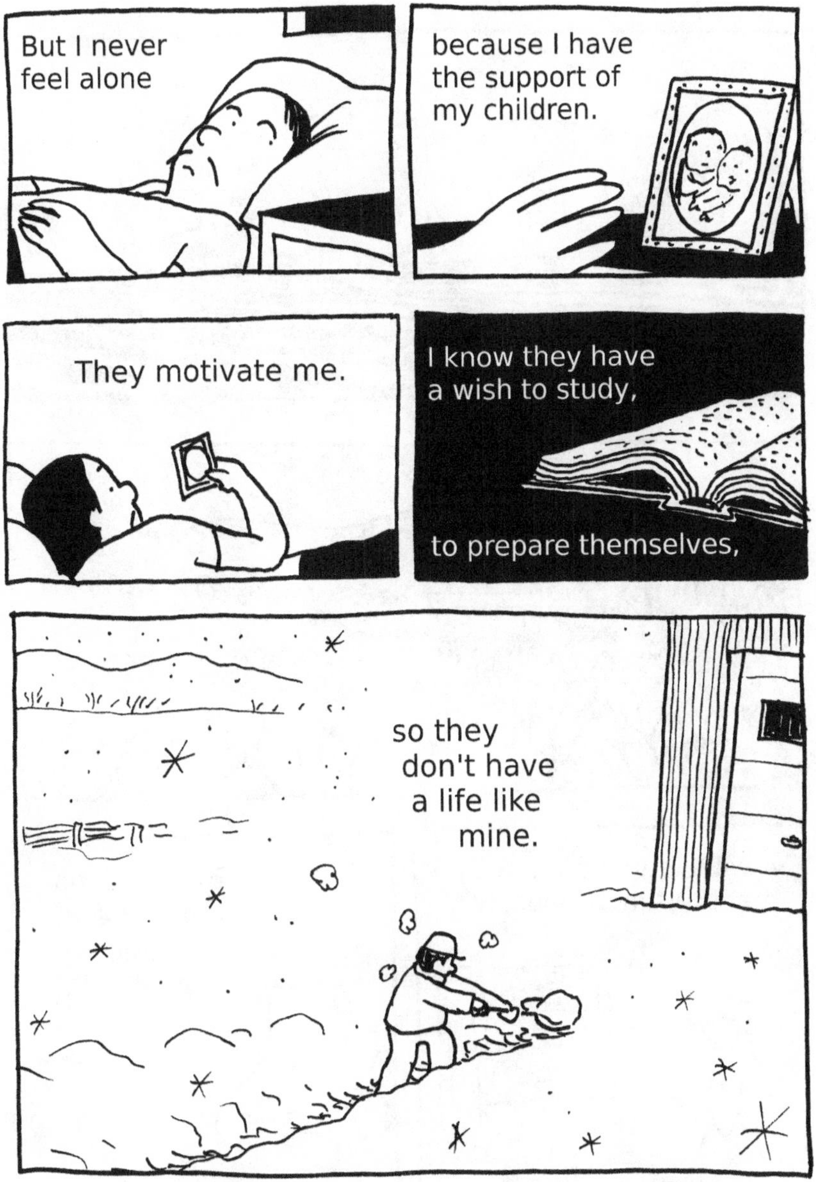
But I never feel alone
because I have the support of my children.
They motivate me.
I know they have a wish to study,
to prepare themselves,
so they don't have a life like mine.

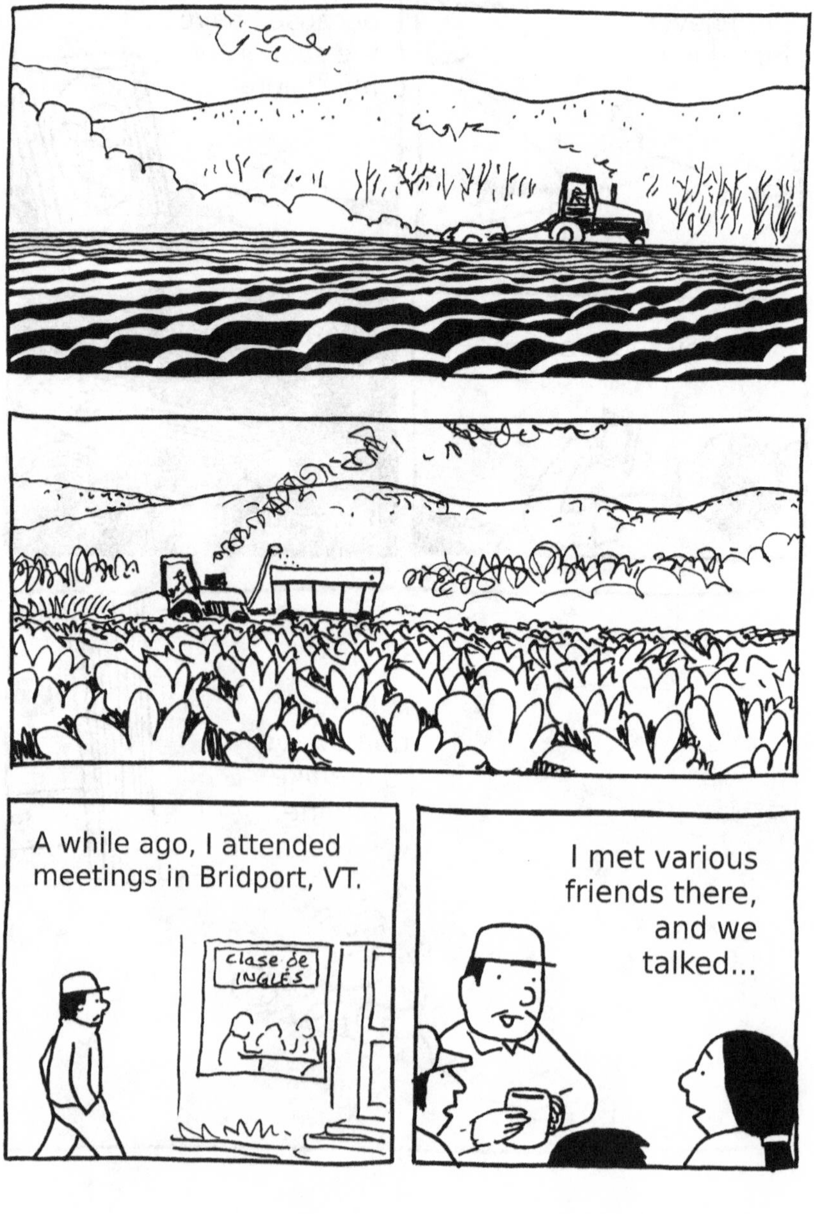
A while ago, I attended meetings in Bridport, VT.
clase de INGLÉS
I met various friends there, and we talked...

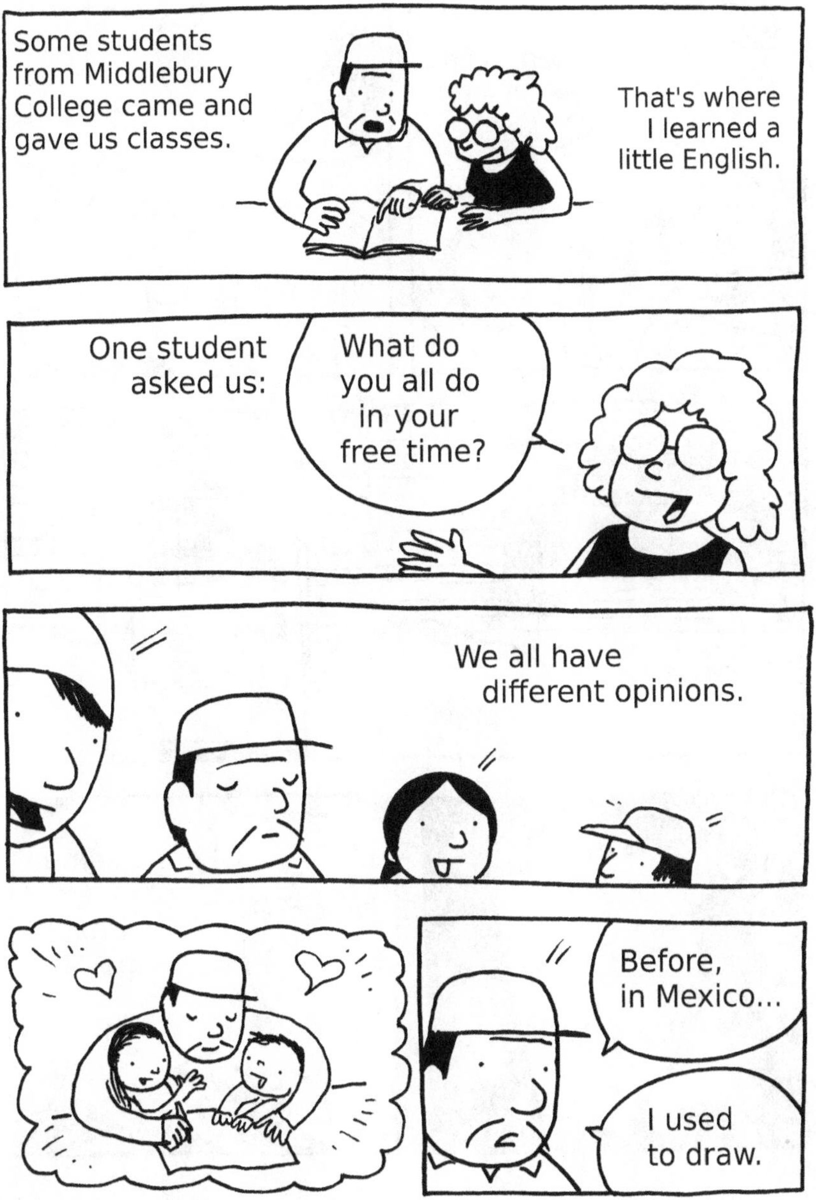
Some students from Middlebury College came and gave us classes.
That's where I learned a little English.
One student asked us:
What do you all do in your free time?
We all have different opinions.
Before, in Mexico...
I used to draw.

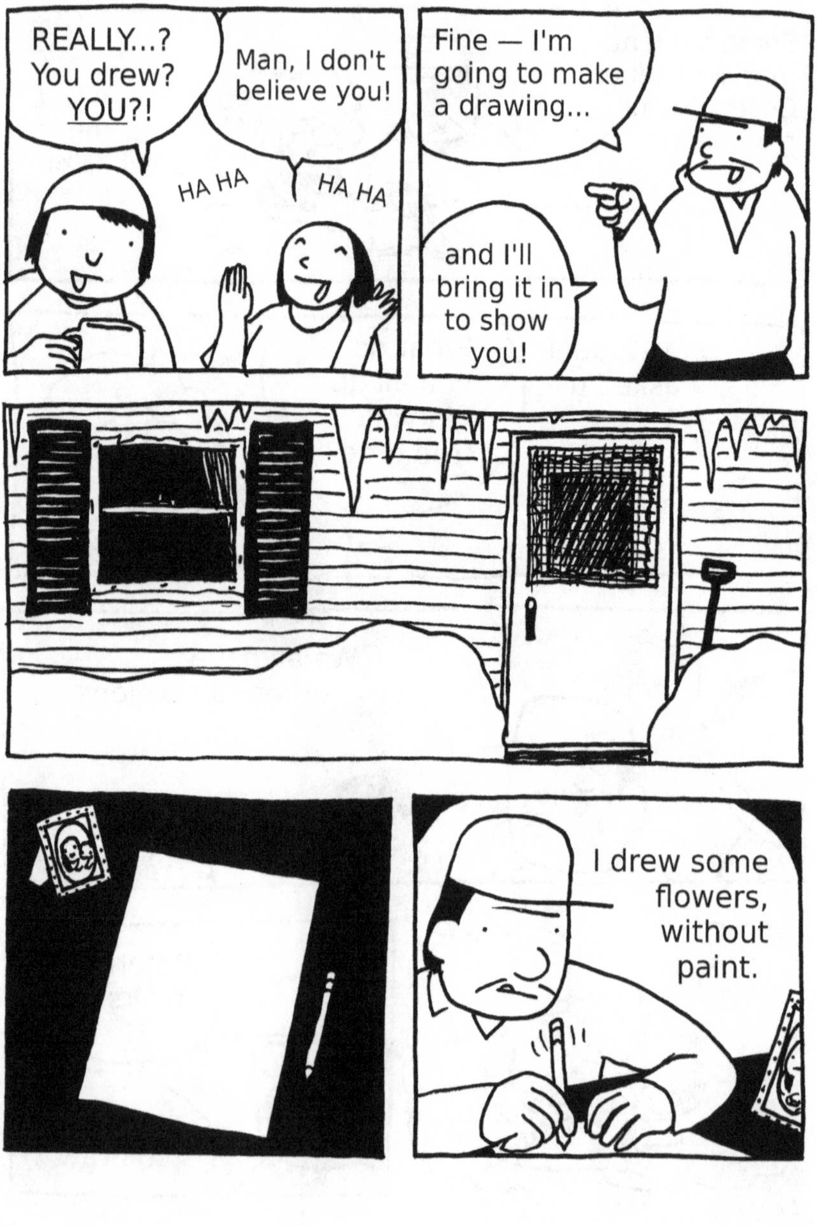
REALLY...? You drew? YOU?!
Man, I don't believe you!
HA HA
HA HA
Fine — I'm going to make a drawing...
and I'll bring it in to show you!
I drew some flowers, without paint.

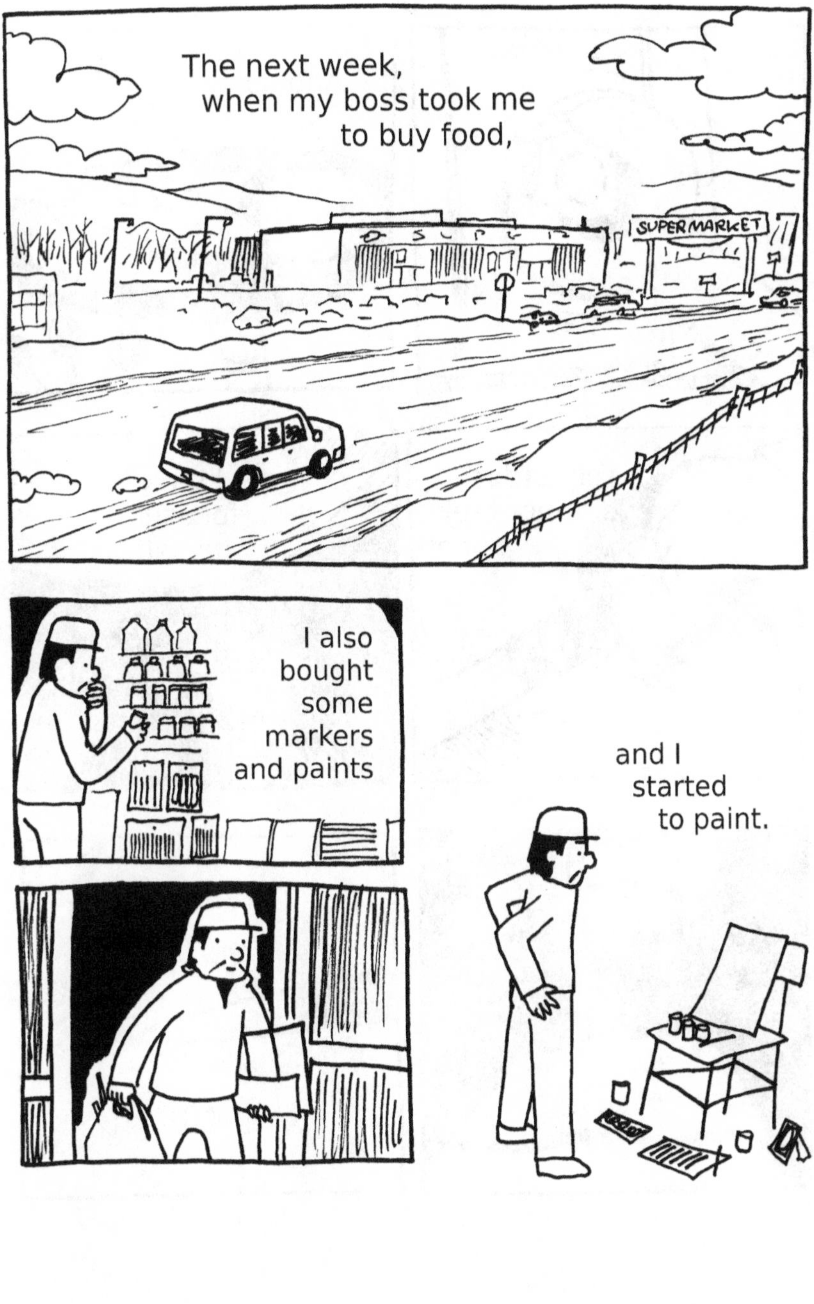
The next week, when my boss took me to buy food,
SUPERMARKET
I also bought some markers and paints
and I started to paint.

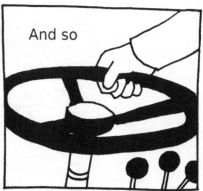

And so

in order to
not feel
alone

I have
focused
myself

on that
which is

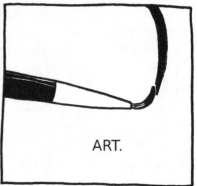

ART.

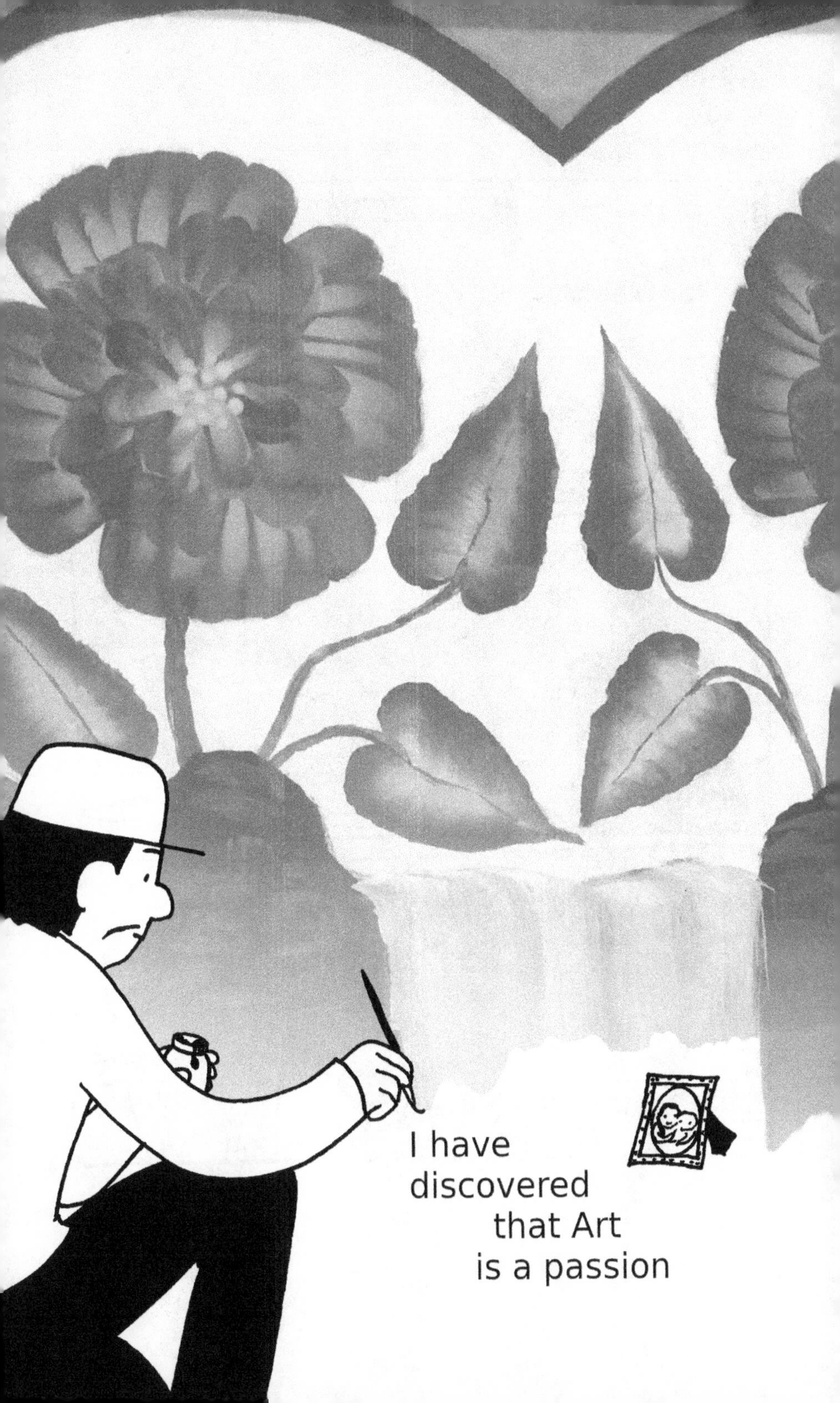
I have
discovered
that Art
is a passion

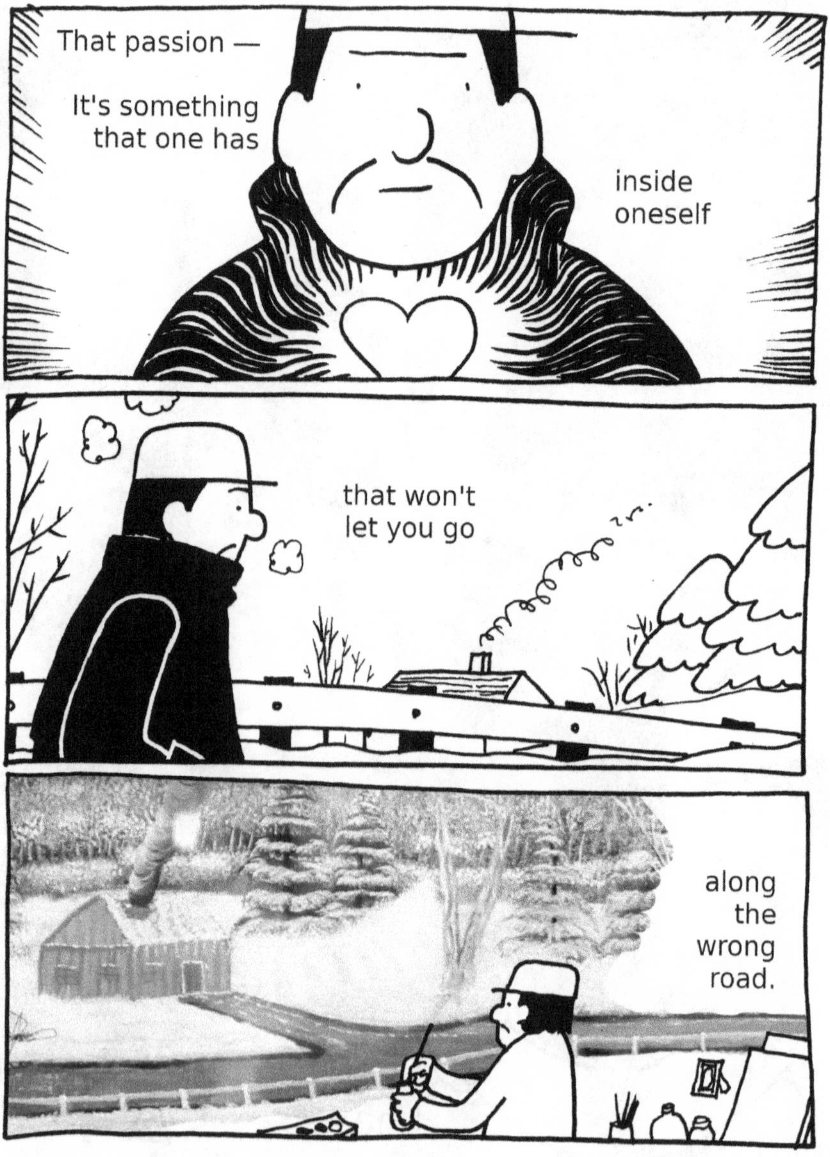
That passion —
It's something that one has
inside oneself
that won't let you go
along the wrong road.

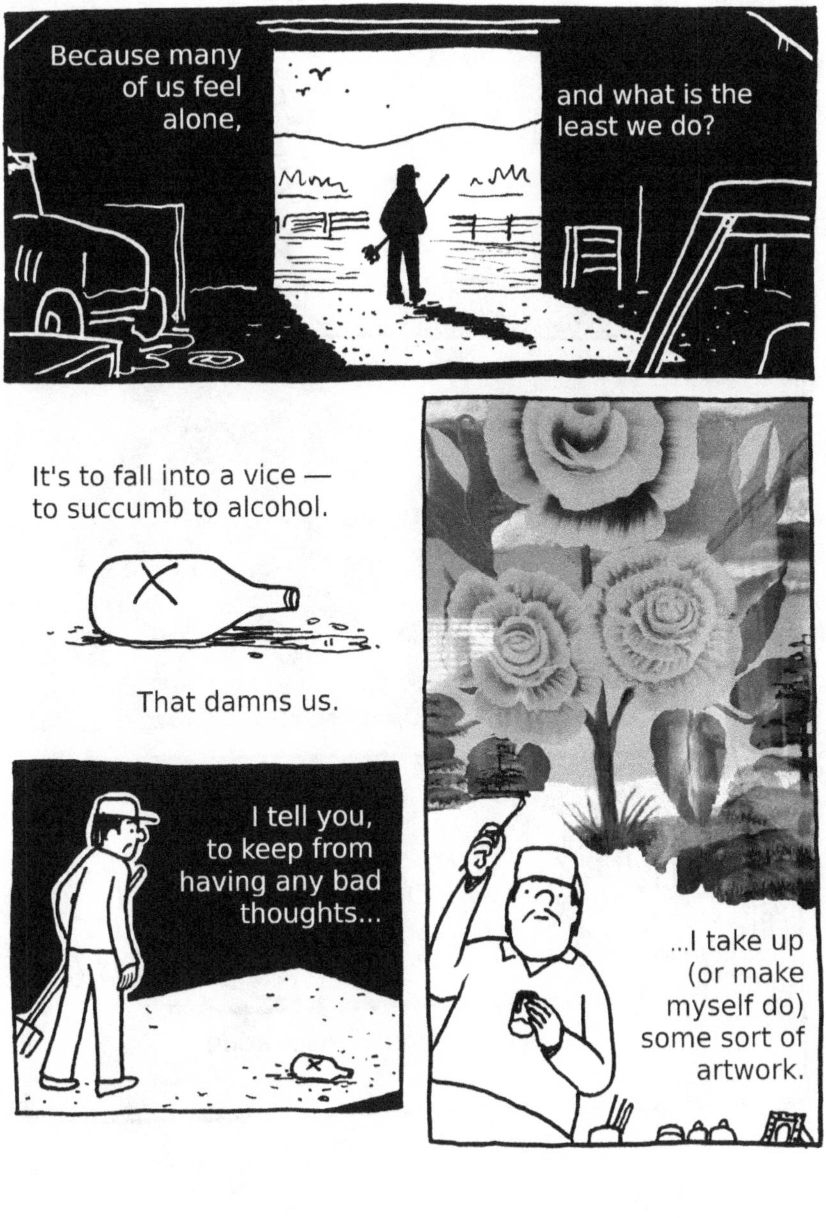
Because many of us feel alone,
and what is the least we do?
It's to fall into a vice — to succumb to alcohol.
That damns us.
I tell you, to keep from having any bad thoughts...
...I take up (or make myself do) some sort of artwork.

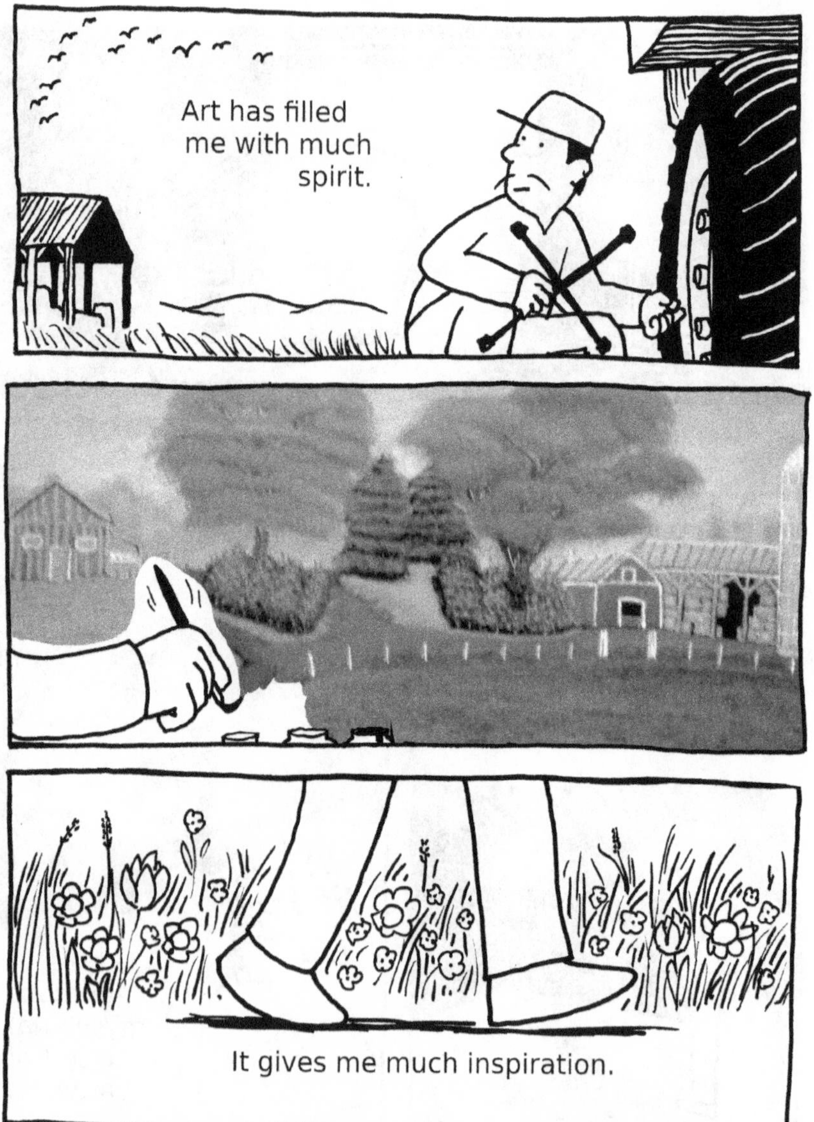
Art has filled me with much spirit.
It gives me much inspiration.

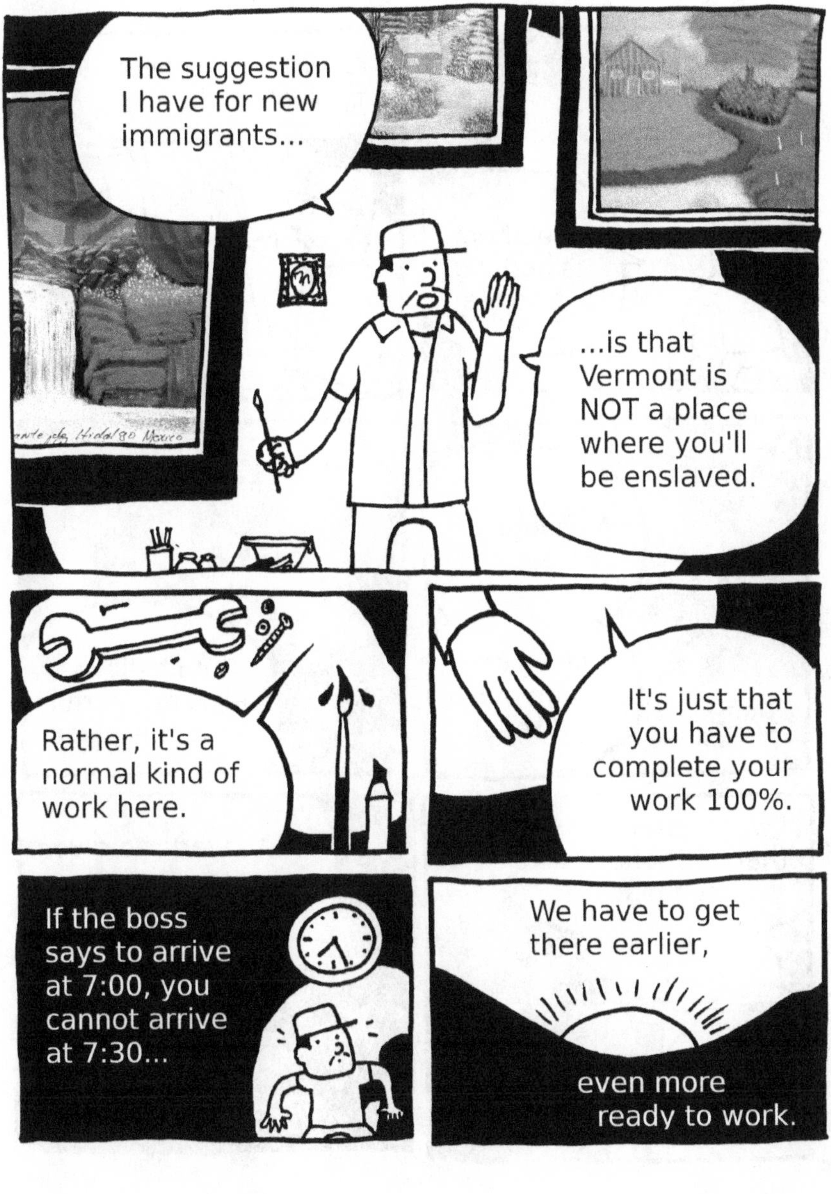
The suggestion I have for new immigrants...
...is that Vermont is NOT a place where you'll be enslaved.
Rather, it's a normal kind of work here.
It's just that you have to complete your work 100%.
If the boss says to arrive at 7:00, you cannot arrive at 7:30...
We have to get there earlier,
even more ready to work.

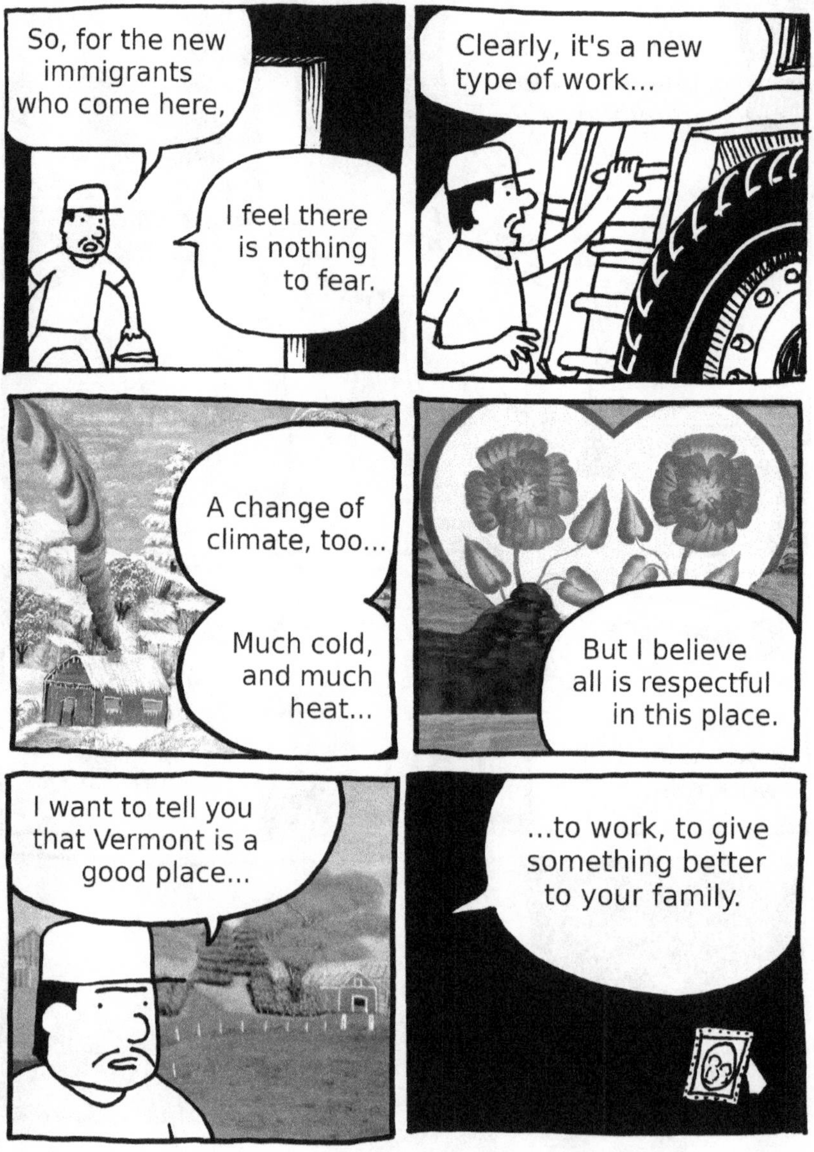
So, for the new immigrants who come here,
I feel there is nothing to fear.
Clearly, it's a new type of work...
A change of climate, too...
Much cold, and much heat...
But I believe all is respectful in this place.
I want to tell you that Vermont is a good place...
...to work, to give something better to your family.

"EL VIAJE MAS CARO" / "THE MOST COSTLY JOURNEY" *presents:*

IN YOUR HANDS

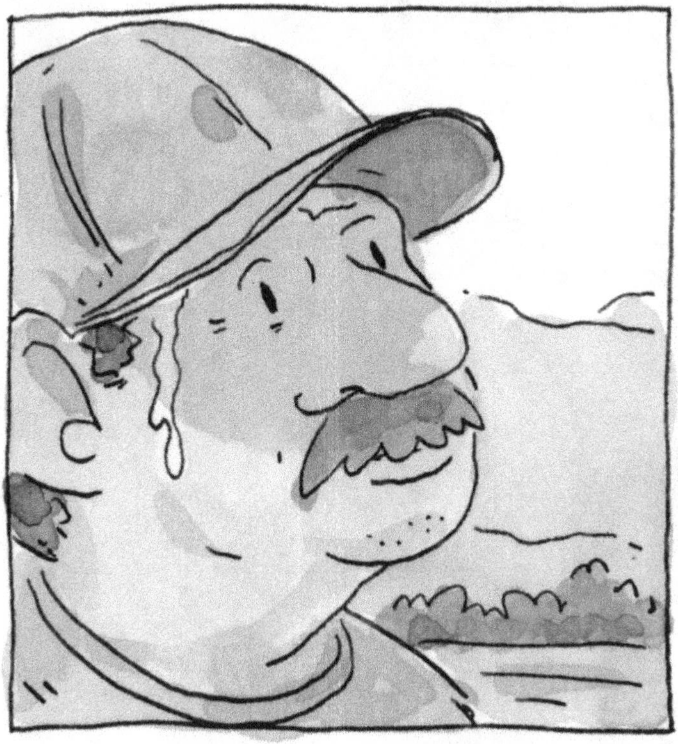

The Story of Jesús

Art by John Carvajal

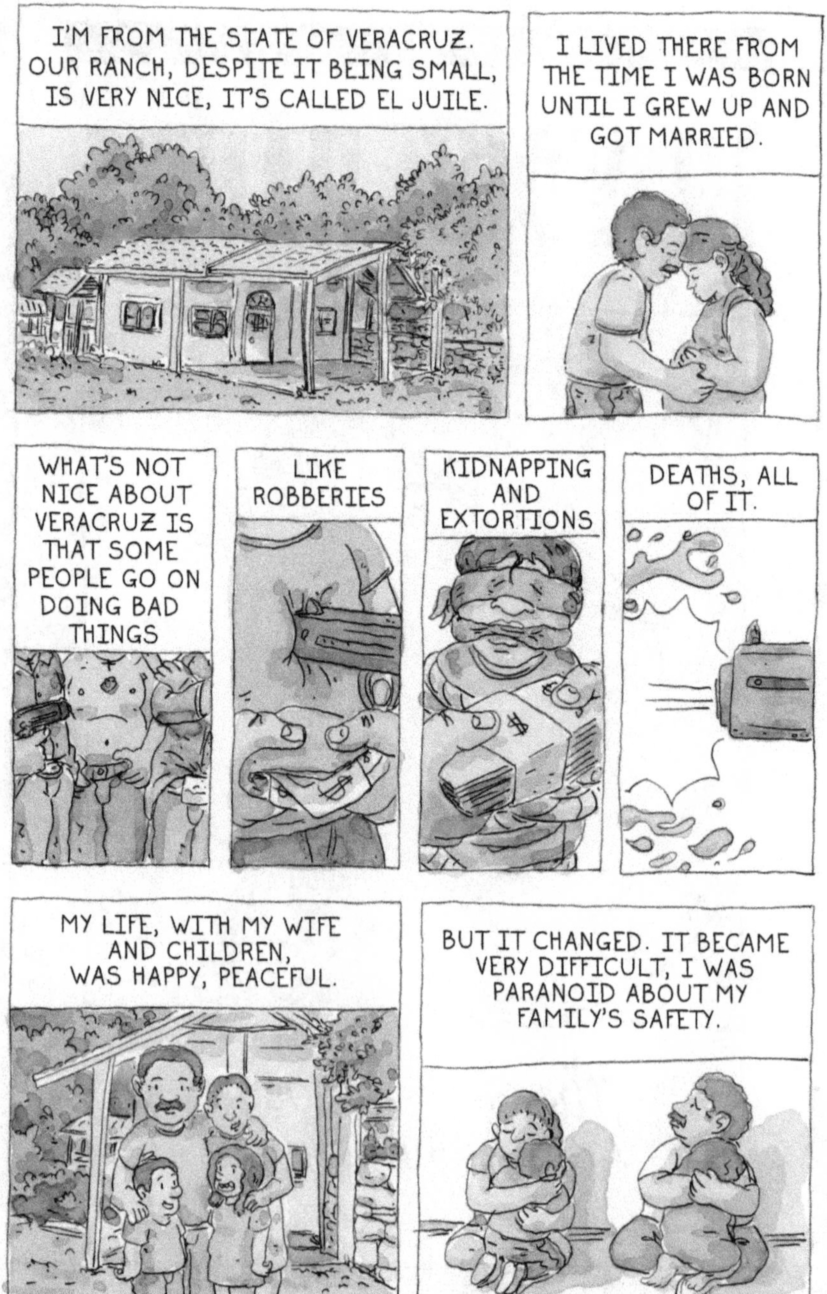
I'M FROM THE STATE OF VERACRUZ. OUR RANCH, DESPITE IT BEING SMALL, IS VERY NICE, IT'S CALLED EL JUILE.
I LIVED THERE FROM THE TIME I WAS BORN UNTIL I GREW UP AND GOT MARRIED.
WHAT'S NOT NICE ABOUT VERACRUZ IS THAT SOME PEOPLE GO ON DOING BAD THINGS
LIKE ROBBERIES
KIDNAPPING AND EXTORTIONS
DEATHS, ALL OF IT.
MY LIFE, WITH MY WIFE AND CHILDREN, WAS HAPPY, PEACEFUL.
BUT IT CHANGED. IT BECAME VERY DIFFICULT, I WAS PARANOID ABOUT MY FAMILY'S SAFETY.

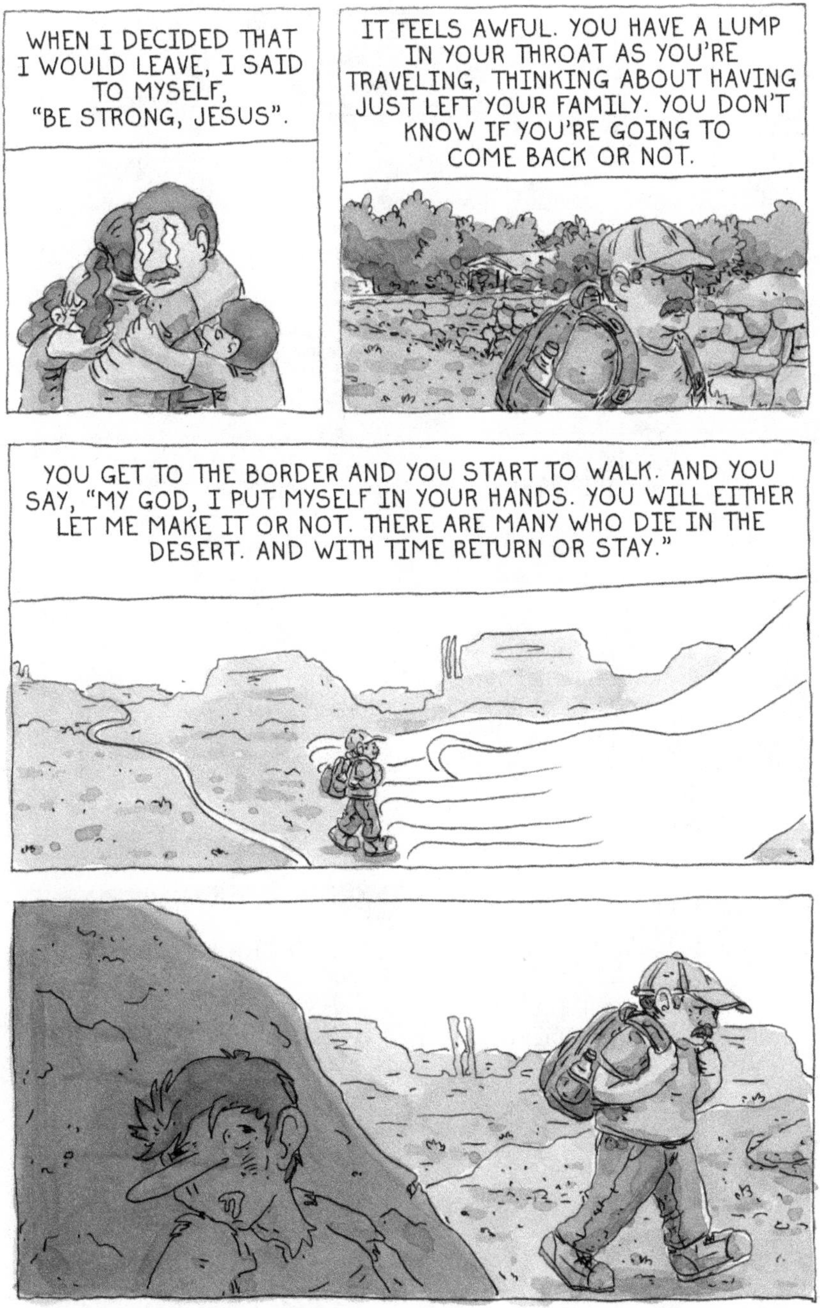
WHEN I DECIDED THAT I WOULD LEAVE, I SAID TO MYSELF, "BE STRONG, JESUS".
IT FEELS AWFUL. YOU HAVE A LUMP IN YOUR THROAT AS YOU'RE TRAVELING, THINKING ABOUT HAVING JUST LEFT YOUR FAMILY. YOU DON'T KNOW IF YOU'RE GOING TO COME BACK OR NOT.
YOU GET TO THE BORDER AND YOU START TO WALK. AND YOU SAY, "MY GOD, I PUT MYSELF IN YOUR HANDS. YOU WILL EITHER LET ME MAKE IT OR NOT. THERE ARE MANY WHO DIE IN THE DESERT. AND WITH TIME RETURN OR STAY."

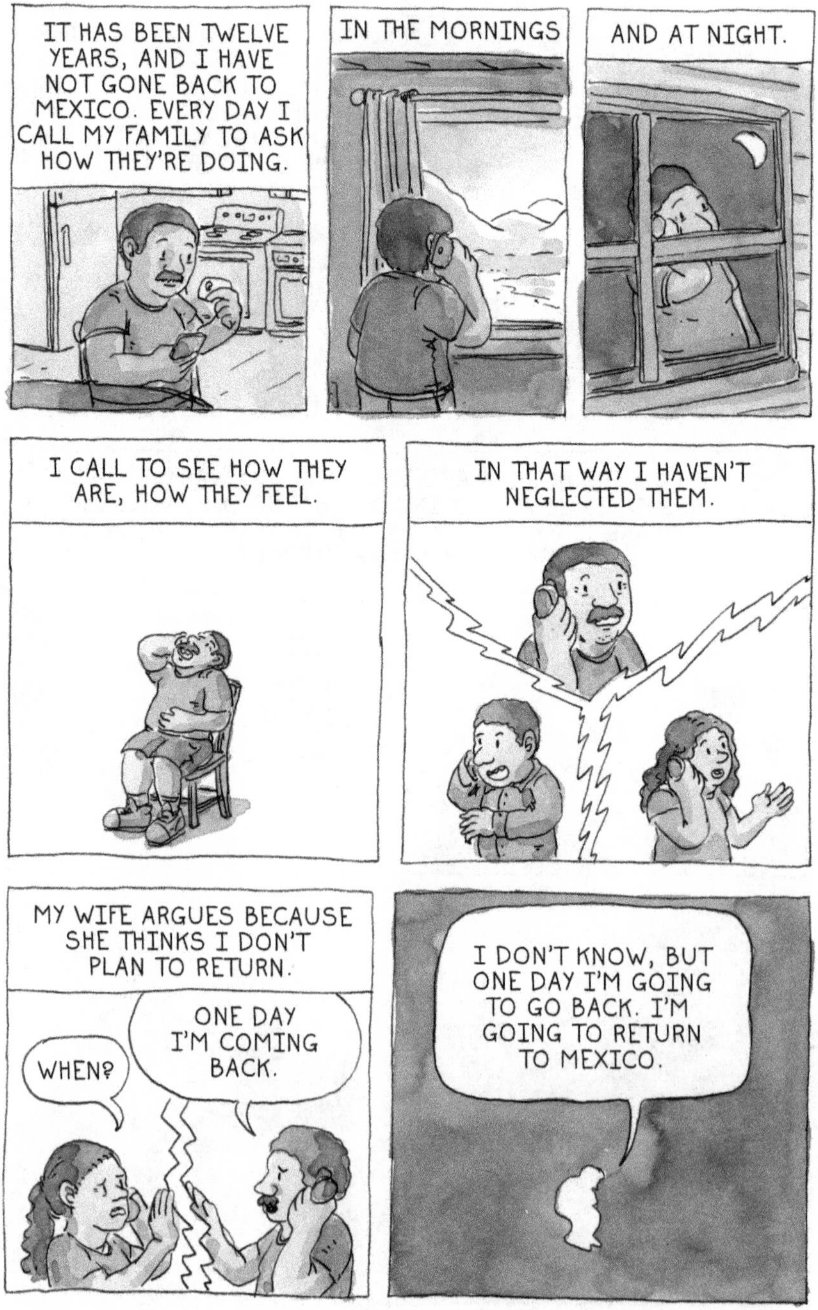
IT HAS BEEN TWELVE YEARS, AND I HAVE NOT GONE BACK TO MEXICO. EVERY DAY I CALL MY FAMILY TO ASK HOW THEY'RE DOING.
IN THE MORNINGS
AND AT NIGHT.
I CALL TO SEE HOW THEY ARE, HOW THEY FEEL.
IN THAT WAY I HAVEN'T NEGLECTED THEM.
MY WIFE ARGUES BECAUSE SHE THINKS I DON'T PLAN TO RETURN.
WHEN?
ONE DAY I'M COMING BACK.
I DON'T KNOW, BUT ONE DAY I'M GOING TO GO BACK. I'M GOING TO RETURN TO MEXICO.

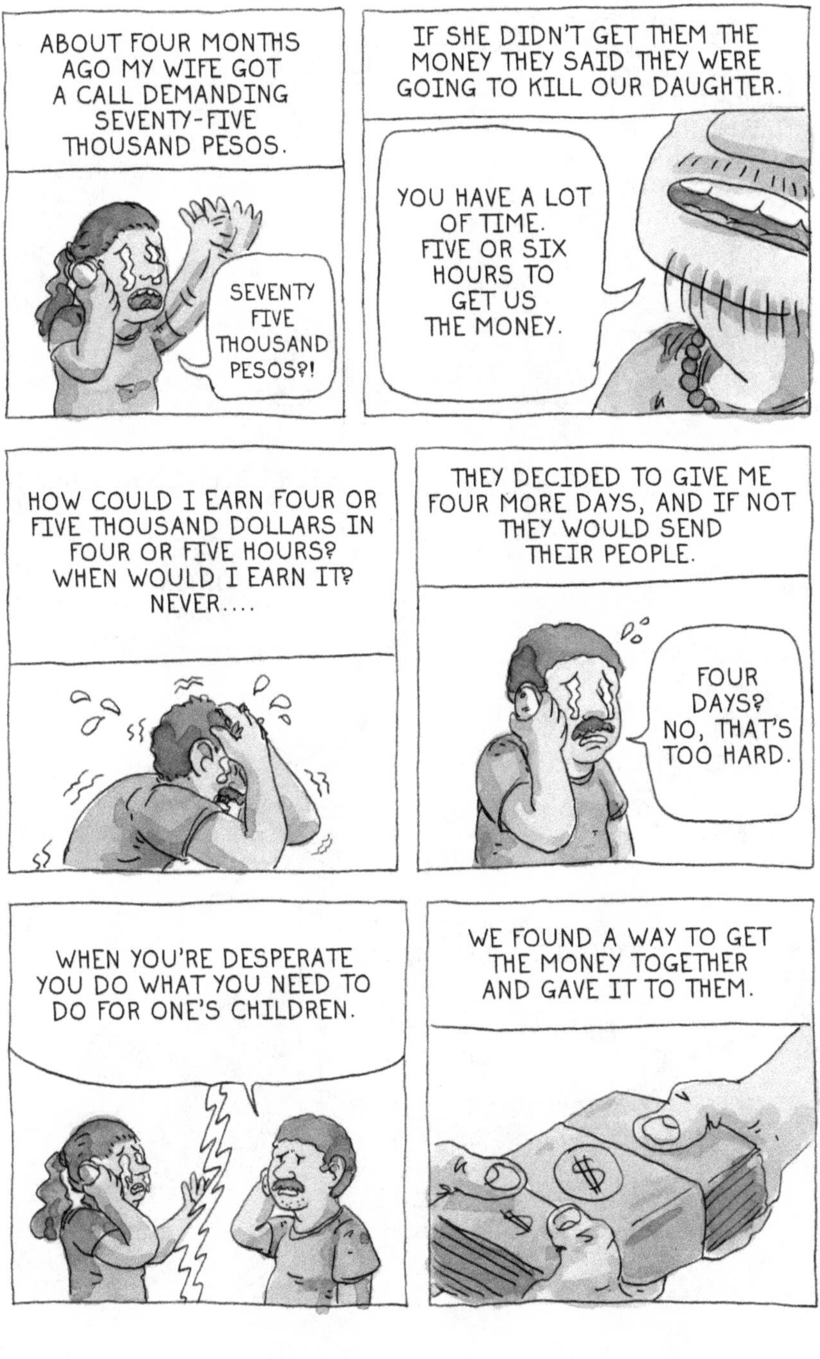
ABOUT FOUR MONTHS AGO MY WIFE GOT A CALL DEMANDING SEVENTY-FIVE THOUSAND PESOS.
SEVENTY FIVE THOUSAND PESOS?!
IF SHE DIDN'T GET THEM THE MONEY THEY SAID THEY WERE GOING TO KILL OUR DAUGHTER.
YOU HAVE A LOT OF TIME. FIVE OR SIX HOURS TO GET US THE MONEY.
HOW COULD I EARN FOUR OR FIVE THOUSAND DOLLARS IN FOUR OR FIVE HOURS? WHEN WOULD I EARN IT? NEVER....
THEY DECIDED TO GIVE ME FOUR MORE DAYS, AND IF NOT THEY WOULD SEND THEIR PEOPLE.
FOUR DAYS? NO, THAT'S TOO HARD.
WHEN YOU'RE DESPERATE YOU DO WHAT YOU NEED TO DO FOR ONE'S CHILDREN.
WE FOUND A WAY TO GET THE MONEY TOGETHER AND GAVE IT TO THEM.

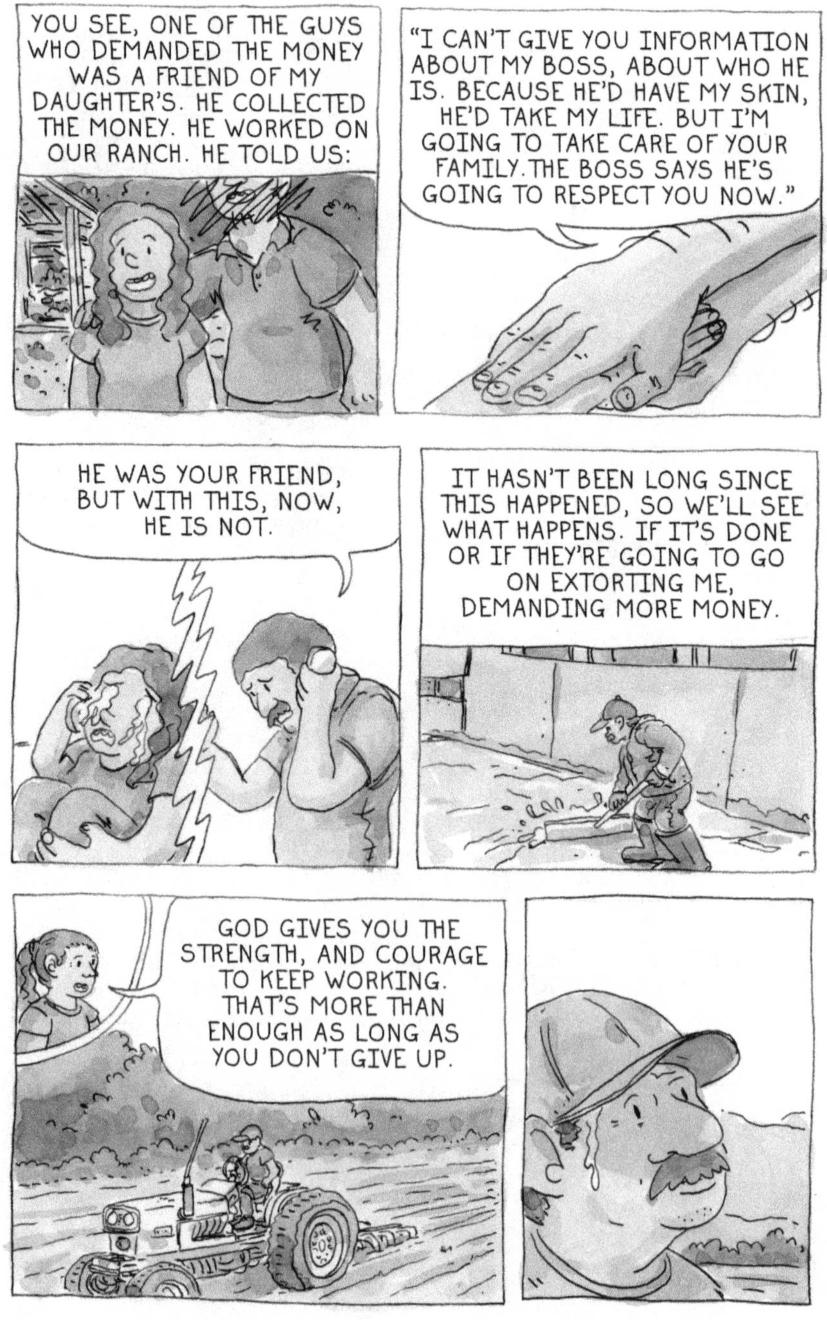
YOU SEE, ONE OF THE GUYS WHO DEMANDED THE MONEY WAS A FRIEND OF MY DAUGHTER'S. HE COLLECTED THE MONEY. HE WORKED ON OUR RANCH. HE TOLD US:
"I CAN'T GIVE YOU INFORMATION ABOUT MY BOSS, ABOUT WHO HE IS. BECAUSE HE'D HAVE MY SKIN, HE'D TAKE MY LIFE. BUT I'M GOING TO TAKE CARE OF YOUR FAMILY. THE BOSS SAYS HE'S GOING TO RESPECT YOU NOW."
HE WAS YOUR FRIEND, BUT WITH THIS, NOW, HE IS NOT.
IT HASN'T BEEN LONG SINCE THIS HAPPENED, SO WE'LL SEE WHAT HAPPENS. IF IT'S DONE OR IF THEY'RE GOING TO GO ON EXTORTING ME, DEMANDING MORE MONEY.
GOD GIVES YOU THE STRENGTH, AND COURAGE TO KEEP WORKING. THAT'S MORE THAN ENOUGH AS LONG AS YOU DON'T GIVE UP.

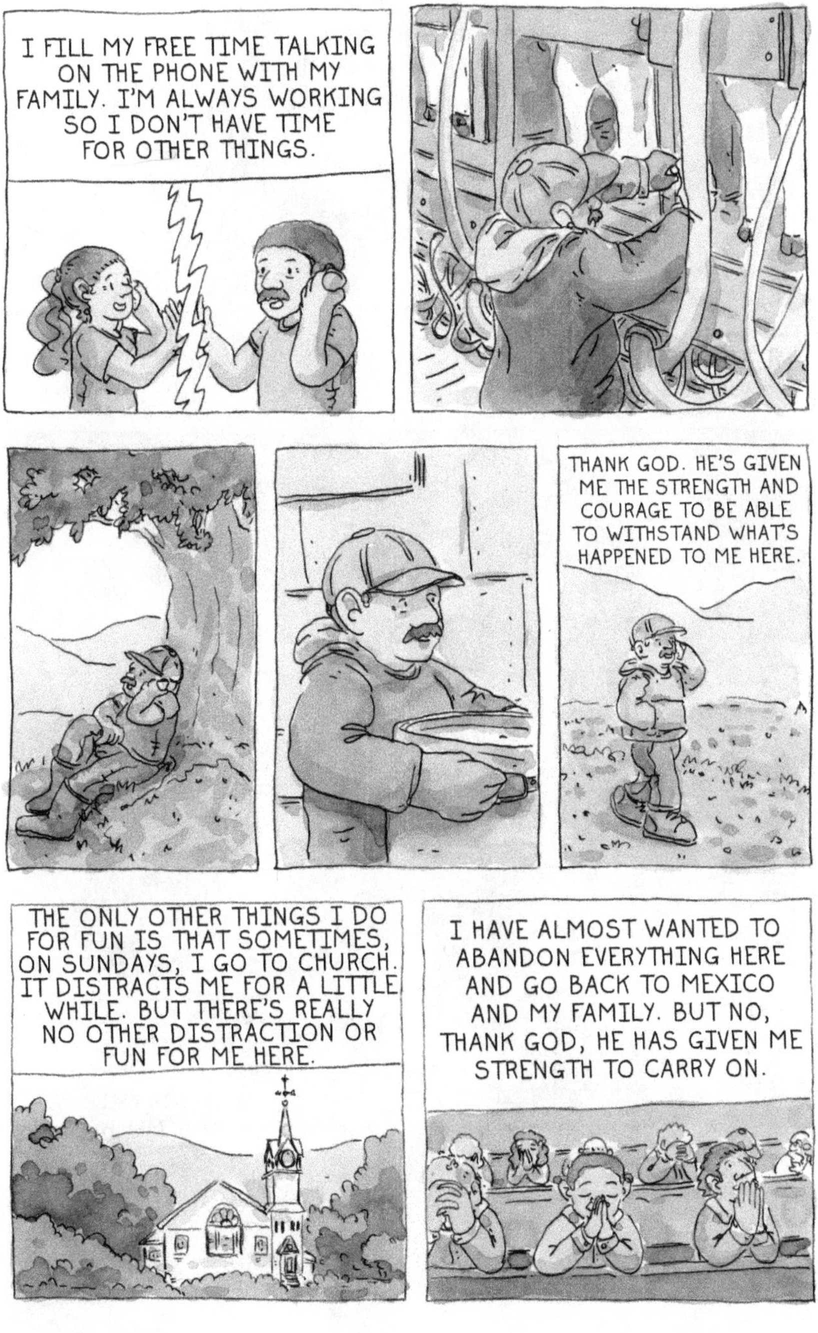
I FILL MY FREE TIME TALKING ON THE PHONE WITH MY FAMILY. I'M ALWAYS WORKING SO I DON'T HAVE TIME FOR OTHER THINGS.
THANK GOD. HE'S GIVEN ME THE STRENGTH AND COURAGE TO BE ABLE TO WITHSTAND WHAT'S HAPPENED TO ME HERE.
THE ONLY OTHER THINGS I DO FOR FUN IS THAT SOMETIMES, ON SUNDAYS, I GO TO CHURCH. IT DISTRACTS ME FOR A LITTLE WHILE. BUT THERE'S REALLY NO OTHER DISTRACTION OR FUN FOR ME HERE.
I HAVE ALMOST WANTED TO ABANDON EVERYTHING HERE AND GO BACK TO MEXICO AND MY FAMILY. BUT NO, THANK GOD, HE HAS GIVEN ME STRENGTH TO CARRY ON.

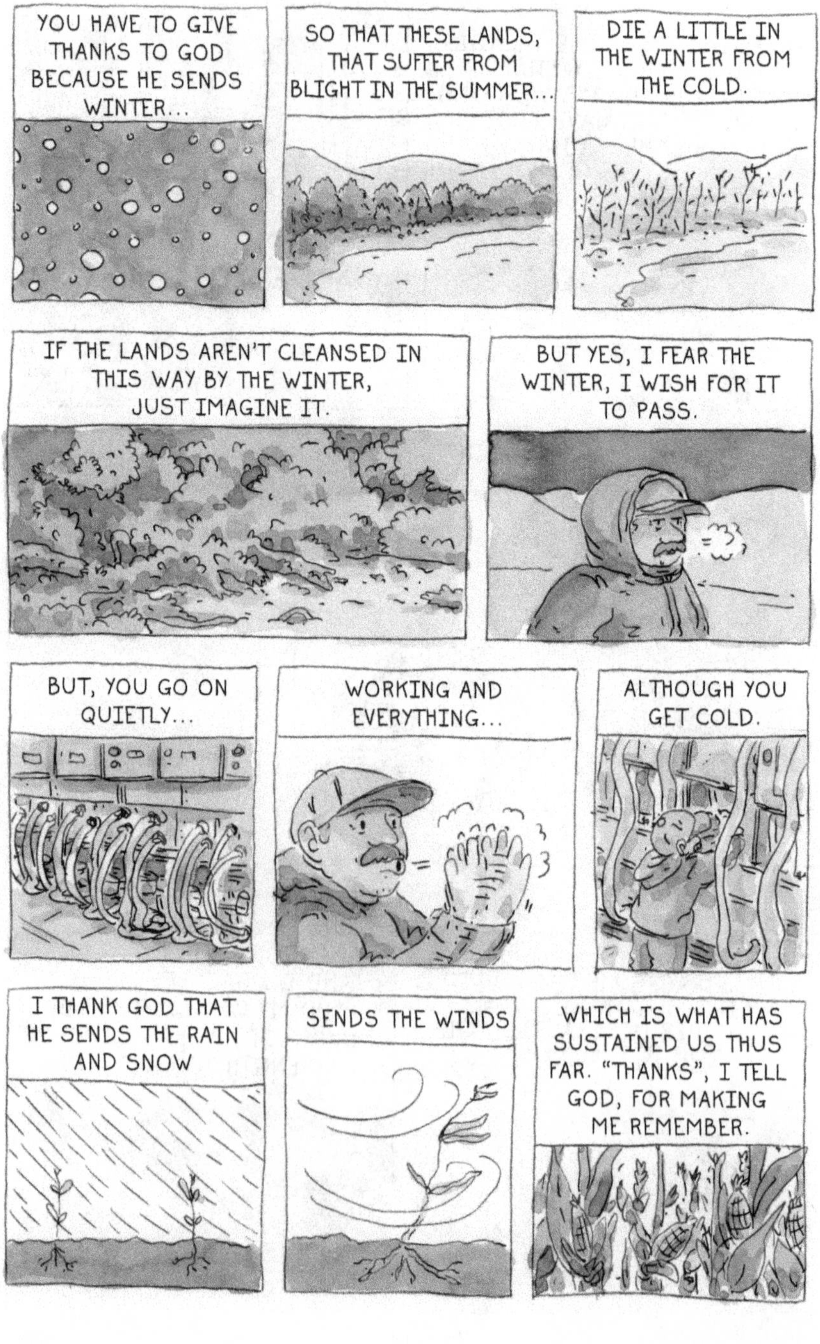
YOU HAVE TO GIVE THANKS TO GOD BECAUSE HE SENDS WINTER...
SO THAT THESE LANDS, THAT SUFFER FROM BLIGHT IN THE SUMMER...
DIE A LITTLE IN THE WINTER FROM THE COLD.
IF THE LANDS AREN'T CLEANSED IN THIS WAY BY THE WINTER, JUST IMAGINE IT.
BUT YES, I FEAR THE WINTER, I WISH FOR IT TO PASS.
BUT, YOU GO ON QUIETLY...
WORKING AND EVERYTHING...
ALTHOUGH YOU GET COLD.
I THANK GOD THAT HE SENDS THE RAIN AND SNOW
SENDS THE WINDS
WHICH IS WHAT HAS SUSTAINED US THUS FAR. "THANKS", I TELL GOD, FOR MAKING ME REMEMBER.

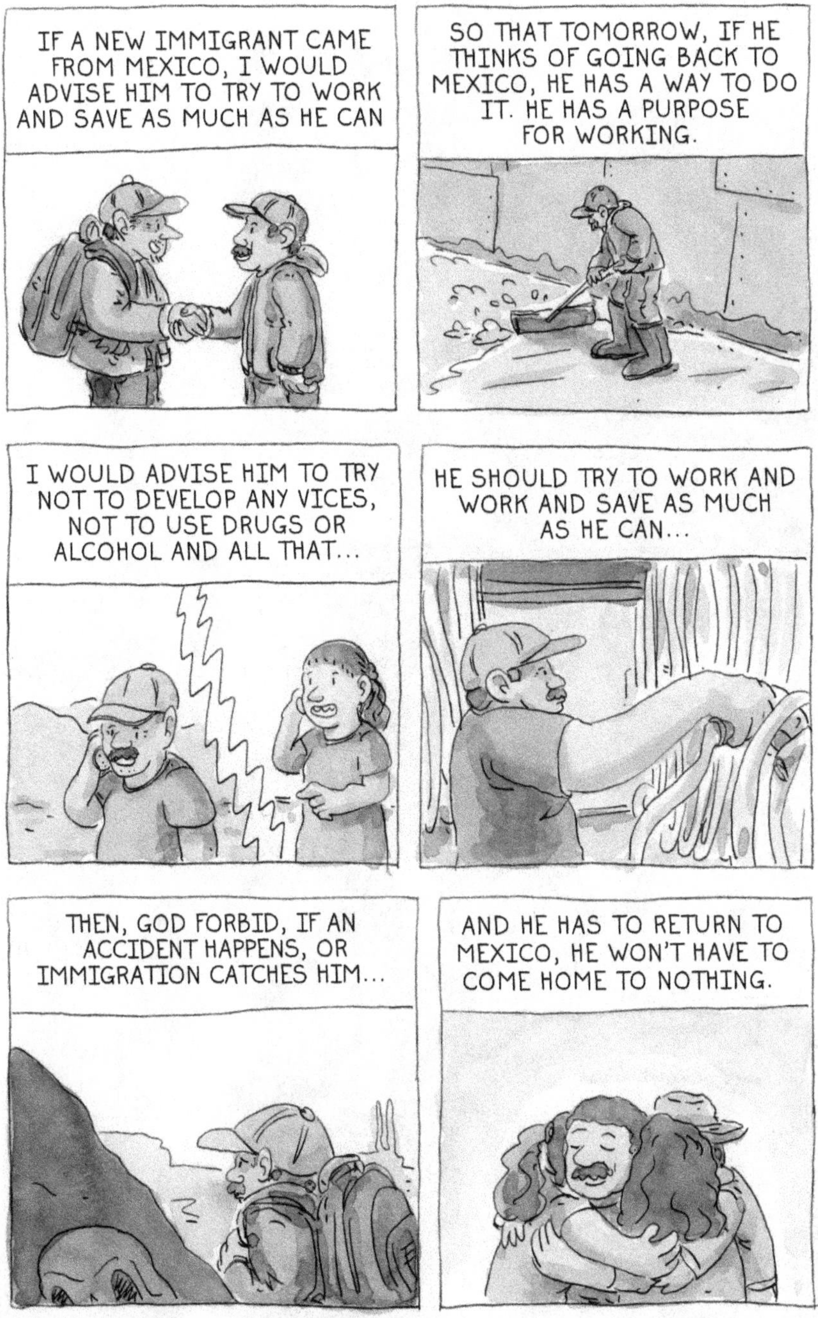
IF A NEW IMMIGRANT CAME FROM MEXICO, I WOULD ADVISE HIM TO TRY TO WORK AND SAVE AS MUCH AS HE CAN
SO THAT TOMORROW, IF HE THINKS OF GOING BACK TO MEXICO, HE HAS A WAY TO DO IT. HE HAS A PURPOSE FOR WORKING.
I WOULD ADVISE HIM TO TRY NOT TO DEVELOP ANY VICES, NOT TO USE DRUGS OR ALCOHOL AND ALL THAT...
HE SHOULD TRY TO WORK AND WORK AND SAVE AS MUCH AS HE CAN...
THEN, GOD FORBID, IF AN ACCIDENT HAPPENS, OR IMMIGRATION CATCHES HIM...
AND HE HAS TO RETURN TO MEXICO, HE WON'T HAVE TO COME HOME TO NOTHING.

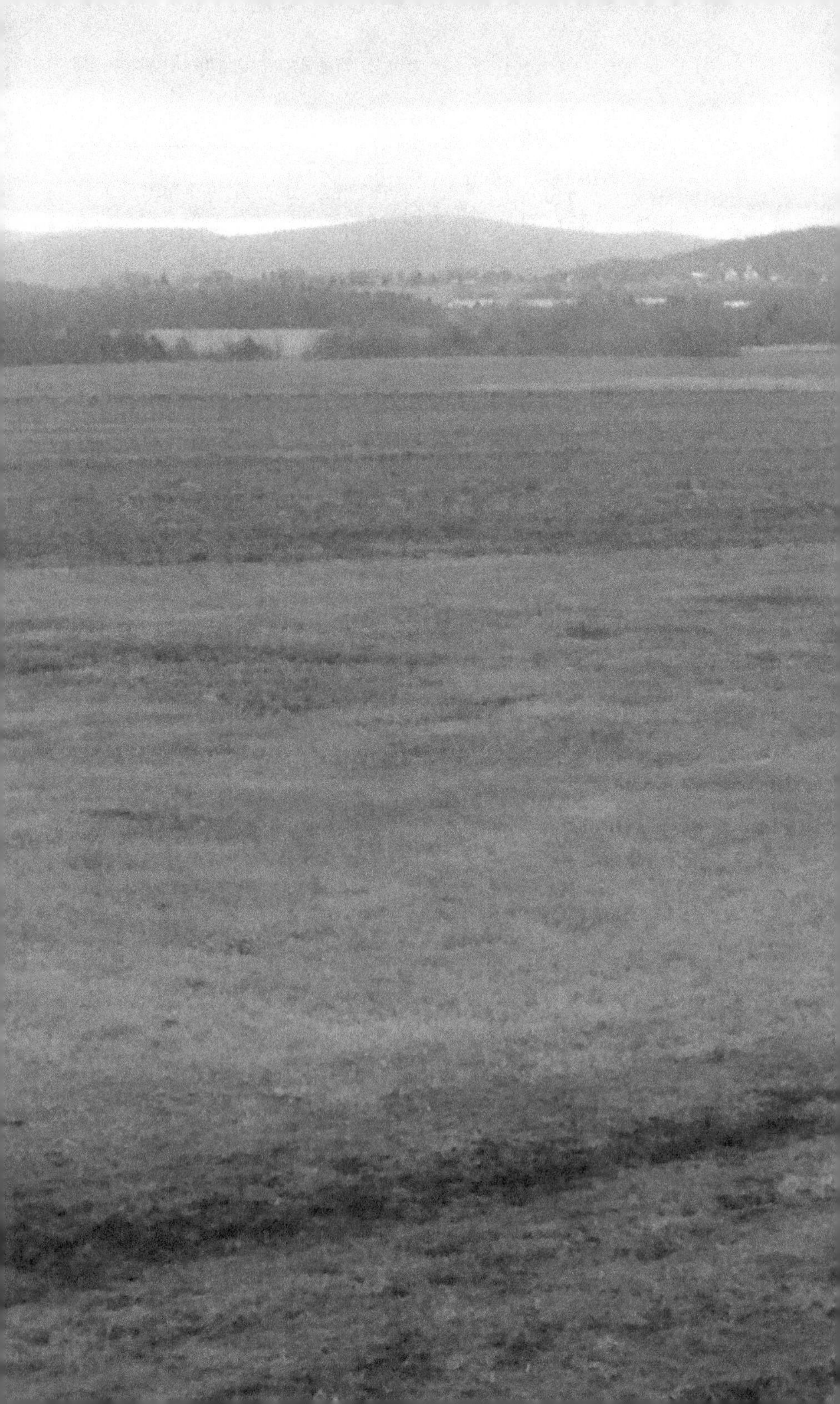

"EL VIAJE MAS CARO" / *"THE MOST COSTLY JOURNEY"* presents:

YOU WILL BE ACCEPTED

The Story of Daniel
Art by Teppi Zuppo

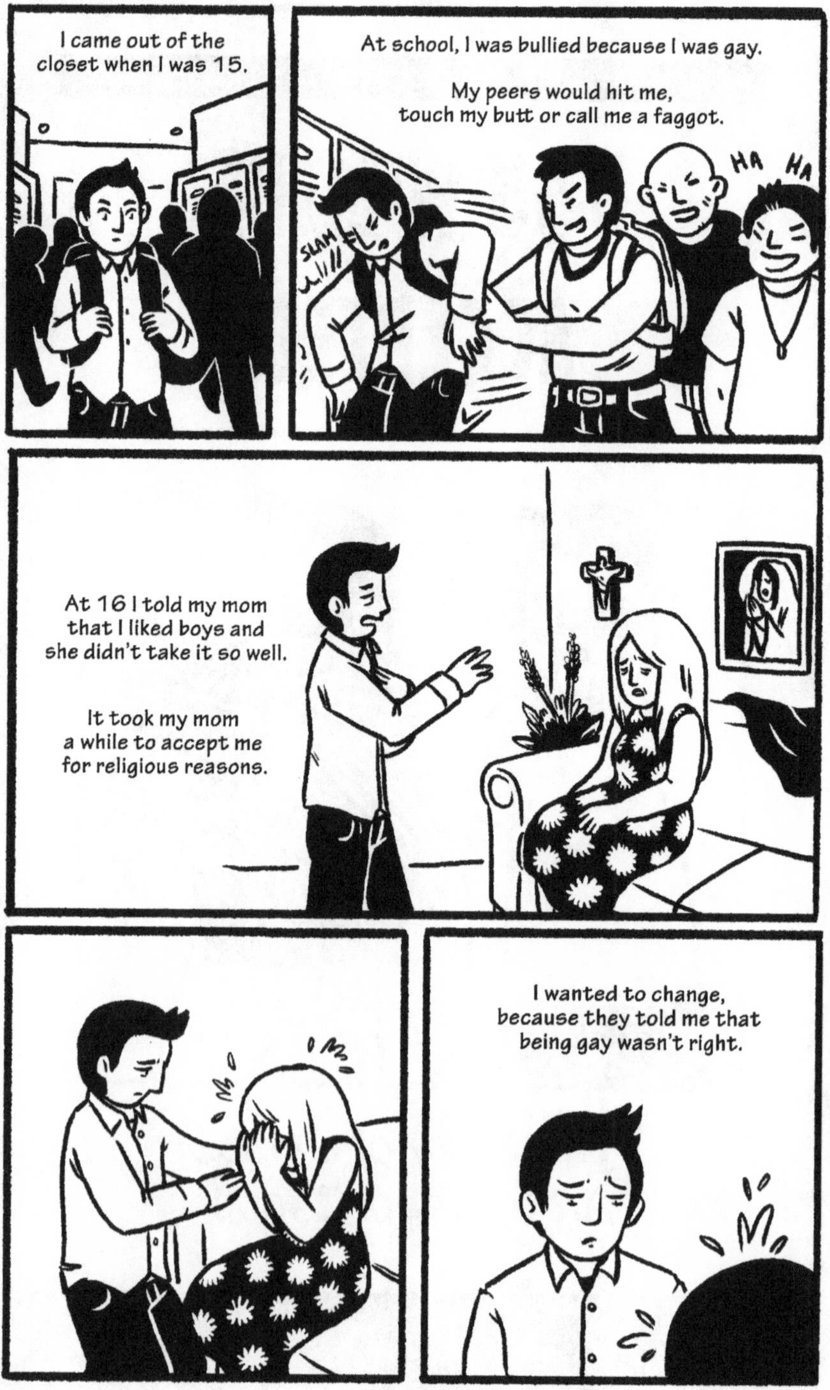
I came out of the closet when I was 15.
At school, I was bullied because I was gay.
My peers would hit me, touch my butt or call me a faggot.
SLAM
HA HA
At 16 I told my mom that I liked boys and she didn't take it so well.
It took my mom a while to accept me for religious reasons.
I wanted to change, because they told me that being gay wasn't right.

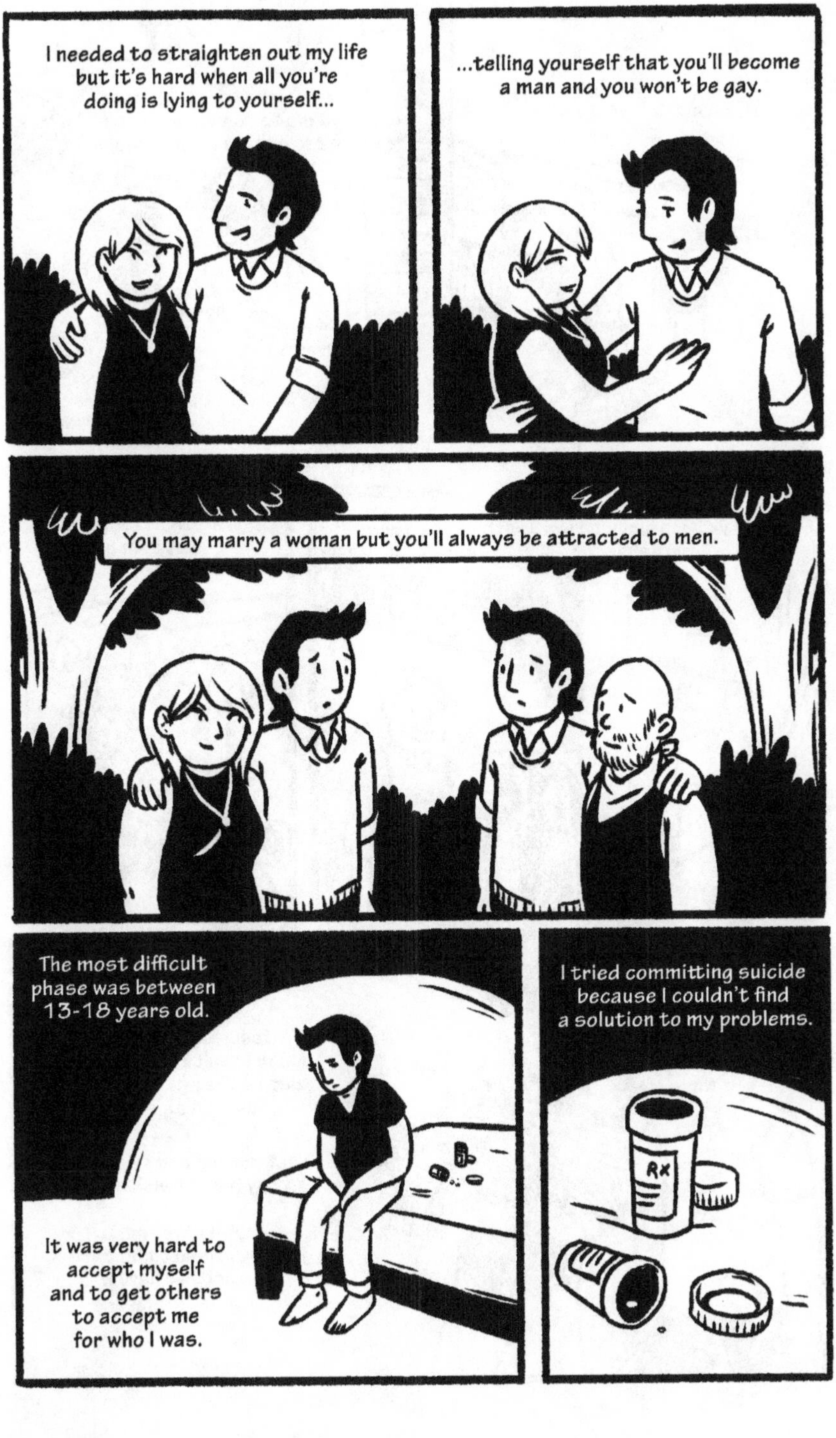
I needed to straighten out my life but it's hard when all you're doing is lying to yourself...
...telling yourself that you'll become a man and you won't be gay.
You may marry a woman but you'll always be attracted to men.
The most difficult phase was between 13-18 years old.
It was very hard to accept myself and to get others to accept me for who I was.
I tried committing suicide because I couldn't find a solution to my problems.
RX

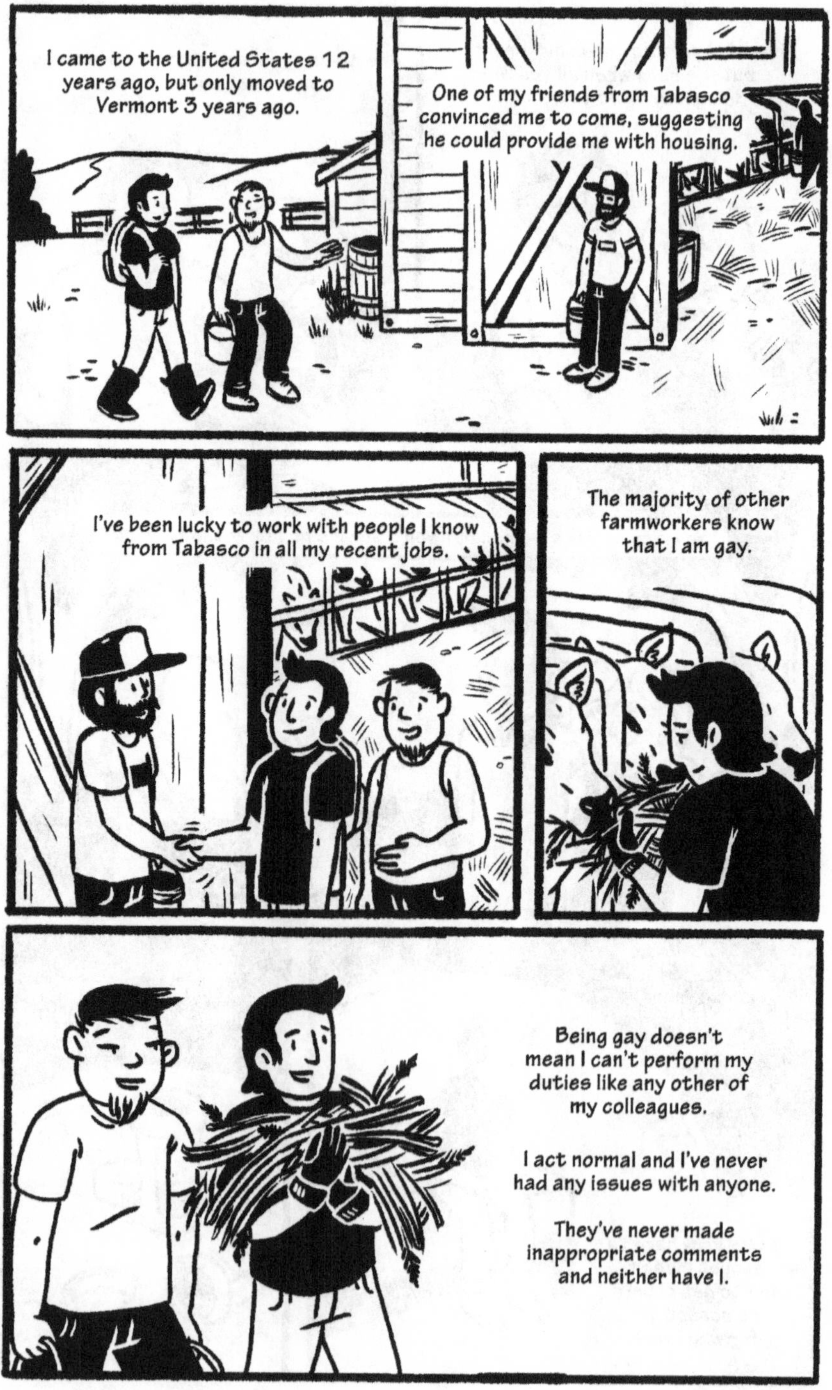
I came to the United States 12 years ago, but only moved to Vermont 3 years ago.
One of my friends from Tabasco convinced me to come, suggesting he could provide me with housing.
I've been lucky to work with people I know from Tabasco in all my recent jobs.
The majority of other farmworkers know that I am gay.
Being gay doesn't mean I can't perform my duties like any other of my colleagues.
I act normal and I've never had any issues with anyone.
They've never made inappropriate comments and neither have I.

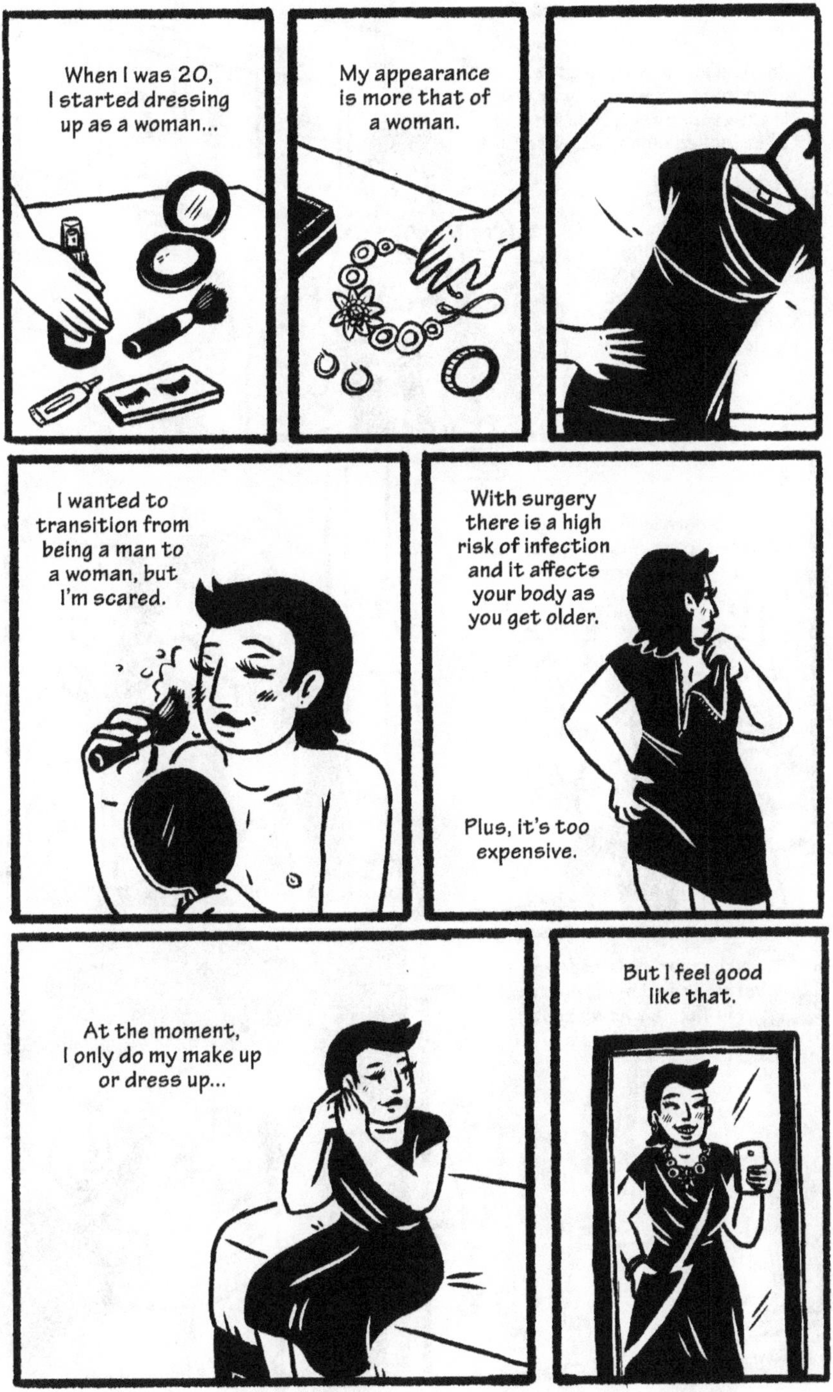
When I was 20, I started dressing up as a woman...
My appearance is more that of a woman.
I wanted to transition from being a man to a woman, but I'm scared.
With surgery there is a high risk of infection and it affects your body as you get older.
Plus, it's too expensive.
At the moment, I only do my make up or dress up...
But I feel good like that.

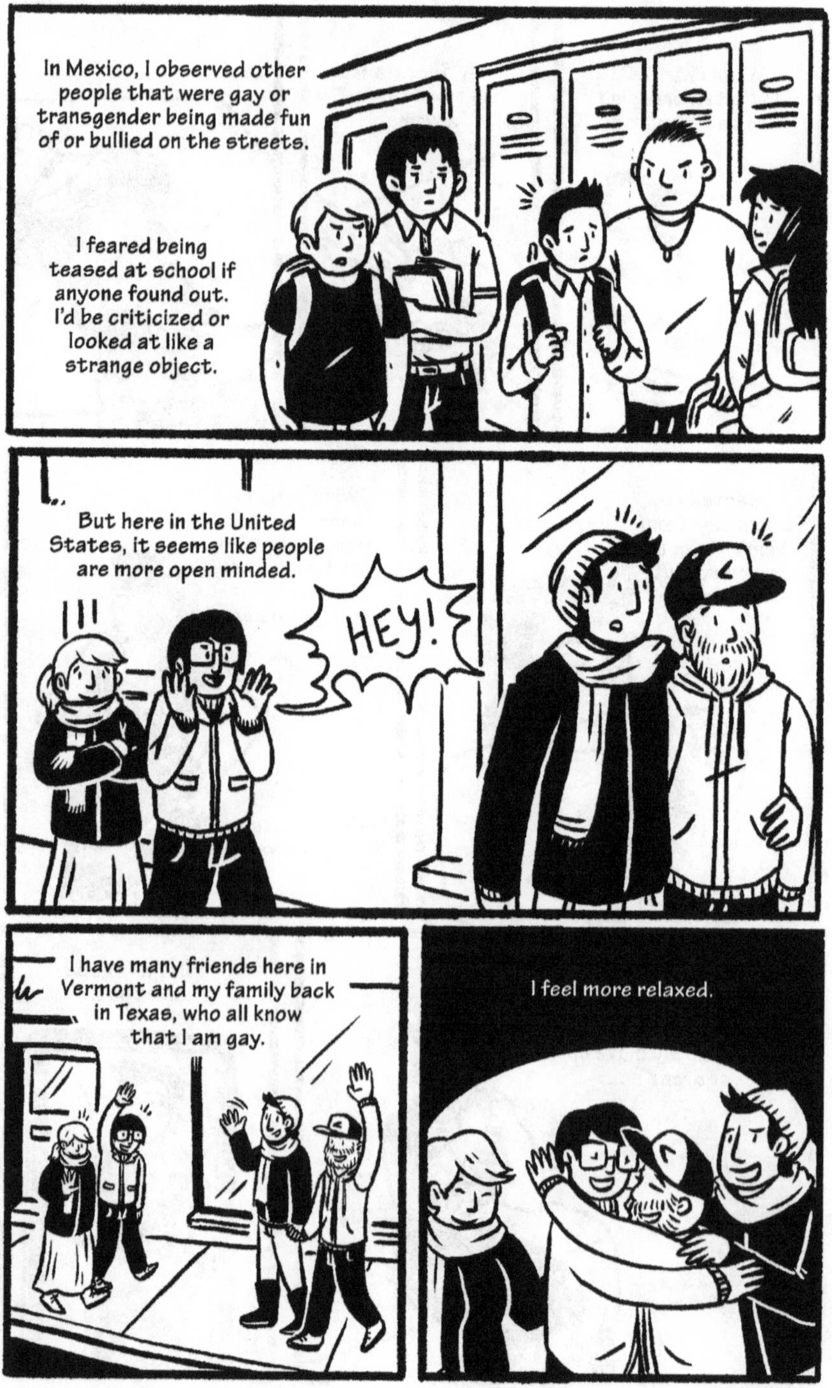
In Mexico, I observed other people that were gay or transgender being made fun of or bullied on the streets.
I feared being teased at school if anyone found out. I'd be criticized or looked at like a strange object.
But here in the United States, it seems like people are more open minded.
HEY!
I have many friends here in Vermont and my family back in Texas, who all know that I am gay.
I feel more relaxed.

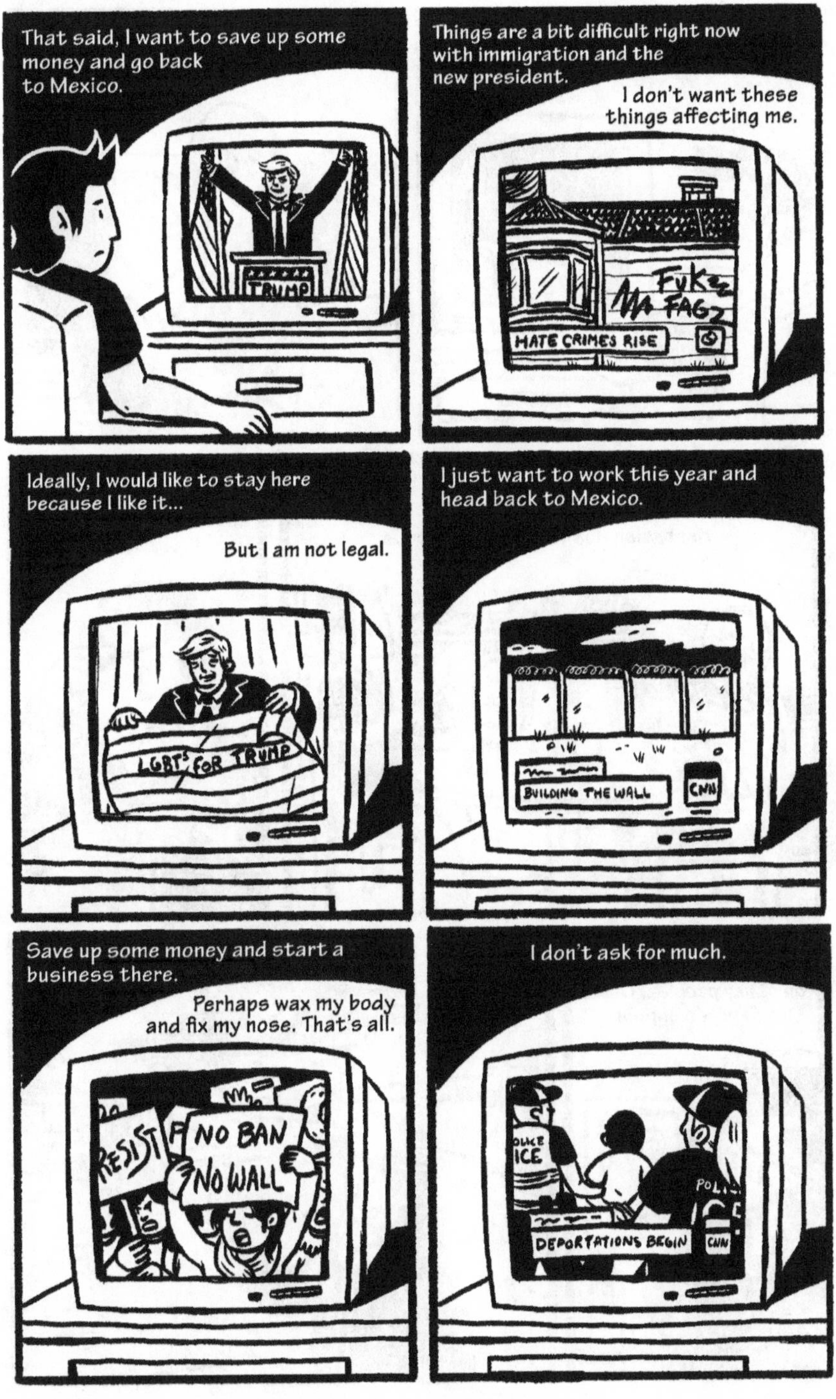
That said, I want to save up some money and go back to Mexico.
TRUMP
Things are a bit difficult right now with immigration and the new president.
I don't want these things affecting me.
FUKz FAGz
HATE CRIMES RISE
Ideally, I would like to stay here because I like it...
But I am not legal.
LGBT's FOR TRUMP
I just want to work this year and head back to Mexico.
BUILDING THE WALL
CNN
Save up some money and start a business there.
Perhaps wax my body and fix my nose. That's all.
RESIST
NO BAN NO WALL
I don't ask for much.
ICE
DEPORTATIONS BEGIN
CNN

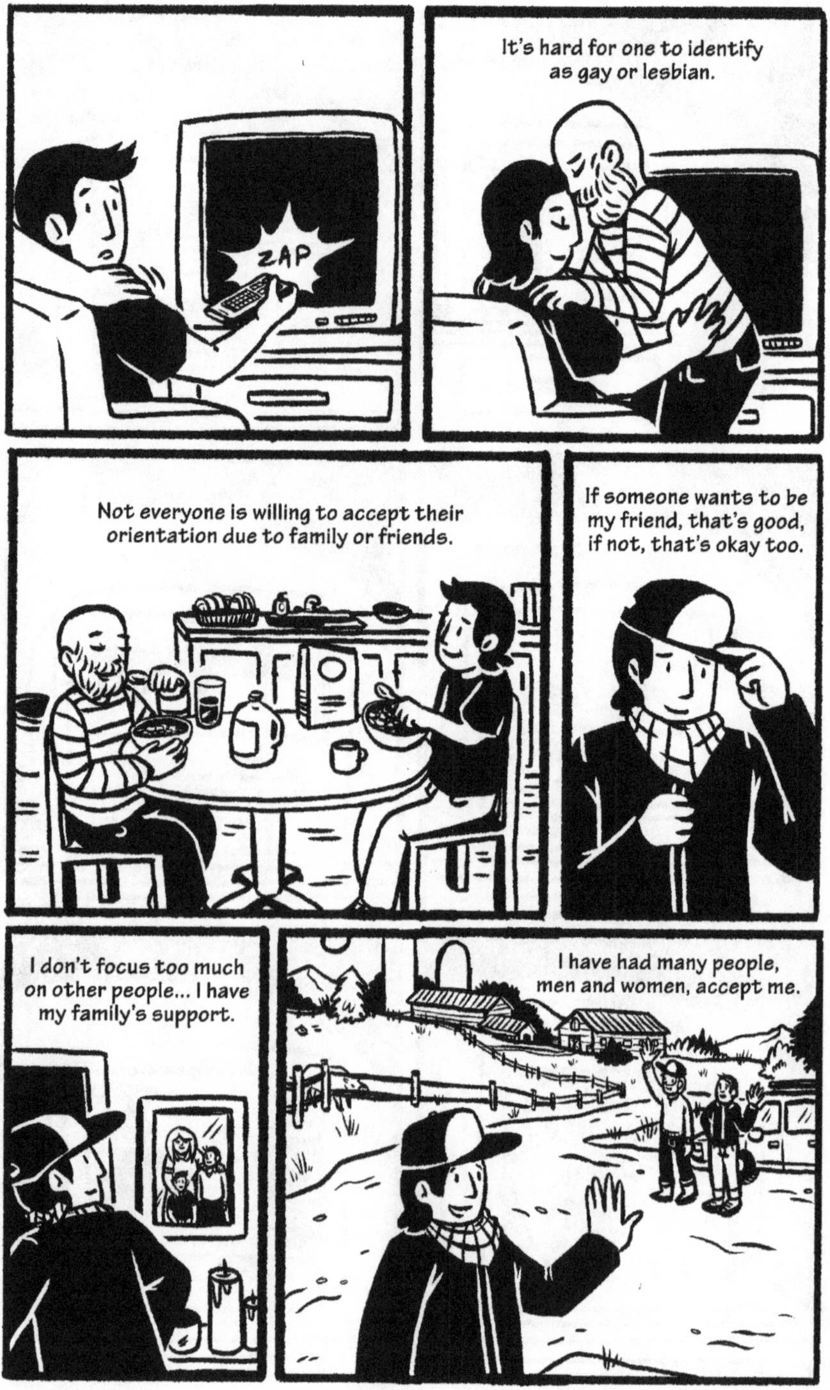
ZAP
It's hard for one to identify as gay or lesbian.
Not everyone is willing to accept their orientation due to family or friends.
If someone wants to be my friend, that's good, if not, that's okay too.
I don't focus too much on other people... I have my family's support.
I have had many people, men and women, accept me.

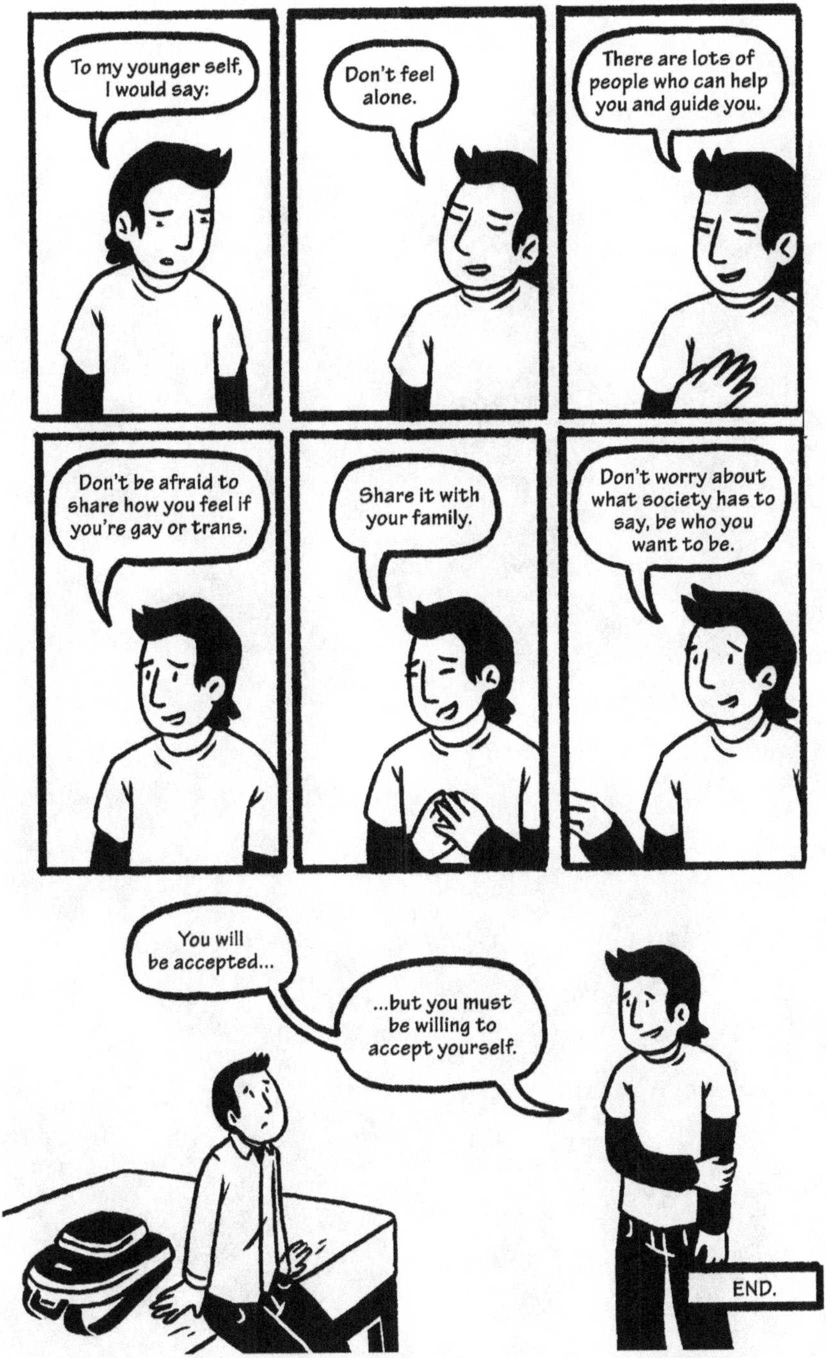
To my younger self, I would say:
Don't feel alone.
There are lots of people who can help you and guide you.
Don't be afraid to share how you feel if you're gay or trans.
Share it with your family.
Don't worry about what society has to say, be who you want to be.
You will be accepted...
...but you must be willing to accept yourself.
END.

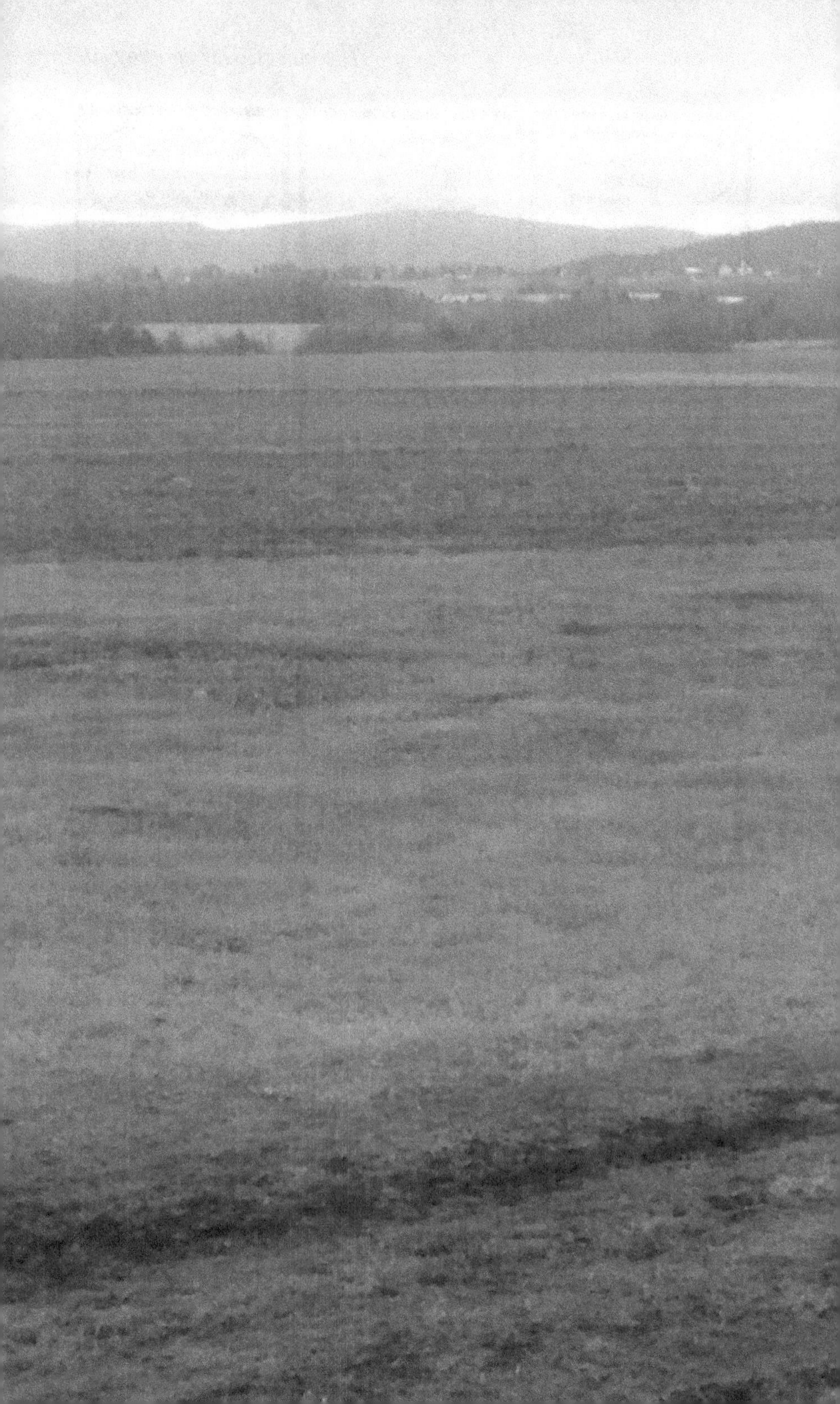

"EL VIAJE MAS CARO" / "THE MOST COSTLY JOURNEY" *presents:*

A HEART
SPLIT IN TWO

*The Story of Juana
Art by Michael Tonn*

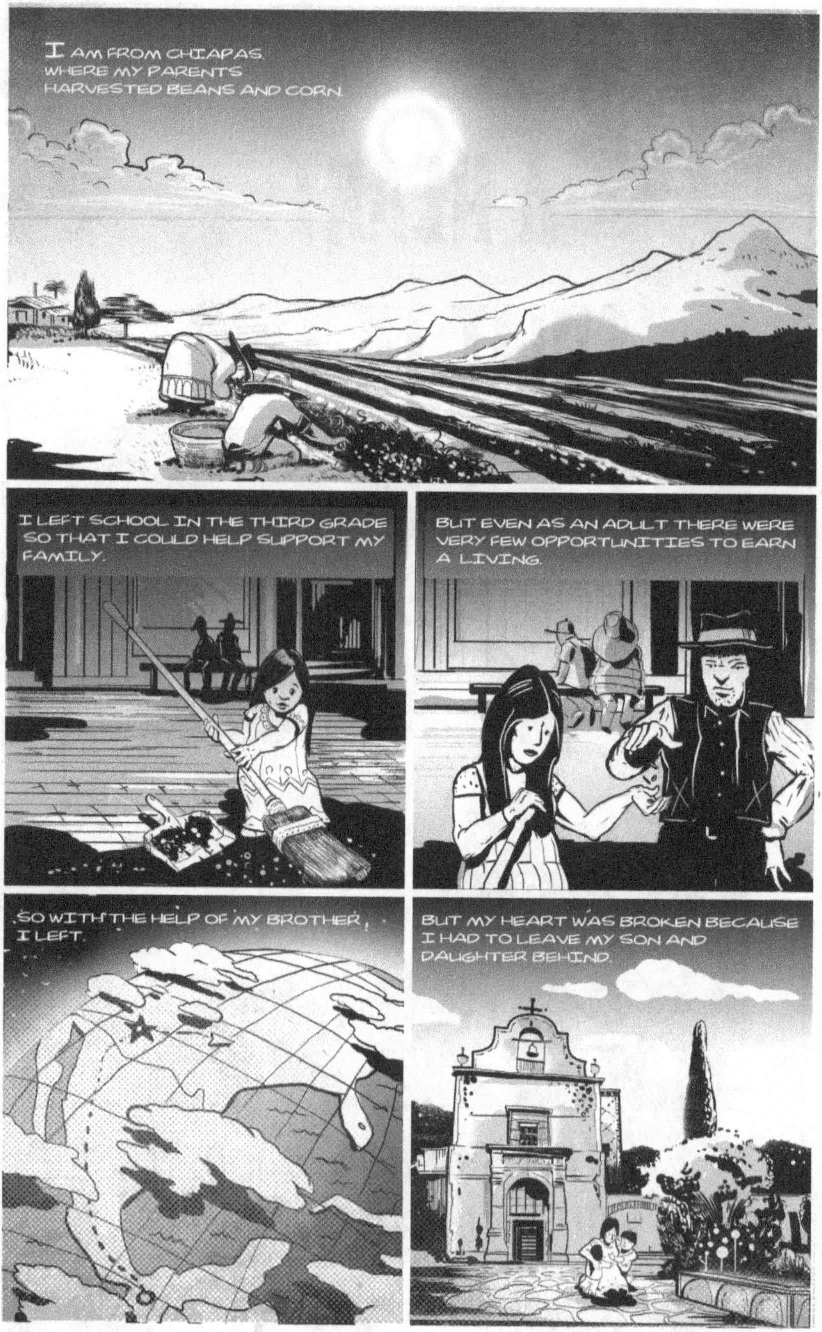
I AM FROM CHIAPAS, WHERE MY PARENTS HARVESTED BEANS AND CORN.
I LEFT SCHOOL IN THE THIRD GRADE SO THAT I COULD HELP SUPPORT MY FAMILY.
BUT EVEN AS AN ADULT THERE WERE VERY FEW OPPORTUNITIES TO EARN A LIVING.
SO WITH THE HELP OF MY BROTHER, I LEFT.
BUT MY HEART WAS BROKEN BECAUSE I HAD TO LEAVE MY SON AND DAUGHTER BEHIND.

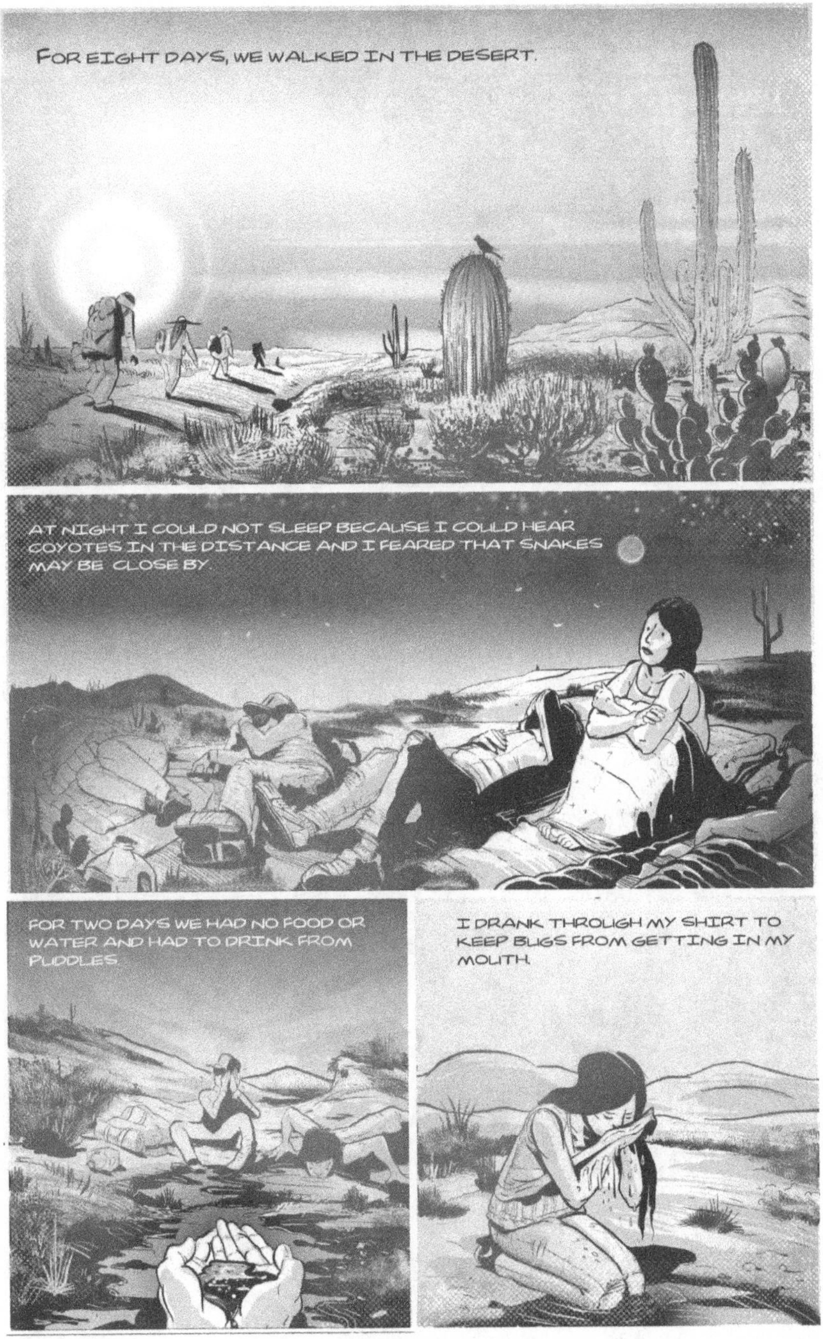
FOR EIGHT DAYS, WE WALKED IN THE DESERT.
AT NIGHT I COULD NOT SLEEP BECAUSE I COULD HEAR COYOTES IN THE DISTANCE AND I FEARED THAT SNAKES MAY BE CLOSE BY.
FOR TWO DAYS WE HAD NO FOOD OR WATER AND HAD TO DRINK FROM PUDDLES.
I DRANK THROUGH MY SHIRT TO KEEP BUGS FROM GETTING IN MY MOUTH.

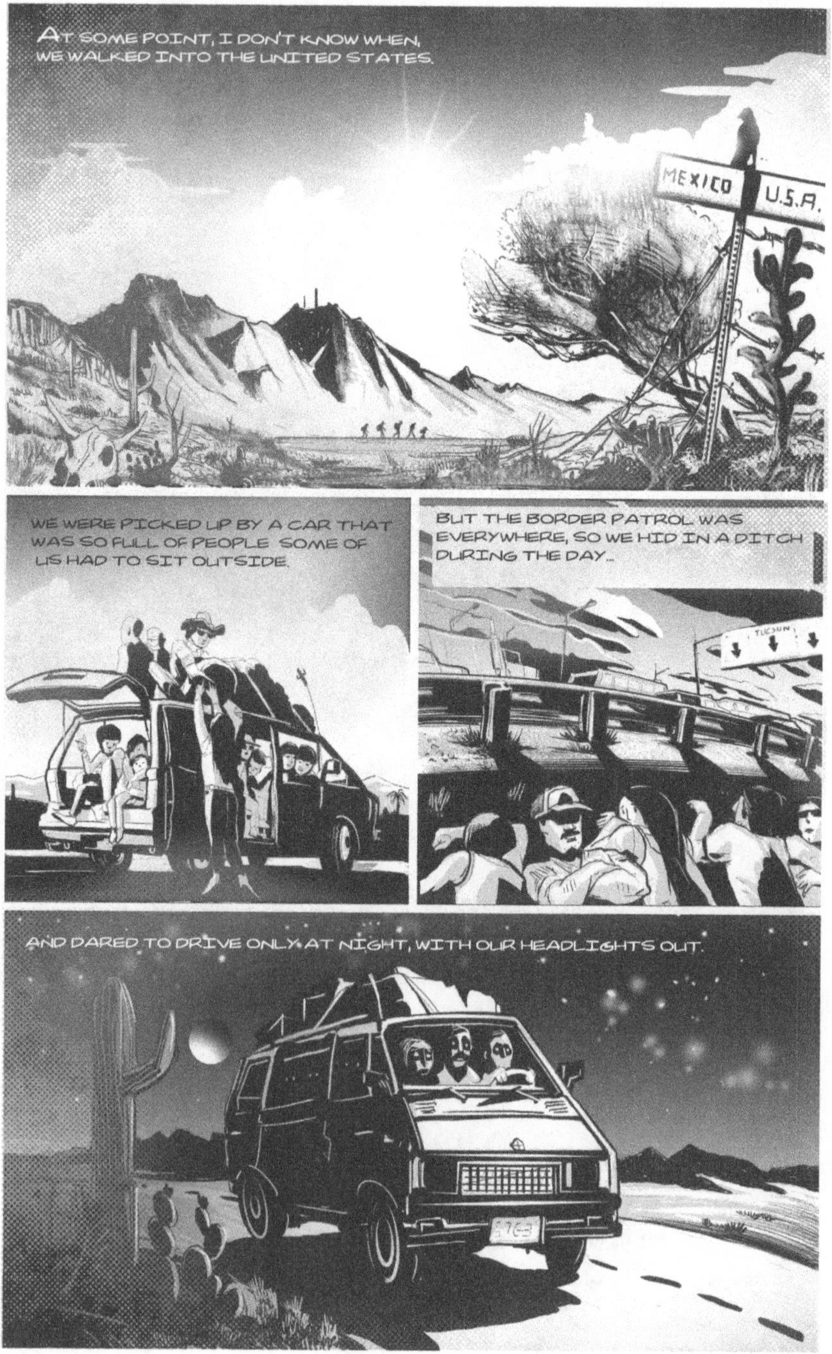
AT SOME POINT, I DON'T KNOW WHEN, WE WALKED INTO THE UNITED STATES.
MEXICO
U.S.A.
WE WERE PICKED UP BY A CAR THAT WAS SO FULL OF PEOPLE SOME OF US HAD TO SIT OUTSIDE.
BUT THE BORDER PATROL WAS EVERYWHERE, SO WE HID IN A DITCH DURING THE DAY...
TUCSON
AND DARED TO DRIVE ONLY AT NIGHT, WITH OUR HEADLIGHTS OUT.

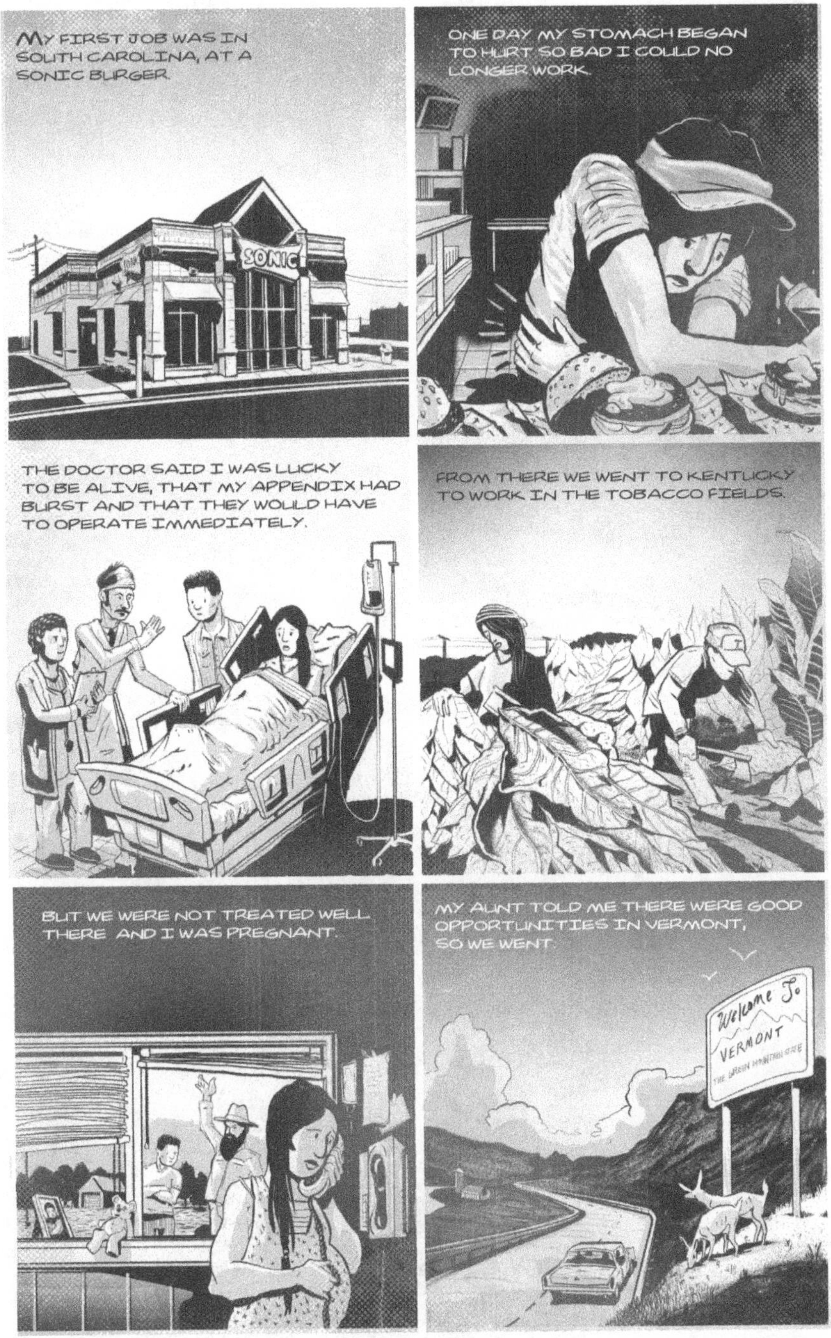
MY FIRST JOB WAS IN SOUTH CAROLINA, AT A SONIC BURGER.
SONIC
ONE DAY MY STOMACH BEGAN TO HURT SO BAD I COULD NO LONGER WORK.
THE DOCTOR SAID I WAS LUCKY TO BE ALIVE, THAT MY APPENDIX HAD BURST AND THAT THEY WOULD HAVE TO OPERATE IMMEDIATELY.
FROM THERE WE WENT TO KENTUCKY TO WORK IN THE TOBACCO FIELDS.
BUT WE WERE NOT TREATED WELL THERE AND I WAS PREGNANT.
MY AUNT TOLD ME THERE WERE GOOD OPPORTUNITIES IN VERMONT, SO WE WENT.
Welcome To
VERMONT

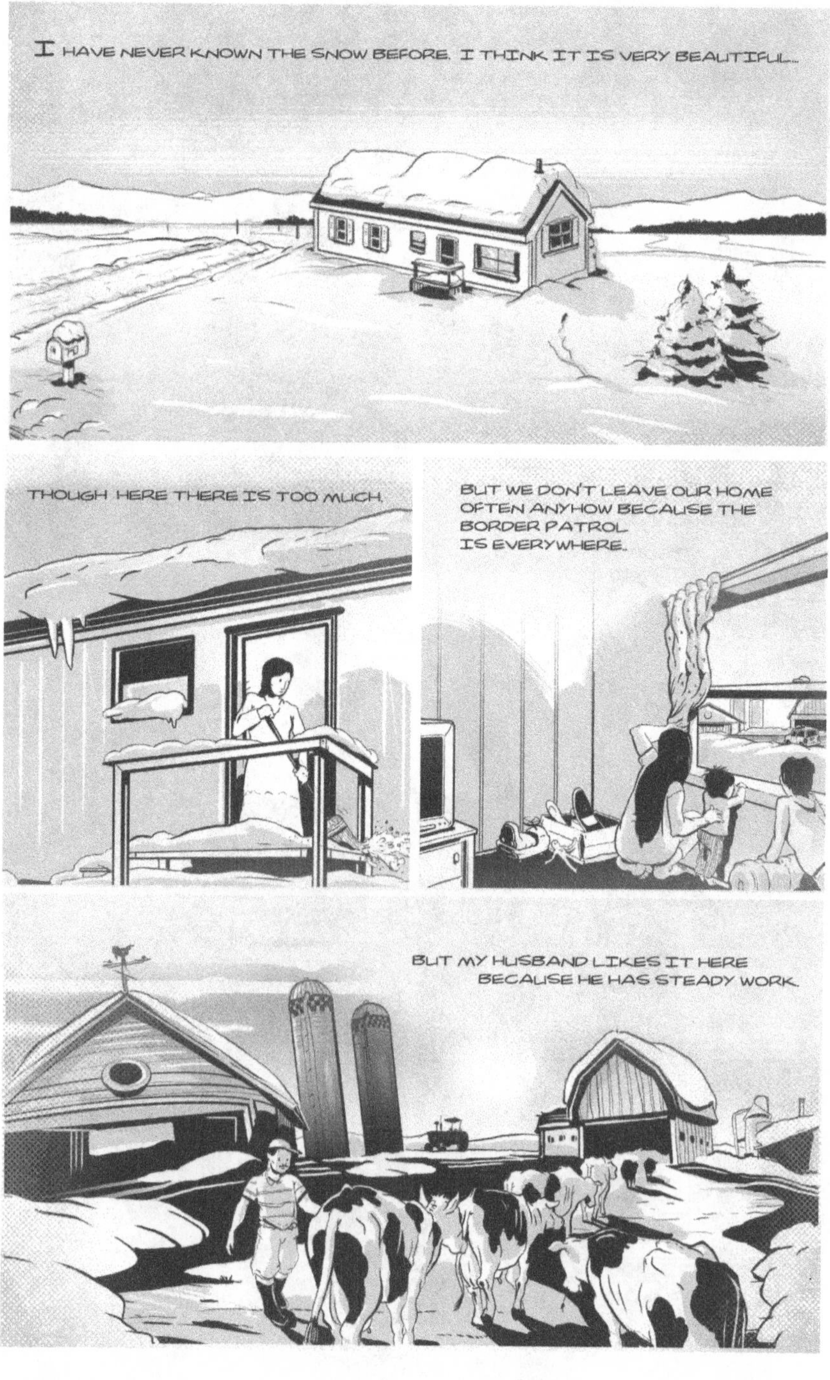
I HAVE NEVER KNOWN THE SNOW BEFORE. I THINK IT IS VERY BEAUTIFUL...
THOUGH HERE THERE IS TOO MUCH.
BUT WE DON'T LEAVE OUR HOME OFTEN ANYHOW BECAUSE THE BORDER PATROL IS EVERYWHERE.
BUT MY HUSBAND LIKES IT HERE BECAUSE HE HAS STEADY WORK.

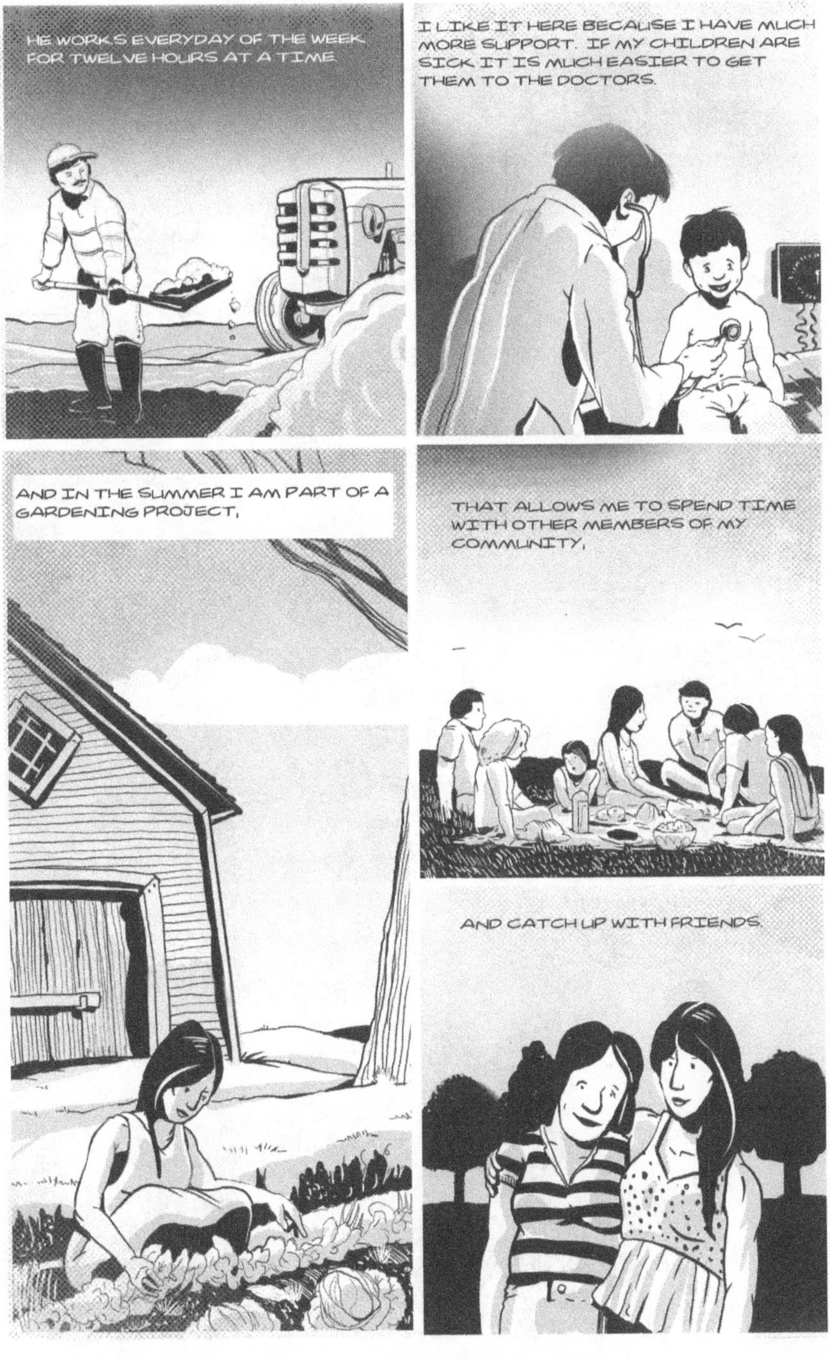
HE WORKS EVERYDAY OF THE WEEK FOR TWELVE HOURS AT A TIME.
I LIKE IT HERE BECAUSE I HAVE MUCH MORE SUPPORT. IF MY CHILDREN ARE SICK IT IS MUCH EASIER TO GET THEM TO THE DOCTORS.
AND IN THE SUMMER I AM PART OF A GARDENING PROJECT,
THAT ALLOWS ME TO SPEND TIME WITH OTHER MEMBERS OF MY COMMUNITY,
AND CATCH UP WITH FRIENDS.

ALSO I AM GLAD TO SAY THAT MY OLDEST SON HAS COME TO VERMONT TOO.

BUT HE WAS ARRESTED BY BORDER PATROL JUST 15 DAYS AFTER ARRIVING.

IT COST US $10,000 TO GET HIM OUT, BUT NOW HE IS HERE WITH US.

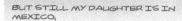

I AM VERY HAPPY.

BUT STILL MY DAUGHTER IS IN MEXICO,

SO MY HEART WILL BE FOREVER SPLIT BETWEEN TWO PLACES.

"EL VIAJE MAS CARO" / "THE MOST COSTLY JOURNEY" presents:

THE BEST THING

The Story of the Cruz Family
Art by Angela Boyle

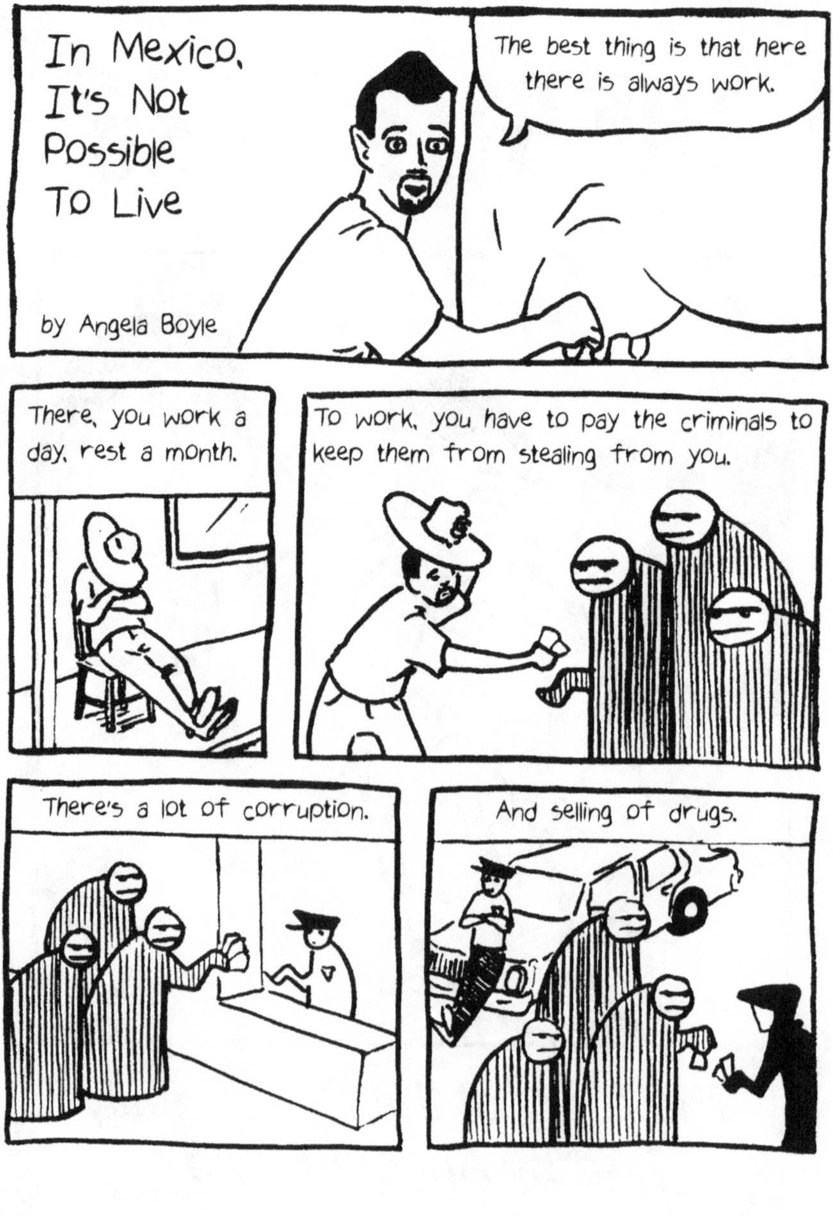
In Mexico, It's Not Possible To Live
by Angela Boyle
The best thing is that here there is always work.
There, you work a day, rest a month.
To work, you have to pay the criminals to keep them from stealing from you.
There's a lot of corruption.
And selling of drugs.

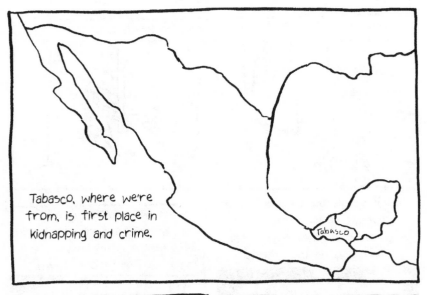

Tabasco, where we're from, is first place in kidnapping and crime.

When I was alone with my son, Alexis, in Mexico, it was too dangerous. I wouldn't let him out of my sight.

I wouldn't let him play with anyone or go out without me.

Just bringing him to school was terrifying for me.

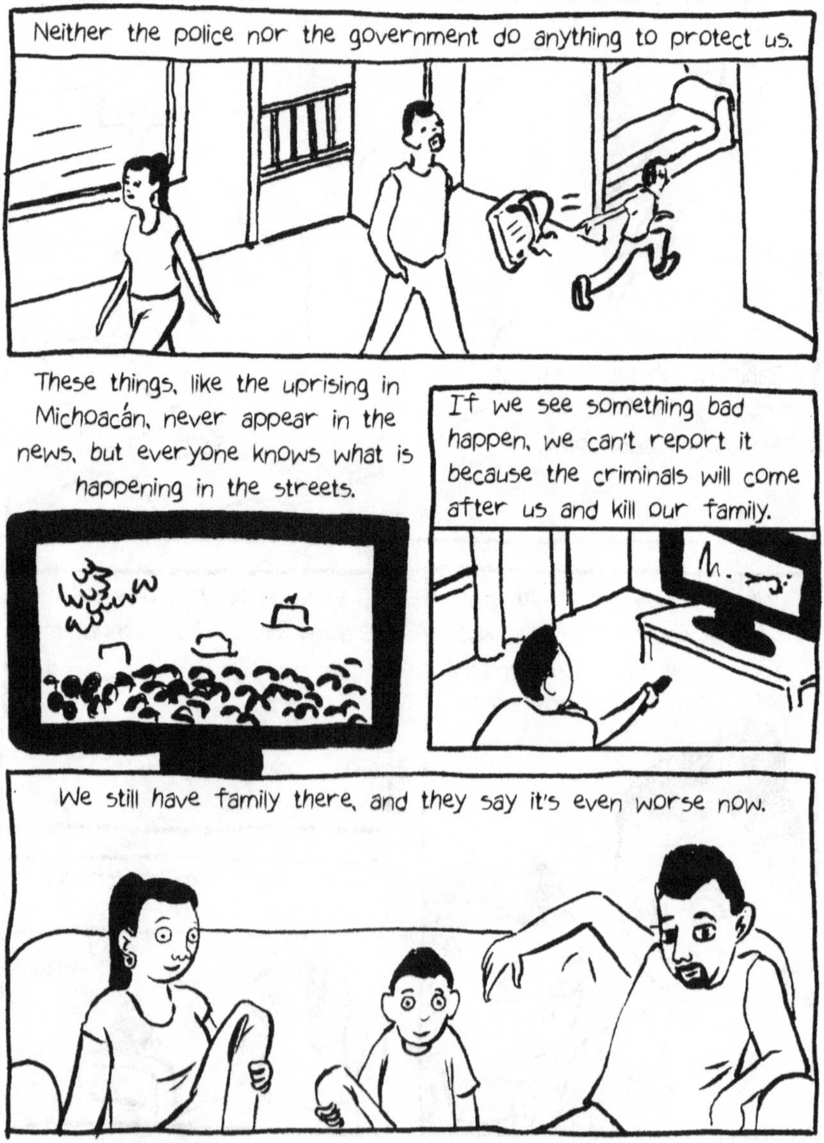
Neither the police nor the government do anything to protect us.
These things, like the uprising in Michoacán, never appear in the news, but everyone knows what is happening in the streets.
If we see something bad happen, we can't report it because the criminals will come after us and kill our family.
We still have family there, and they say it's even worse now.

Our families still have land. They harvest cacao outside the city and sell the harvest.

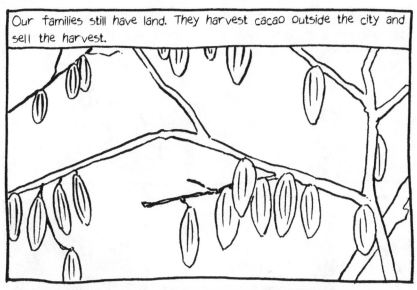

But criminals also take part of the harvest. You have to pay them with either money or cacao.

It's because the police and the criminals are the same thing.

They extort us in exchange for "protection."

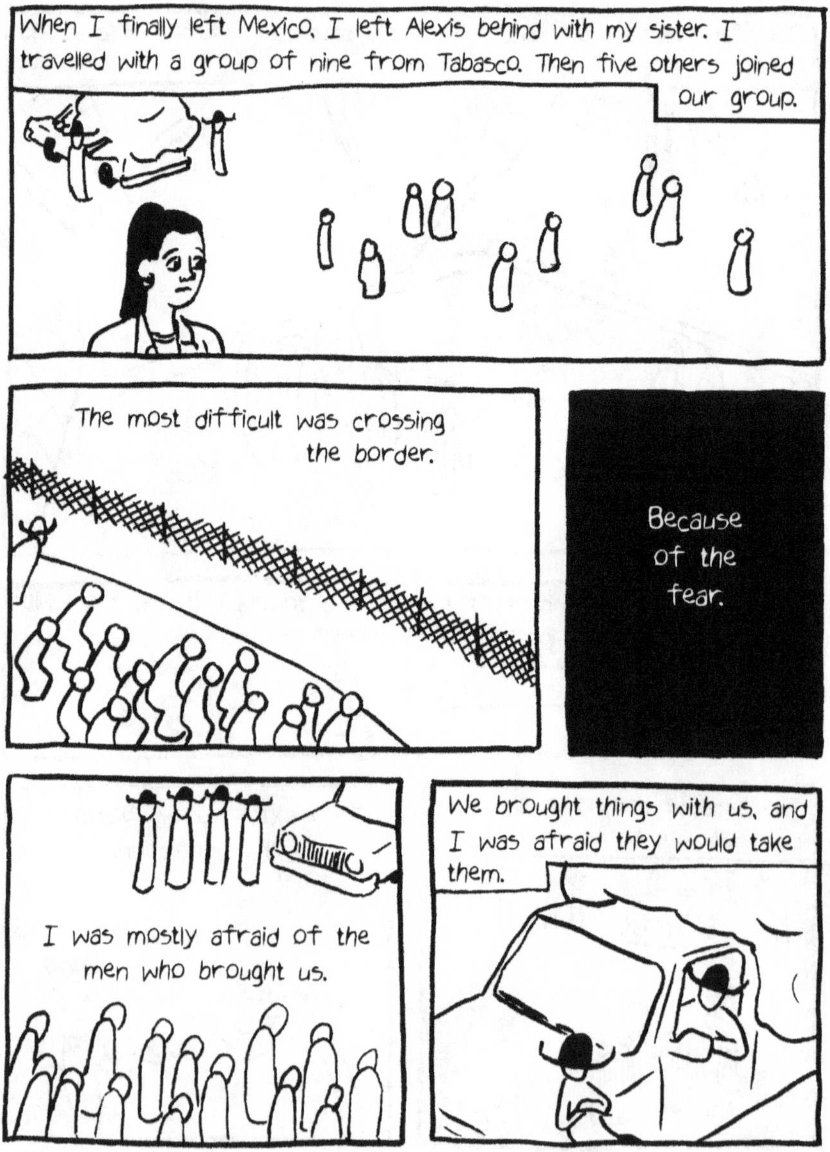
When I finally left Mexico, I left Alexis behind with my sister. I travelled with a group of nine from Tabasco. Then five others joined our group.
The most difficult was crossing the border.
Because of the fear.
I was mostly afraid of the men who brought us.
We brought things with us, and I was afraid they would take them.

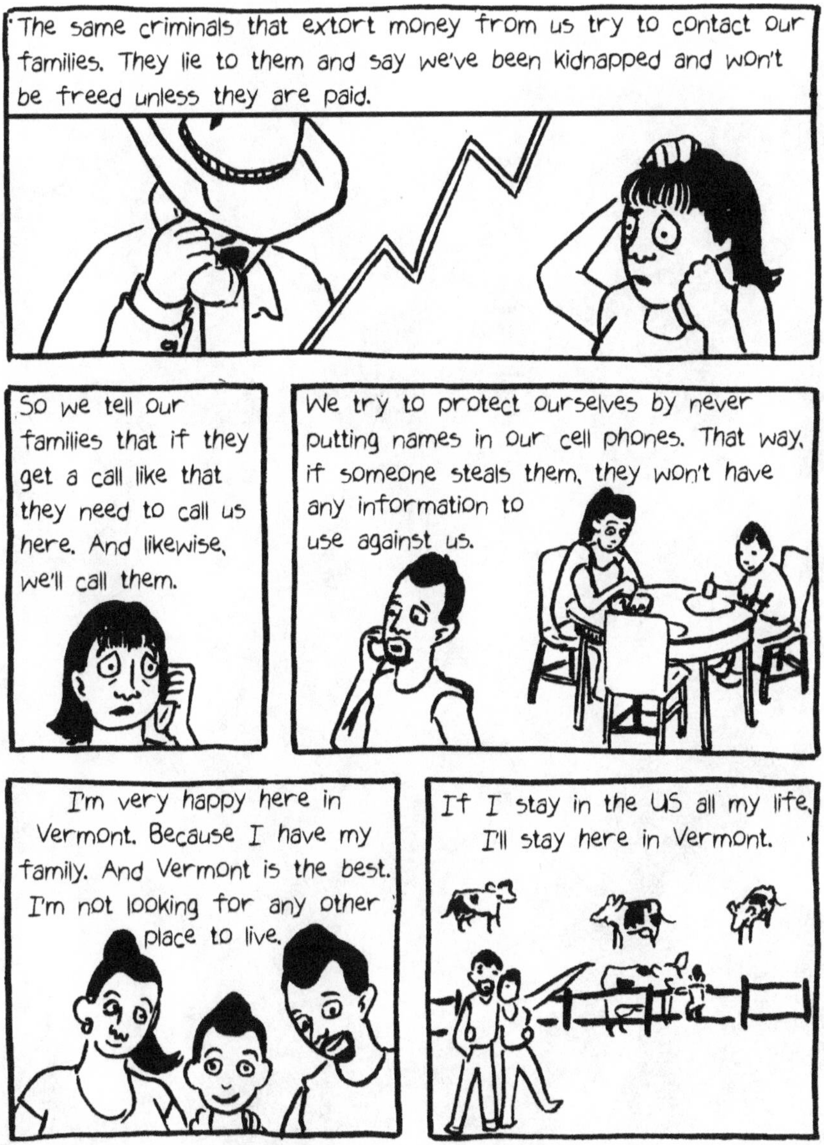
The same criminals that extort money from us try to contact our families. They lie to them and say we've been kidnapped and won't be freed unless they are paid.
So we tell our families that if they get a call like that they need to call us here. And likewise, we'll call them.
We try to protect ourselves by never putting names in our cell phones. That way, if someone steals them, they won't have any information to use against us.
I'm very happy here in Vermont. Because I have my family. And Vermont is the best. I'm not looking for any other place to live.
If I stay in the US all my life, I'll stay here in Vermont.

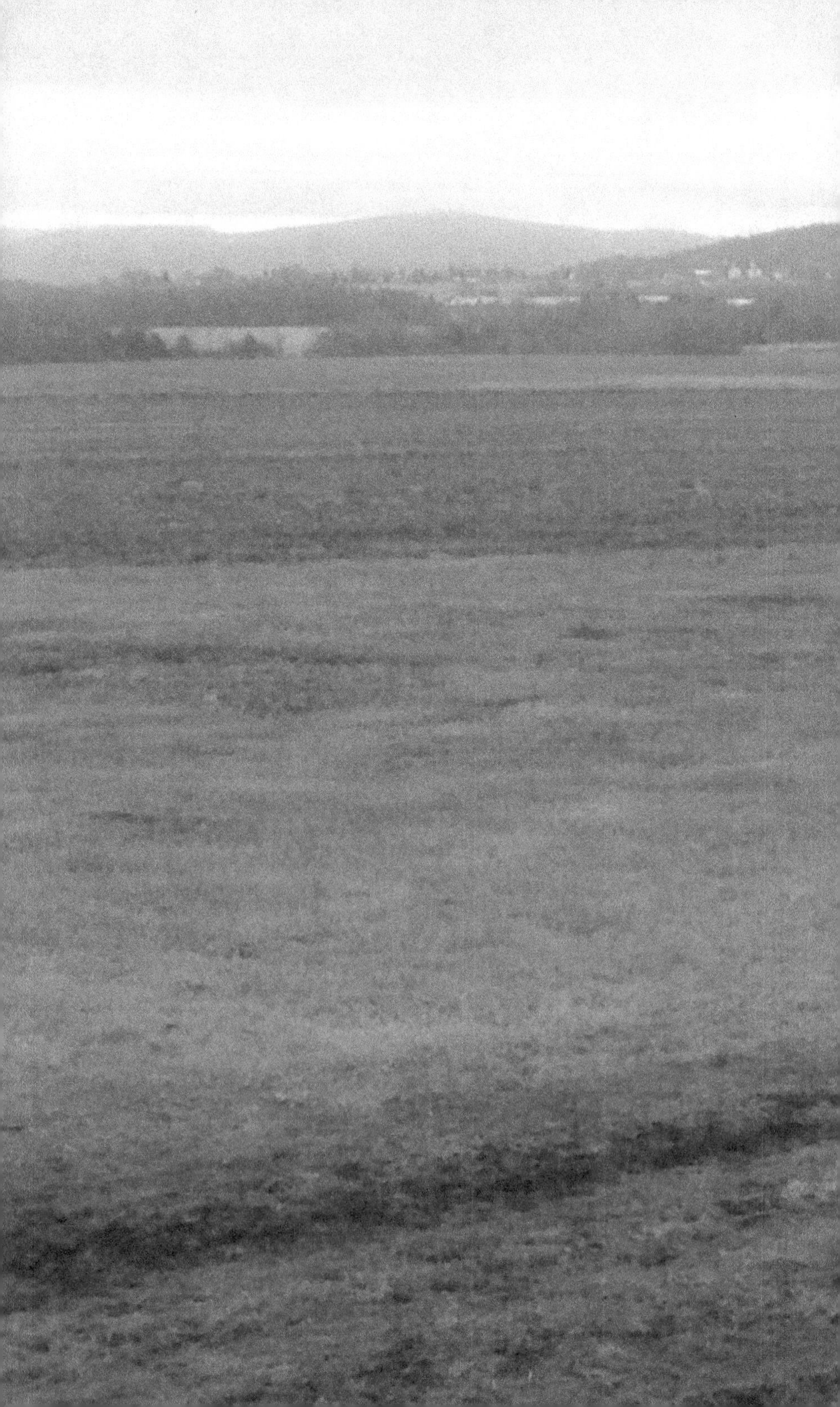

"EL VIAJE MAS CARO" / "THE MOST COSTLY JOURNEY" *presents:*

"ONE SUFFERS TO PROVIDE FOR THE FAMILY"

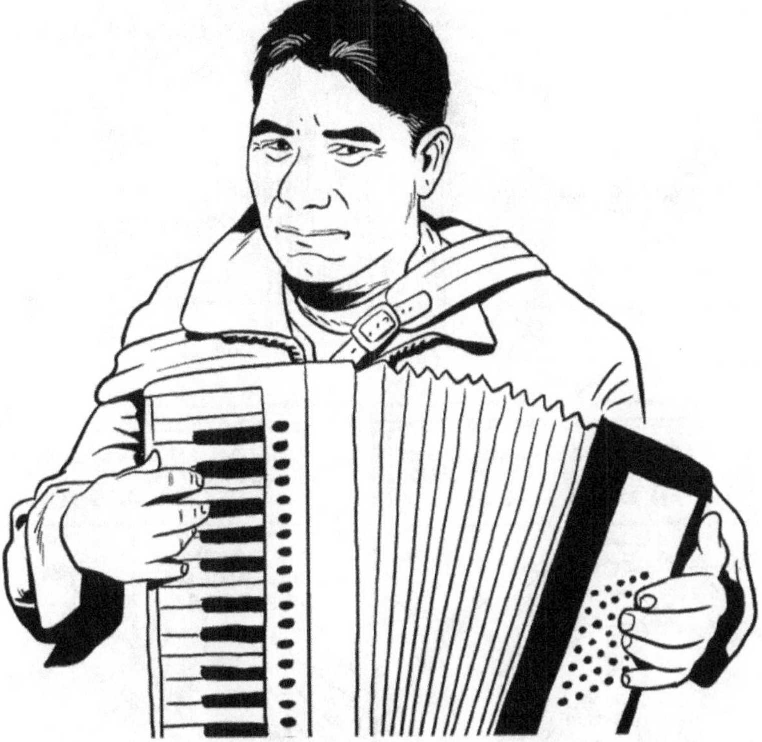

Pablo's Story

Comics by Rick Veitch

A Eureka Comics Production

PABLO'S STORY

I COME FROM *OAXACA*, A VILLAGE THAT IS CALLED *SAN FRANCISCO LOGUECHE MIAHUATLAN*.

WE WERE A BIG FAMILY, ALL SLEEPING IN ONE ROOM MADE WITH METAL SHEETS.

MY MOTHER COOKED OVER A WOOD FIRE.

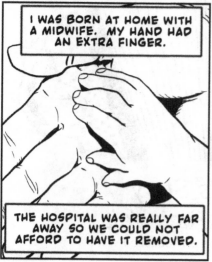

I WAS BORN AT HOME WITH A MIDWIFE. MY HAND HAD AN EXTRA FINGER.

THE HOSPITAL WAS REALLY FAR AWAY SO WE COULD NOT AFFORD TO HAVE IT REMOVED.

FROM AN EARLY AGE I WORKED IN THE FIELDS CUTTING *MAGUEY*.

IT'S THE MAIN INGREDIENT OF *MEZCAL*.

I HAD TO WORK TO FEED MY FIVE YOUNGER SIBLINGS.
MY FATHER HAD LEFT US AND LEFT DEBT BUT I EARNED SO LITTLE I COULDN'T PAY IT.
I WANTED TO STUDY COMPUTERS BUT MY SITUATION WOULDN'T ALLOW IT.
I QUIT SCHOOL AT FOURTEEN.
AT SEVENTEEN I ENTERED THE UNITED STATES.
IT WAS THE ONLY WAY TO PAY OFF THE DEBT.
I CROSSED THE BORDER IN ALTA SONORA.
WE WALKED THREE DAYS AND TWO NIGHTS.

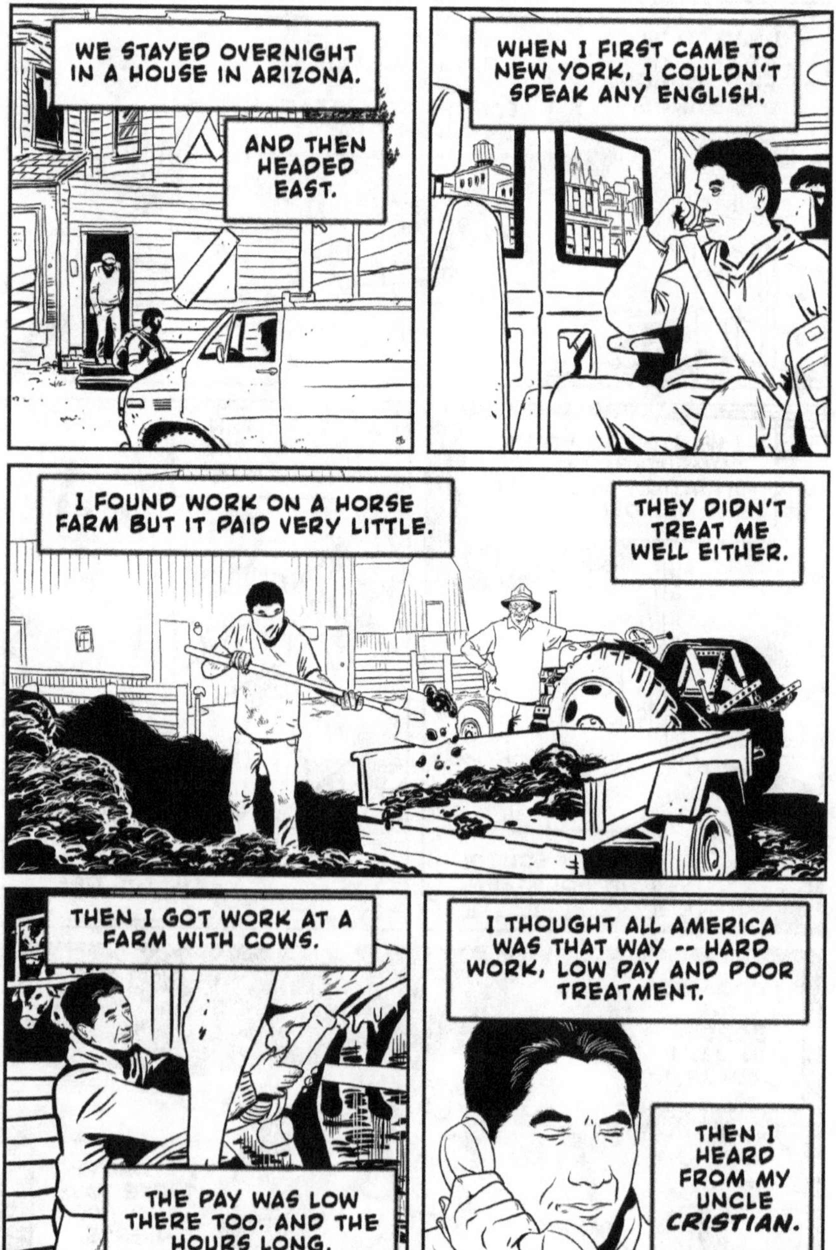
WE STAYED OVERNIGHT IN A HOUSE IN ARIZONA.
AND THEN HEADED EAST.
WHEN I FIRST CAME TO NEW YORK, I COULDN'T SPEAK ANY ENGLISH.
I FOUND WORK ON A HORSE FARM BUT IT PAID VERY LITTLE.
THEY DIDN'T TREAT ME WELL EITHER.
THEN I GOT WORK AT A FARM WITH COWS.
THE PAY WAS LOW THERE TOO. AND THE HOURS LONG.
I THOUGHT ALL AMERICA WAS THAT WAY -- HARD WORK, LOW PAY AND POOR TREATMENT.
THEN I HEARD FROM MY UNCLE *CRISTIAN*.

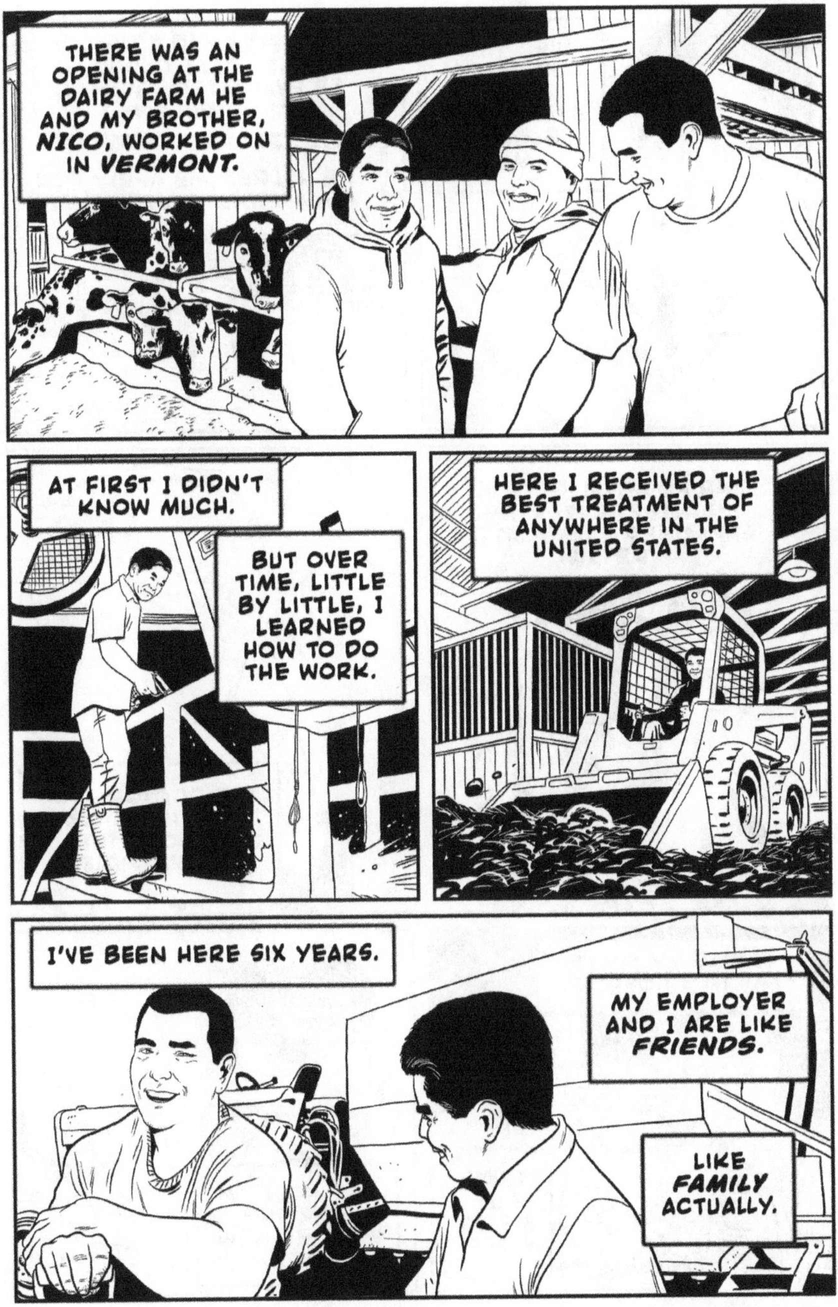
THERE WAS AN OPENING AT THE DAIRY FARM HE AND MY BROTHER, NICO, WORKED ON IN VERMONT.
AT FIRST I DIDN'T KNOW MUCH.
BUT OVER TIME, LITTLE BY LITTLE, I LEARNED HOW TO DO THE WORK.
HERE I RECEIVED THE BEST TREATMENT OF ANYWHERE IN THE UNITED STATES.
I'VE BEEN HERE SIX YEARS.
MY EMPLOYER AND I ARE LIKE FRIENDS.
LIKE FAMILY ACTUALLY.

OVER TIME, MY EXTRA FINGER STARTED TO BOTHER ME.

MY EMPLOYER TOOK ME TO THE LOCAL CLINIC TO BE EVALUATED. THEN TO THE *SPECIALIST.*

HE HELPED ME APPLY FOR *FINANCIAL ASSISTANCE.*

THE HOSPITAL GAVE ME AN INTERPRETER WHO EXPLAINED EVERY LITTLE DETAIL.

THE DOCTOR SAID THAT HE COULD REMOVE THE EXTRA DIGIT.

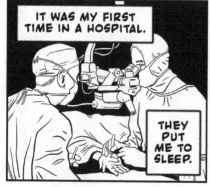

IT WAS MY FIRST TIME IN A HOSPITAL.

THEY PUT ME TO SLEEP.

AND NOW I'M STARTING WITH MY NEW HAND.

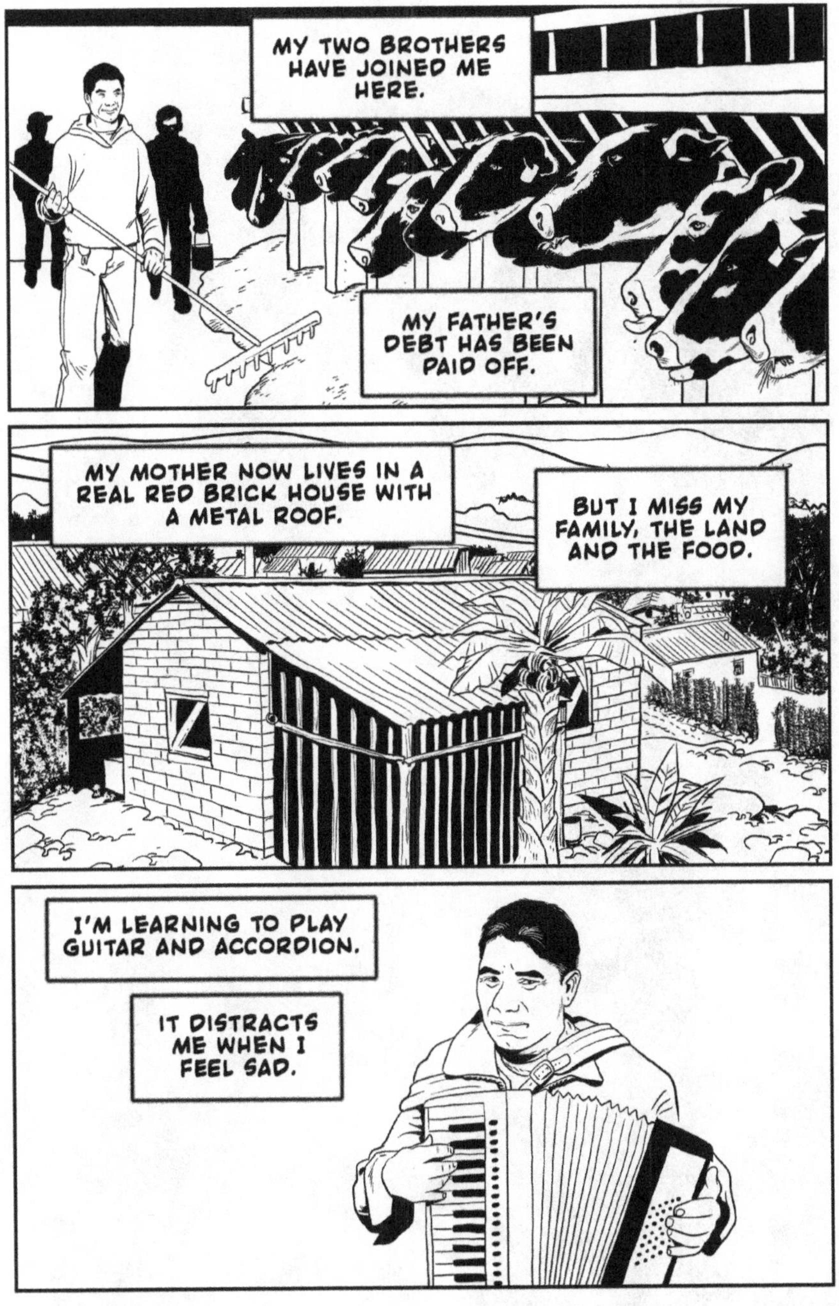
MY TWO BROTHERS HAVE JOINED ME HERE.
MY FATHER'S DEBT HAS BEEN PAID OFF.
MY MOTHER NOW LIVES IN A REAL RED BRICK HOUSE WITH A METAL ROOF.
BUT I MISS MY FAMILY, THE LAND AND THE FOOD.
I'M LEARNING TO PLAY GUITAR AND ACCORDION.
IT DISTRACTS ME WHEN I FEEL SAD.

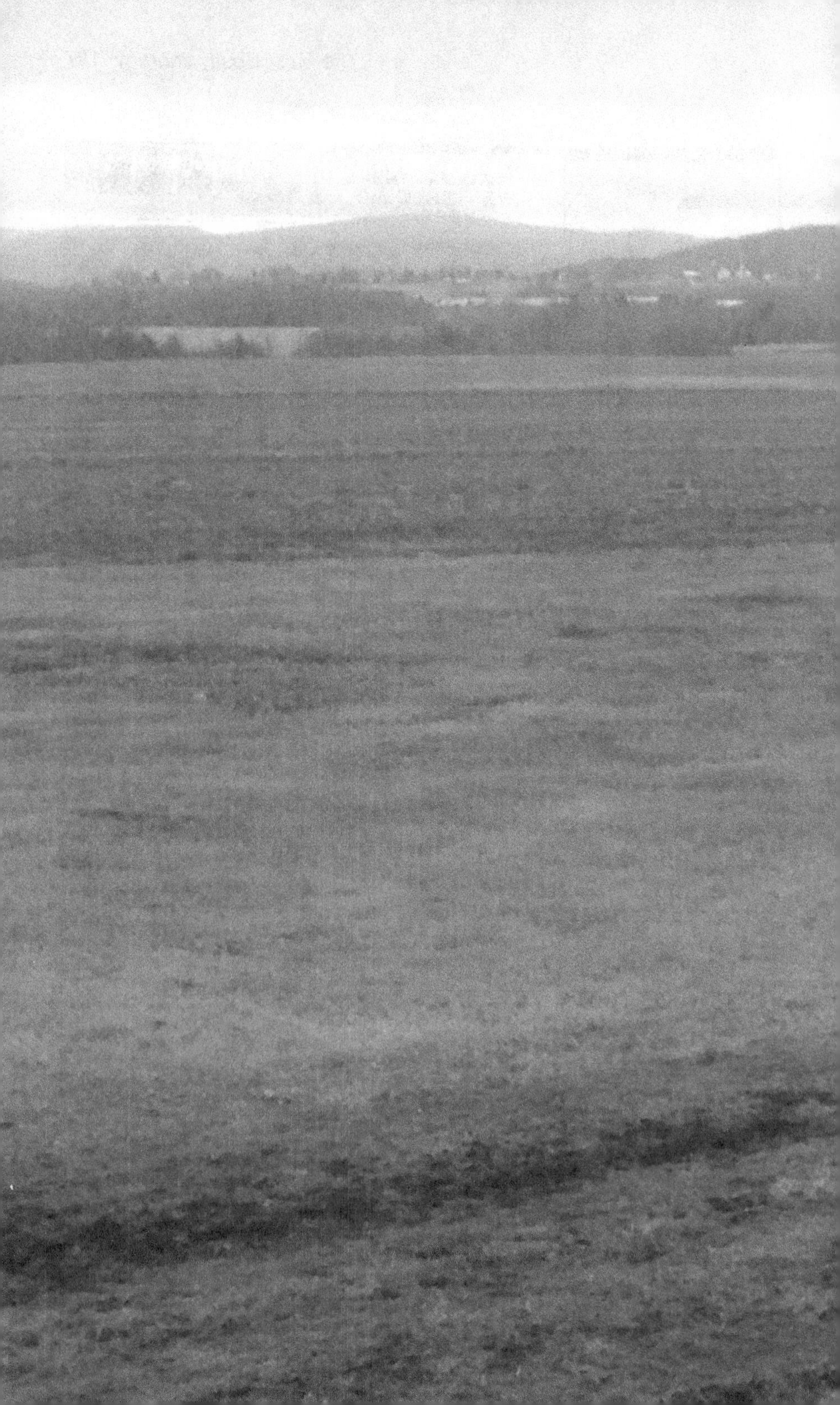

"EL VIAJE MAS CARO" / "THE MOST COSTLY JOURNEY" presents:

IT WASN'T OUR PLAN

The Story of Ana
Art by Glynnis Fawkes

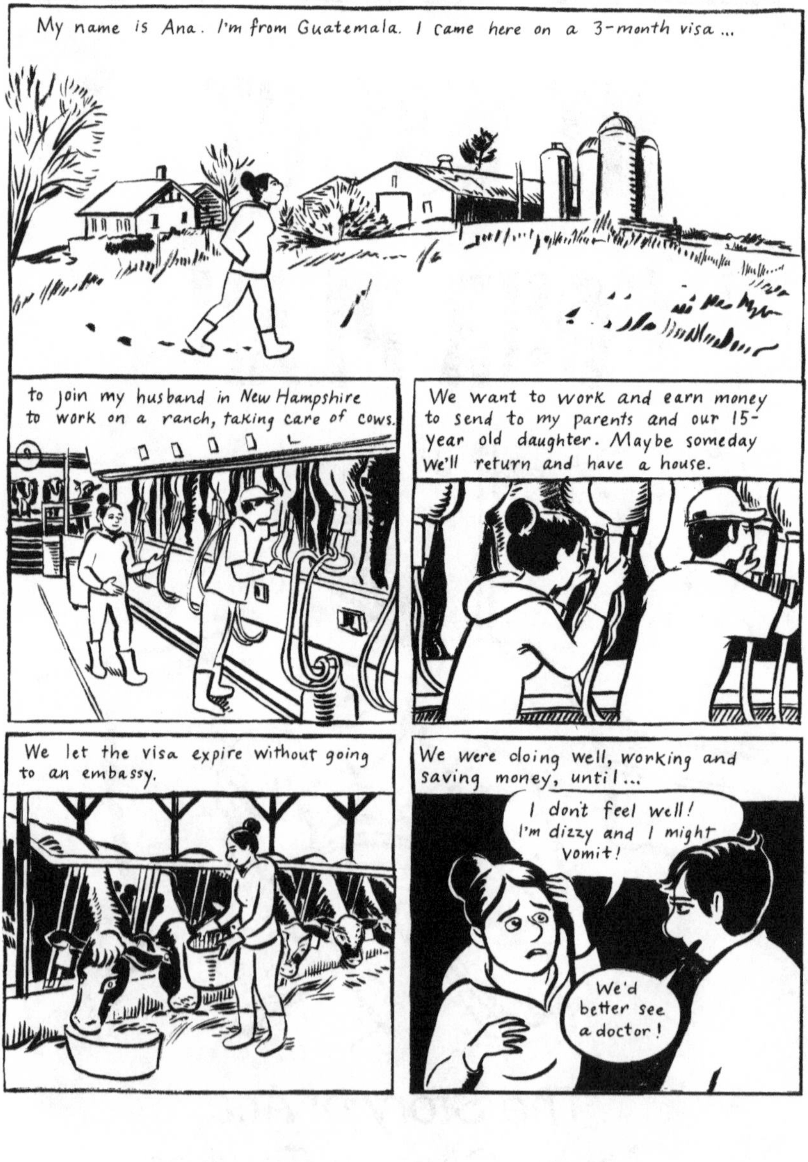
My name is Ana. I'm from Guatemala. I came here on a 3-month visa ...
to join my husband in New Hampshire to work on a ranch, taking care of cows.
We want to work and earn money to send to my parents and our 15-year old daughter. Maybe someday we'll return and have a house.
We let the visa expire without going to an embassy.
We were doing well, working and saving money, until...
I don't feel well! I'm dizzy and I might vomit!
We'd better see a doctor!

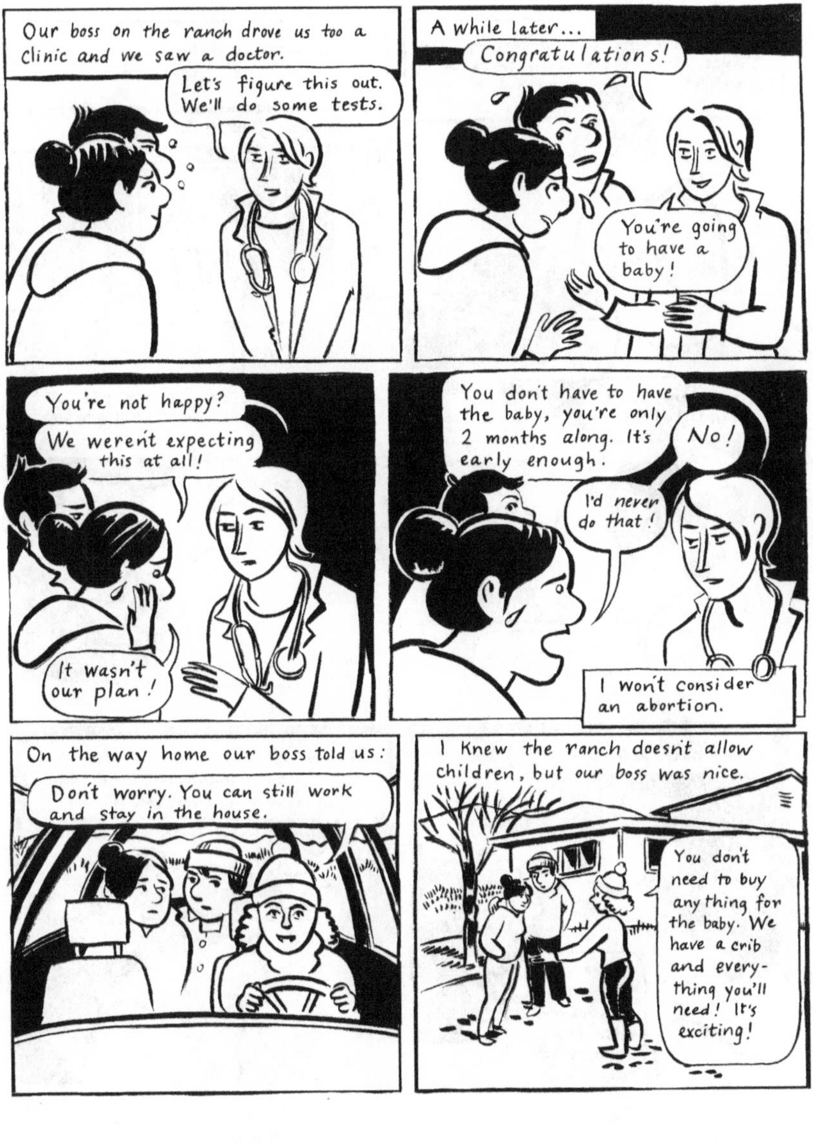
Our boss on the ranch drove us too a clinic and we saw a doctor.
Let's figure this out. We'll do some tests.
A while later...
Congratulations!
You're going to have a baby!
You're not happy?
We weren't expecting this at all!
It wasn't our plan!
You don't have to have the baby, you're only 2 months along. It's early enough.
No!
I'd never do that!
I won't consider an abortion.
On the way home our boss told us:
Don't worry. You can still work and stay in the house.
I knew the ranch doesn't allow children, but our boss was nice.
You don't need to buy anything for the baby. We have a crib and everything you'll need! It's exciting!

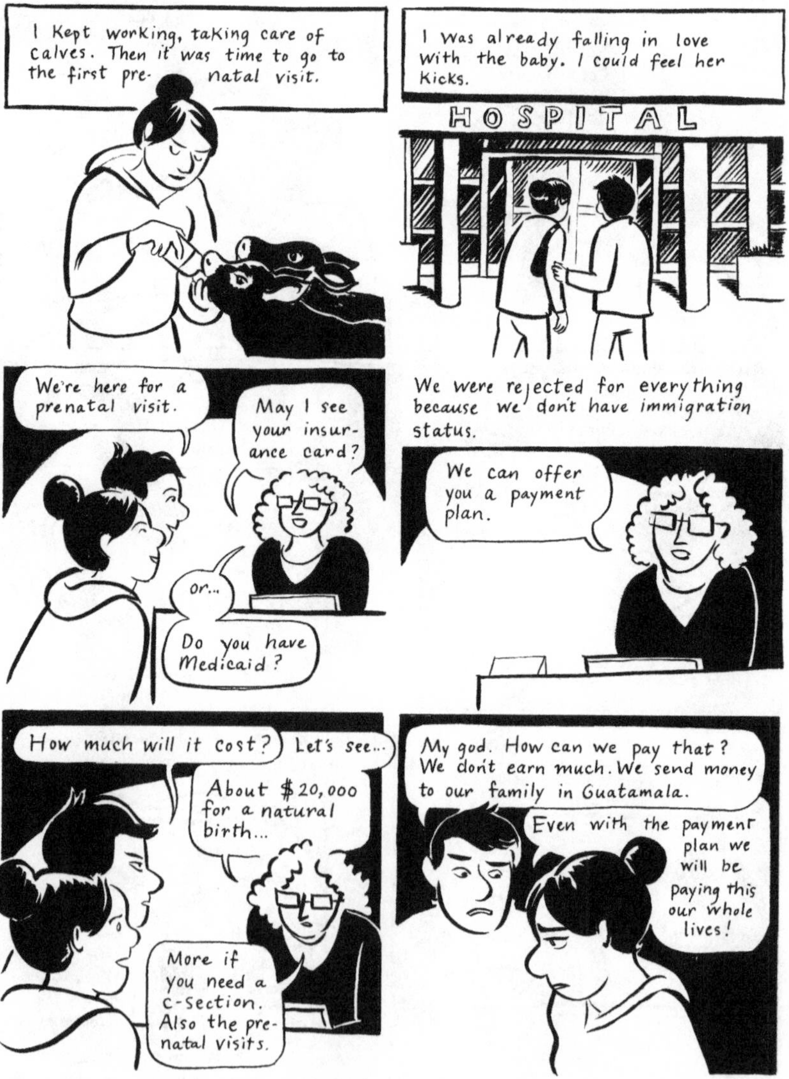
I Kept working, taking care of calves. Then it was time to go to the first pre-natal visit.
I was already falling in love with the baby. I could feel her Kicks.
HOSPITAL
We're here for a prenatal visit.
May I see your insurance card?
or...
Do you have Medicaid?
We were rejected for everything because we don't have immigration status.
We can offer you a payment plan.
How much will it cost?
Let's see...
About $20,000 for a natural birth...
More if you need a C-section. Also the prenatal visits.
My god. How can we pay that? We don't earn much. We send money to our family in Guatamala.
Even with the payment plan we will be paying this our whole lives!

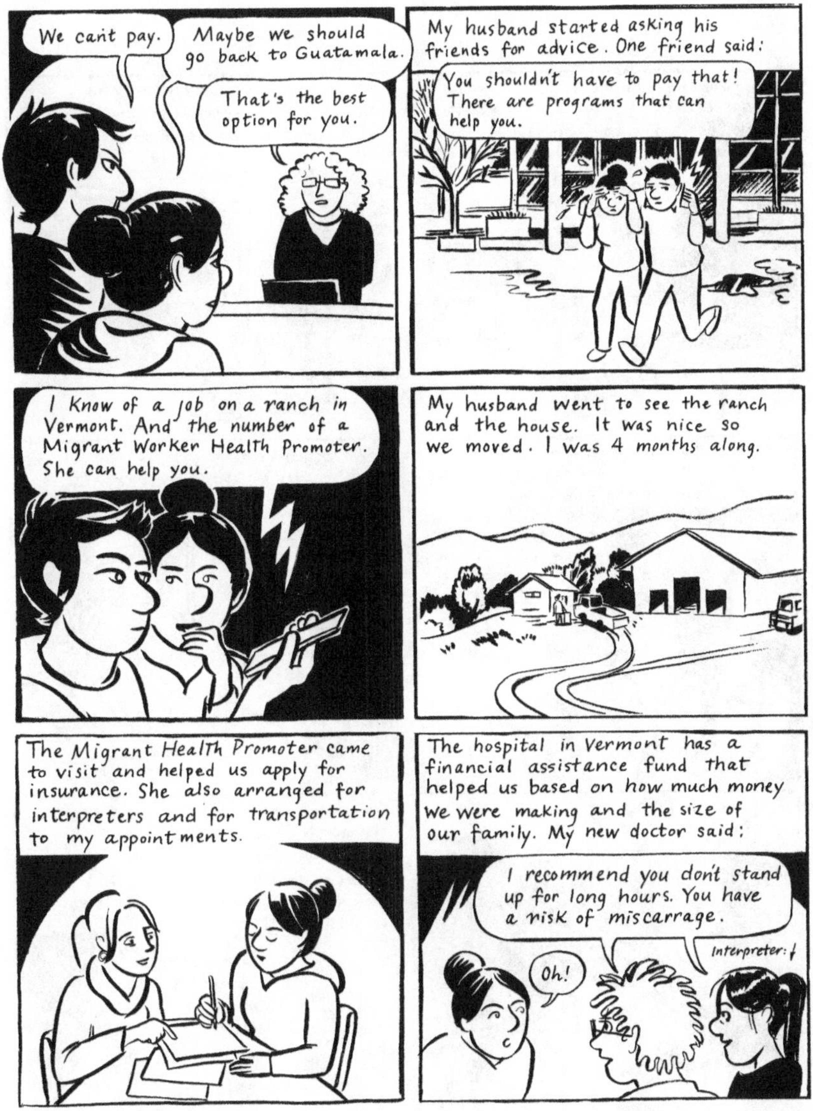
We can't pay.
Maybe we should go back to Guatamala.
That's the best option for you.
My husband started asking his friends for advice. One friend said:
You shouldn't have to pay that! There are programs that can help you.
I know of a job on a ranch in Vermont. And the number of a Migrant Worker Health Promoter. She can help you.
My husband went to see the ranch and the house. It was nice so we moved. I was 4 months along.
The Migrant Health Promoter came to visit and helped us apply for insurance. She also arranged for interpreters and for transportation to my appointments.
The hospital in Vermont has a financial assistance fund that helped us based on how much money we were making and the size of our family. My new doctor said:
I recommend you don't stand up for long hours. You have a risk of miscarrage.
Interpreter:
Oh!

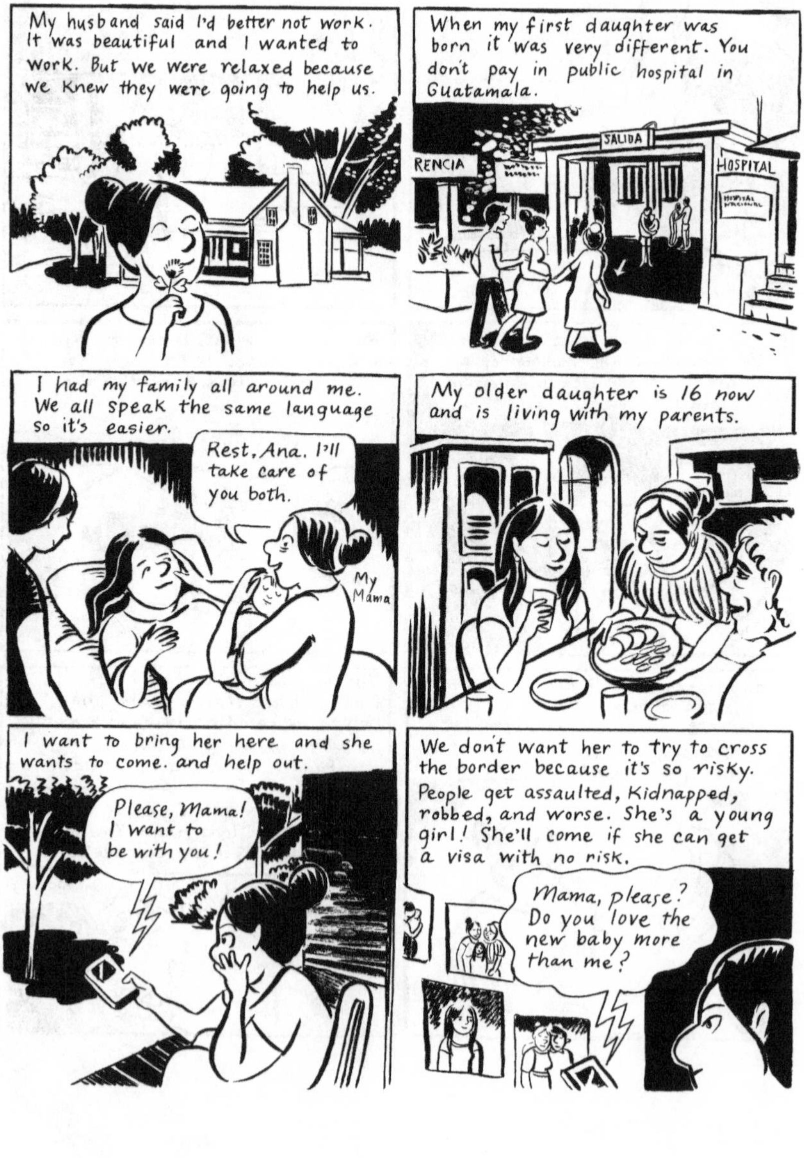
My husband said I'd better not work. It was beautiful and I wanted to work. But we were relaxed because we knew they were going to help us.
When my first daughter was born it was very different. You don't pay in public hospital in Guatamala.
SALIDA
RENCIA
HOSPITAL
I had my family all around me. We all speak the same language so it's easier.
Rest, Ana. I'll take care of you both.
My Mama
My older daughter is 16 now and is living with my parents.
I want to bring her here and she wants to come. and help out.
Please, Mama! I want to be with you!
We don't want her to try to cross the border because it's so risky. People get assaulted, kidnapped, robbed, and worse. She's a young girl! She'll come if she can get a visa with no risk.
Mama, please? Do you love the new baby more than me?

My baby was born in December.

She had Medicaid because she was born here. We take her to her appointments every 2 months and receive financial assistance and an interpreter and transportation!

She's growing well!

We also have help from WIC – They gave her formula and food; food for me too while I'm breastfeeding that I can buy at the store through a debit card that they gave us.

The pediatrician came to our house and gave me a book in Spanish about the baby's food.

You'll want to feed yourself soon!

They also organized a group of Hispanic women so we wouldn't feel too isolated. We meet about once a month. We talk about our stories.

Some are sadder than mine, some better. We offer advice and help and friendship. We need friendship always.

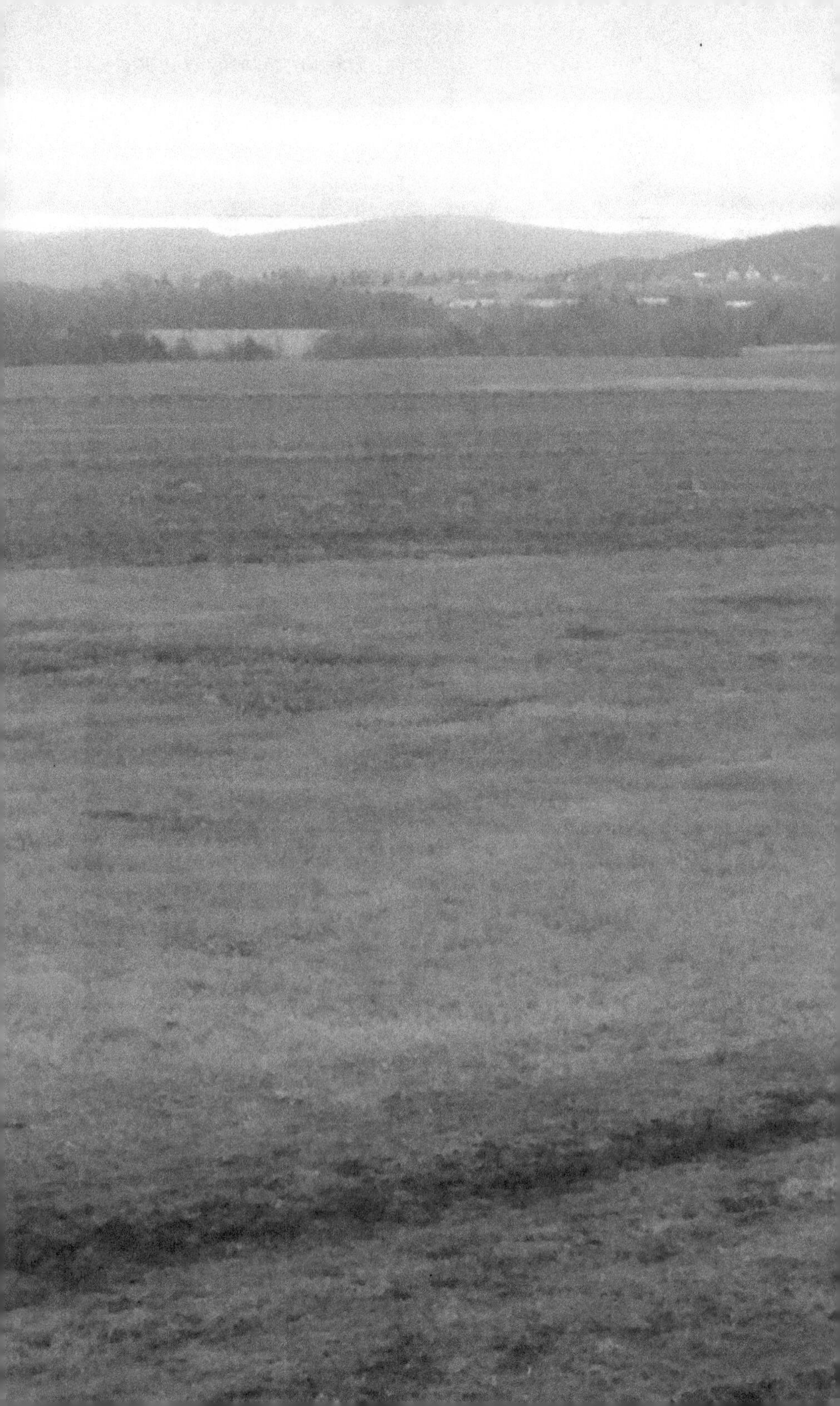

"EL VIAJE MAS CARO" / "THE MOST COSTLY JOURNEY" presents:

NOW THAT I HAVE MY LICENSE

Reflections on Driving
Art by Marek Bennett

PIERO

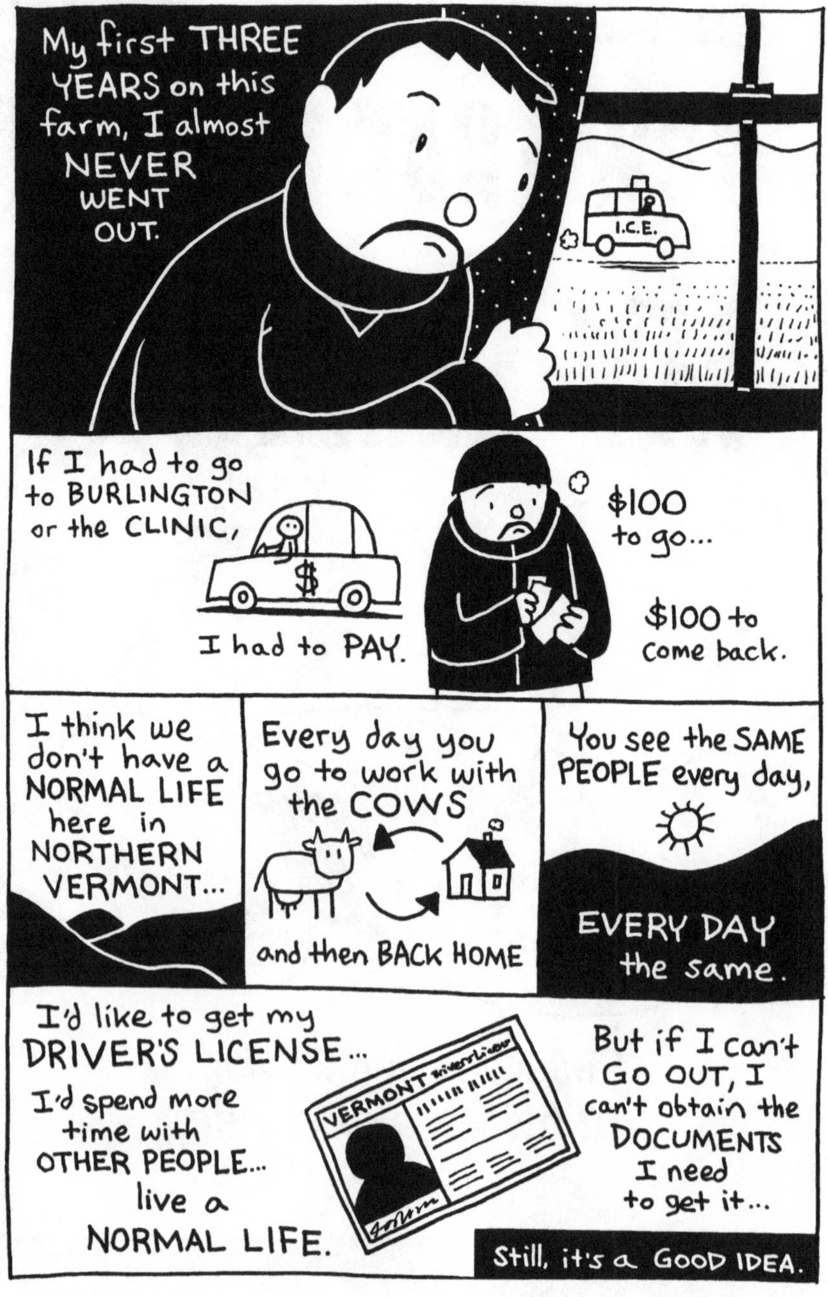
My first THREE YEARS on this farm, I almost NEVER WENT OUT.
I.C.E.
If I had to go to BURLINGTON or the CLINIC,
$
I had to PAY.
$100 to go...
$100 to come back.
I think we don't have a NORMAL LIFE here in NORTHERN VERMONT...
Every day you go to work with the COWS
and then BACK HOME
You see the SAME PEOPLE every day,
EVERY DAY the same.
I'd like to get my DRIVER'S LICENSE...
I'd spend more time with OTHER PEOPLE... live a NORMAL LIFE.
VERMONT
But if I can't GO OUT, I can't obtain the DOCUMENTS I need to get it...
Still, it's a GOOD IDEA.

SAUL + OLIVIA

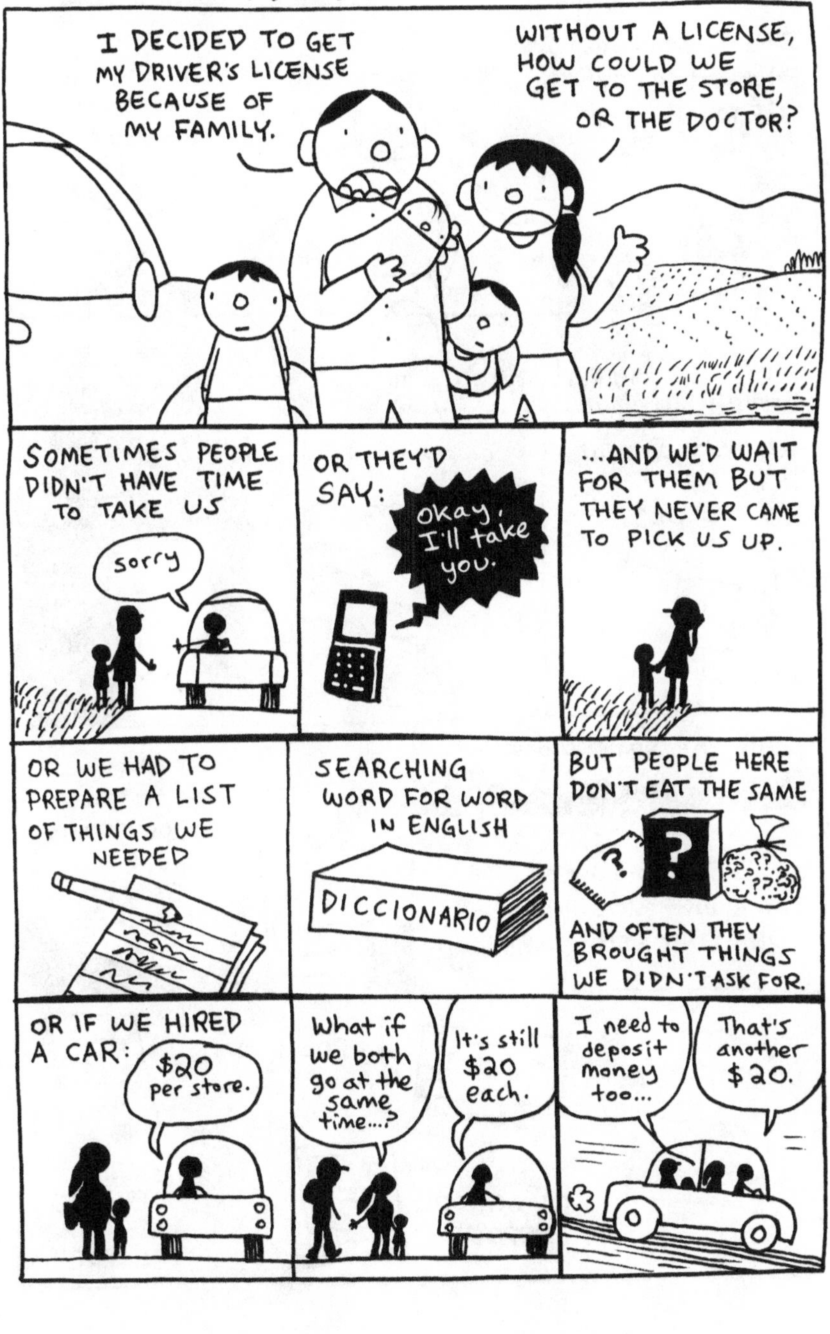
I DECIDED TO GET MY DRIVER'S LICENSE BECAUSE OF MY FAMILY.
WITHOUT A LICENSE, HOW COULD WE GET TO THE STORE, OR THE DOCTOR?
SOMETIMES PEOPLE DIDN'T HAVE TIME TO TAKE US
sorry
OR THEY'D SAY:
okay, I'll take you.
...AND WE'D WAIT FOR THEM BUT THEY NEVER CAME TO PICK US UP.
OR WE HAD TO PREPARE A LIST OF THINGS WE NEEDED
SEARCHING WORD FOR WORD IN ENGLISH
DICCIONARIO
BUT PEOPLE HERE DON'T EAT THE SAME
AND OFTEN THEY BROUGHT THINGS WE DIDN'T ASK FOR.
OR IF WE HIRED A CAR:
$20 per store.
What if we both go at the same time...?
It's still $20 each.
I need to deposit money too...
That's another $20.

PACO

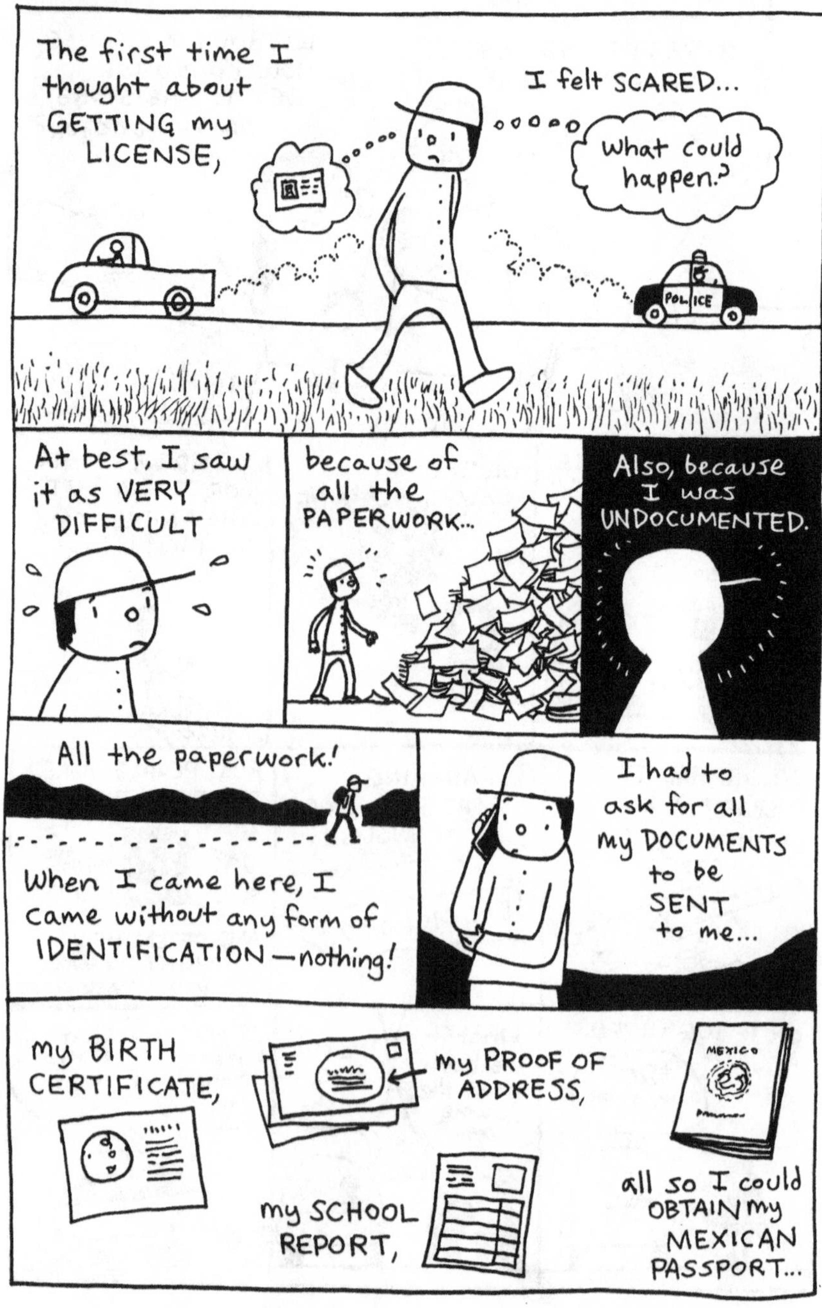
The first time I thought about GETTING my LICENSE,
I felt SCARED...
What could happen?
POLICE
At best, I saw it as VERY DIFFICULT
because of all the PAPERWORK...
Also, because I was UNDOCUMENTED.
All the paperwork!
When I came here, I came without any form of IDENTIFICATION—nothing!
I had to ask for all my DOCUMENTS to be SENT to me...
my BIRTH CERTIFICATE,
my PROOF OF ADDRESS,
MEXICO
my SCHOOL REPORT,
all so I could OBTAIN my MEXICAN PASSPORT...

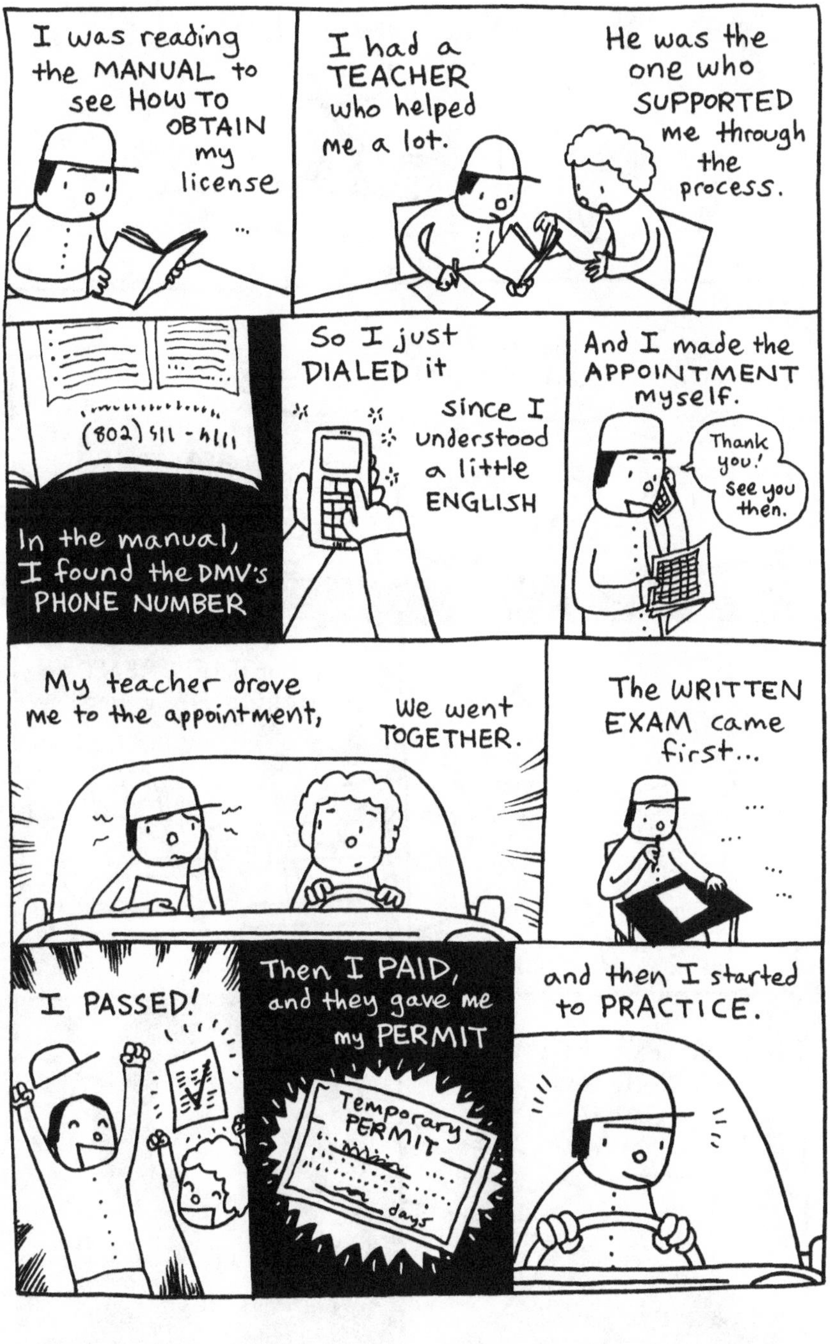
I was reading the MANUAL to see HOW TO OBTAIN my license
...
I had a TEACHER who helped me a lot.
He was the one who SUPPORTED me through the process.
(802) 511 - 4111
In the manual, I found the DMV's PHONE NUMBER
So I just DIALED it
since I understood a little ENGLISH
And I made the APPOINTMENT myself.
Thank you! See you then.
My teacher drove me to the appointment,
We went TOGETHER.
The WRITTEN EXAM came first...
I PASSED!
Then I PAID, and they gave me my PERMIT
Temporary PERMIT
days
and then I started to PRACTICE.

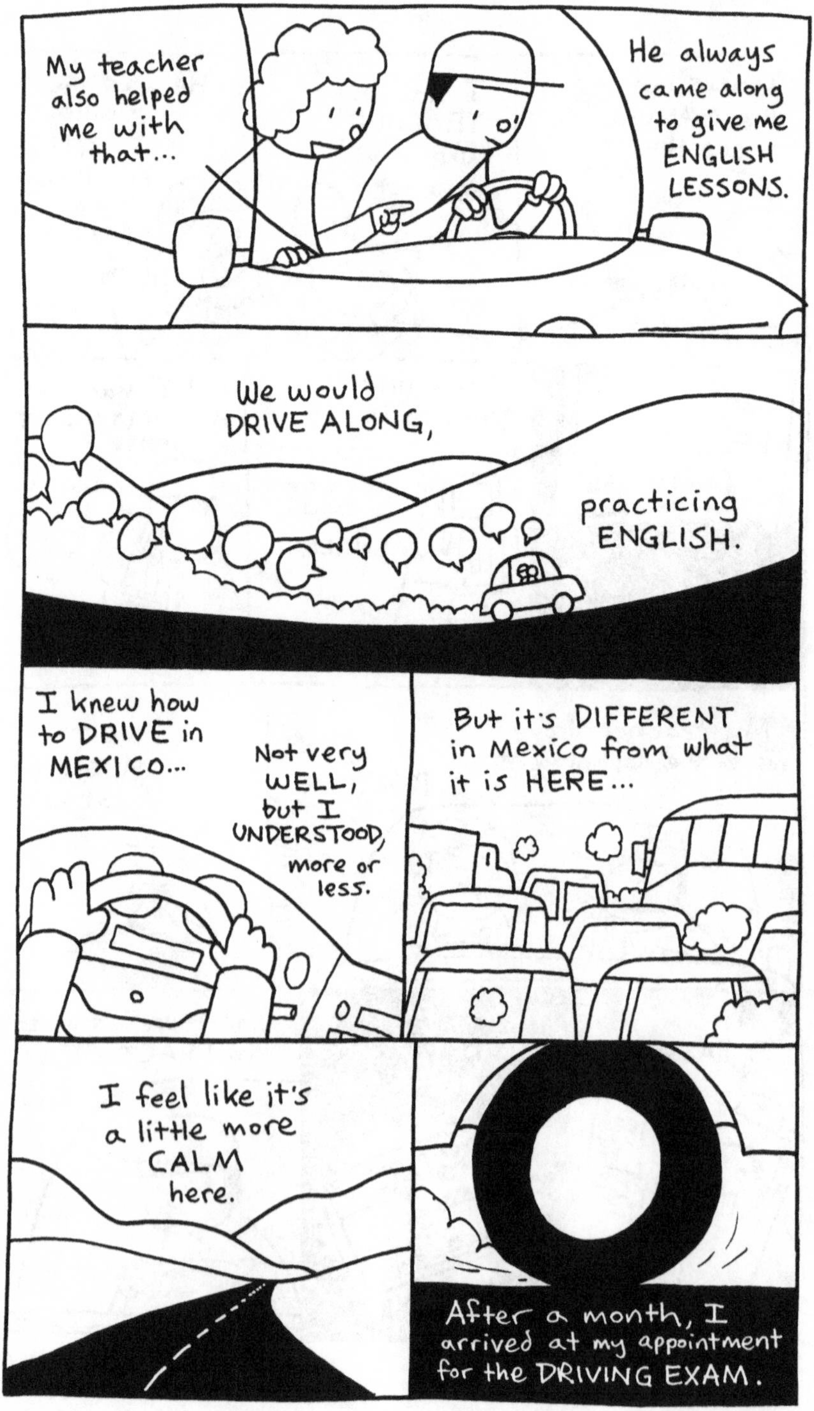
My teacher also helped me with that...
He always came along to give me ENGLISH LESSONS.
We would DRIVE ALONG,
practicing ENGLISH.
I knew how to DRIVE in MEXICO...
Not very WELL, but I UNDERSTOOD, more or less.
But it's DIFFERENT in Mexico from what it is HERE...
I feel like it's a little more CALM here.
After a month, I arrived at my appointment for the DRIVING EXAM.

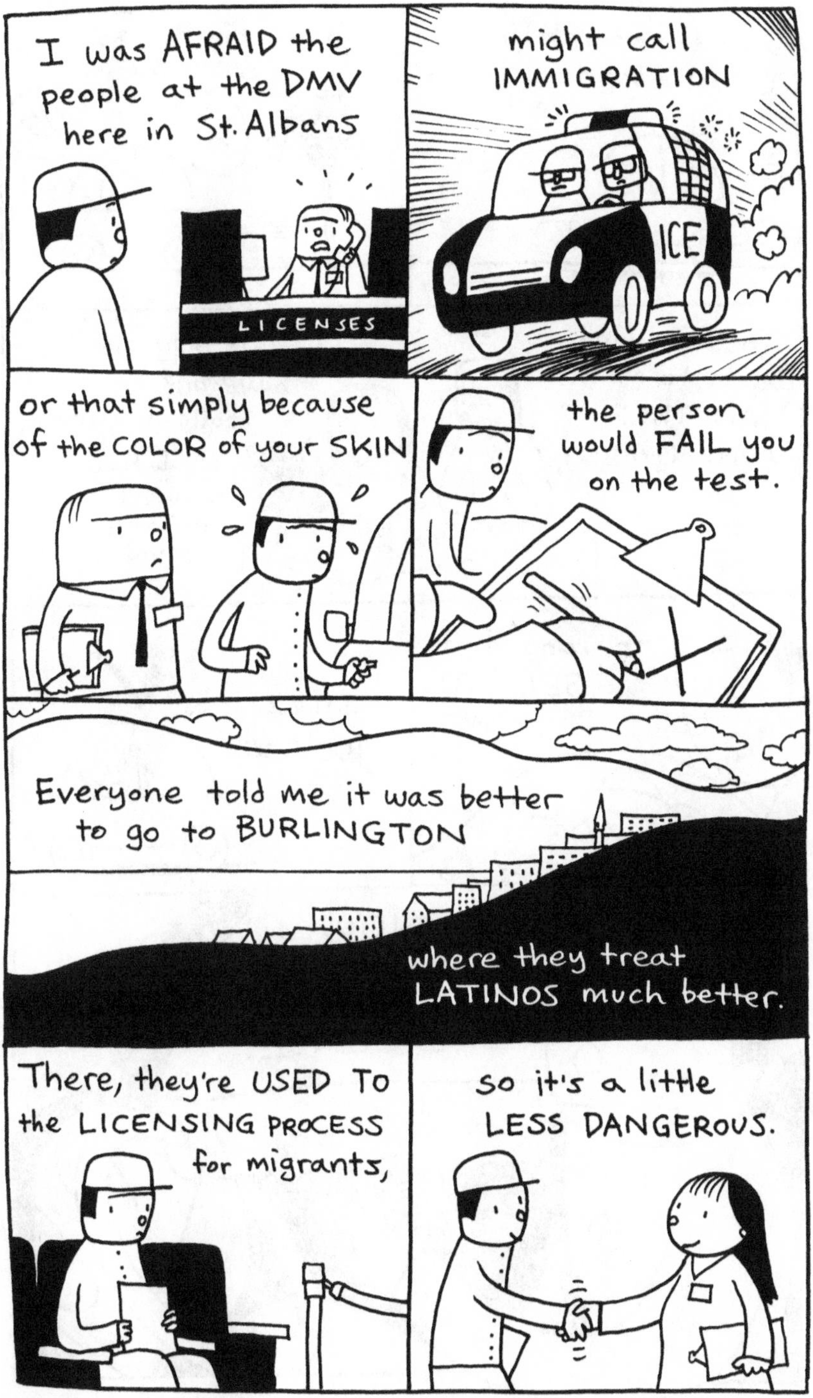
I was AFRAID the people at the DMV here in St. Albans
LICENSES
might call IMMIGRATION
ICE
or that simply because of the COLOR of your SKIN
the person would FAIL you on the test.
Everyone told me it was better to go to BURLINGTON
where they treat LATINOS much better.
There, they're USED TO the LICENSING PROCESS for migrants,
so it's a little LESS DANGEROUS.

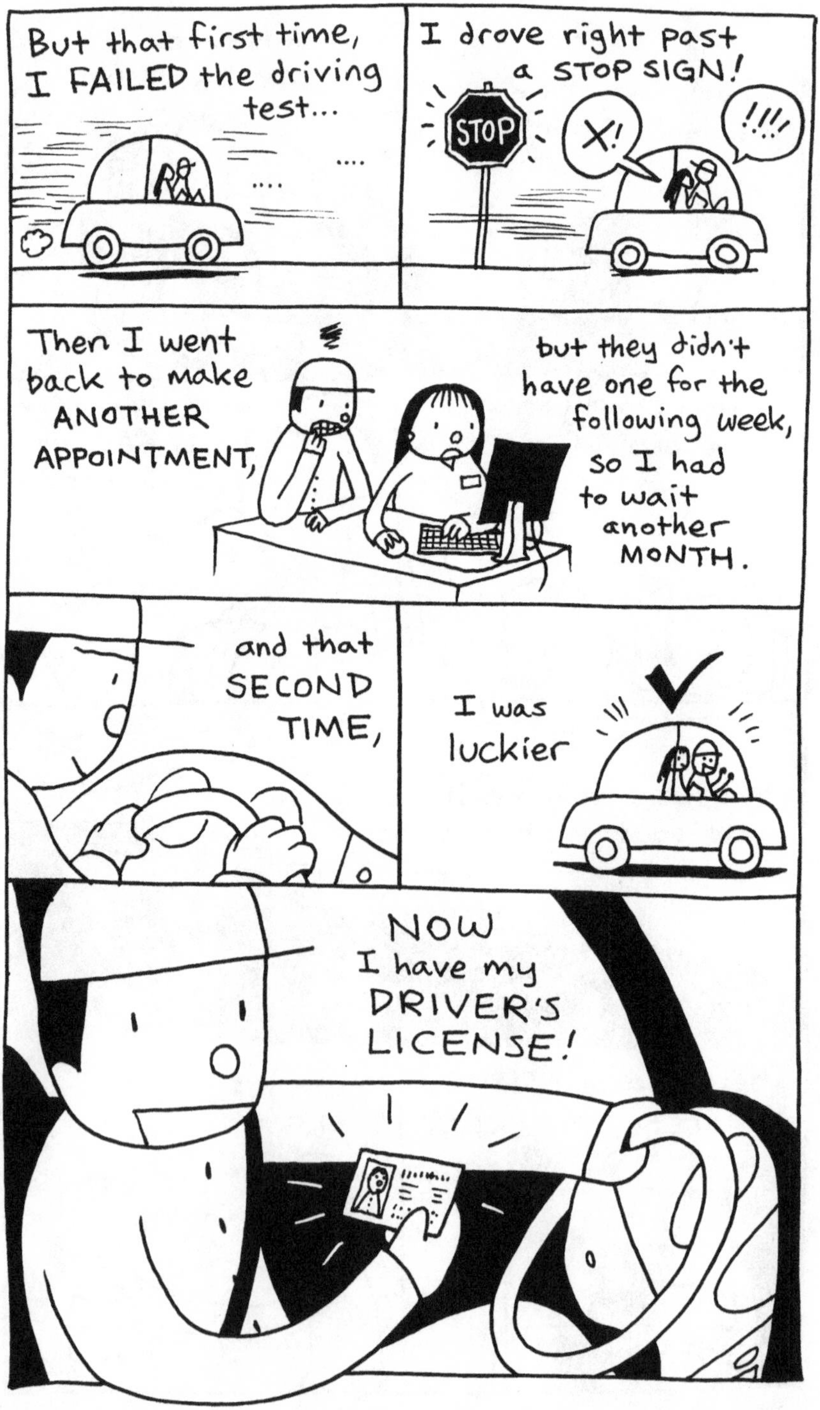

But that first time, I FAILED the driving test...
....
....
I drove right past a STOP SIGN!
STOP
X!
!!!!
Then I went back to make ANOTHER APPOINTMENT,
but they didn't have one for the following week,
so I had to wait another MONTH.
and that SECOND TIME,
I was luckier
NOW I have my DRIVER'S LICENSE!

OLIVIA

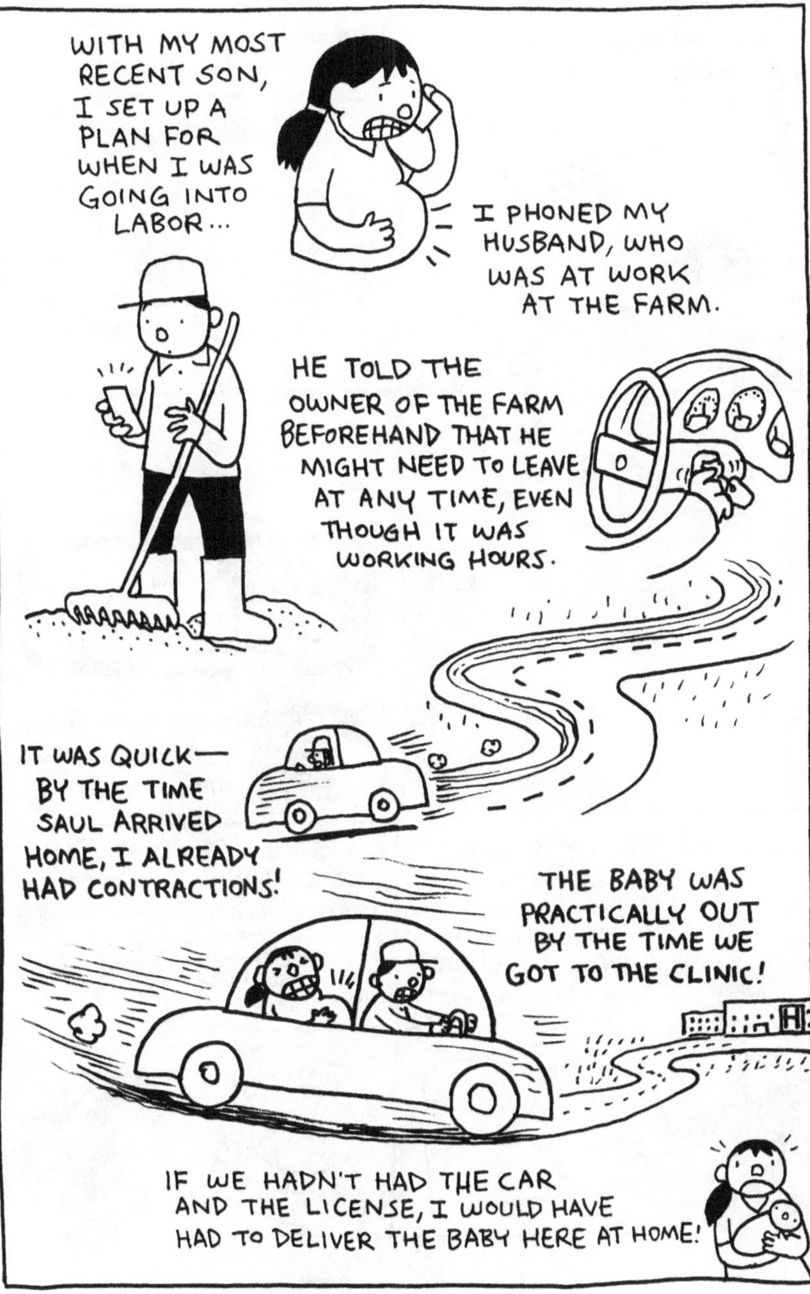
WITH MY MOST RECENT SON, I SET UP A PLAN FOR WHEN I WAS GOING INTO LABOR...
I PHONED MY HUSBAND, WHO WAS AT WORK AT THE FARM.
HE TOLD THE OWNER OF THE FARM BEFOREHAND THAT HE MIGHT NEED TO LEAVE AT ANY TIME, EVEN THOUGH IT WAS WORKING HOURS.
IT WAS QUICK— BY THE TIME SAUL ARRIVED HOME, I ALREADY HAD CONTRACTIONS!
THE BABY WAS PRACTICALLY OUT BY THE TIME WE GOT TO THE CLINIC!
IF WE HADN'T HAD THE CAR AND THE LICENSE, I WOULD HAVE HAD TO DELIVER THE BABY HERE AT HOME!

SAUL

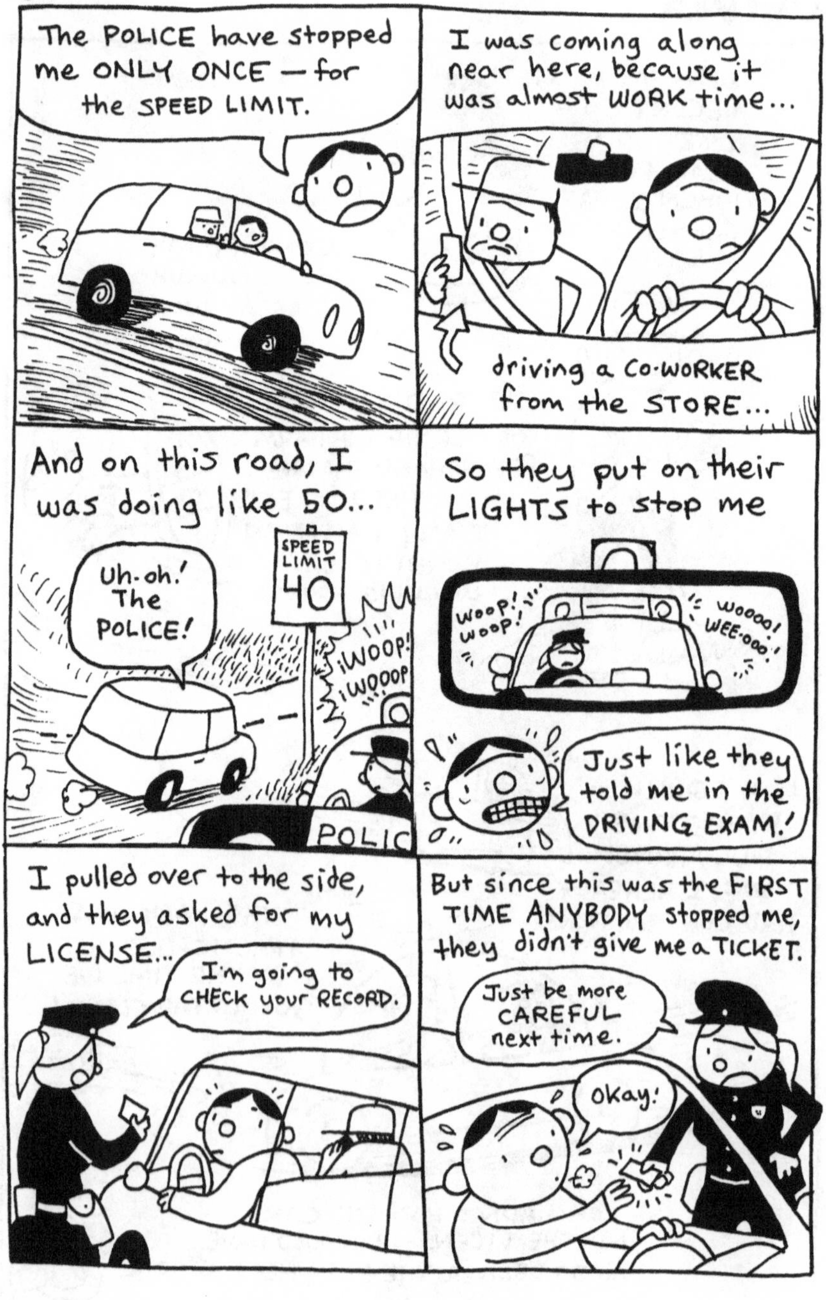
The POLICE have stopped me ONLY ONCE — for the SPEED LIMIT.
I was coming along near here, because it was almost WORK time...
driving a CO-WORKER from the STORE...
And on this road, I was doing like 50...
Uh-oh! The POLICE!
SPEED LIMIT 40
¡WOOP! ¡WOOOP
POLIC
So they put on their LIGHTS to stop me
WOOP! WOOP!
WOOOO! WEE-OOO!
Just like they told me in the DRIVING EXAM!
I pulled over to the side, and they asked for my LICENSE...
I'm going to CHECK your RECORD.
But since this was the FIRST TIME ANYBODY stopped me, they didn't give me a TICKET.
Just be more CAREFUL next time.
Okay!

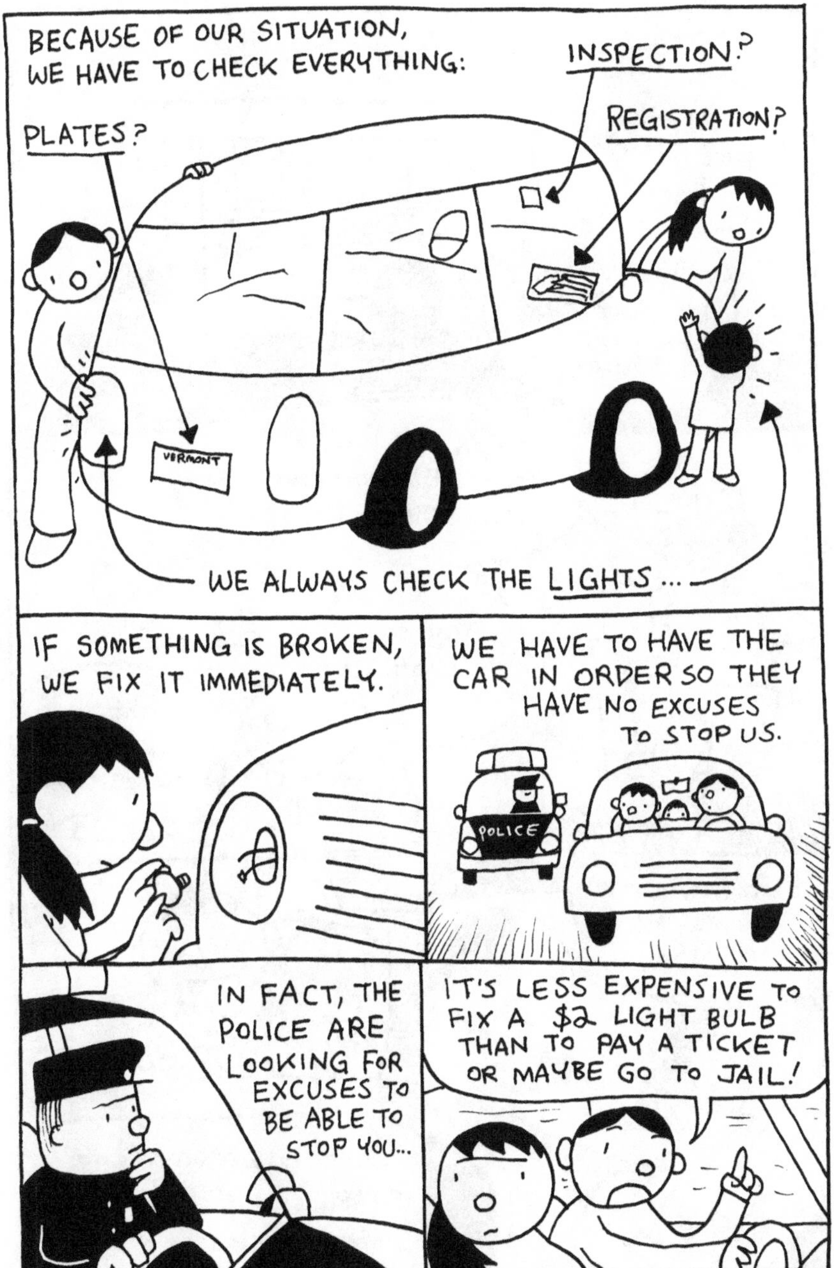
BECAUSE OF OUR SITUATION, WE HAVE TO CHECK EVERYTHING:
INSPECTION?
PLATES?
REGISTRATION?
VERMONT
WE ALWAYS CHECK THE LIGHTS...
IF SOMETHING IS BROKEN, WE FIX IT IMMEDIATELY.
WE HAVE TO HAVE THE CAR IN ORDER SO THEY HAVE NO EXCUSES TO STOP US.
POLICE
IN FACT, THE POLICE ARE LOOKING FOR EXCUSES TO BE ABLE TO STOP YOU...
IT'S LESS EXPENSIVE TO FIX A $2 LIGHT BULB THAN TO PAY A TICKET OR MAYBE GO TO JAIL!

OLIVIA

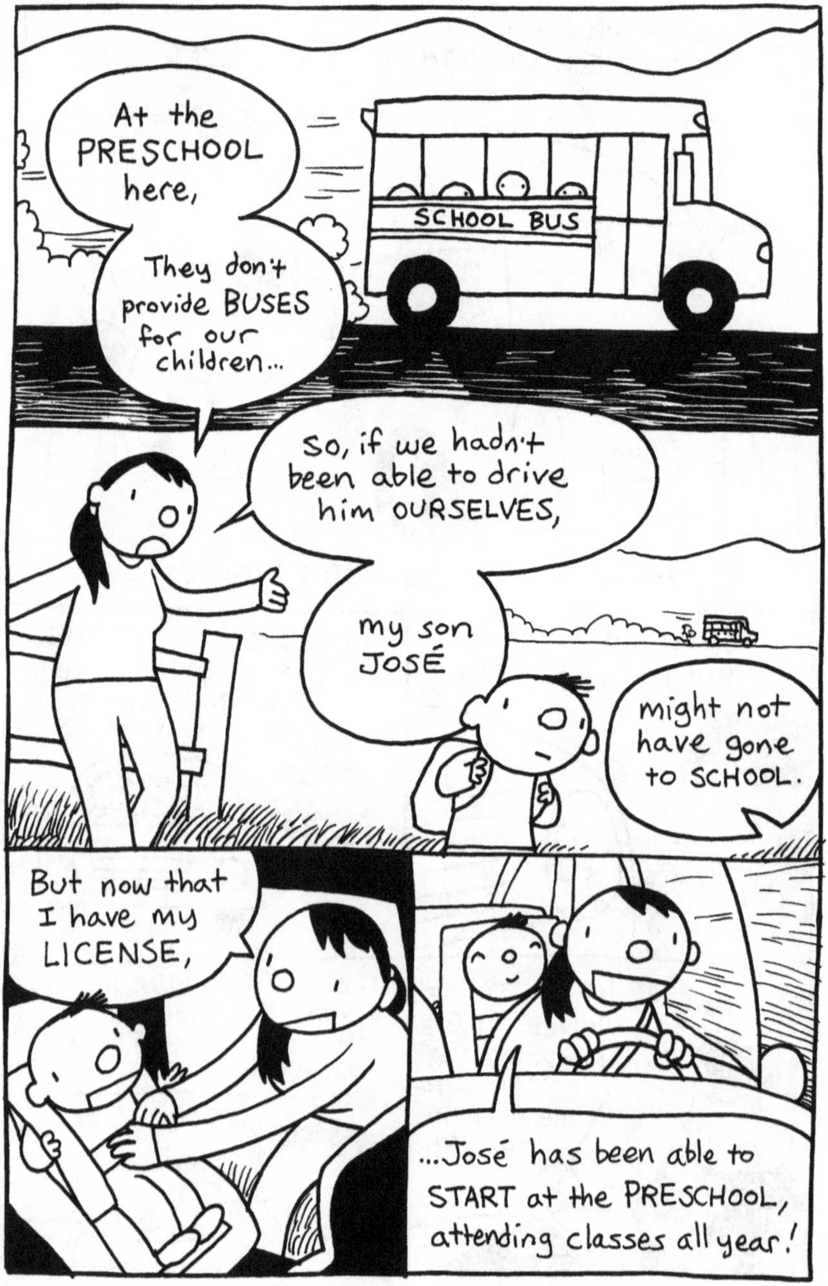
At the PRESCHOOL here,
They don't provide BUSES for our children...
SCHOOL BUS
So, if we hadn't been able to drive him OURSELVES,
my son JOSÉ
might not have gone to SCHOOL.
But now that I have my LICENSE,
...José has been able to START at the PRESCHOOL, attending classes all year!

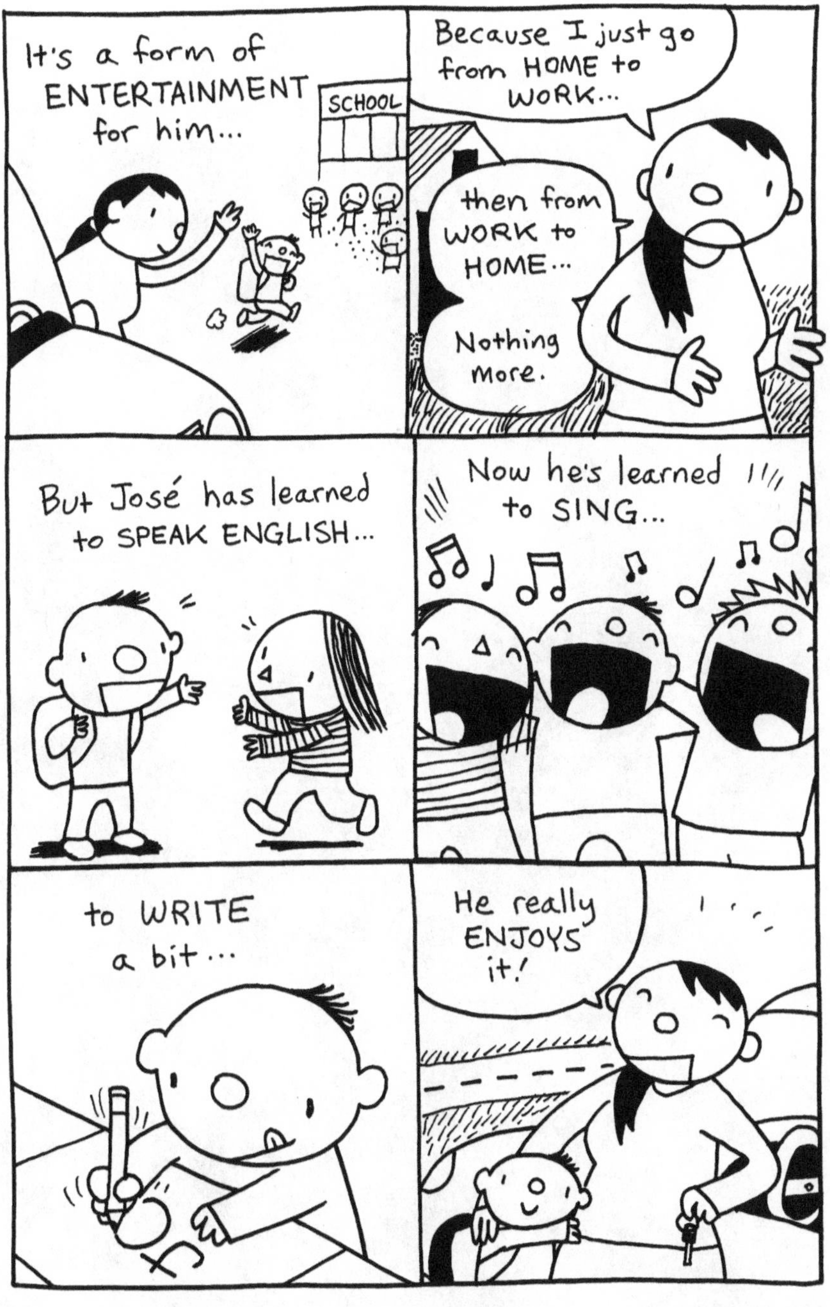
It's a form of ENTERTAINMENT for him...
SCHOOL
Because I just go from HOME to WORK...
then from WORK to HOME...
Nothing more.
But José has learned to SPEAK ENGLISH...
Now he's learned to SING...
to WRITE a bit...
He really ENJOYS it!

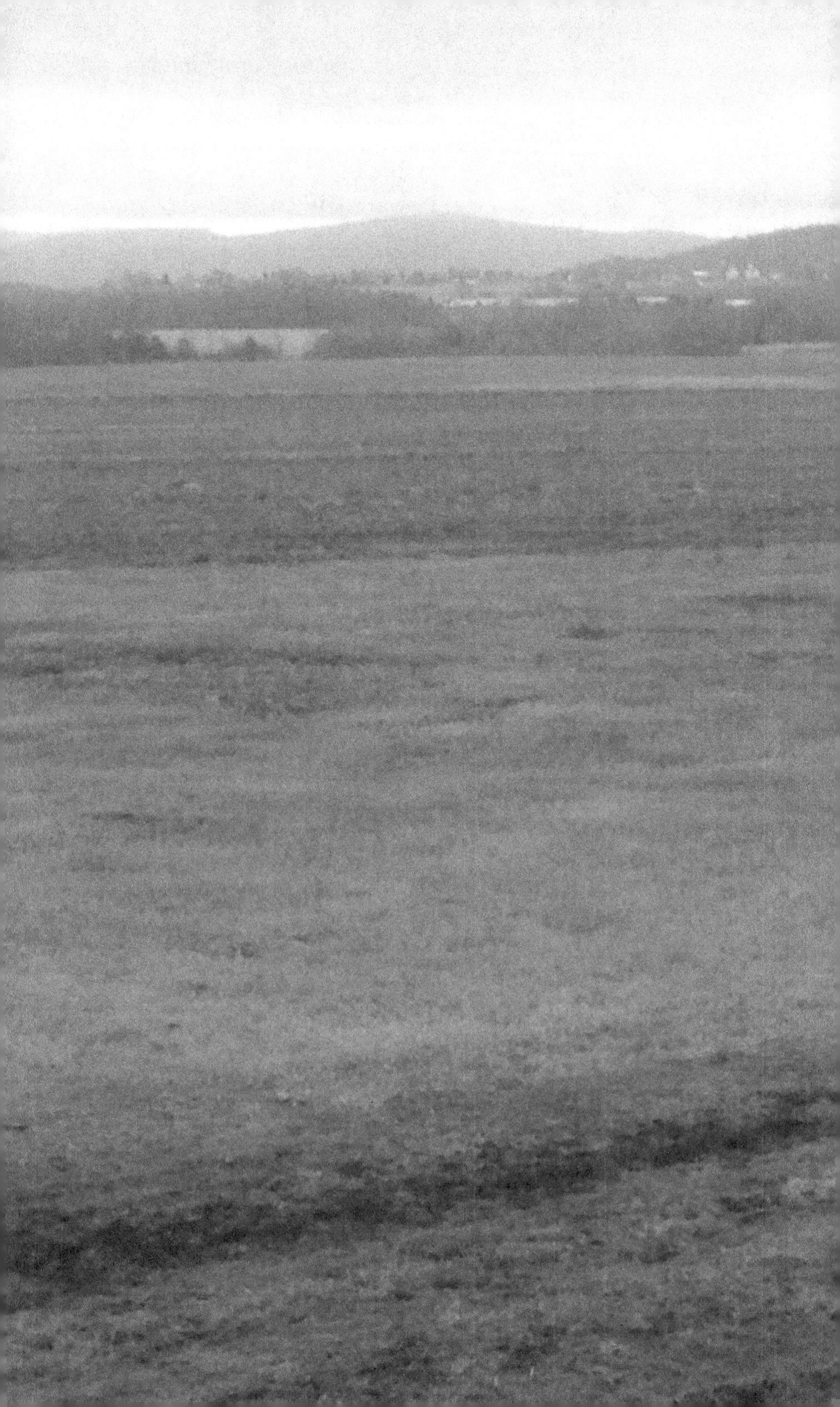

"EL VIAJE MAS CARO" / "THE MOST COSTLY JOURNEY" presents:

THE TWO OF US
TOGETHER
(MEXICAN AMERICAN)

The story of Felix & Alejandro
Art by Greg Giordano
Script by William Woodcock

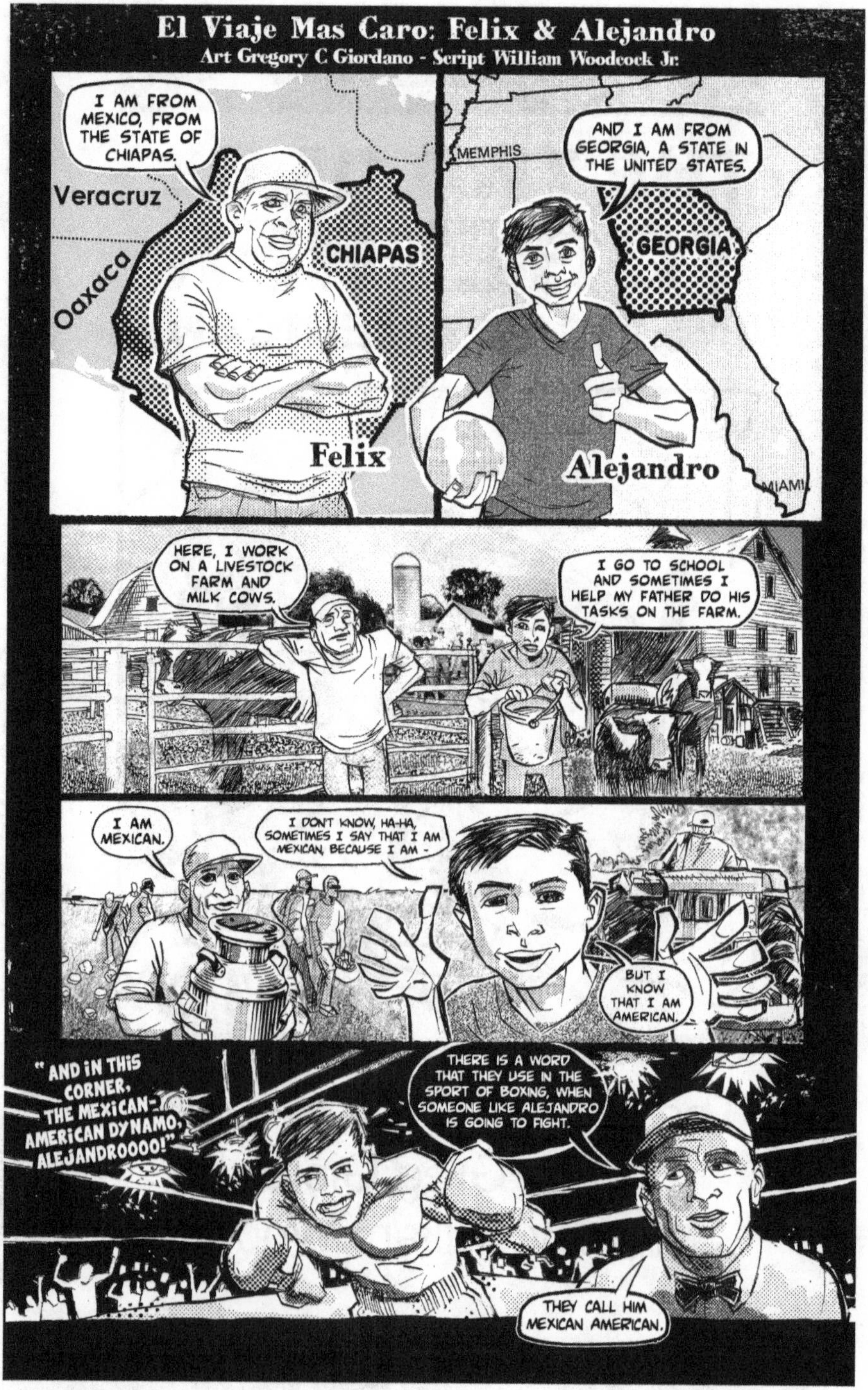
El Viaje Mas Caro: Felix & Alejandro
Art Gregory C Giordano - Script William Woodcock Jr.
I AM FROM MEXICO, FROM THE STATE OF CHIAPAS.
Veracruz
Oaxaca
CHIAPAS
Felix
MEMPHIS
AND I AM FROM GEORGIA, A STATE IN THE UNITED STATES.
GEORGIA
Alejandro
MIAMI
HERE, I WORK ON A LIVESTOCK FARM AND MILK COWS.
I GO TO SCHOOL AND SOMETIMES I HELP MY FATHER DO HIS TASKS ON THE FARM.
I AM MEXICAN.
I DON'T KNOW, HA-HA, SOMETIMES I SAY THAT I AM MEXICAN, BECAUSE I AM -
BUT I KNOW THAT I AM AMERICAN.
"AND IN THIS CORNER, THE MEXICAN-AMERICAN DYNAMO, ALEJANDROOOO!"
THERE IS A WORD THAT THEY USE IN THE SPORT OF BOXING, WHEN SOMEONE LIKE ALEJANDRO IS GOING TO FIGHT.
THEY CALL HIM MEXICAN AMERICAN.

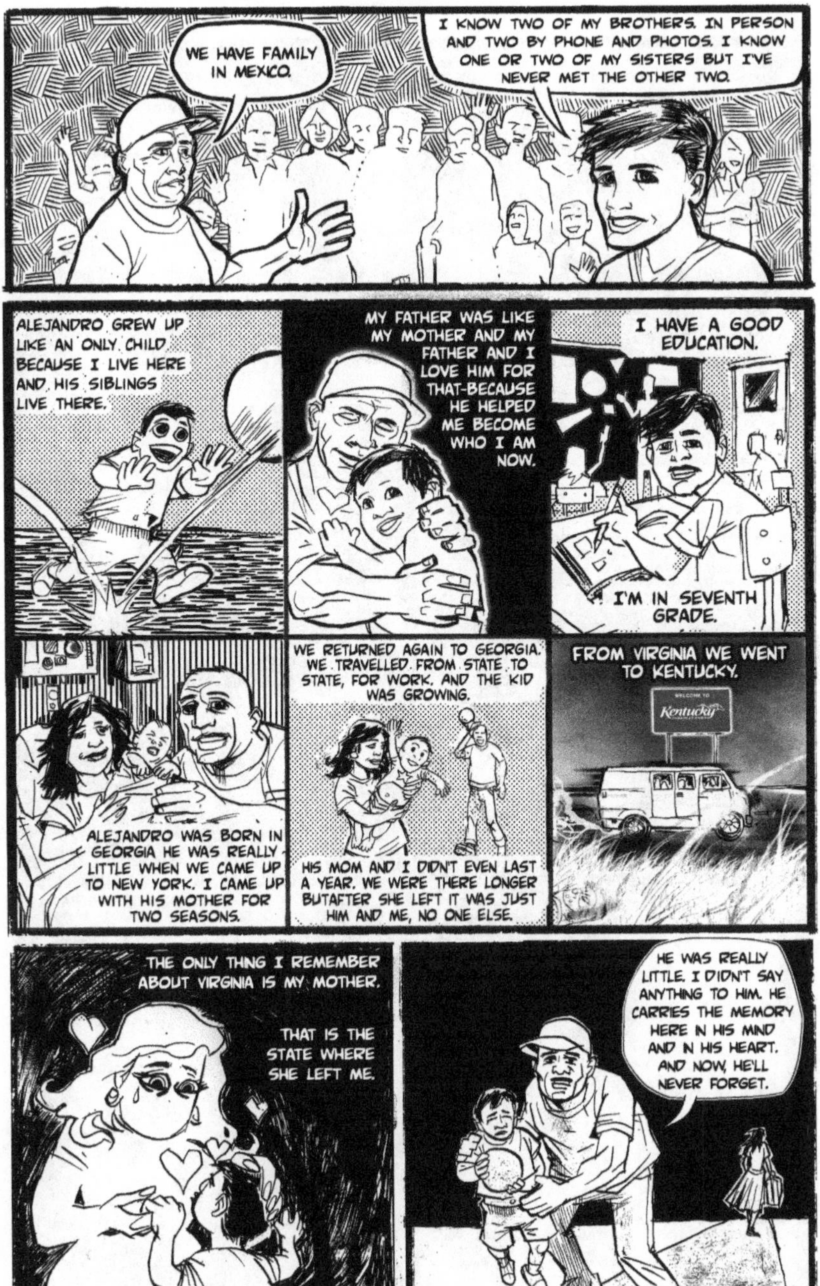
WE HAVE FAMILY IN MEXICO.
I KNOW TWO OF MY BROTHERS IN PERSON AND TWO BY PHONE AND PHOTOS. I KNOW ONE OR TWO OF MY SISTERS BUT I'VE NEVER MET THE OTHER TWO.
ALEJANDRO GREW UP LIKE AN ONLY CHILD BECAUSE I LIVE HERE AND HIS SIBLINGS LIVE THERE.
MY FATHER WAS LIKE MY MOTHER AND MY FATHER AND I LOVE HIM FOR THAT-BECAUSE HE HELPED ME BECOME WHO I AM NOW.
I HAVE A GOOD EDUCATION.
I'M IN SEVENTH GRADE.
ALEJANDRO WAS BORN IN GEORGIA HE WAS REALLY LITTLE WHEN WE CAME UP TO NEW YORK. I CAME UP WITH HIS MOTHER FOR TWO SEASONS.
WE RETURNED AGAIN TO GEORGIA. WE TRAVELLED FROM STATE TO STATE, FOR WORK. AND THE KID WAS GROWING.
HIS MOM AND I DIDN'T EVEN LAST A YEAR. WE WERE THERE LONGER BUTAFTER SHE LEFT IT WAS JUST HIM AND ME, NO ONE ELSE.
FROM VIRGINIA WE WENT TO KENTUCKY.
Kentucky
THE ONLY THING I REMEMBER ABOUT VIRGINIA IS MY MOTHER.
THAT IS THE STATE WHERE SHE LEFT ME.
HE WAS REALLY LITTLE. I DIDN'T SAY ANYTHING TO HIM. HE CARRIES THE MEMORY HERE IN HIS MIND AND IN HIS HEART. AND NOW, HE'LL NEVER FORGET.

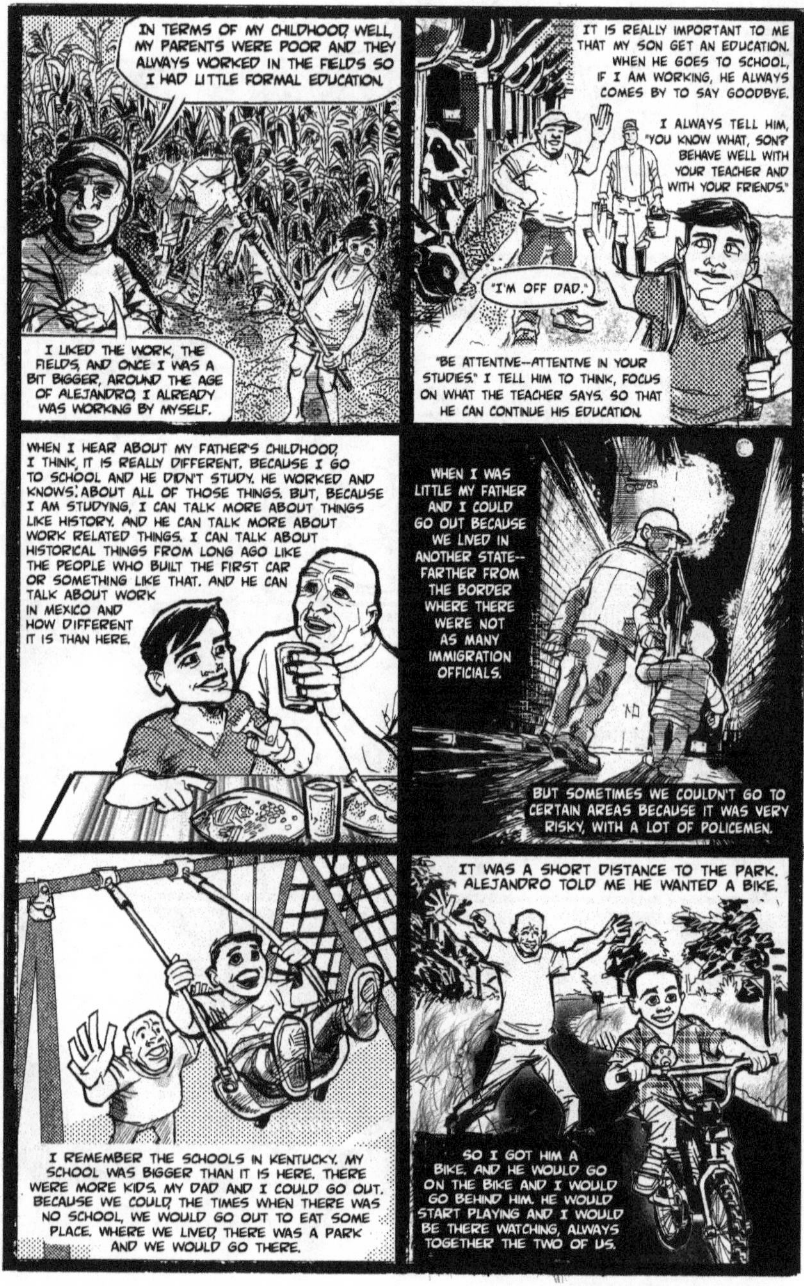
IN TERMS OF MY CHILDHOOD, WELL, MY PARENTS WERE POOR AND THEY ALWAYS WORKED IN THE FIELDS SO I HAD LITTLE FORMAL EDUCATION.
I LIKED THE WORK, THE FIELDS, AND ONCE I WAS A BIT BIGGER, AROUND THE AGE OF ALEJANDRO, I ALREADY WAS WORKING BY MYSELF.
IT IS REALLY IMPORTANT TO ME THAT MY SON GET AN EDUCATION. WHEN HE GOES TO SCHOOL, IF I AM WORKING, HE ALWAYS COMES BY TO SAY GOODBYE.
I ALWAYS TELL HIM, "YOU KNOW WHAT, SON? BEHAVE WELL WITH YOUR TEACHER AND WITH YOUR FRIENDS."
"I'M OFF DAD."
"BE ATTENTIVE--ATTENTIVE IN YOUR STUDIES." I TELL HIM TO THINK, FOCUS ON WHAT THE TEACHER SAYS. SO THAT HE CAN CONTINUE HIS EDUCATION.
WHEN I HEAR ABOUT MY FATHER'S CHILDHOOD, I THINK, IT IS REALLY DIFFERENT. BECAUSE I GO TO SCHOOL AND HE DIDN'T STUDY. HE WORKED AND KNOWS ABOUT ALL OF THOSE THINGS. BUT, BECAUSE I AM STUDYING, I CAN TALK MORE ABOUT THINGS LIKE HISTORY. AND HE CAN TALK MORE ABOUT WORK RELATED THINGS. I CAN TALK ABOUT HISTORICAL THINGS FROM LONG AGO LIKE THE PEOPLE WHO BUILT THE FIRST CAR OR SOMETHING LIKE THAT. AND HE CAN TALK ABOUT WORK IN MEXICO AND HOW DIFFERENT IT IS THAN HERE.
WHEN I WAS LITTLE MY FATHER AND I COULD GO OUT BECAUSE WE LIVED IN ANOTHER STATE-- FARTHER FROM THE BORDER WHERE THERE WERE NOT AS MANY IMMIGRATION OFFICIALS.
BUT SOMETIMES WE COULDN'T GO TO CERTAIN AREAS BECAUSE IT WAS VERY RISKY, WITH A LOT OF POLICEMEN.
I REMEMBER THE SCHOOLS IN KENTUCKY. MY SCHOOL WAS BIGGER THAN IT IS HERE. THERE WERE MORE KIDS. MY DAD AND I COULD GO OUT. BECAUSE WE COULD, THE TIMES WHEN THERE WAS NO SCHOOL, WE WOULD GO OUT TO EAT SOME PLACE. WHERE WE LIVED, THERE WAS A PARK AND WE WOULD GO THERE.
IT WAS A SHORT DISTANCE TO THE PARK. ALEJANDRO TOLD ME HE WANTED A BIKE.
SO I GOT HIM A BIKE, AND HE WOULD GO ON THE BIKE AND I WOULD GO BEHIND HIM. HE WOULD START PLAYING AND I WOULD BE THERE WATCHING, ALWAYS TOGETHER THE TWO OF US.

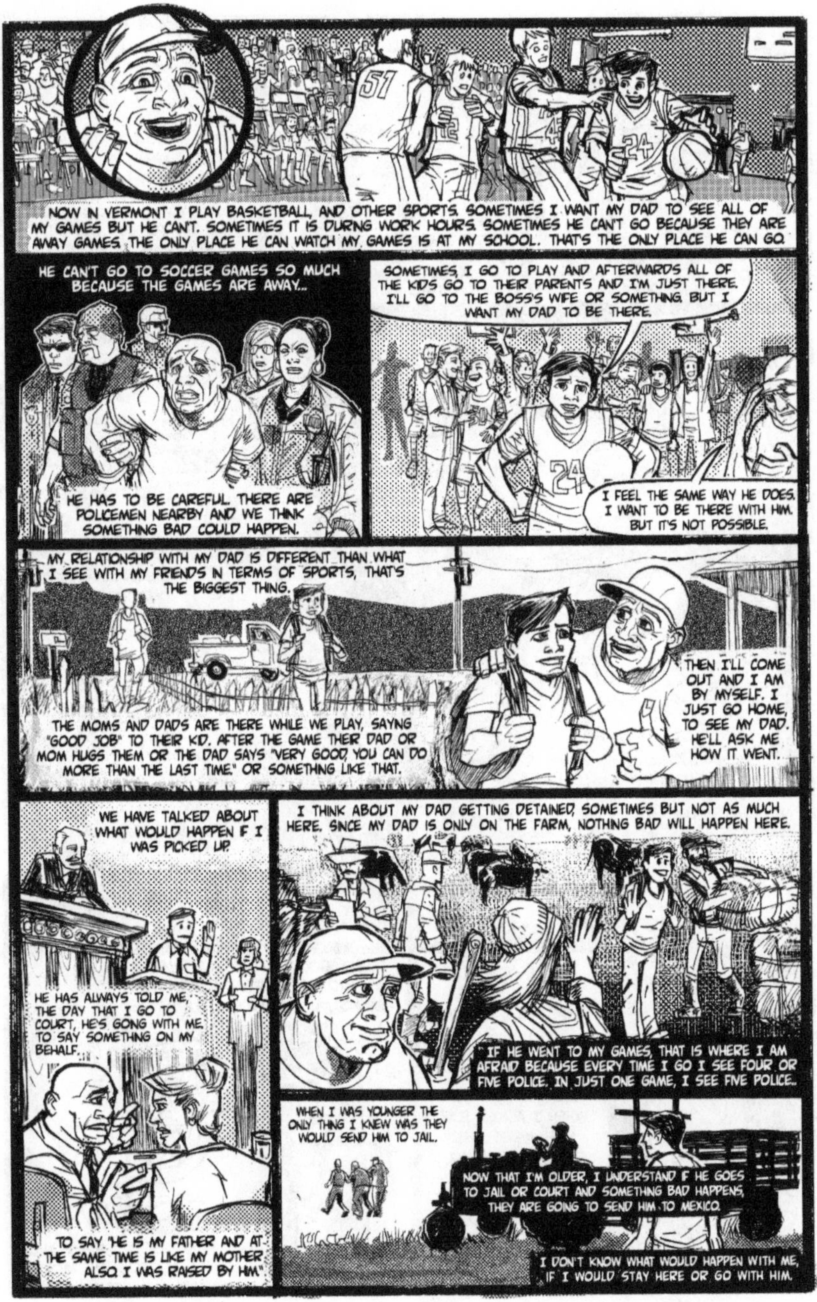
NOW IN VERMONT I PLAY BASKETBALL AND OTHER SPORTS. SOMETIMES I WANT MY DAD TO SEE ALL OF MY GAMES BUT HE CAN'T. SOMETIMES IT IS DURING WORK HOURS. SOMETIMES HE CAN'T GO BECAUSE THEY ARE AWAY GAMES. THE ONLY PLACE HE CAN WATCH MY GAMES IS AT MY SCHOOL. THAT'S THE ONLY PLACE HE CAN GO.
HE CAN'T GO TO SOCCER GAMES SO MUCH BECAUSE THE GAMES ARE AWAY...
HE HAS TO BE CAREFUL. THERE ARE POLICEMEN NEARBY AND WE THINK SOMETHING BAD COULD HAPPEN.
SOMETIMES, I GO TO PLAY AND AFTERWARDS ALL OF THE KIDS GO TO THEIR PARENTS AND I'M JUST THERE. I'LL GO TO THE BOSS'S WIFE OR SOMETHING. BUT I WANT MY DAD TO BE THERE.
I FEEL THE SAME WAY HE DOES. I WANT TO BE THERE WITH HIM. BUT IT'S NOT POSSIBLE.
MY RELATIONSHIP WITH MY DAD IS DIFFERENT THAN WHAT I SEE WITH MY FRIENDS IN TERMS OF SPORTS, THAT'S THE BIGGEST THING.
THE MOMS AND DADS ARE THERE WHILE WE PLAY, SAYING "GOOD JOB" TO THEIR KID. AFTER THE GAME THEIR DAD OR MOM HUGS THEM OR THE DAD SAYS "VERY GOOD, YOU CAN DO MORE THAN THE LAST TIME." OR SOMETHING LIKE THAT.
THEN I'LL COME OUT AND I AM BY MYSELF. I JUST GO HOME, TO SEE MY DAD. HE'LL ASK ME HOW IT WENT.
WE HAVE TALKED ABOUT WHAT WOULD HAPPEN IF I WAS PICKED UP.
HE HAS ALWAYS TOLD ME, THE DAY THAT I GO TO COURT, HE'S GOING WITH ME TO SAY SOMETHING ON MY BEHALF...
TO SAY "HE IS MY FATHER AND AT THE SAME TIME IS LIKE MY MOTHER ALSO. I WAS RAISED BY HIM."
I THINK ABOUT MY DAD GETTING DETAINED, SOMETIMES BUT NOT AS MUCH HERE. SINCE MY DAD IS ONLY ON THE FARM, NOTHING BAD WILL HAPPEN HERE.
IF HE WENT TO MY GAMES, THAT IS WHERE I AM AFRAID BECAUSE EVERY TIME I GO I SEE FOUR OR FIVE POLICE. IN JUST ONE GAME, I SEE FIVE POLICE.
WHEN I WAS YOUNGER THE ONLY THING I KNEW WAS THEY WOULD SEND HIM TO JAIL.
NOW THAT I'M OLDER, I UNDERSTAND IF HE GOES TO JAIL OR COURT AND SOMETHING BAD HAPPENS, THEY ARE GOING TO SEND HIM TO MEXICO.
I DON'T KNOW WHAT WOULD HAPPEN WITH ME, IF I WOULD STAY HERE OR GO WITH HIM.

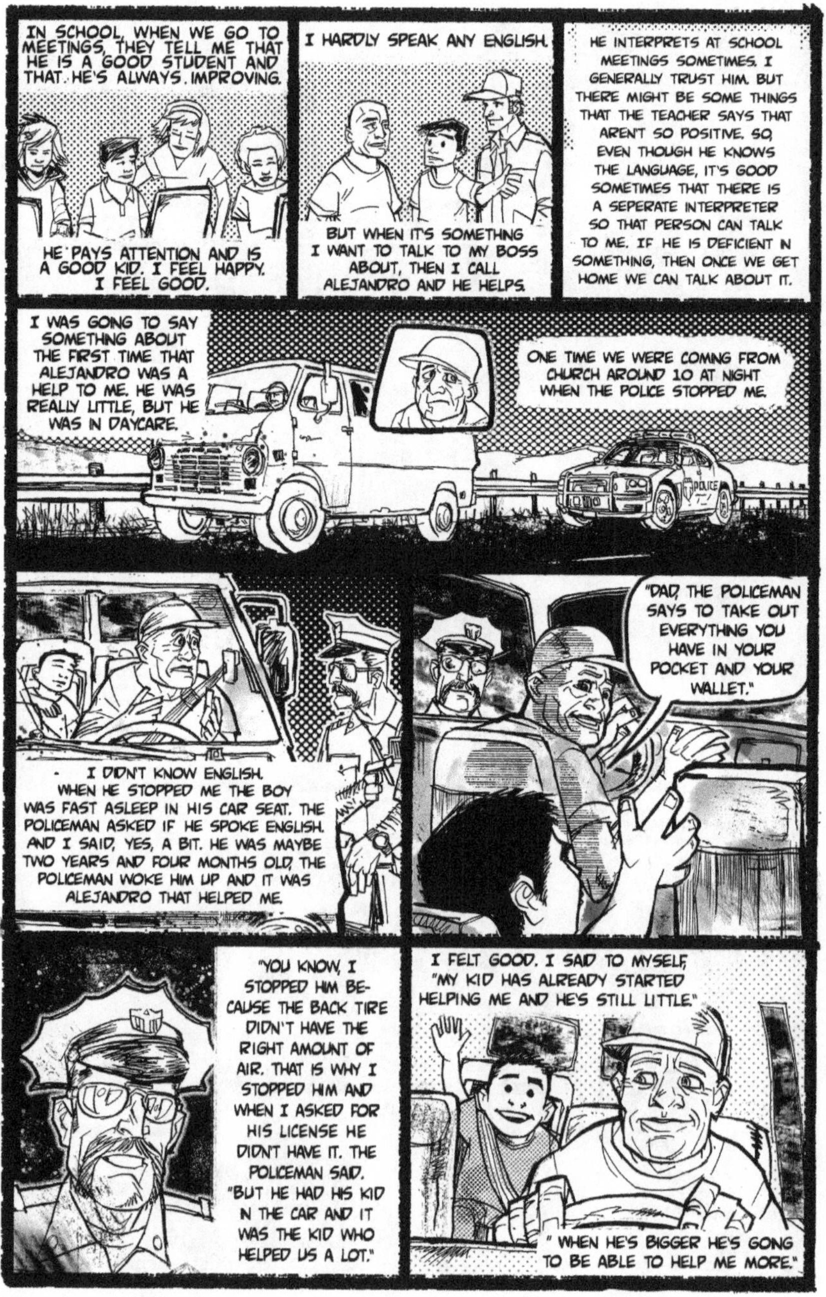
IN SCHOOL, WHEN WE GO TO MEETINGS, THEY TELL ME THAT HE IS A GOOD STUDENT AND THAT HE'S ALWAYS IMPROVING.
HE PAYS ATTENTION AND IS A GOOD KID. I FEEL HAPPY. I FEEL GOOD.
I HARDLY SPEAK ANY ENGLISH.
BUT WHEN IT'S SOMETHING I WANT TO TALK TO MY BOSS ABOUT, THEN I CALL ALEJANDRO AND HE HELPS.
HE INTERPRETS AT SCHOOL MEETINGS SOMETIMES. I GENERALLY TRUST HIM. BUT THERE MIGHT BE SOME THINGS THAT THE TEACHER SAYS THAT AREN'T SO POSITIVE. SO, EVEN THOUGH HE KNOWS THE LANGUAGE, IT'S GOOD SOMETIMES THAT THERE IS A SEPERATE INTERPRETER SO THAT PERSON CAN TALK TO ME. IF HE IS DEFICIENT IN SOMETHING, THEN ONCE WE GET HOME WE CAN TALK ABOUT IT.
I WAS GOING TO SAY SOMETHING ABOUT THE FIRST TIME THAT ALEJANDRO WAS A HELP TO ME. HE WAS REALLY LITTLE, BUT HE WAS IN DAYCARE.
ONE TIME WE WERE COMING FROM CHURCH AROUND 10 AT NIGHT WHEN THE POLICE STOPPED ME.
POLICE
I DIDN'T KNOW ENGLISH. WHEN HE STOPPED ME THE BOY WAS FAST ASLEEP IN HIS CAR SEAT. THE POLICEMAN ASKED IF HE SPOKE ENGLISH. AND I SAID, YES, A BIT. HE WAS MAYBE TWO YEARS AND FOUR MONTHS OLD, THE POLICEMAN WOKE HIM UP AND IT WAS ALEJANDRO THAT HELPED ME.
"DAD, THE POLICEMAN SAYS TO TAKE OUT EVERYTHING YOU HAVE IN YOUR POCKET AND YOUR WALLET."
"YOU KNOW, I STOPPED HIM BECAUSE THE BACK TIRE DIDN'T HAVE THE RIGHT AMOUNT OF AIR. THAT IS WHY I STOPPED HIM AND WHEN I ASKED FOR HIS LICENSE HE DIDN'T HAVE IT. THE POLICEMAN SAID. "BUT HE HAD HIS KID IN THE CAR AND IT WAS THE KID WHO HELPED US A LOT."
I FELT GOOD. I SAID TO MYSELF, "MY KID HAS ALREADY STARTED HELPING ME AND HE'S STILL LITTLE."
" WHEN HE'S BIGGER HE'S GONG TO BE ABLE TO HELP ME MORE."

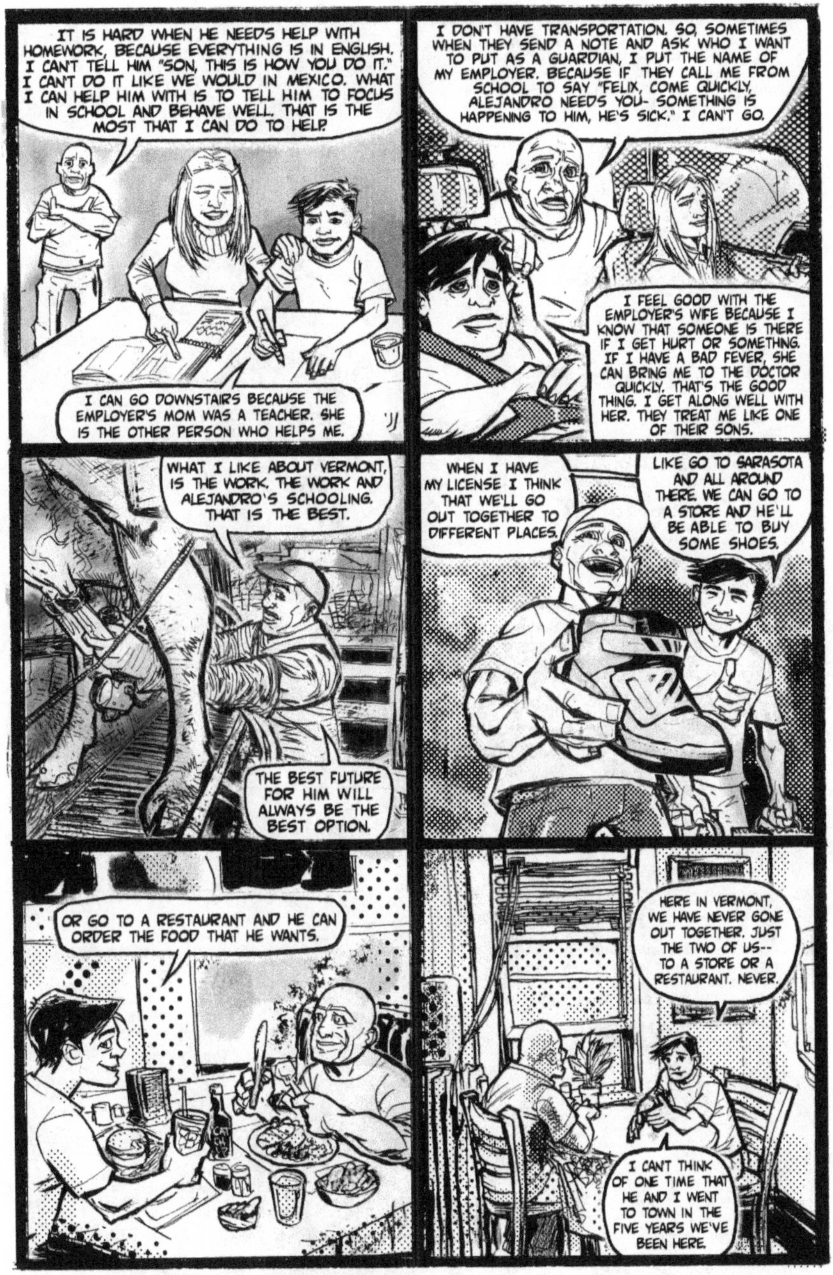
IT IS HARD WHEN HE NEEDS HELP WITH HOMEWORK, BECAUSE EVERYTHING IS IN ENGLISH. I CAN'T TELL HIM "SON, THIS IS HOW YOU DO IT." I CAN'T DO IT LIKE WE WOULD IN MEXICO. WHAT I CAN HELP HIM WITH IS TO TELL HIM TO FOCUS IN SCHOOL AND BEHAVE WELL. THAT IS THE MOST THAT I CAN DO TO HELP.
I CAN GO DOWNSTAIRS BECAUSE THE EMPLOYER'S MOM WAS A TEACHER. SHE IS THE OTHER PERSON WHO HELPS ME.
I DON'T HAVE TRANSPORTATION. SO, SOMETIMES WHEN THEY SEND A NOTE AND ASK WHO I WANT TO PUT AS A GUARDIAN, I PUT THE NAME OF MY EMPLOYER. BECAUSE IF THEY CALL ME FROM SCHOOL TO SAY "FELIX, COME QUICKLY, ALEJANDRO NEEDS YOU- SOMETHING IS HAPPENING TO HIM, HE'S SICK." I CAN'T GO.
I FEEL GOOD WITH THE EMPLOYER'S WIFE BECAUSE I KNOW THAT SOMEONE IS THERE IF I GET HURT OR SOMETHING. IF I HAVE A BAD FEVER, SHE CAN BRING ME TO THE DOCTOR QUICKLY. THAT'S THE GOOD THING. I GET ALONG WELL WITH HER. THEY TREAT ME LIKE ONE OF THEIR SONS.
WHAT I LIKE ABOUT VERMONT, IS THE WORK. THE WORK AND ALEJANDRO'S SCHOOLING. THAT IS THE BEST.
THE BEST FUTURE FOR HIM WILL ALWAYS BE THE BEST OPTION.
WHEN I HAVE MY LICENSE I THINK THAT WE'LL GO OUT TOGETHER TO DIFFERENT PLACES,
LIKE GO TO SARASOTA AND ALL AROUND THERE. WE CAN GO TO A STORE AND HE'LL BE ABLE TO BUY SOME SHOES.
OR GO TO A RESTAURANT AND HE CAN ORDER THE FOOD THAT HE WANTS.
HERE IN VERMONT, WE HAVE NEVER GONE OUT TOGETHER, JUST THE TWO OF US-- TO A STORE OR A RESTAURANT. NEVER.
I CAN'T THINK OF ONE TIME THAT HE AND I WENT TO TOWN IN THE FIVE YEARS WE'VE BEEN HERE.

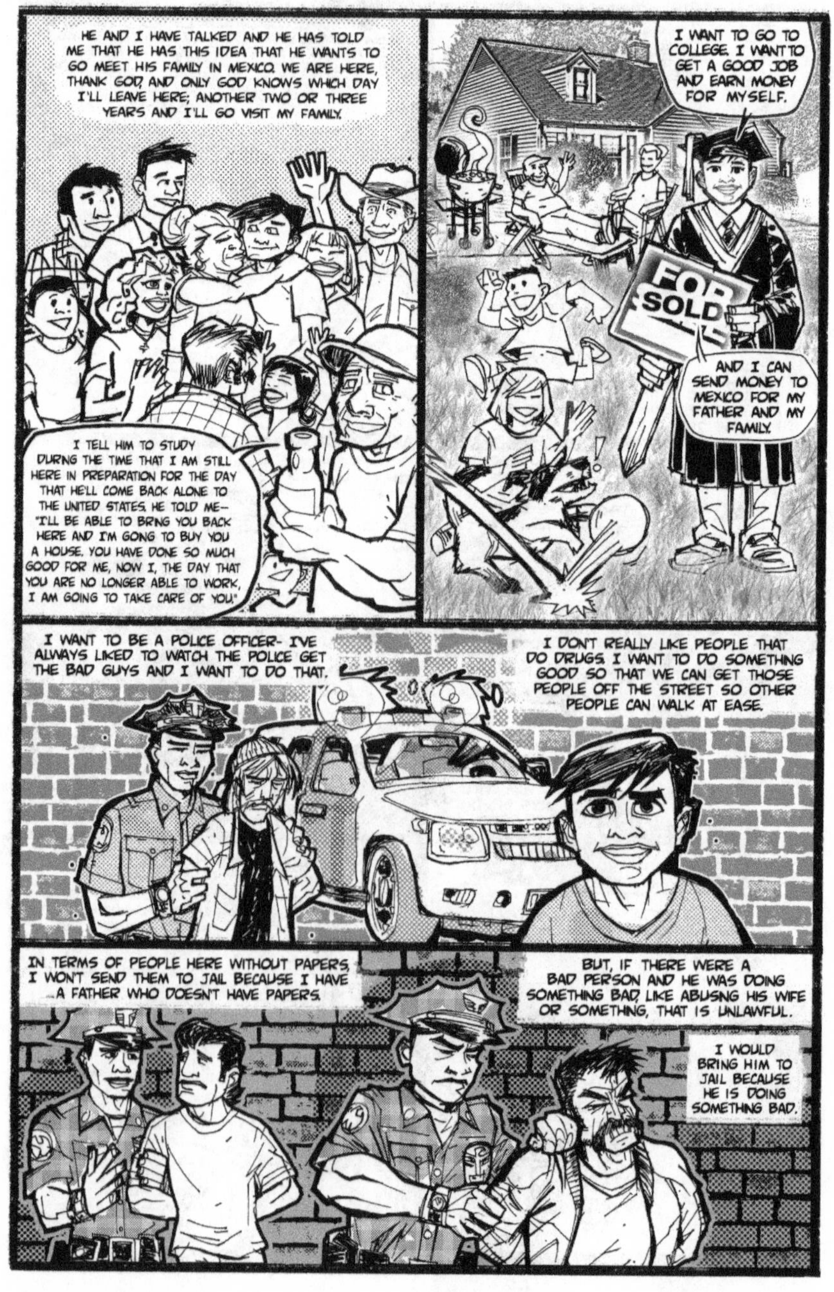
HE AND I HAVE TALKED AND HE HAS TOLD ME THAT HE HAS THIS IDEA THAT HE WANTS TO GO MEET HIS FAMILY IN MEXICO. WE ARE HERE, THANK GOD, AND ONLY GOD KNOWS WHICH DAY I'LL LEAVE HERE; ANOTHER TWO OR THREE YEARS AND I'LL GO VISIT MY FAMILY.
I TELL HIM TO STUDY DURING THE TIME THAT I AM STILL HERE IN PREPARATION FOR THE DAY THAT HE'LL COME BACK ALONE TO THE UNITED STATES. HE TOLD ME- "I'LL BE ABLE TO BRING YOU BACK HERE AND I'M GONG TO BUY YOU A HOUSE. YOU HAVE DONE SO MUCH GOOD FOR ME, NOW I, THE DAY THAT YOU ARE NO LONGER ABLE TO WORK, I AM GOING TO TAKE CARE OF YOU."
I WANT TO GO TO COLLEGE. I WANT TO GET A GOOD JOB AND EARN MONEY FOR MYSELF.
SOLD
AND I CAN SEND MONEY TO MEXICO FOR MY FATHER AND MY FAMILY.
I WANT TO BE A POLICE OFFICER- I'VE ALWAYS LIKED TO WATCH THE POLICE GET THE BAD GUYS AND I WANT TO DO THAT.
I DON'T REALLY LIKE PEOPLE THAT DO DRUGS. I WANT TO DO SOMETHING GOOD SO THAT WE CAN GET THOSE PEOPLE OFF THE STREET SO OTHER PEOPLE CAN WALK AT EASE.
IN TERMS OF PEOPLE HERE WITHOUT PAPERS, I WON'T SEND THEM TO JAIL BECAUSE I HAVE A FATHER WHO DOESN'T HAVE PAPERS.
BUT, IF THERE WERE A BAD PERSON AND HE WAS DOING SOMETHING BAD, LIKE ABUSNG HIS WIFE OR SOMETHING, THAT IS UNLAWFUL.
I WOULD BRING HIM TO JAIL BECAUSE HE IS DOING SOMETHING BAD.

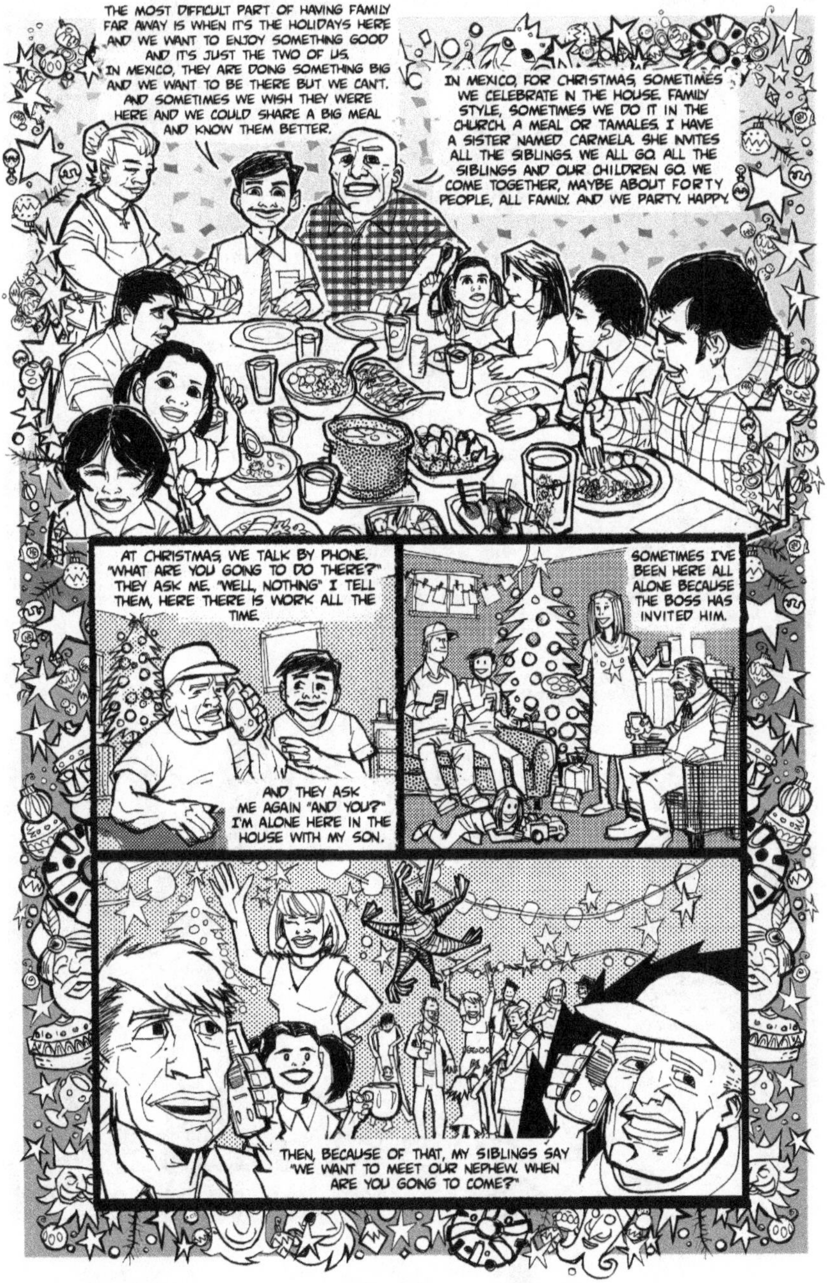
THE MOST DIFFICULT PART OF HAVING FAMILY FAR AWAY IS WHEN IT'S THE HOLIDAYS HERE AND WE WANT TO ENJOY SOMETHING GOOD AND IT'S JUST THE TWO OF US. IN MEXICO, THEY ARE DOING SOMETHING BIG AND WE WANT TO BE THERE BUT WE CAN'T. AND SOMETIMES WE WISH THEY WERE HERE AND WE COULD SHARE A BIG MEAL AND KNOW THEM BETTER.
IN MEXICO, FOR CHRISTMAS, SOMETIMES WE CELEBRATE IN THE HOUSE, FAMILY STYLE, SOMETIMES WE DO IT IN THE CHURCH. A MEAL OR TAMALES. I HAVE A SISTER NAMED CARMELA. SHE INVITES ALL THE SIBLINGS. WE ALL GO. ALL THE SIBLINGS AND OUR CHILDREN GO. WE COME TOGETHER, MAYBE ABOUT FORTY PEOPLE, ALL FAMILY. AND WE PARTY. HAPPY.
AT CHRISTMAS, WE TALK BY PHONE. "WHAT ARE YOU GOING TO DO THERE?" THEY ASK ME. "WELL, NOTHING" I TELL THEM, HERE THERE IS WORK ALL THE TIME.
AND THEY ASK ME AGAIN "AND YOU?" I'M ALONE HERE IN THE HOUSE WITH MY SON.
SOMETIMES I'VE BEEN HERE ALL ALONE BECAUSE THE BOSS HAS INVITED HIM.
THEN, BECAUSE OF THAT, MY SIBLINGS SAY "WE WANT TO MEET OUR NEPHEW. WHEN ARE YOU GONG TO COME?"

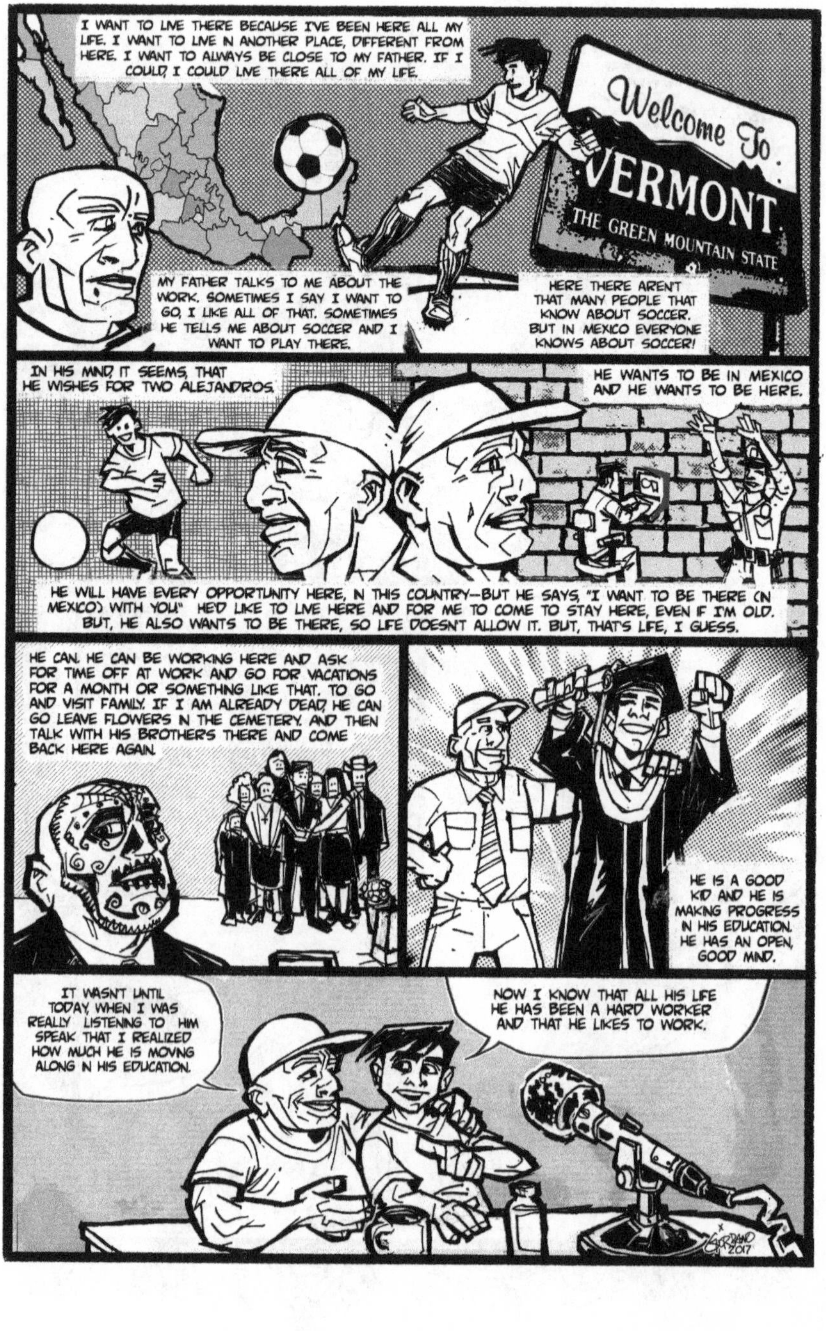
I WANT TO LIVE THERE BECAUSE I'VE BEEN HERE ALL MY LIFE. I WANT TO LIVE IN ANOTHER PLACE, DIFFERENT FROM HERE. I WANT TO ALWAYS BE CLOSE TO MY FATHER. IF I COULD, I COULD LIVE THERE ALL OF MY LIFE.
Welcome To VERMONT THE GREEN MOUNTAIN STATE
MY FATHER TALKS TO ME ABOUT THE WORK. SOMETIMES I SAY I WANT TO GO, I LIKE ALL OF THAT. SOMETIMES HE TELLS ME ABOUT SOCCER AND I WANT TO PLAY THERE.
HERE THERE AREN'T THAT MANY PEOPLE THAT KNOW ABOUT SOCCER. BUT IN MEXICO EVERYONE KNOWS ABOUT SOCCER!
IN HIS MIND, IT SEEMS, THAT HE WISHES FOR TWO ALEJANDROS.
HE WANTS TO BE IN MEXICO AND HE WANTS TO BE HERE.
HE WILL HAVE EVERY OPPORTUNITY HERE, IN THIS COUNTRY--BUT HE SAYS, "I WANT TO BE THERE (IN MEXICO) WITH YOU." HE'D LIKE TO LIVE HERE AND FOR ME TO COME TO STAY HERE, EVEN IF I'M OLD. BUT, HE ALSO WANTS TO BE THERE, SO LIFE DOESN'T ALLOW IT. BUT, THAT'S LIFE, I GUESS.
HE CAN. HE CAN BE WORKING HERE AND ASK FOR TIME OFF AT WORK AND GO FOR VACATIONS FOR A MONTH OR SOMETHING LIKE THAT. TO GO AND VISIT FAMILY. IF I AM ALREADY DEAD, HE CAN GO LEAVE FLOWERS IN THE CEMETERY. AND THEN TALK WITH HIS BROTHERS THERE AND COME BACK HERE AGAIN.
HE IS A GOOD KID AND HE IS MAKING PROGRESS IN HIS EDUCATION. HE HAS AN OPEN, GOOD MIND.
IT WASN'T UNTIL TODAY, WHEN I WAS REALLY LISTENING TO HIM SPEAK THAT I REALIZED HOW MUCH HE IS MOVING ALONG IN HIS EDUCATION.
NOW I KNOW THAT ALL HIS LIFE HE HAS BEEN A HARD WORKER AND THAT HE LIKES TO WORK.
GIORDANO 2017

"EL VIAJE MAS CARO" / "THE MOST COSTLY JOURNEY" presents:

LANGUAGE IS POWER

The Story of Carlos and Bob
Art by Ezra Veitch

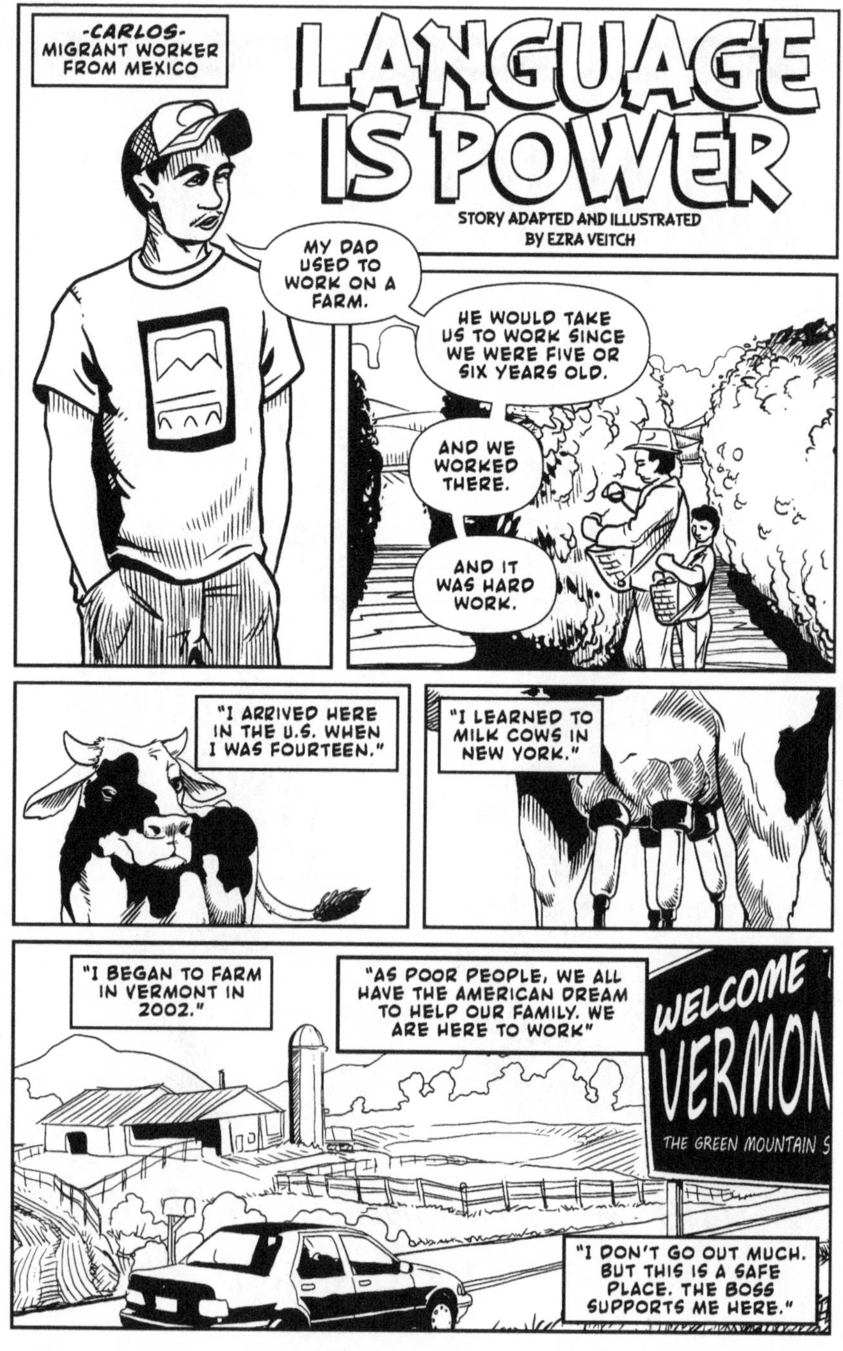
-CARLOS-
MIGRANT WORKER FROM MEXICO
LANGUAGE IS POWER
STORY ADAPTED AND ILLUSTRATED BY EZRA VEITCH
MY DAD USED TO WORK ON A FARM.
HE WOULD TAKE US TO WORK SINCE WE WERE FIVE OR SIX YEARS OLD.
AND WE WORKED THERE.
AND IT WAS HARD WORK.
"I ARRIVED HERE IN THE U.S. WHEN I WAS FOURTEEN."
"I LEARNED TO MILK COWS IN NEW YORK."
"I BEGAN TO FARM IN VERMONT IN 2002."
"AS POOR PEOPLE, WE ALL HAVE THE AMERICAN DREAM TO HELP OUR FAMILY. WE ARE HERE TO WORK"
WELCOME
VERMON
THE GREEN MOUNTAIN S
"I DON'T GO OUT MUCH. BUT THIS IS A SAFE PLACE. THE BOSS SUPPORTS ME HERE."

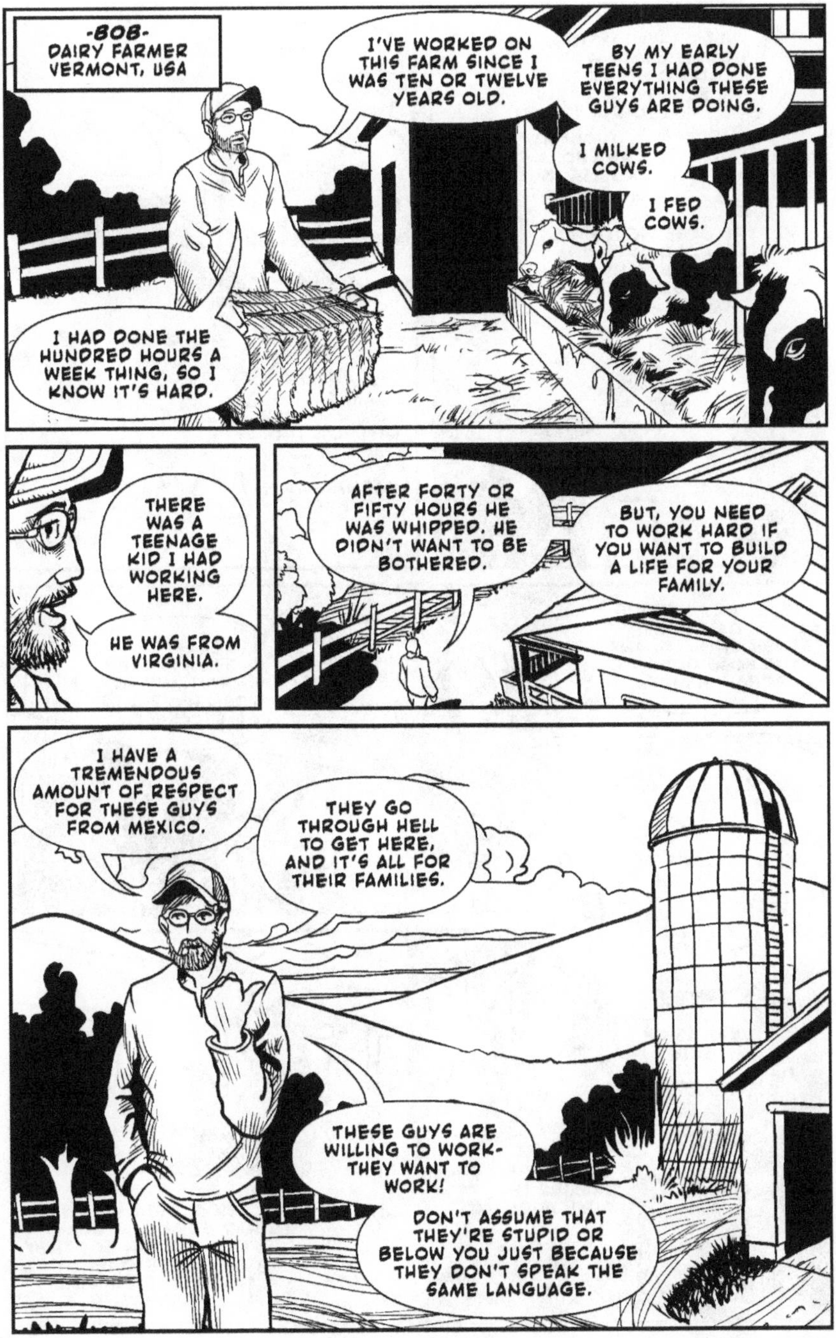
-BOB-
DAIRY FARMER
VERMONT, USA
I'VE WORKED ON THIS FARM SINCE I WAS TEN OR TWELVE YEARS OLD.
BY MY EARLY TEENS I HAD DONE EVERYTHING THESE GUYS ARE DOING.
I MILKED COWS.
I FED COWS.
I HAD DONE THE HUNDRED HOURS A WEEK THING, SO I KNOW IT'S HARD.
THERE WAS A TEENAGE KID I HAD WORKING HERE.
HE WAS FROM VIRGINIA.
AFTER FORTY OR FIFTY HOURS HE WAS WHIPPED. HE DIDN'T WANT TO BE BOTHERED.
BUT, YOU NEED TO WORK HARD IF YOU WANT TO BUILD A LIFE FOR YOUR FAMILY.
I HAVE A TREMENDOUS AMOUNT OF RESPECT FOR THESE GUYS FROM MEXICO.
THEY GO THROUGH HELL TO GET HERE, AND IT'S ALL FOR THEIR FAMILIES.
THESE GUYS ARE WILLING TO WORK- THEY WANT TO WORK!
DON'T ASSUME THAT THEY'RE STUPID OR BELOW YOU JUST BECAUSE THEY DON'T SPEAK THE SAME LANGUAGE.

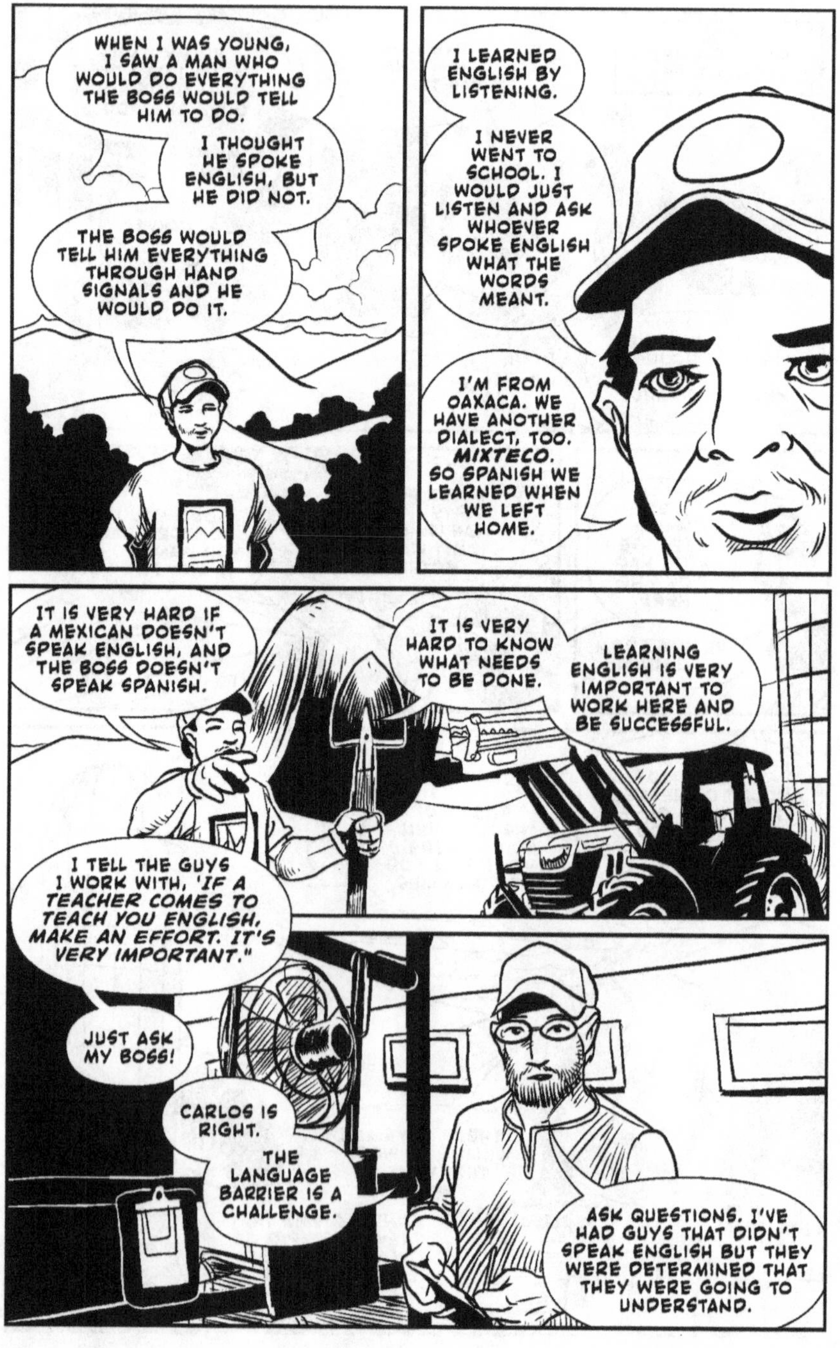
WHEN I WAS YOUNG, I SAW A MAN WHO WOULD DO EVERYTHING THE BOSS WOULD TELL HIM TO DO.
I THOUGHT HE SPOKE ENGLISH, BUT HE DID NOT.
THE BOSS WOULD TELL HIM EVERYTHING THROUGH HAND SIGNALS AND HE WOULD DO IT.
I LEARNED ENGLISH BY LISTENING.
I NEVER WENT TO SCHOOL. I WOULD JUST LISTEN AND ASK WHOEVER SPOKE ENGLISH WHAT THE WORDS MEANT.
I'M FROM OAXACA. WE HAVE ANOTHER DIALECT, TOO. *MIXTECO*. SO SPANISH WE LEARNED WHEN WE LEFT HOME.
IT IS VERY HARD IF A MEXICAN DOESN'T SPEAK ENGLISH, AND THE BOSS DOESN'T SPEAK SPANISH.
IT IS VERY HARD TO KNOW WHAT NEEDS TO BE DONE.
LEARNING ENGLISH IS VERY IMPORTANT TO WORK HERE AND BE SUCCESSFUL.
I TELL THE GUYS I WORK WITH, '*IF A TEACHER COMES TO TEACH YOU ENGLISH, MAKE AN EFFORT. IT'S VERY IMPORTANT.*"
JUST ASK MY BOSS!
CARLOS IS RIGHT.
THE LANGUAGE BARRIER IS A CHALLENGE.
ASK QUESTIONS. I'VE HAD GUYS THAT DIDN'T SPEAK ENGLISH BUT THEY WERE DETERMINED THAT THEY WERE GOING TO UNDERSTAND.

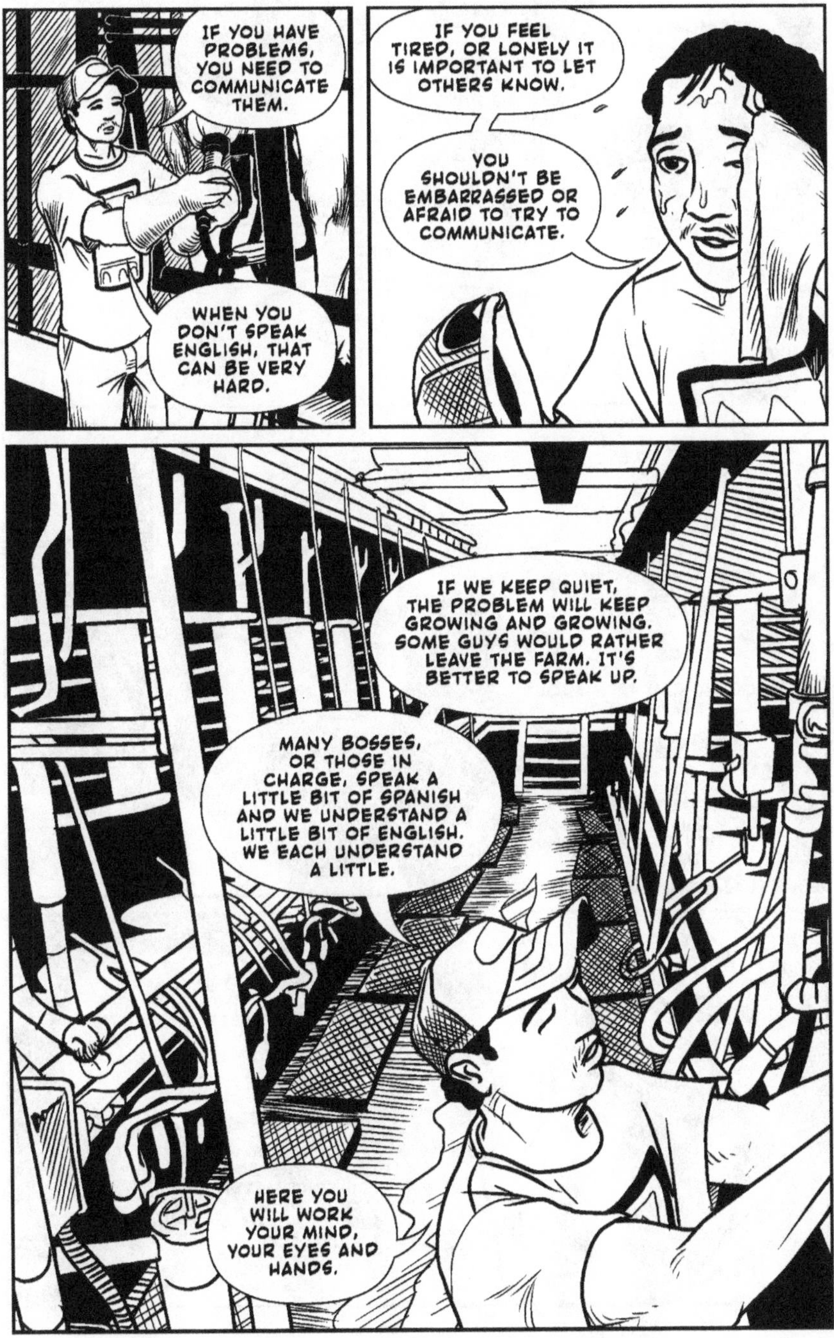
IF YOU HAVE PROBLEMS, YOU NEED TO COMMUNICATE THEM.
WHEN YOU DON'T SPEAK ENGLISH, THAT CAN BE VERY HARD.
IF YOU FEEL TIRED, OR LONELY IT IS IMPORTANT TO LET OTHERS KNOW.
YOU SHOULDN'T BE EMBARRASSED OR AFRAID TO TRY TO COMMUNICATE.
IF WE KEEP QUIET, THE PROBLEM WILL KEEP GROWING AND GROWING. SOME GUYS WOULD RATHER LEAVE THE FARM. IT'S BETTER TO SPEAK UP.
MANY BOSSES, OR THOSE IN CHARGE, SPEAK A LITTLE BIT OF SPANISH AND WE UNDERSTAND A LITTLE BIT OF ENGLISH. WE EACH UNDERSTAND A LITTLE.
HERE YOU WILL WORK YOUR MIND, YOUR EYES AND HANDS.

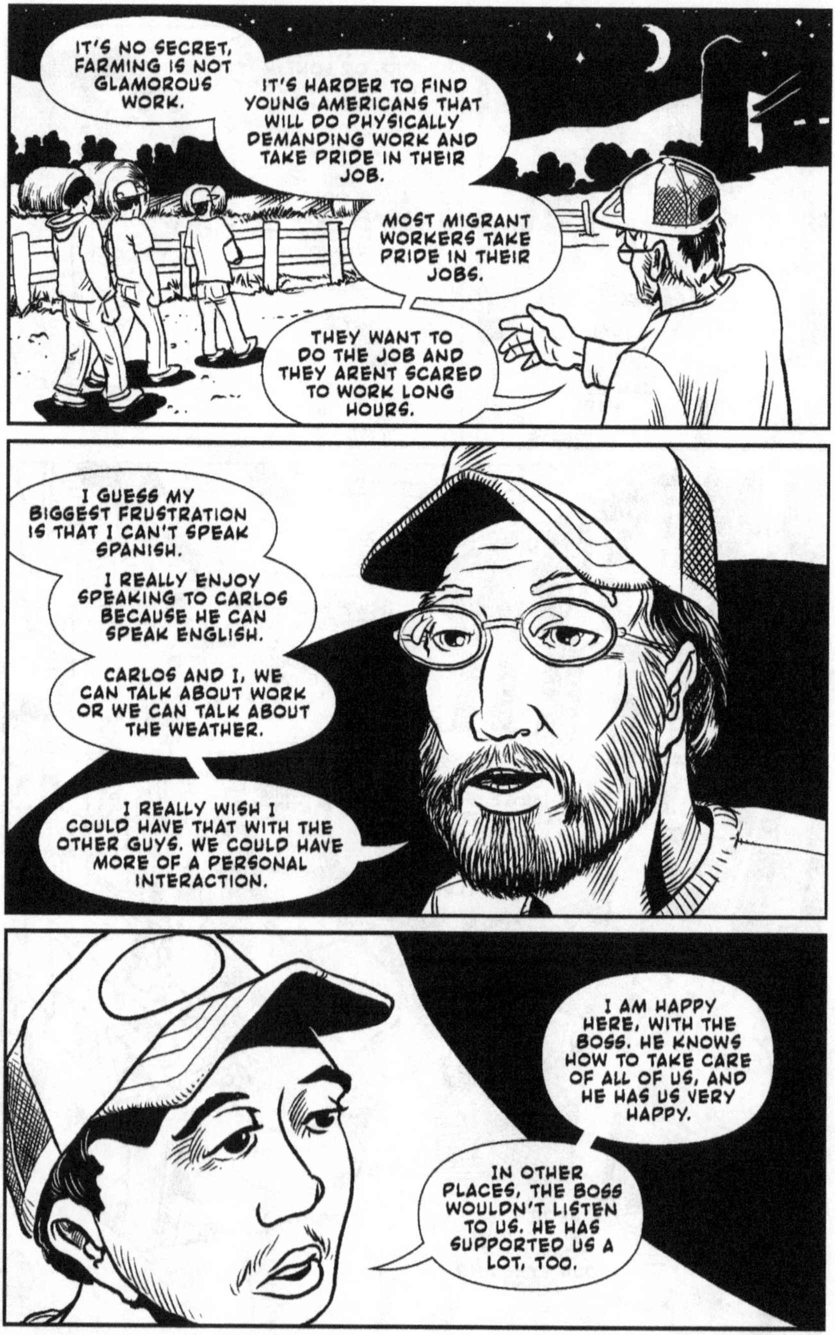
IT'S NO SECRET, FARMING IS NOT GLAMOROUS WORK.
IT'S HARDER TO FIND YOUNG AMERICANS THAT WILL DO PHYSICALLY DEMANDING WORK AND TAKE PRIDE IN THEIR JOB.
MOST MIGRANT WORKERS TAKE PRIDE IN THEIR JOBS.
THEY WANT TO DO THE JOB AND THEY ARENT SCARED TO WORK LONG HOURS.
I GUESS MY BIGGEST FRUSTRATION IS THAT I CAN'T SPEAK SPANISH.
I REALLY ENJOY SPEAKING TO CARLOS BECAUSE HE CAN SPEAK ENGLISH.
CARLOS AND I, WE CAN TALK ABOUT WORK OR WE CAN TALK ABOUT THE WEATHER.
I REALLY WISH I COULD HAVE THAT WITH THE OTHER GUYS. WE COULD HAVE MORE OF A PERSONAL INTERACTION.
I AM HAPPY HERE, WITH THE BOSS. HE KNOWS HOW TO TAKE CARE OF ALL OF US, AND HE HAS US VERY HAPPY.
IN OTHER PLACES, THE BOSS WOULDN'T LISTEN TO US. HE HAS SUPPORTED US A LOT, TOO.

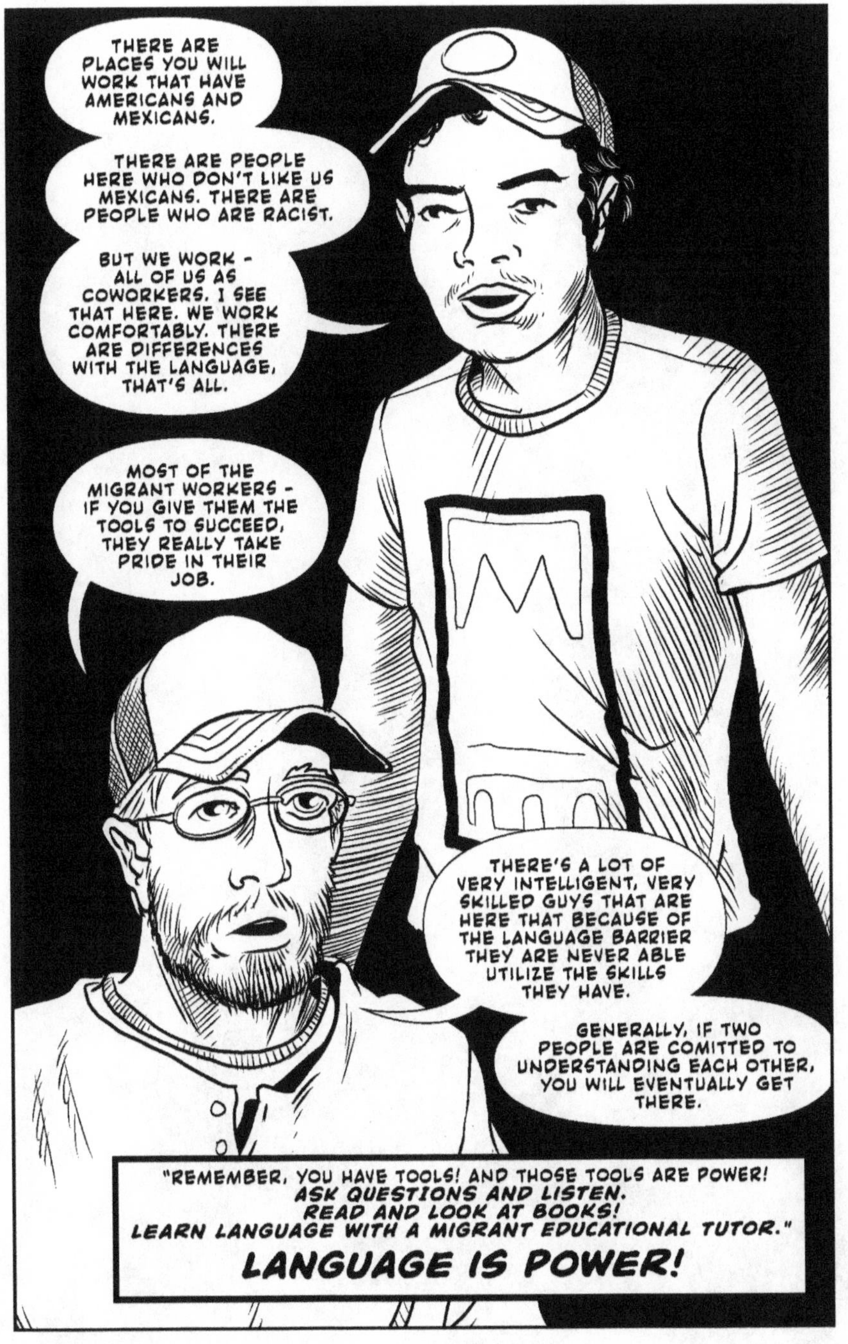
THERE ARE PLACES YOU WILL WORK THAT HAVE AMERICANS AND MEXICANS.
THERE ARE PEOPLE HERE WHO DON'T LIKE US MEXICANS. THERE ARE PEOPLE WHO ARE RACIST.
BUT WE WORK - ALL OF US AS COWORKERS. I SEE THAT HERE. WE WORK COMFORTABLY. THERE ARE DIFFERENCES WITH THE LANGUAGE, THAT'S ALL.
MOST OF THE MIGRANT WORKERS - IF YOU GIVE THEM THE TOOLS TO SUCCEED, THEY REALLY TAKE PRIDE IN THEIR JOB.
THERE'S A LOT OF VERY INTELLIGENT, VERY SKILLED GUYS THAT ARE HERE THAT BECAUSE OF THE LANGUAGE BARRIER THEY ARE NEVER ABLE UTILIZE THE SKILLS THEY HAVE.
GENERALLY, IF TWO PEOPLE ARE COMITTED TO UNDERSTANDING EACH OTHER, YOU WILL EVENTUALLY GET THERE.
"REMEMBER, YOU HAVE TOOLS! AND THOSE TOOLS ARE POWER!
ASK QUESTIONS AND LISTEN.
READ AND LOOK AT BOOKS!
LEARN LANGUAGE WITH A MIGRANT EDUCATIONAL TUTOR."
LANGUAGE IS POWER!

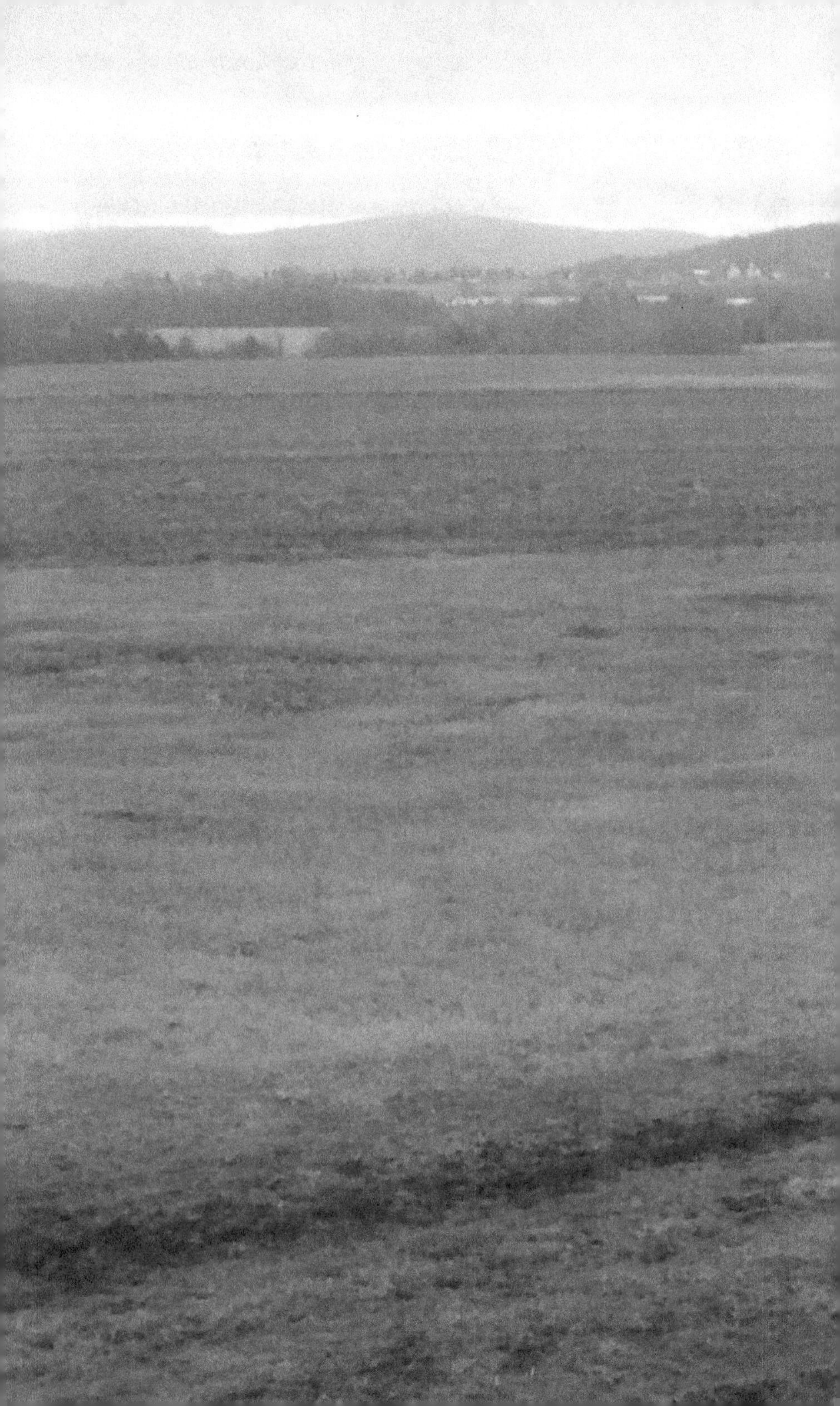

"EL VIAJE MÁS CARO" / "THE MOST COSTLY JOURNEY"

¿CÓMO EXPLICAS ESTO?

HOW DO YOU EXPLAIN THIS?

Historia por:
Story by: **Ana Teresa**

Historieta por:
Comics by: **Shashwat Mishra**

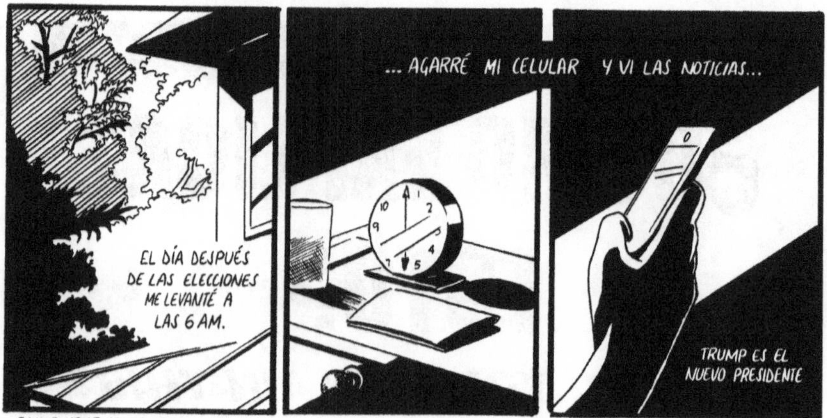
EL DÍA DESPUÉS DE LAS ELECCIONES ME LEVANTÉ A LAS 6 AM.
... AGARRÉ MI CELULAR Y VI LAS NOTICIAS...
TRUMP ES EL NUEVO PRESIDENTE

I WOKE UP AT 6AM THAT DAY... AFTER THE ELECTION.

... I PICKED UP MY PHONE AND SAW THE NEWS... TRUMP WAS PRESIDENT.

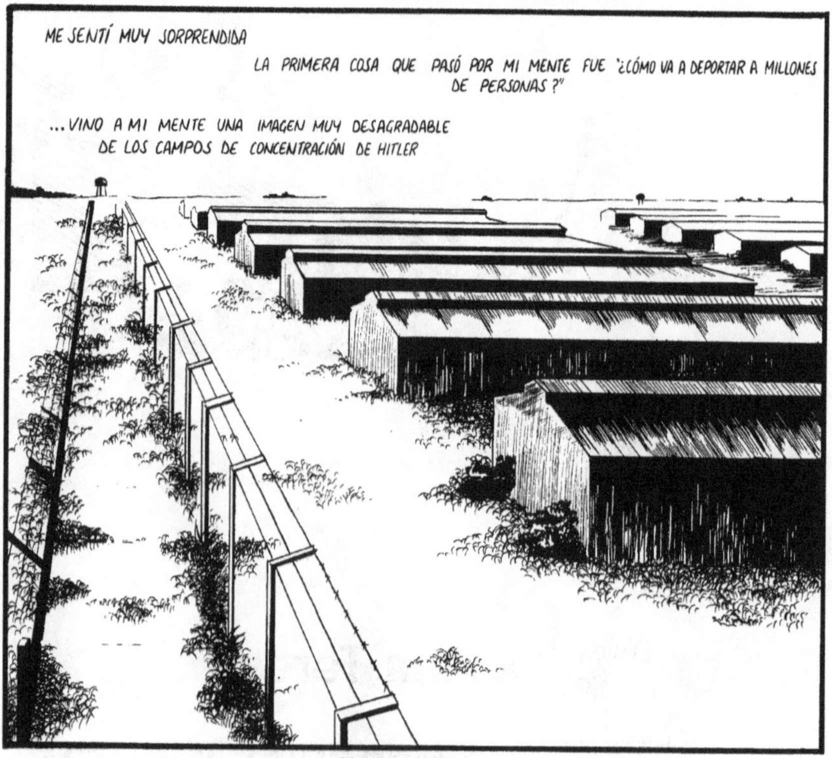
ME SENTÍ MUY SORPRENDIDA
LA PRIMERA COSA QUE PASÓ POR MI MENTE FUE "¿CÓMO VA A DEPORTAR A MILLONES DE PERSONAS?"
...VINO A MI MENTE UNA IMAGEN MUY DESAGRADABLE DE LOS CAMPOS DE CONCENTRACIÓN DE HITLER

I WAS IN SHOCK.
THE FIRST THING THAT CAME TO MY MIND WAS "HOW IS HE GOING TO DEPORT MILLIONS OF PEOPLE?"...
... THEN CAME AN IMAGE OF HITLER'S CONCENTRATION CAMPS.

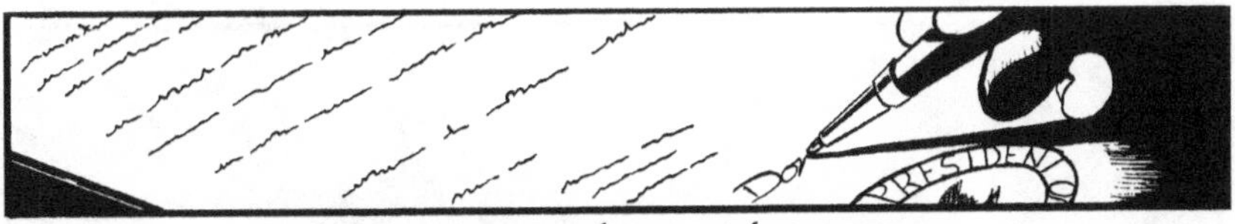

NOSOTROS NO SABEMOS QUÉ ES LO QUE ÉL PUEDE HACER.
WE DON'T KNOW WHAT HE CAN DO.

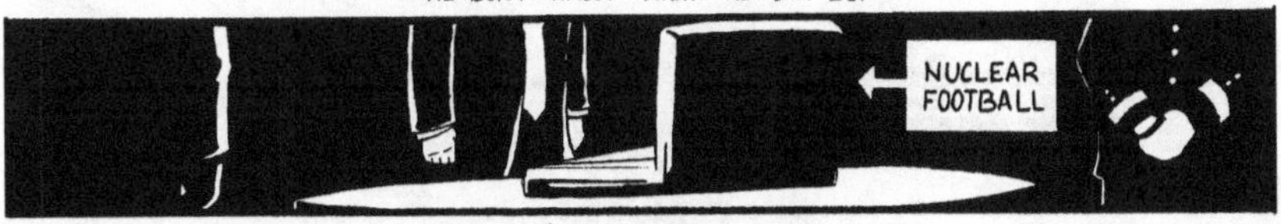
NUCLEAR FOOTBALL

... O LO QUE ÉL SEA CAPAZ DE HACER.
... WHAT HE'S CAPABLE OF DOING.

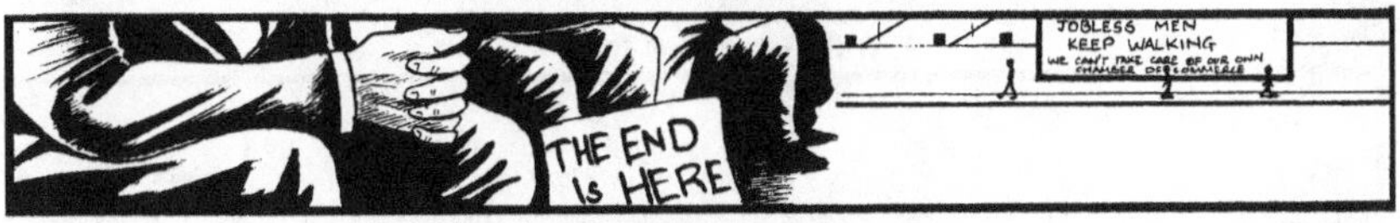
THE END Is HERE
JOBLESS MEN KEEP WALKING

ÉL DESPIERTA EMOCIONES EN LA GENTE.
HE STIRRED UP EMOTIONS IN PEOPLE.

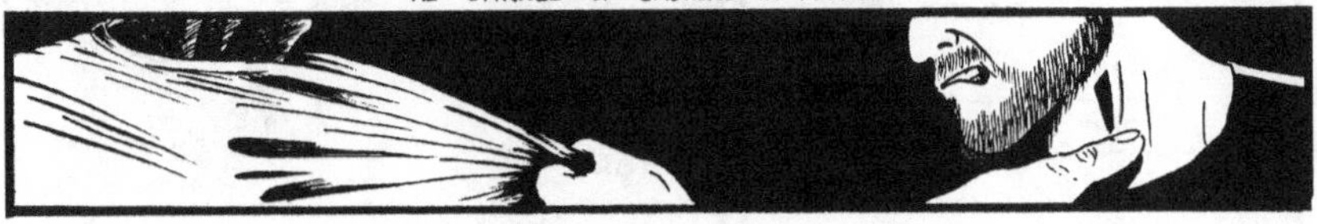

... LA GENTE QUE ODIA A OTRA GENTE.
... PEOPLE WHO HATE OTHER PEOPLE.

NOSOTROS VIVIMOS EN VT, ES UN ESTADO MUY BUENO PERO... NUNCA SABES SI LAS PERSONAS CON LAS QUE PLATICAS SON PARTIDARIAS DE TRUMP.
WE LIVE IN VT, IT'S A NICE STATE BUT... YOU DON'T KNOW IF THE PEOPLE YOU ARE TALKING TO ARE TRUMP SUPPORTERS

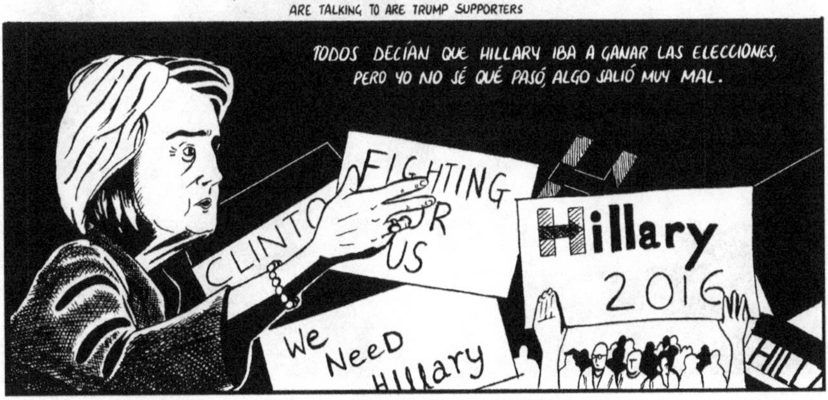
TODOS DECÍAN QUE HILLARY IBA A GANAR LAS ELECCIONES, PERO YO NO SÉ QUÉ PASÓ, ALGO SALIÓ MUY MAL.
Hillary 2016
We NeeD Hillary

EVERYBODY SAID HILLARY WAS GOING TO WIN BUT I DON'T KNOW WHAT HAPPENED... WHAT WENT WRONG...

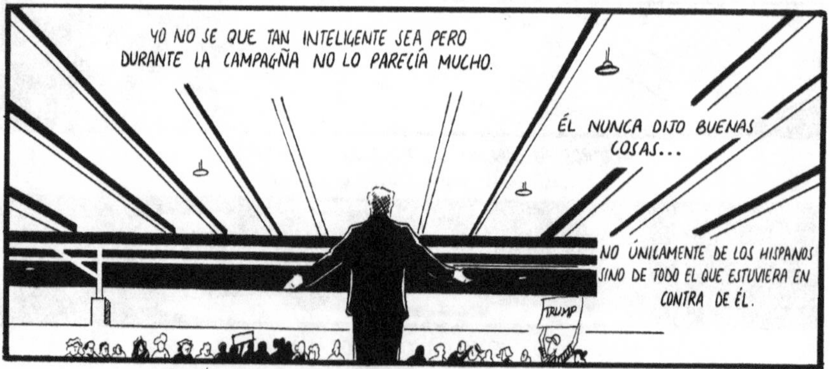
YO NO SE QUE TAN INTELIGENTE SEA PERO DURANTE LA CAMPAGÑA NO LO PARECÍA MUCHO.
ÉL NUNCA DIJO BUENAS COSAS...
NO ÚNICAMENTE DE LOS HISPANOS SINO DE TODO EL QUE ESTUVIERA EN CONTRA DE ÉL.
TRUMP

I DON'T KNOW HOW SMART HE IS BUT DURING THE CAMPAIGN HE DIDN'T SEEM THAT SMART.
HE WASN'T SAYING GOOD THINGS...
TO NOT JUST HISPANICS BUT TO EVERYBODY ELSE.

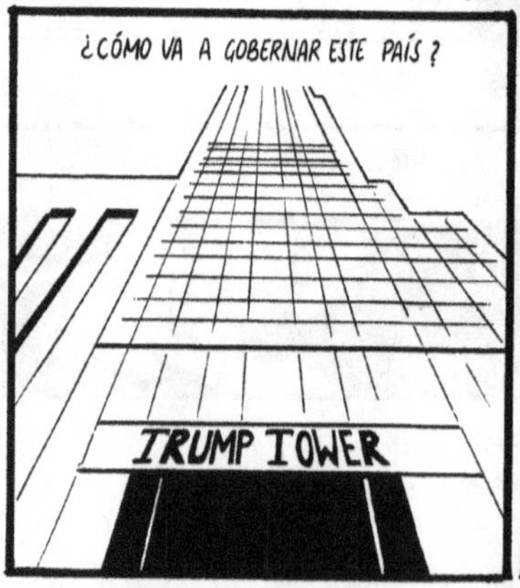
¿CÓMO VA A GOBERNAR ESTE PAÍS ?
TRUMP TOWER

HOW IS HE GOING TO RUN THIS COUNTRY?

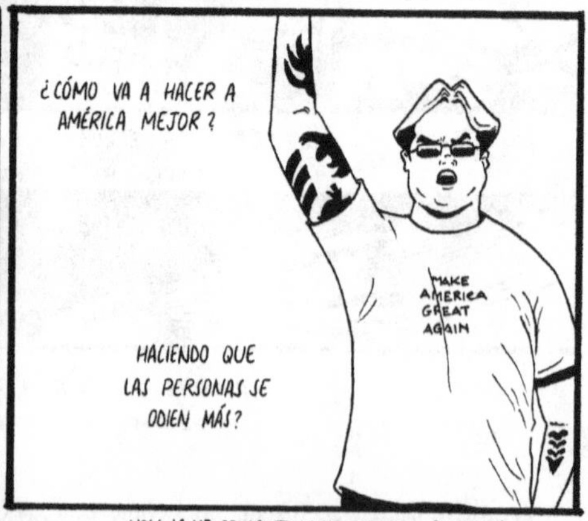
¿CÓMO VA A HACER A AMÉRICA MEJOR ?
HACIENDO QUE LAS PERSONAS SE ODIEN MÁS ?
MAKE AMERICA GREAT AGAIN

HOW IS HE GOING TO MAKE AMERICA BETTER?
BY MAKING PEOPLE ANGRY?

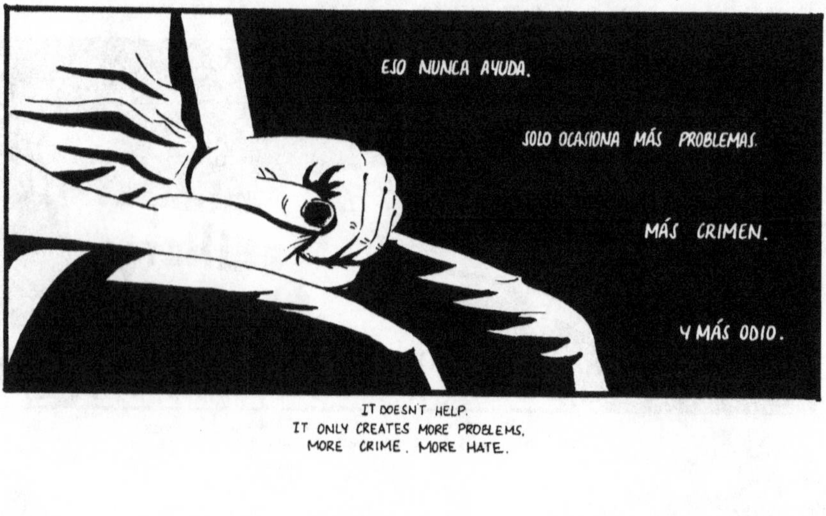
ESO NUNCA AYUDA.
SOLO OCASIONA MÁS PROBLEMAS.
MÁS CRIMEN.
Y MÁS ODIO.

IT DOESN'T HELP.
IT ONLY CREATES MORE PROBLEMS.
MORE CRIME. MORE HATE.

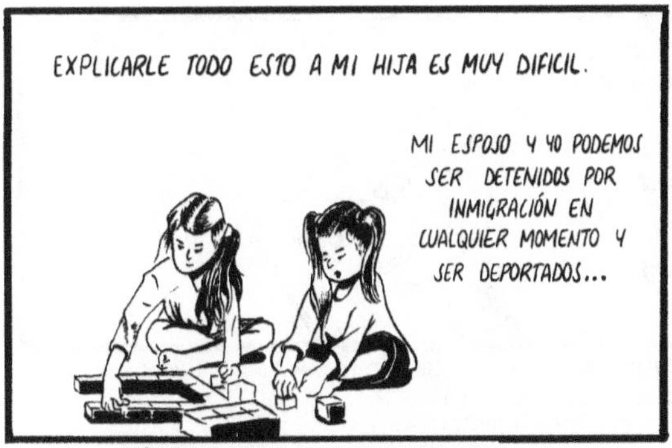
EXPLICARLE TODO ESTO A MI HIJA ES MUY DIFICIL.
MI ESPOSO Y YO PODEMOS SER DETENIDOS POR INMIGRACIÓN EN CUALQUIER MOMENTO Y SER DEPORTADOS...

EXPLAINING ALL THIS TO MY DAUGHTER IS VERY HARD.
MY HUSBAND AND I CAN BE DEPORTED OR CAUGHT BY IMMIGRATION AT ANY TIME...

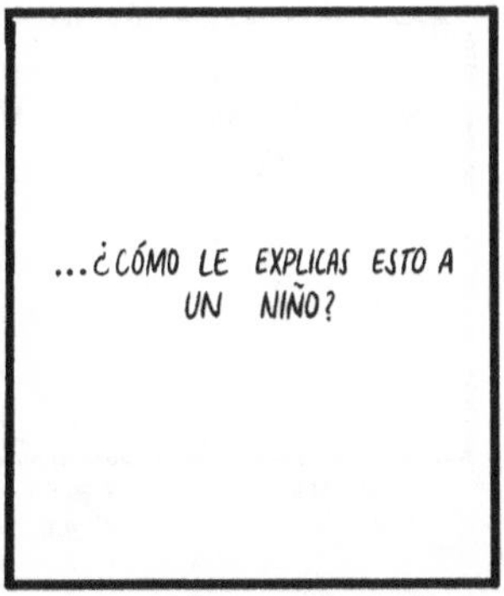
...¿CÓMO LE EXPLICAS ESTO A UN NIÑO?

...HOW DO YOU EXPLAIN THIS TO A KID?

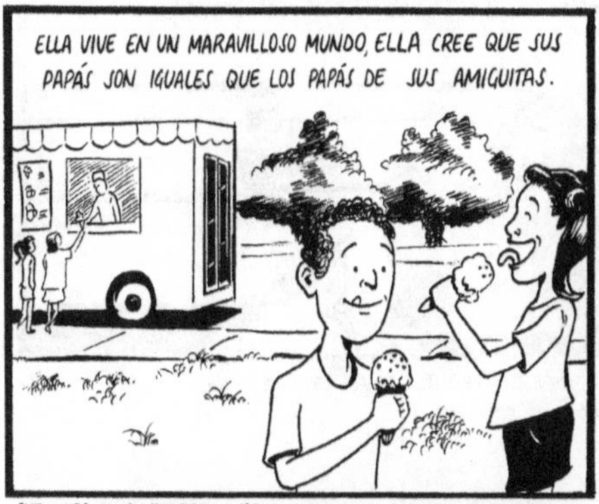
ELLA VIVE EN UN MARAVILLOSO MUNDO, ELLA CREE QUE SUS PAPÁS SON IGUALES QUE LOS PAPÁS DE SUS AMIGUITAS.

SHE LIVES IN A WONDERFUL WORLD. SHE THINKS PAPI AND MAMI ARE EQUAL AS HER FRIENDS' PARENTS.

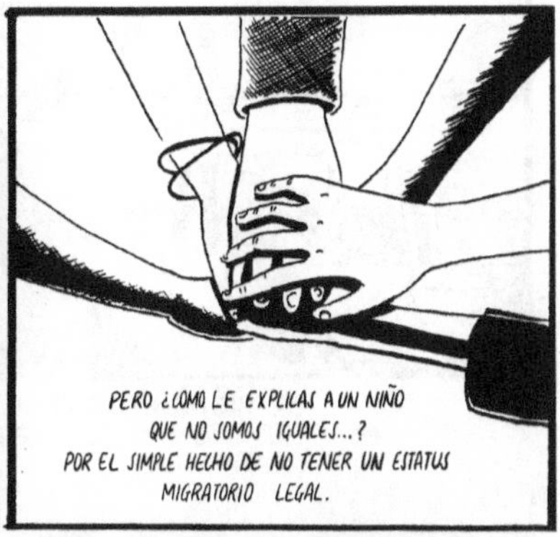
PERO ¿CÓMO LE EXPLICAS A UN NIÑO QUE NO SOMOS IGUALES...?
POR EL SIMPLE HECHO DE NO TENER UN ESTATUS MIGRATORIO LEGAL.

BUT HOW DO YOU TELL A KID THAT WE ARE NOT EQUAL...?
THAT WE ARE NOT THE SAME...?

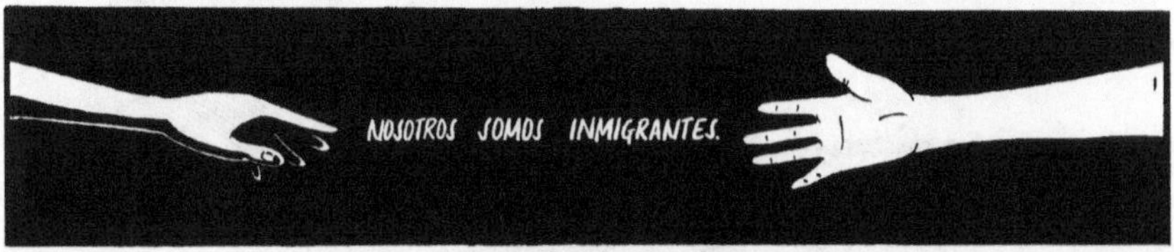
NOSOTROS SOMOS INMIGRANTES.

WE ARE IMMIGRANTS.

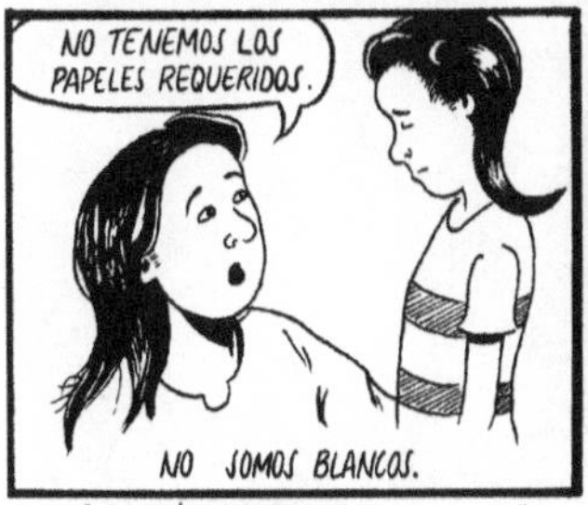
NO TENEMOS LOS PAPELES REQUERIDOS.
NO SOMOS BLANCOS.

"WE DON'T HAVE THE REQUIRED PAPERS."
WE ARE NOT WHITE.

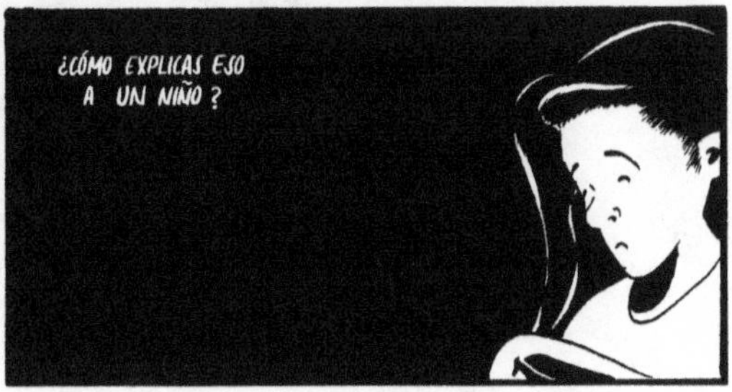
¿CÓMO EXPLICAS ESO A UN NIÑO?

HOW CAN YOU EXPLAIN THAT TO A KID?

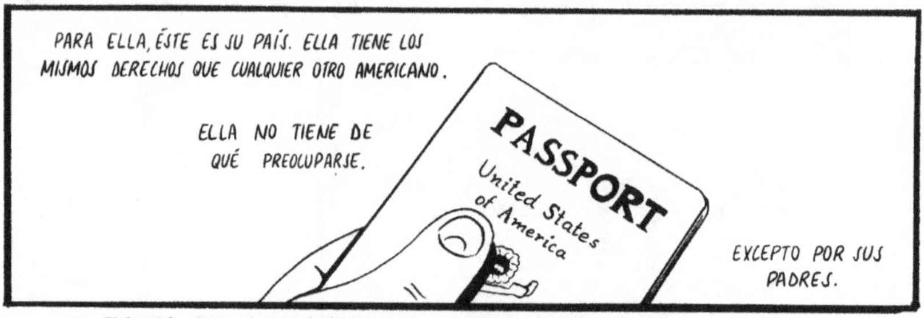
PARA ELLA, ÉSTE ES SU PAÍS. ELLA TIENE LOS MISMOS DERECHOS QUE CUALQUIER OTRO AMERICANO.
ELLA NO TIENE DE QUÉ PREOCUPARSE.
PASSPORT
United States of America
EXCEPTO POR SUS PADRES.

FOR HER, THIS IS HER COUNTRY, SHE HAS RIGHTS, LIKE OTHER AMERICAN CITIZENS.
SHE DOESN'T HAVE ANYTHING TO WORRY ABOUT.
EXCEPT FOR HER PARENTS.

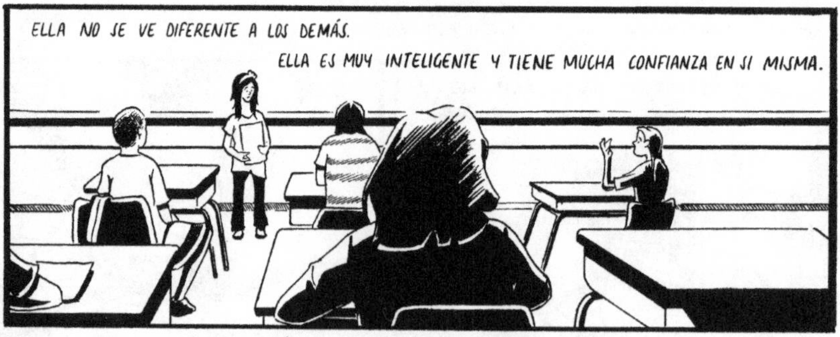
ELLA NO SE VE DIFERENTE A LOS DEMÁS.
ELLA ES MUY INTELIGENTE Y TIENE MUCHA CONFIANZA EN SI MISMA.

SHE DOESN'T SEE HERSELF ANY DIFFERENTLY THAN OTHERS.
SHE'S SMART AND CONFIDENT.

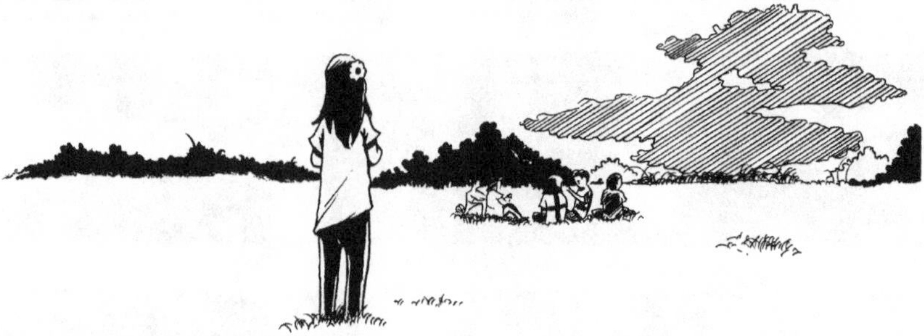

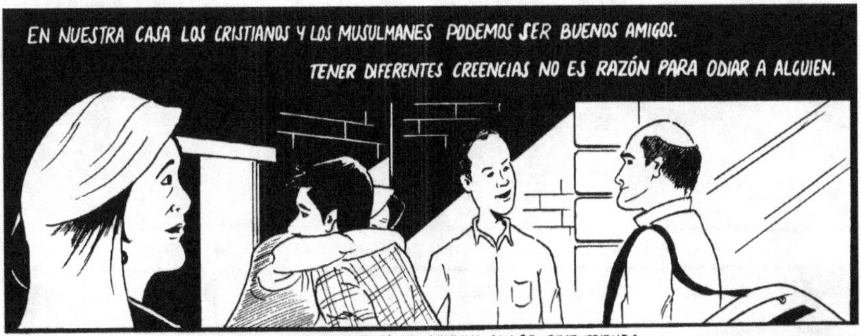
EN NUESTRA CASA LOS CRISTIANOS Y LOS MUSULMANES PODEMOS SER BUENOS AMIGOS.
TENER DIFERENTES CREENCIAS NO ES RAZÓN PARA ODIAR A ALGUIEN.

IN OUR HOUSE CHRISTIANS AND MUSLIMS CAN BE BEST FRIENDS.
HAVING DIFFERENT BELIEFS IS NO REASON TO HATE SOMEBODY.

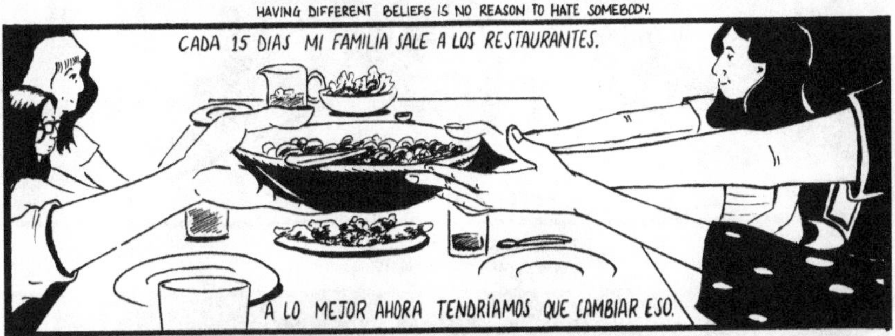
CADA 15 DIAS MI FAMILIA SALE A LOS RESTAURANTES.
A LO MEJOR AHORA TENDRÍAMOS QUE CAMBIAR ESO.

EVERY OTHER SATURDAY OUR FAMILY GOES ON OUTINGS, OR TO RESTAURANTS.
MAYBE NOW WE'LL HAVE TO CHANGE THAT.

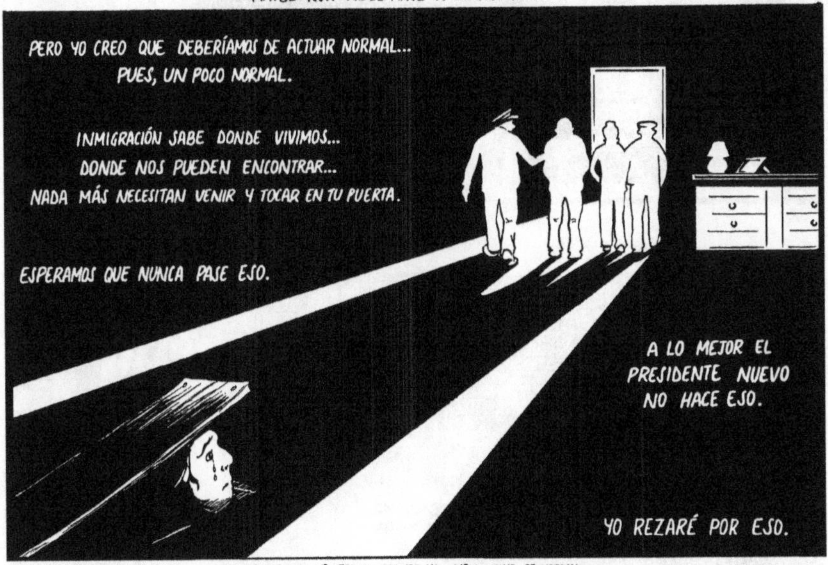
PERO YO CREO QUE DEBERÍAMOS DE ACTUAR NORMAL... PUES, UN POCO NORMAL.
INMIGRACIÓN SABE DONDE VIVIMOS... DONDE NOS PUEDEN ENCONTRAR... NADA MÁS NECESITAN VENIR Y TOCAR EN TU PUERTA.
ESPERAMOS QUE NUNCA PASE ESO.
A LO MEJOR EL PRESIDENTE NUEVO NO HACE ESO.
YO REZARÉ POR ESO.

BUT I FEEL WE NEED TO STAY NORMAL... WELL, KIND OF NORMAL.
IMMIGRATION KNOWS WHERE WE LIVE... WHERE TO FIND US... THEY'LL JUST COME KNOCKING.
WE HOPE THAT NEVER HAPPENS.
MAYBE THE NEW PRESIDENT WON'T DO THAT. MAYBE HE'LL CHANGE.
I'LL PRAY FOR THAT.

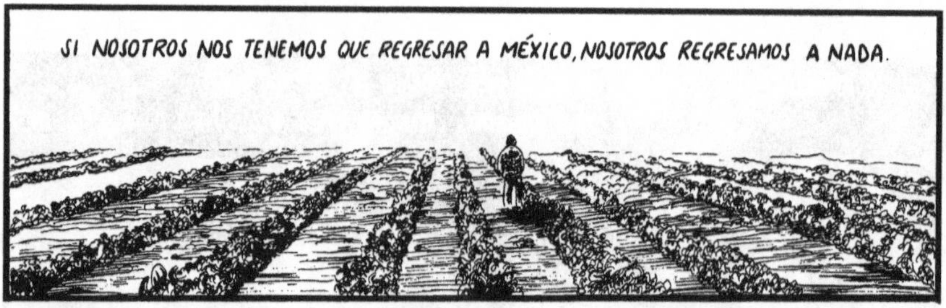
SI NOSOTROS NOS TENEMOS QUE REGRESAR A MÉXICO, NOSOTROS REGRESAMOS A NADA.

IF WE **HAVE** TO GO BACK TO MEXICO THEN WE GO BACK TO NOTHING.

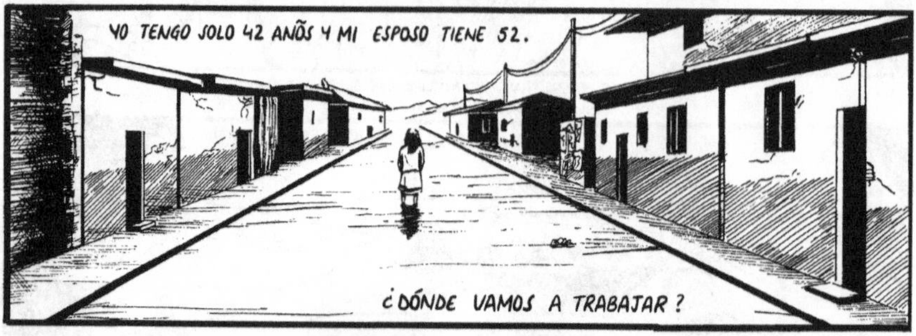
YO TENGO SOLO 42 AÑOS Y MI ESPOSO TIENE 52.
¿DÓNDE VAMOS A TRABAJAR?

I AM 42 YEARS OLD, MY HUSBAND IS 52.
WHERE ARE WE GOING TO WORK?

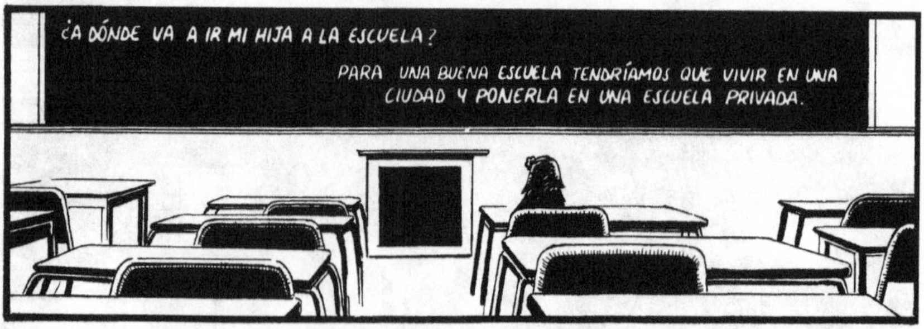
¿A DÓNDE VA A IR MI HIJA A LA ESCUELA?
PARA UNA BUENA ESCUELA TENDRÍAMOS QUE VIVIR EN UNA CIUDAD Y PONERLA EN UNA ESCUELA PRIVADA.

WHERE WILL MY DAUGHTER GO TO SCHOOL?
FOR A GOOD SCHOOL WE HAVE TO LIVE IN THE CITY, ENROLL HER IN A PRIVATE SCHOOL.

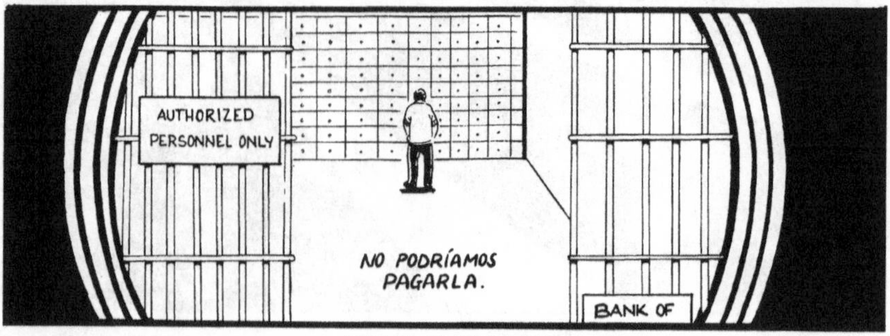
AUTHORIZED PERSONNEL ONLY
NO PODRÍAMOS PAGARLA.
BANK OF

HOW WILL WE PAY FOR THAT?

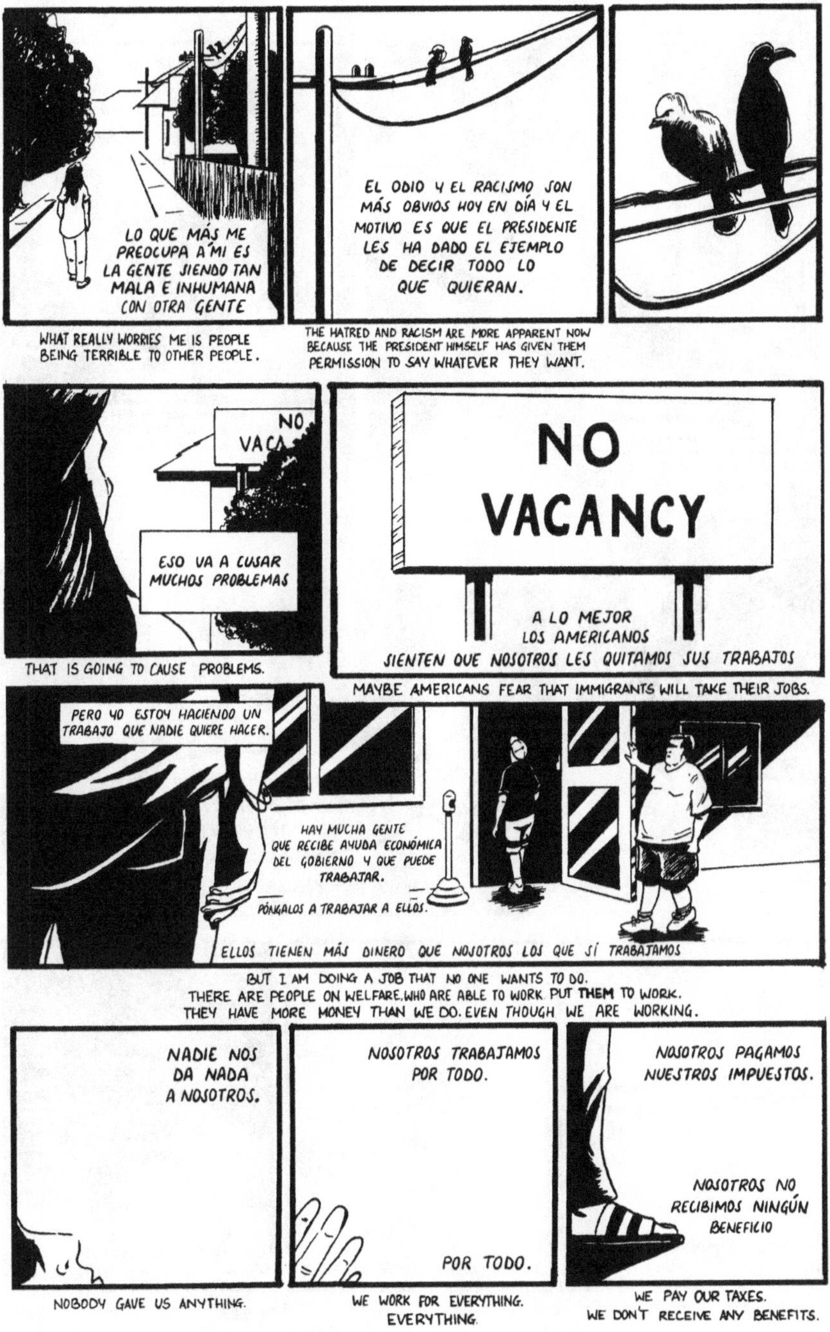
LO QUE MÁS ME PREOCUPA A MÍ ES LA GENTE SIENDO TAN MALA E INHUMANA CON OTRA GENTE
WHAT REALLY WORRIES ME IS PEOPLE BEING TERRIBLE TO OTHER PEOPLE.
EL ODIO Y EL RACISMO SON MÁS OBVIOS HOY EN DÍA Y EL MOTIVO ES QUE EL PRESIDENTE LES HA DADO EL EJEMPLO DE DECIR TODO LO QUE QUIERAN.
THE HATRED AND RACISM ARE MORE APPARENT NOW BECAUSE THE PRESIDENT HIMSELF HAS GIVEN THEM PERMISSION TO SAY WHATEVER THEY WANT.
NO VACA
ESO VA A CUSAR MUCHOS PROBLEMAS
THAT IS GOING TO CAUSE PROBLEMS.
NO VACANCY
A LO MEJOR LOS AMERICANOS SIENTEN QUE NOSOTROS LES QUITAMOS SUS TRABAJOS
MAYBE AMERICANS FEAR THAT IMMIGRANTS WILL TAKE THEIR JOBS.
PERO YO ESTOY HACIENDO UN TRABAJO QUE NADIE QUIERE HACER.
HAY MUCHA GENTE QUE RECIBE AYUDA ECONÓMICA DEL GOBIERNO Y QUE PUEDE TRABAJAR.
PÓNGALOS A TRABAJAR A ELLOS.
ELLOS TIENEN MÁS DINERO QUE NOSOTROS LOS QUE SÍ TRABAJAMOS
BUT I AM DOING A JOB THAT NO ONE WANTS TO DO.
THERE ARE PEOPLE ON WELFARE, WHO ARE ABLE TO WORK PUT THEM TO WORK.
THEY HAVE MORE MONEY THAN WE DO. EVEN THOUGH WE ARE WORKING.
NADIE NOS DA NADA A NOSOTROS.
NOBODY GAVE US ANYTHING.
NOSOTROS TRABAJAMOS POR TODO.
POR TODO.
WE WORK FOR EVERYTHING.
EVERYTHING.
NOSOTROS PAGAMOS NUESTROS IMPUESTOS.
NOSOTROS NO RECIBIMOS NINGÚN BENEFICIO
WE PAY OUR TAXES.
WE DON'T RECEIVE ANY BENEFITS.

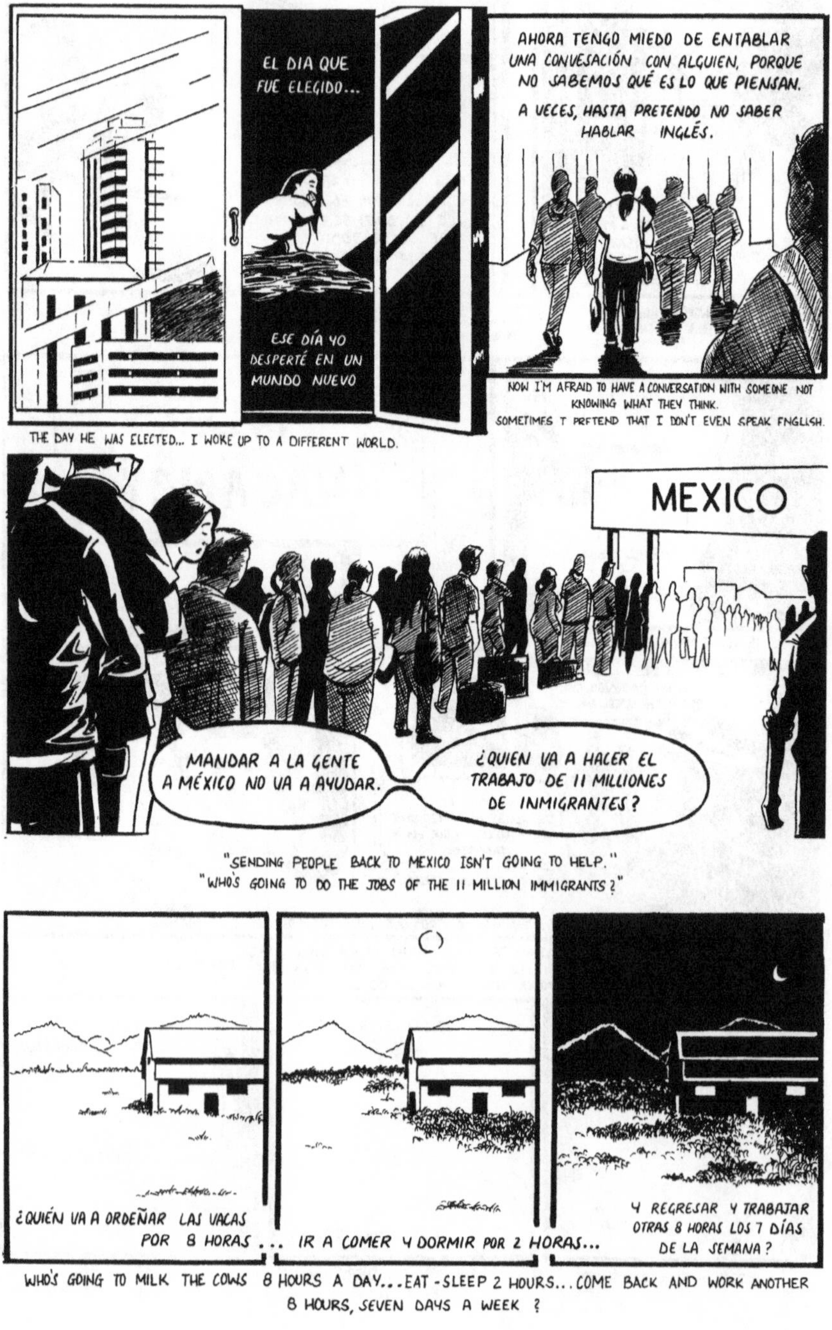
EL DIA QUE FUE ELEGIDO...
ESE DÍA YO DESPERTÉ EN UN MUNDO NUEVO
THE DAY HE WAS ELECTED... I WOKE UP TO A DIFFERENT WORLD.
AHORA TENGO MIEDO DE ENTABLAR UNA CONVESACIÓN CON ALGUIEN, PORQUE NO SABEMOS QUÉ ES LO QUE PIENSAN.
A VECES, HASTA PRETENDO NO SABER HABLAR INGLÉS.
NOW I'M AFRAID TO HAVE A CONVERSATION WITH SOMEONE NOT KNOWING WHAT THEY THINK.
SOMETIMES I PRETEND THAT I DON'T EVEN SPEAK ENGLISH.
MEXICO
MANDAR A LA GENTE A MÉXICO NO VA A AYUDAR.
¿QUIEN VA A HACER EL TRABAJO DE 11 MILLIONES DE INMIGRANTES?
"SENDING PEOPLE BACK TO MEXICO ISN'T GOING TO HELP."
"WHO'S GOING TO DO THE JOBS OF THE 11 MILLION IMMIGRANTS?"
¿QUIÉN VA A ORDEÑAR LAS VACAS POR 8 HORAS ...
IR A COMER Y DORMIR POR 2 HORAS...
Y REGRESAR Y TRABAJAR OTRAS 8 HORAS LOS 7 DÍAS DE LA SEMANA?
WHO'S GOING TO MILK THE COWS 8 HOURS A DAY... EAT-SLEEP 2 HOURS... COME BACK AND WORK ANOTHER 8 HOURS, SEVEN DAYS A WEEK?

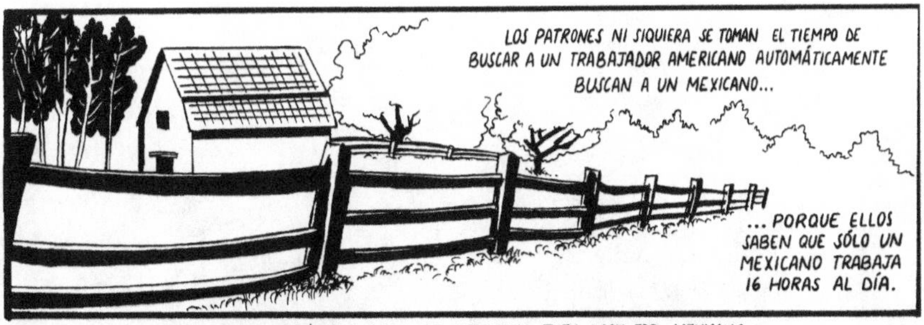
LOS PATRONES NI SIQUIERA SE TOMAN EL TIEMPO DE BUSCAR A UN TRABAJADOR AMERICANO AUTOMÁTICAMENTE BUSCAN A UN MEXICANO...
... PORQUE ELLOS SABEN QUE SÓLO UN MEXICANO TRABAJA 16 HORAS AL DÍA.

THE BOSSES DON'T EVEN LOOK FOR AMERICANS, THEY LOOK FOR MEXICANS...
...BECAUSE THEY KNOW ONLY MEXICANS WILL WORK 16 HOURS A DAY.

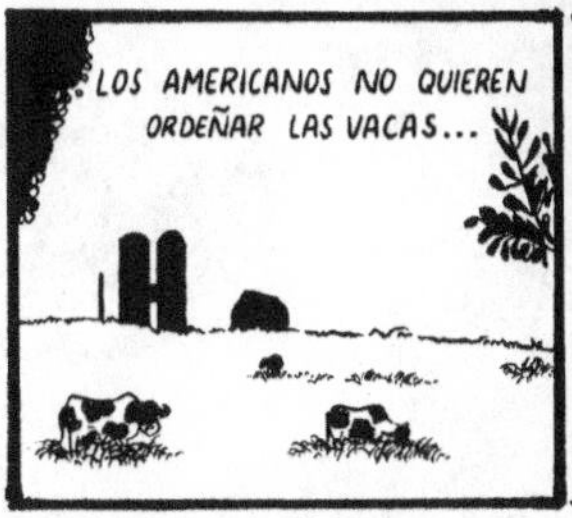
LOS AMERICANOS NO QUIEREN ORDEÑAR LAS VACAS...

NO AMERICAN WANTS TO MILK COWS...

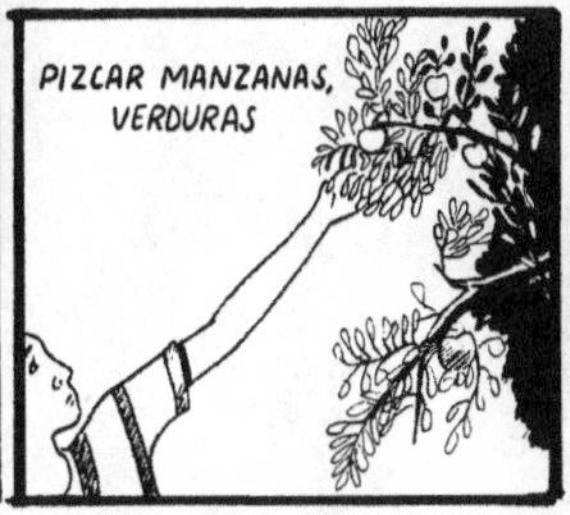
PIZCAR MANZANAS, VERDURAS

PICK APPLES, VEGETABLES.

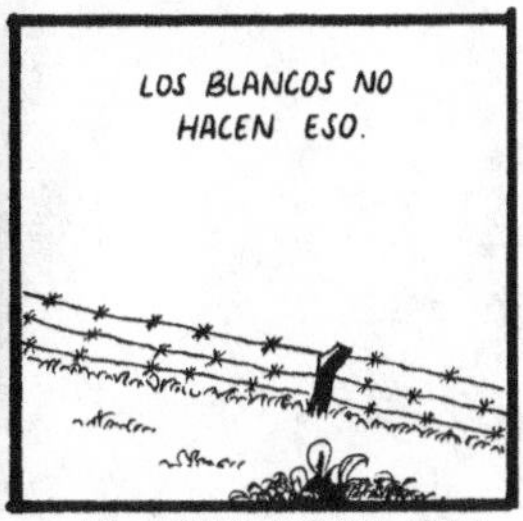
LOS BLANCOS NO HACEN ESO.

NO WHITES DO THOSE JOBS.

SI NOSOTROS VAMOS A SUFRIR, TAMBIÉN LOS BLANCOS PORQUE NO VAN A HACER EL TRABAJO.

IF WE ARE GOING TO SUFFER THEN SO WILL THE WHITE PEOPLE BECAUSE NO ONE'S GOING TO DO THOSE JOBS.

ESTE PAÍS DESAPARECERÍA.

THIS COUNTRY WILL DISAPPEAR.

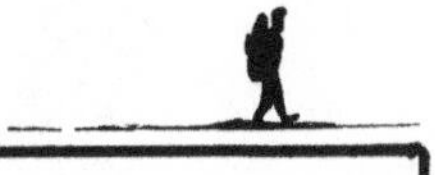

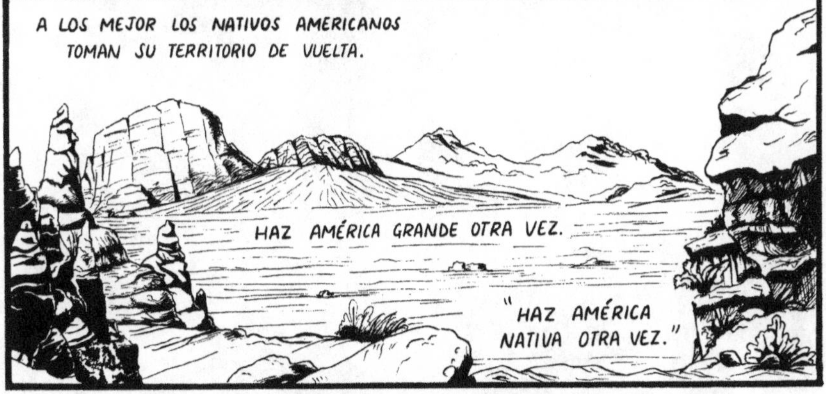
A LOS MEJOR LOS NATIVOS AMERICANOS TOMAN SU TERRITORIO DE VUELTA.
HAZ AMÉRICA GRANDE OTRA VEZ.
"HAZ AMÉRICA NATIVA OTRA VEZ."

MAYBE THE NATIVE AMERICANS WILL TAKE THEIR TERRITORY BACK.
MAKE THIS COUNTRY GREAT AGAIN.
"MAKE AMERICA NATIVE AGAIN."

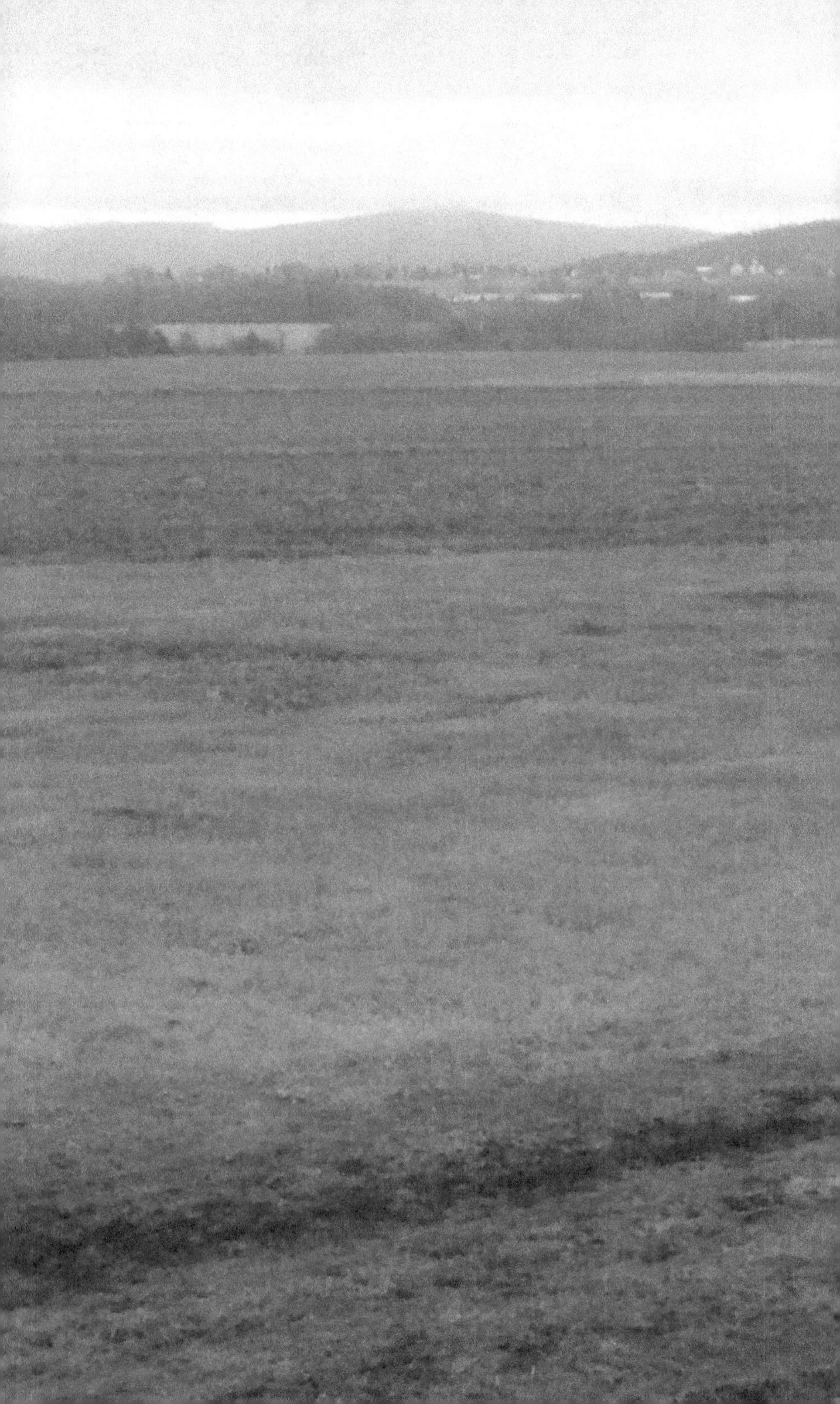

"EL VIAJE MAS CARO" / "THE MOST COSTLY JOURNEY" presents:

THE SCHOOL OF LIFE

The Story of Ponciano
Art by Michelle Sayles

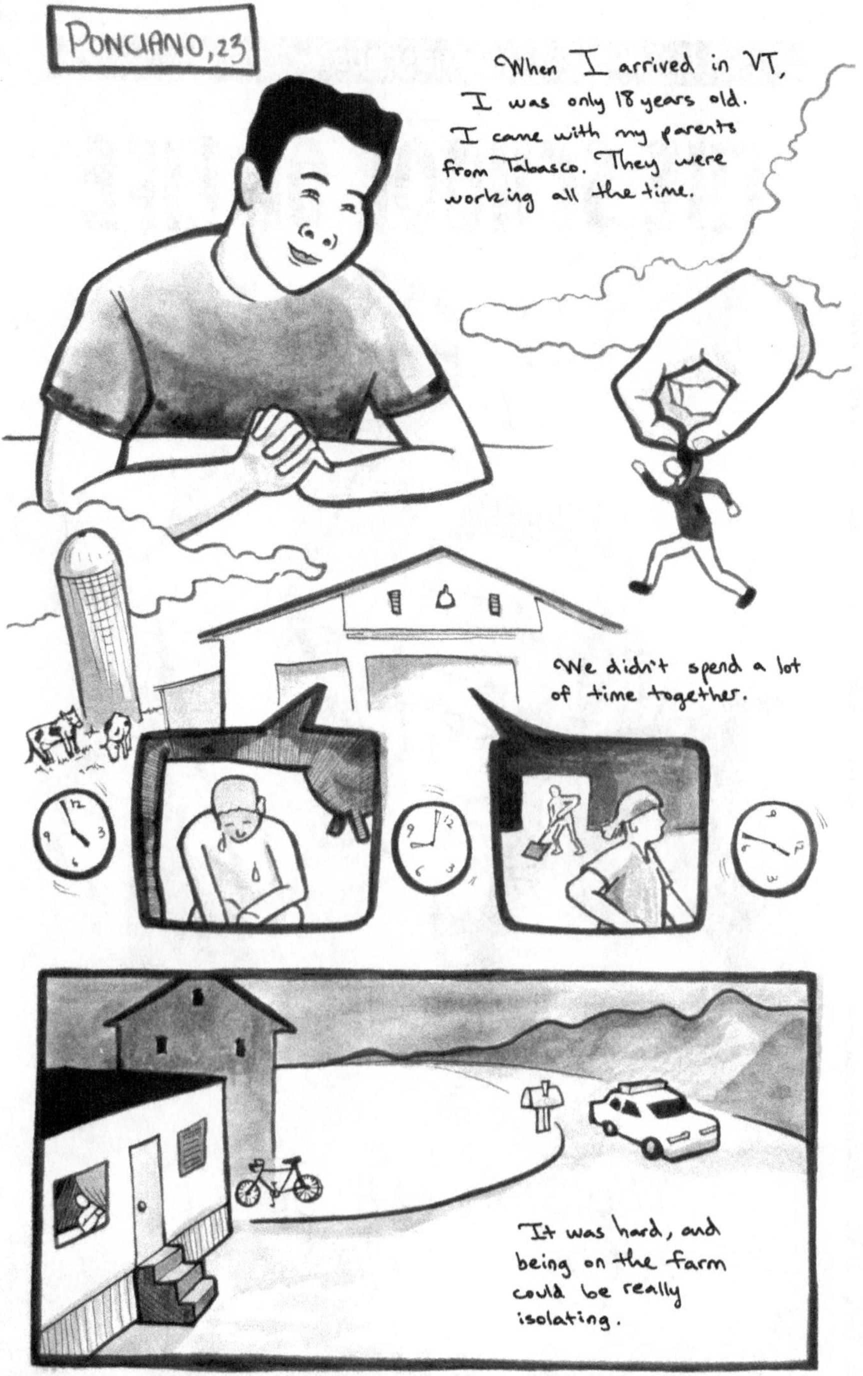
PONCIANO, 23
When I arrived in VT, I was only 18 years old. I came with my parents from Tabasco. They were working all the time.
We didn't spend a lot of time together.
It was hard, and being on the farm could be really isolating.

I come from a community that is fairly marginalized. Tabasco- like Vermont - is far from big cities, meaning less access to health care and education.

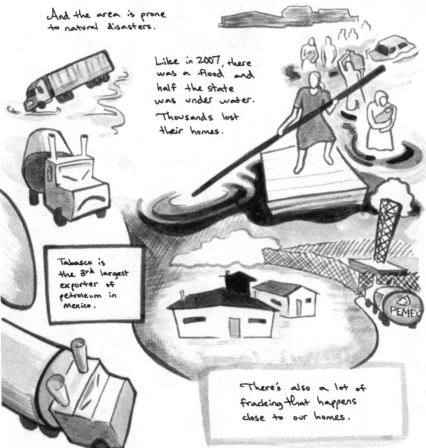

And the area is prone to natural disasters.

Like in 2007, there was a flood and half the state was under water.

Thousands lost their homes.

Tabasco is the 3rd largest exporter of petroleum in Mexico.

There's also a lot of fracking that happens close to our homes.

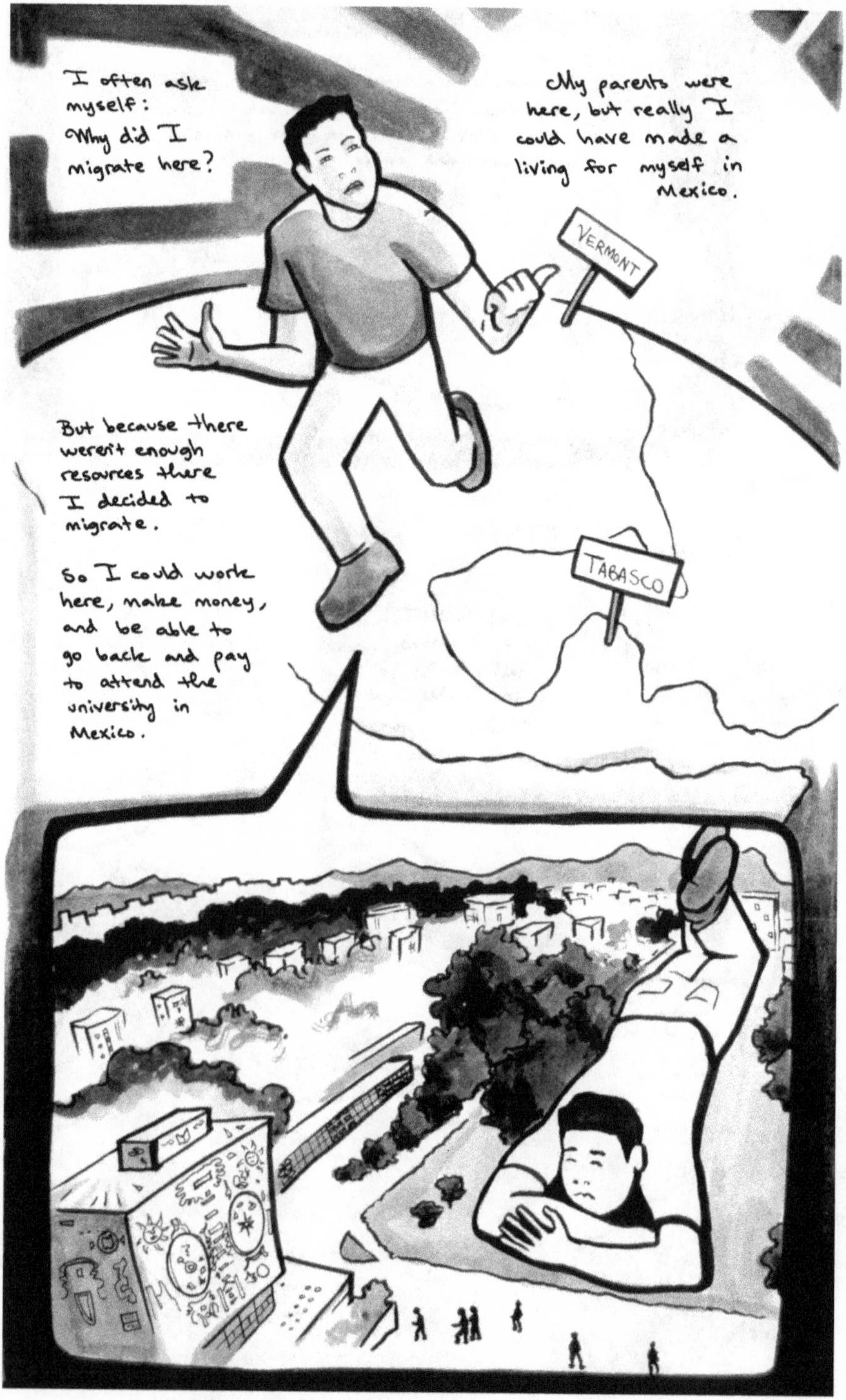
I often ask myself:
Why did I migrate here?
My parents were here, but really I could have made a living for myself in Mexico.
VERMONT
TABASCO
But because there weren't enough resources there I decided to migrate.
So I could work here, make money, and be able to go back and pay to attend the university in Mexico.

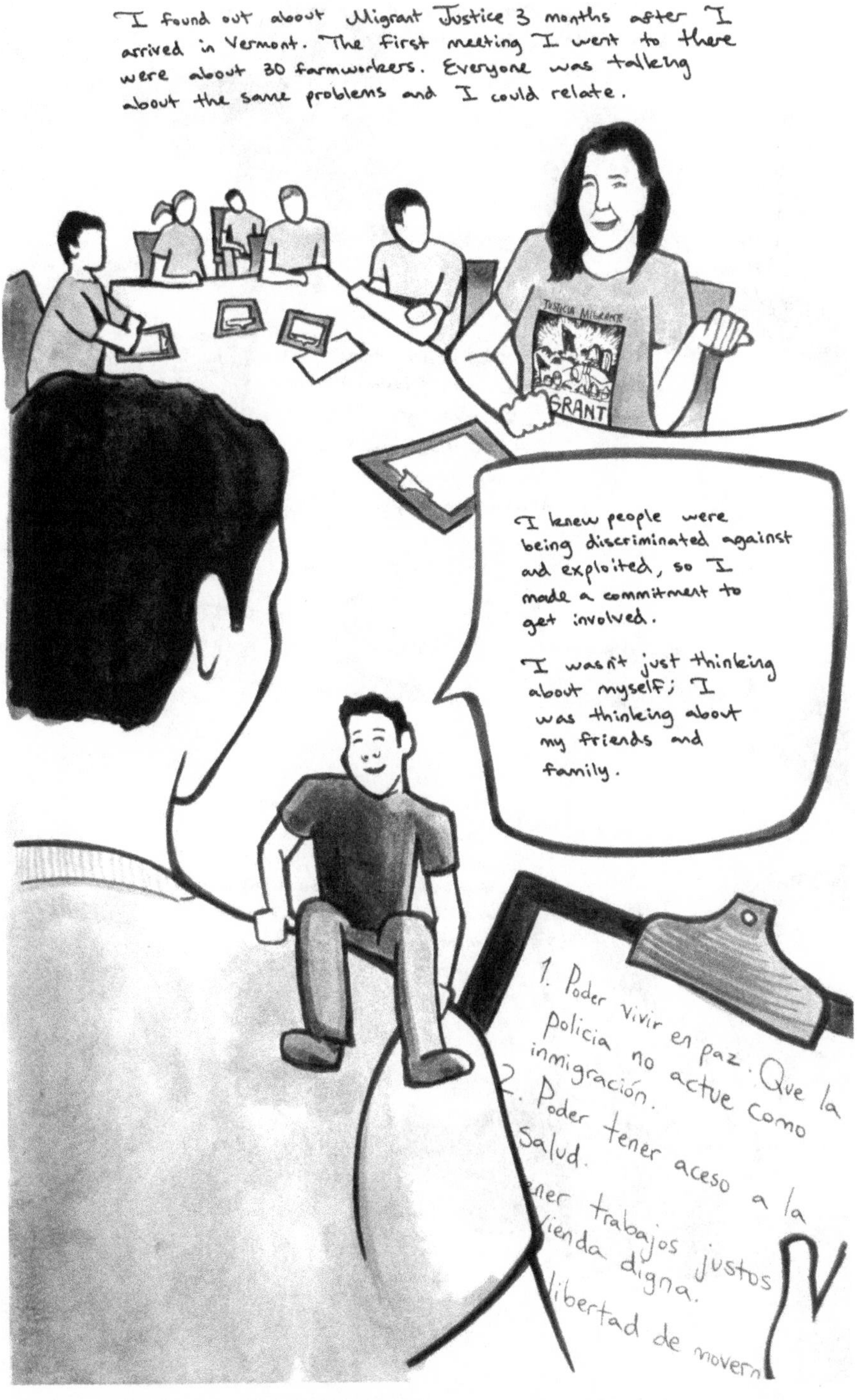
I found out about Migrant Justice 3 months after I arrived in Vermont. The first meeting I went to there were about 30 farmworkers. Everyone was talking about the same problems and I could relate.
I knew people were being discriminated against and exploited, so I made a commitment to get involved.
I wasn't just thinking about myself; I was thinking about my friends and family.
1. Poder vivir en paz. Que la policia no actue como inmigración.
2. Poder tener aceso a la salud.
ener trabajos justos
ienda digna.
libertad de movern

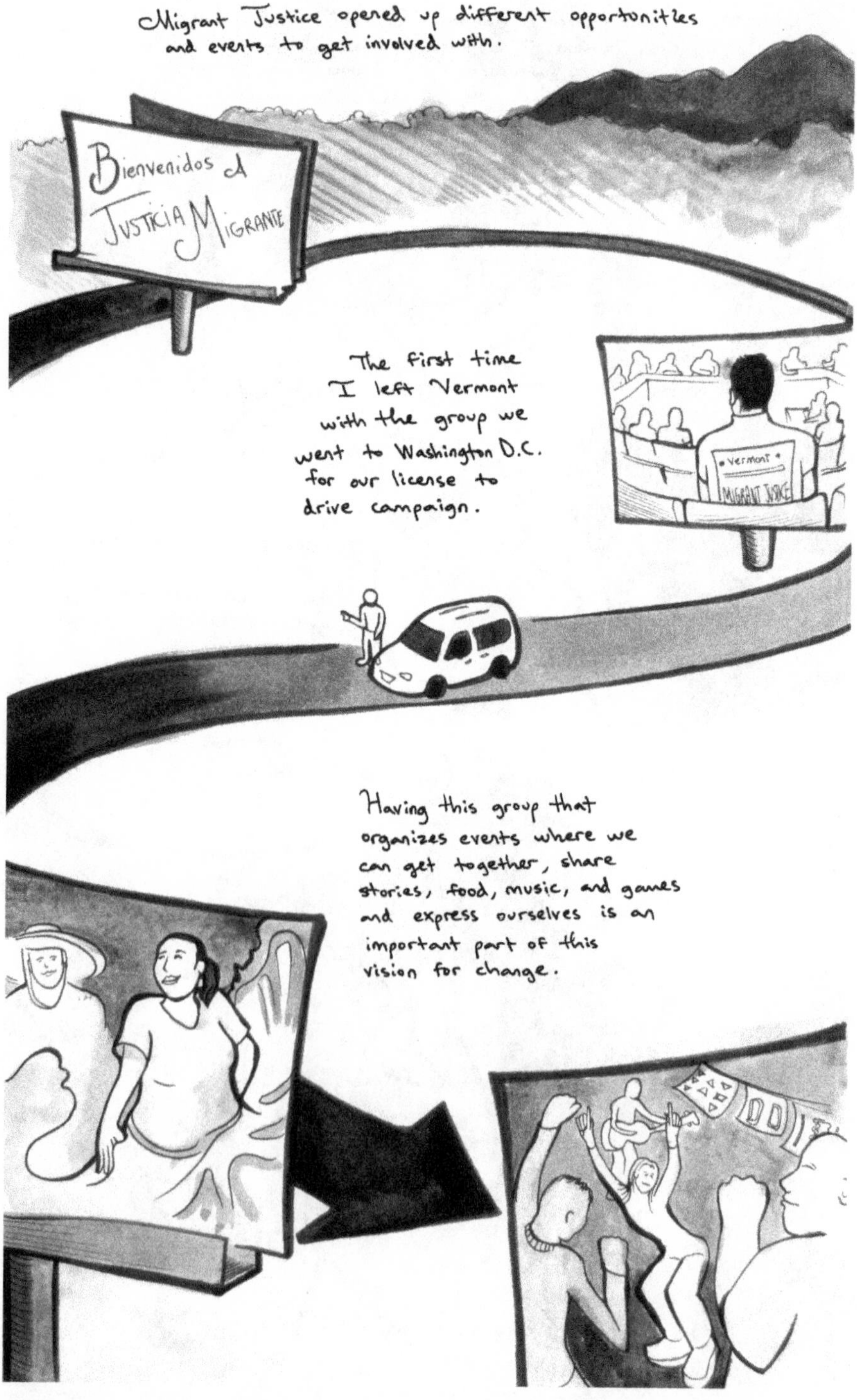

Migrant Justice opened up different opportunities and events to get involved with.
Bienvenidos a Justicia Migrante
The first time I left Vermont with the group we went to Washington D.C. for our license to drive campaign.
Vermont
Migrant Justice
Having this group that organizes events where we can get together, share stories, food, music, and games and express ourselves is an important part of this vision for change.

With the Milk With Dignity program, we follow a model that gives a voice to the worker that has never been recognized.

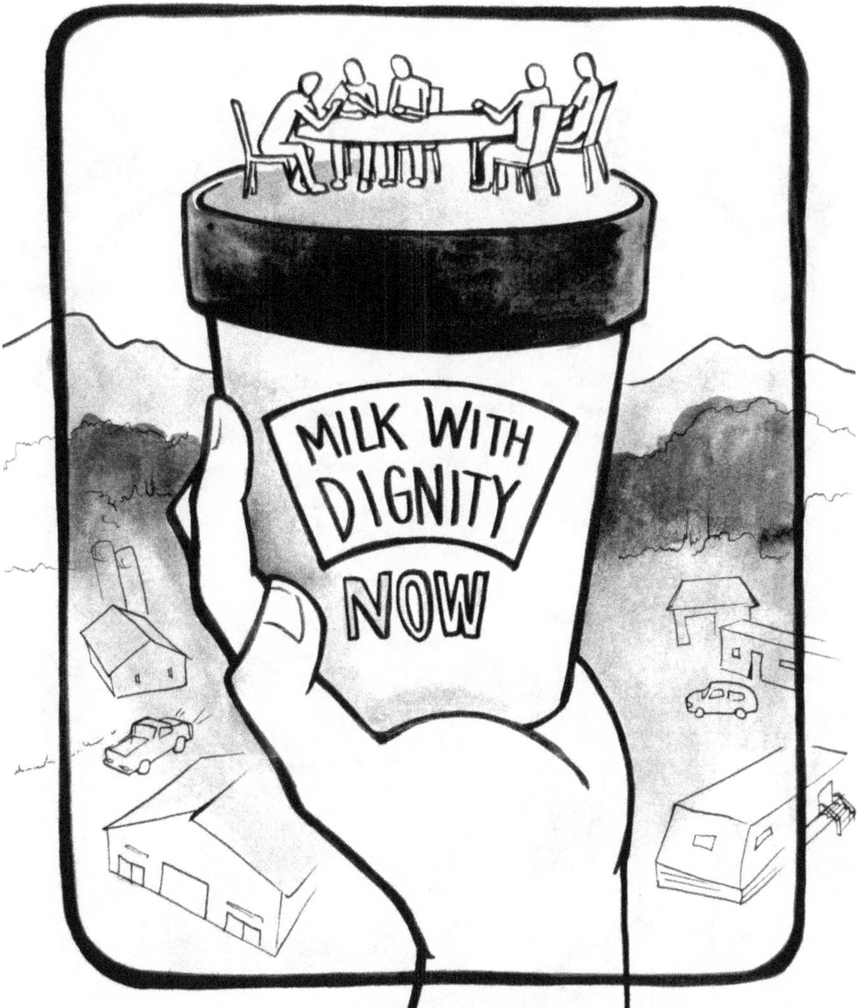
MILK WITH
DIGNITY
NOW

There are over 1500 dairy workers in Vermont and it's really our hands, our work, that sustains the industry.

When I started participating with Migrant Justice I began learning about the reasons people were migrating and the connections between migrant workers and these systems.

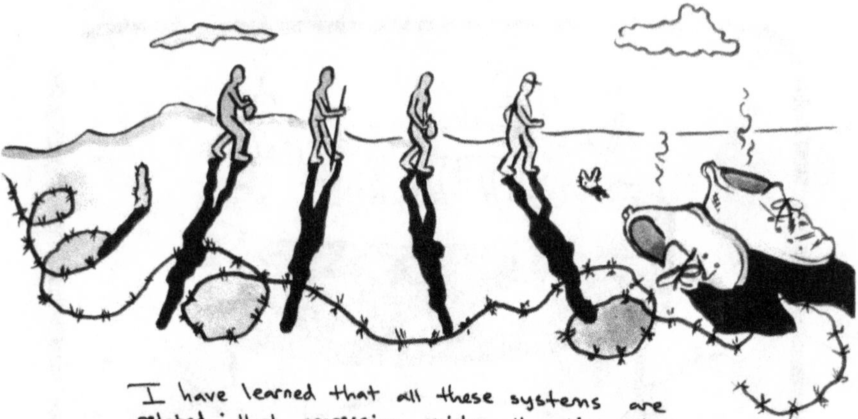

I have learned that all these systems are related: that oppression exists, the idea that the rich have power, the exploitation of labor, and also how immigration is caused by a lot of these issues.

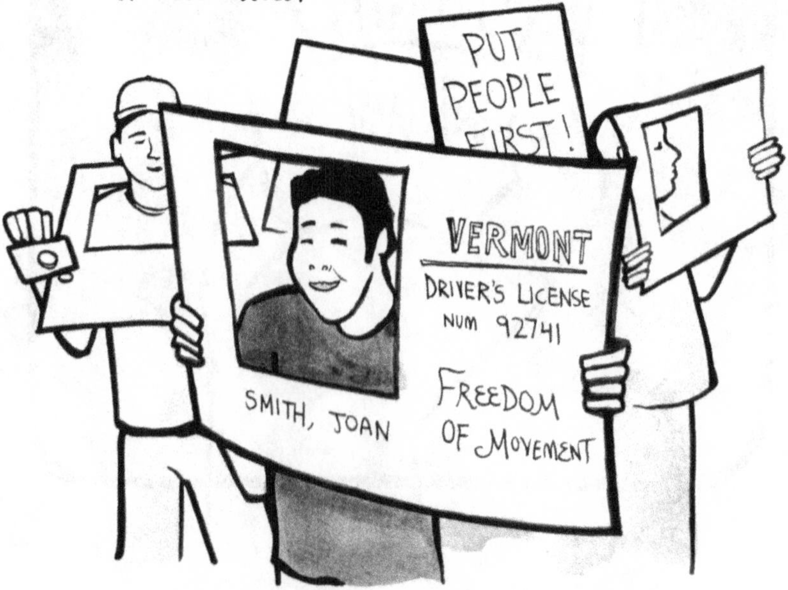
PUT PEOPLE FIRST!
VERMONT
DRIVER'S LICENSE
NUM 92741
FREEDOM OF MOVEMENT
SMITH, JOAN

Migrant Justice is like the "School of Life" because the things I learned here I would not have learned as easily in school.

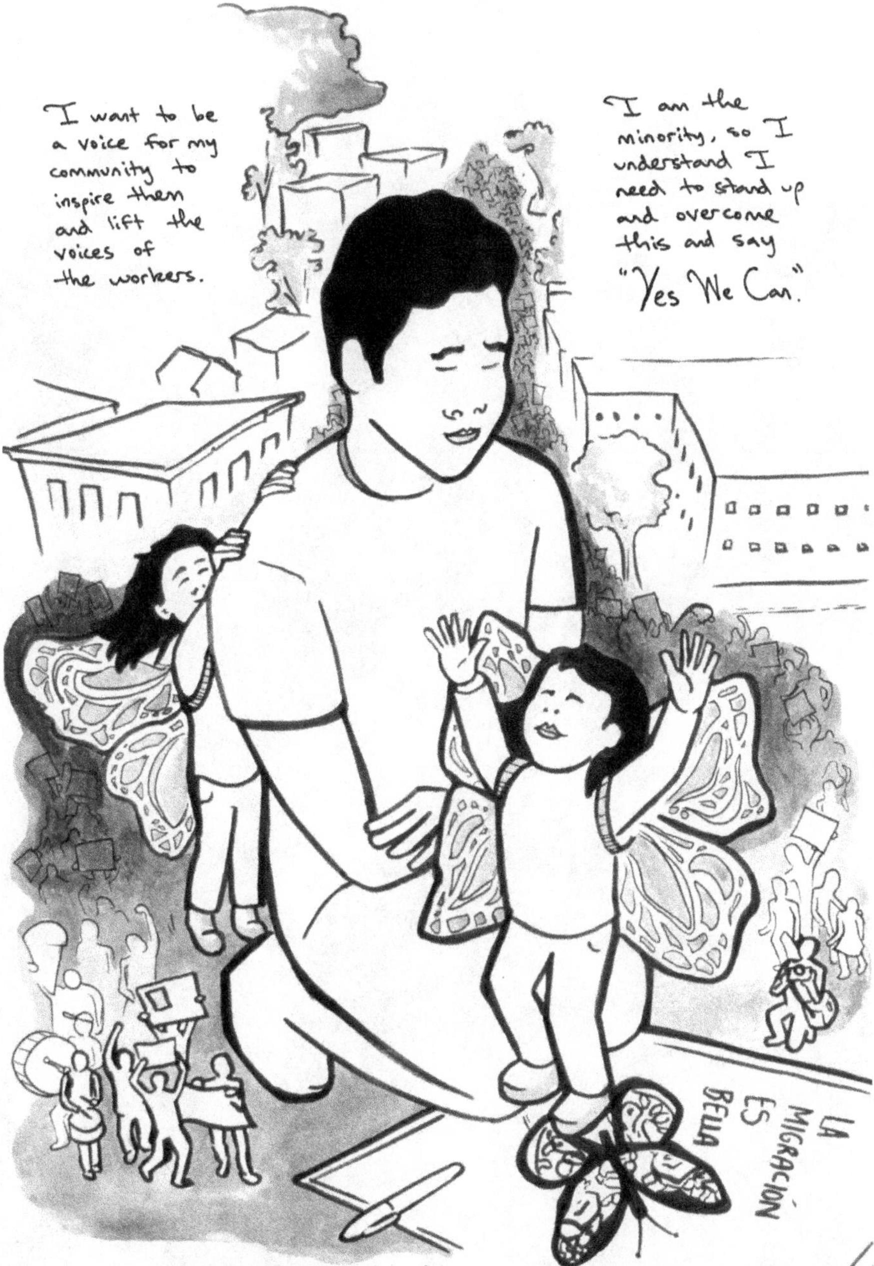
I want to be a voice for my community to inspire them and lift the voices of the workers.
I am the minority, so I understand I need to stand up and overcome this and say "Yes We Can".
LA MIGRACIÓN ES BELLA
Migrant Justice is the voice of the community, and together, little by little, we are creating a new day.

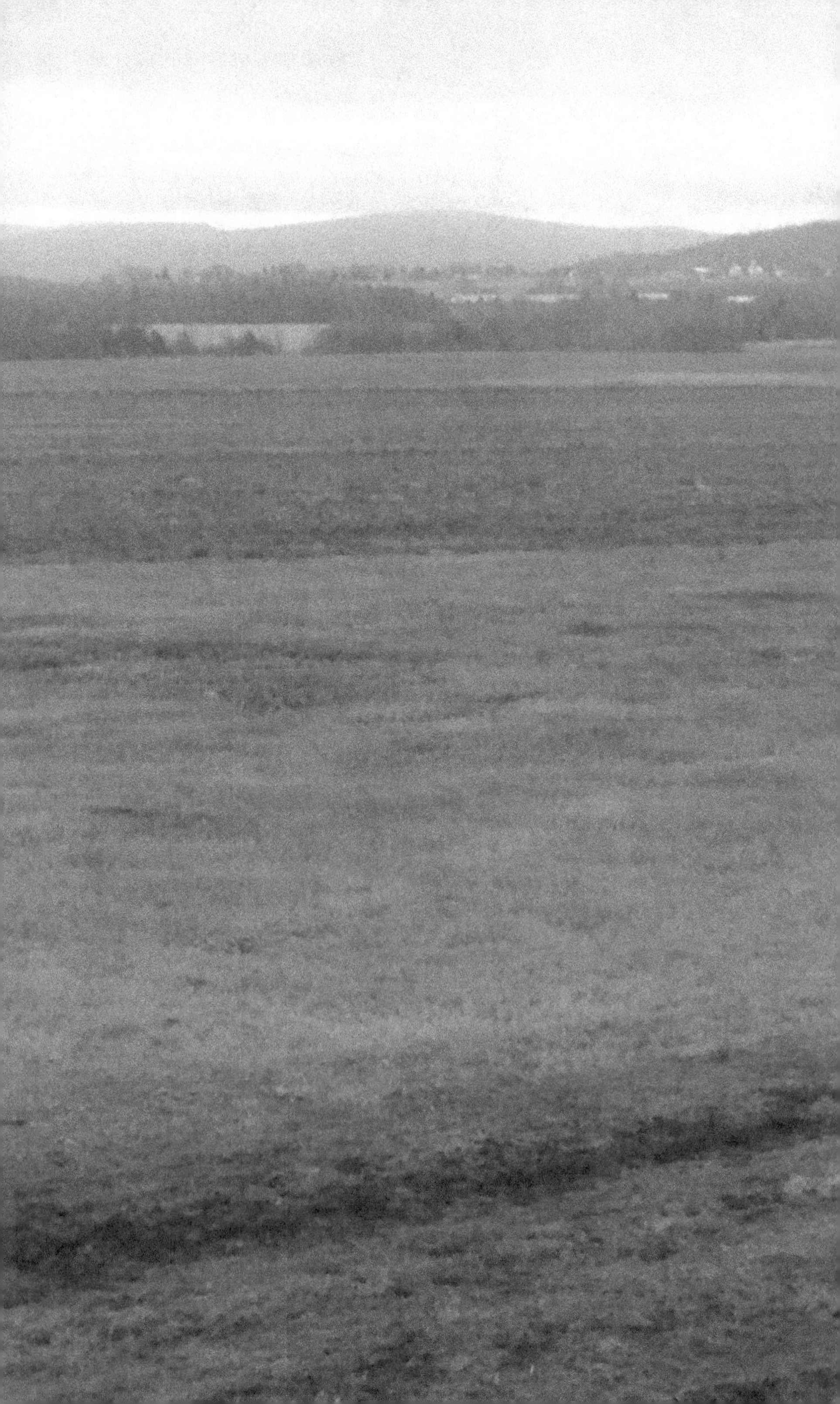

"EL VIAJE MAS CARO" / "THE MOST COSTLY JOURNEY" *presents:*

WHAT I'VE PLANTED HERE

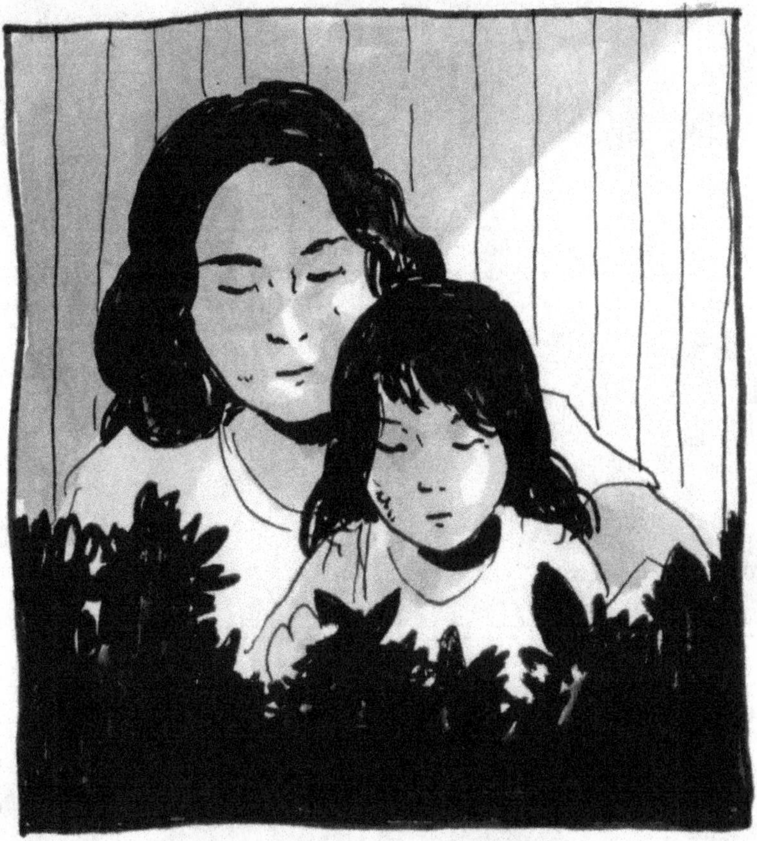

The Story of Lara

Art by Tillie Walden

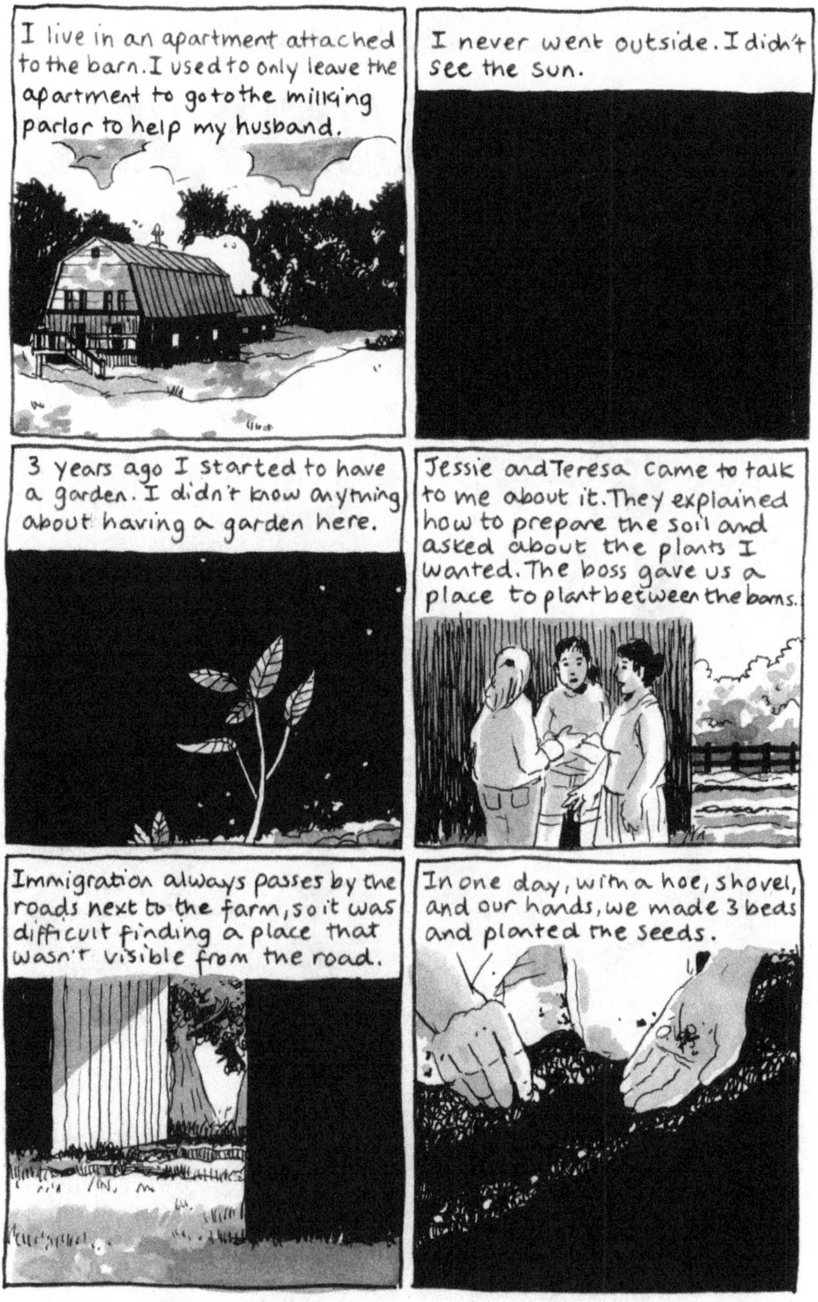
I live in an apartment attached to the barn. I used to only leave the apartment to go to the milking parlor to help my husband.
I never went outside. I didn't see the sun.
3 years ago I started to have a garden. I didn't know anything about having a garden here.
Jessie and Teresa came to talk to me about it. They explained how to prepare the soil and asked about the plants I wanted. The boss gave us a place to plant between the barns.
Immigration always passes by the roads next to the farm, so it was difficult finding a place that wasn't visible from the road.
In one day, with a hoe, shovel, and our hands, we made 3 beds and planted the seeds.

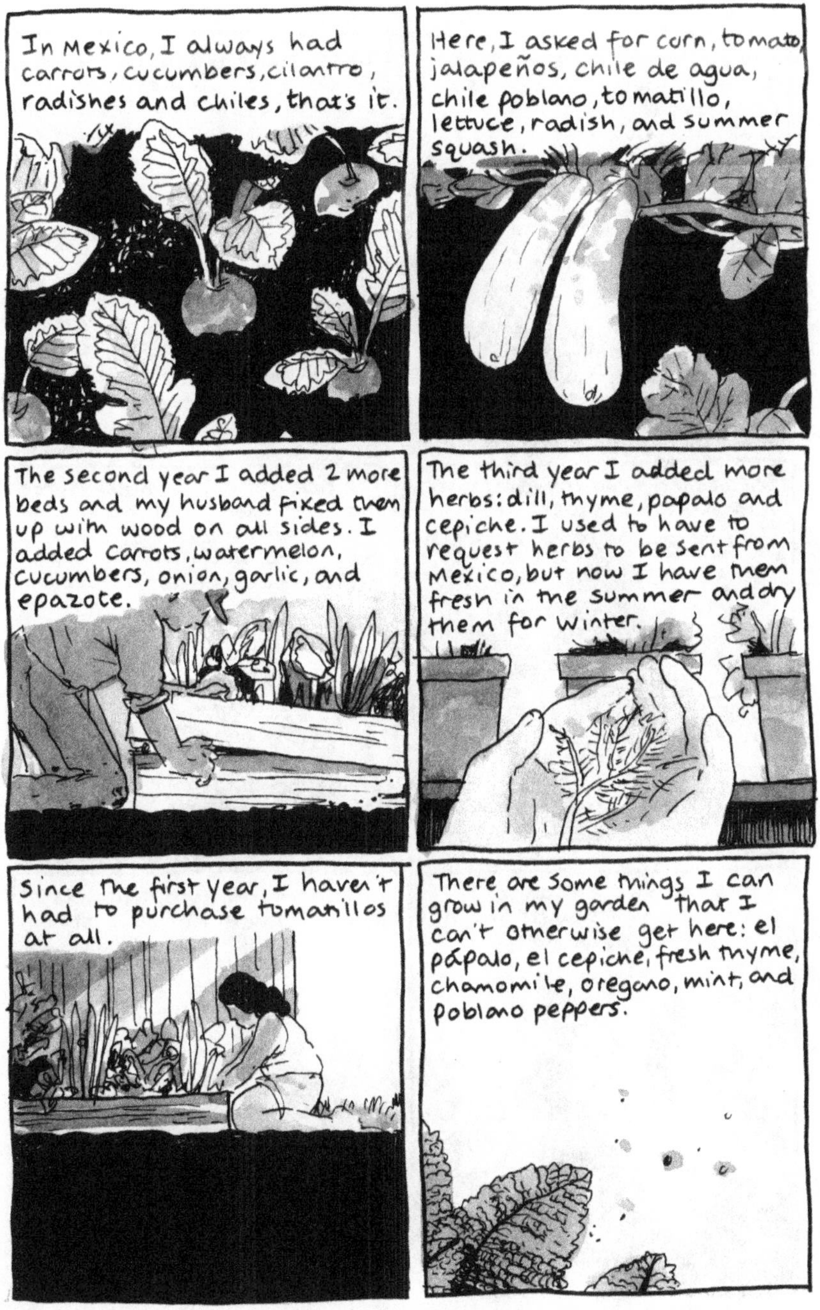
In Mexico, I always had carrots, cucumbers, cilantro, radishes and chiles, that's it.
Here, I asked for corn, tomato, jalapeños, chile de agua, chile poblano, tomatillo, lettuce, radish, and summer squash.
The second year I added 2 more beds and my husband fixed them up with wood on all sides. I added carrots, watermelon, cucumbers, onion, garlic, and epazote.
The third year I added more herbs: dill, thyme, papalo and cepiche. I used to have to request herbs to be sent from Mexico, but now I have them fresh in the summer and dry them for winter.
Since the first year, I haven't had to purchase tomatillos at all.
There are some things I can grow in my garden that I can't otherwise get here: el pápalo, el cepiche, fresh thyme, chamomile, oregano, mint, and poblano peppers.

The first year I brought my daughter out to the garden in a carriage; she wasn't walking yet.

I'd go twice a day: in the morning to pull weeds and pick the vegetables I was going to use in the day's food, and in the afternoon to water.

The second year my daughter had started walking.

The first time I planted carrots she went along pulling the tops off. I had to teach her what they were and little by little she began to understand.

This year, she no longer pulled up my plants! She has started to help me.

I taught her about weeds and showed her how to get rid of them.

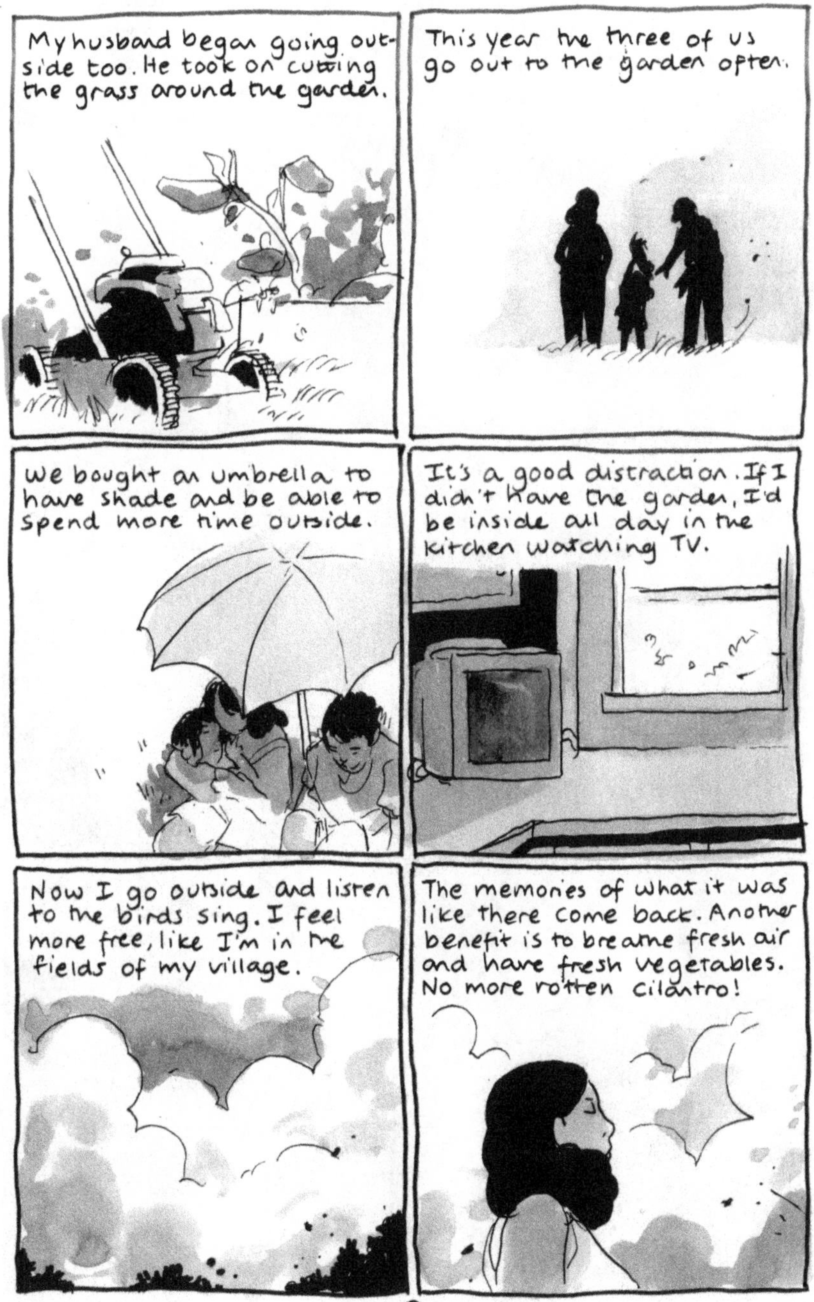
My husband began going outside too. He took on cutting the grass around the garden.
This year the three of us go out to the garden often.
We bought an umbrella to have shade and be able to spend more time outside.
It's a good distraction. If I didn't have the garden, I'd be inside all day in the kitchen watching TV.
Now I go outside and listen to the birds sing. I feel more free, like I'm in the fields of my village.
The memories of what it was like there come back. Another benefit is to breathe fresh air and have fresh vegetables. No more rotten cilantro!

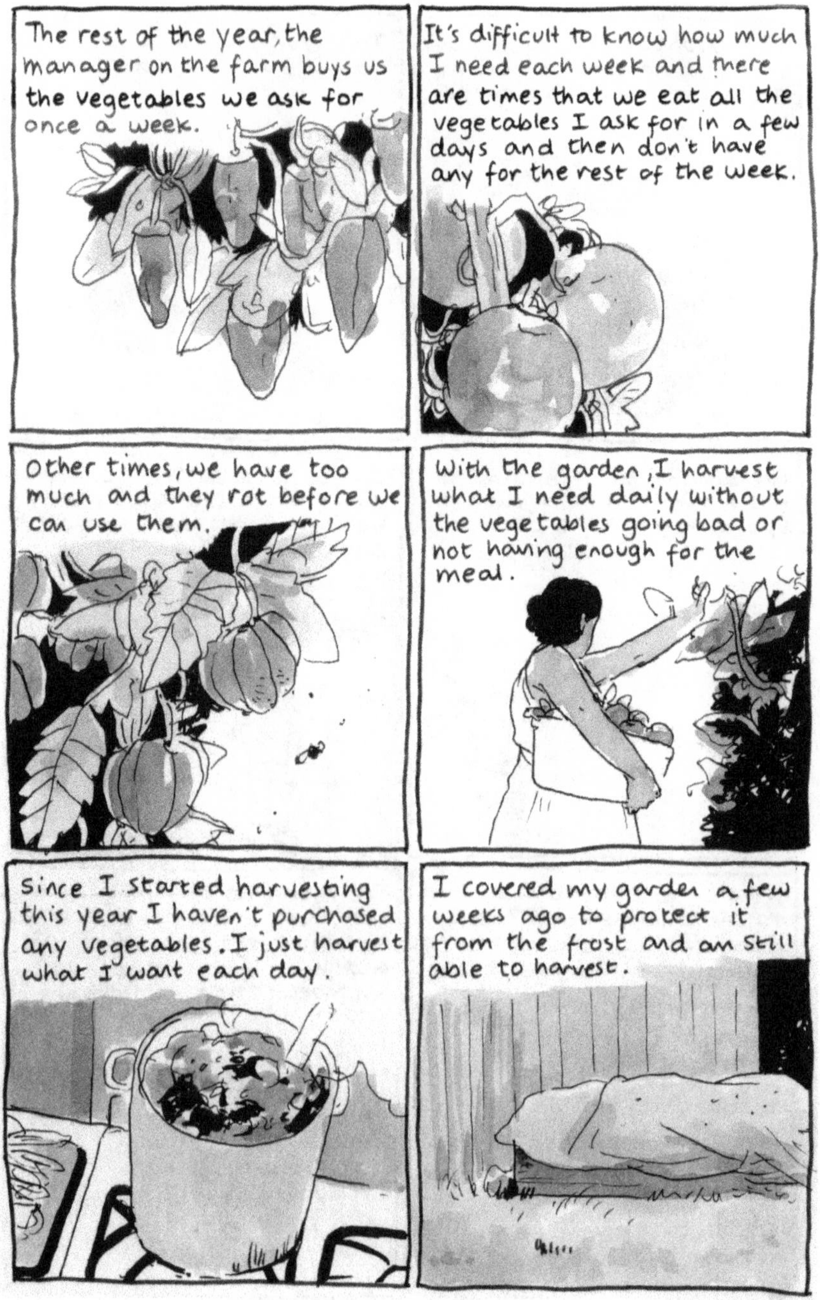
The rest of the year, the manager on the farm buys us the vegetables we ask for once a week.
It's difficult to know how much I need each week and there are times that we eat all the vegetables I ask for in a few days and then don't have any for the rest of the week.
Other times, we have too much and they rot before we can use them.
With the garden, I harvest what I need daily without the vegetables going bad or not having enough for the meal.
Since I started harvesting this year I haven't purchased any vegetables. I just harvest what I want each day.
I covered my garden a few weeks ago to protect it from the frost and am still able to harvest.

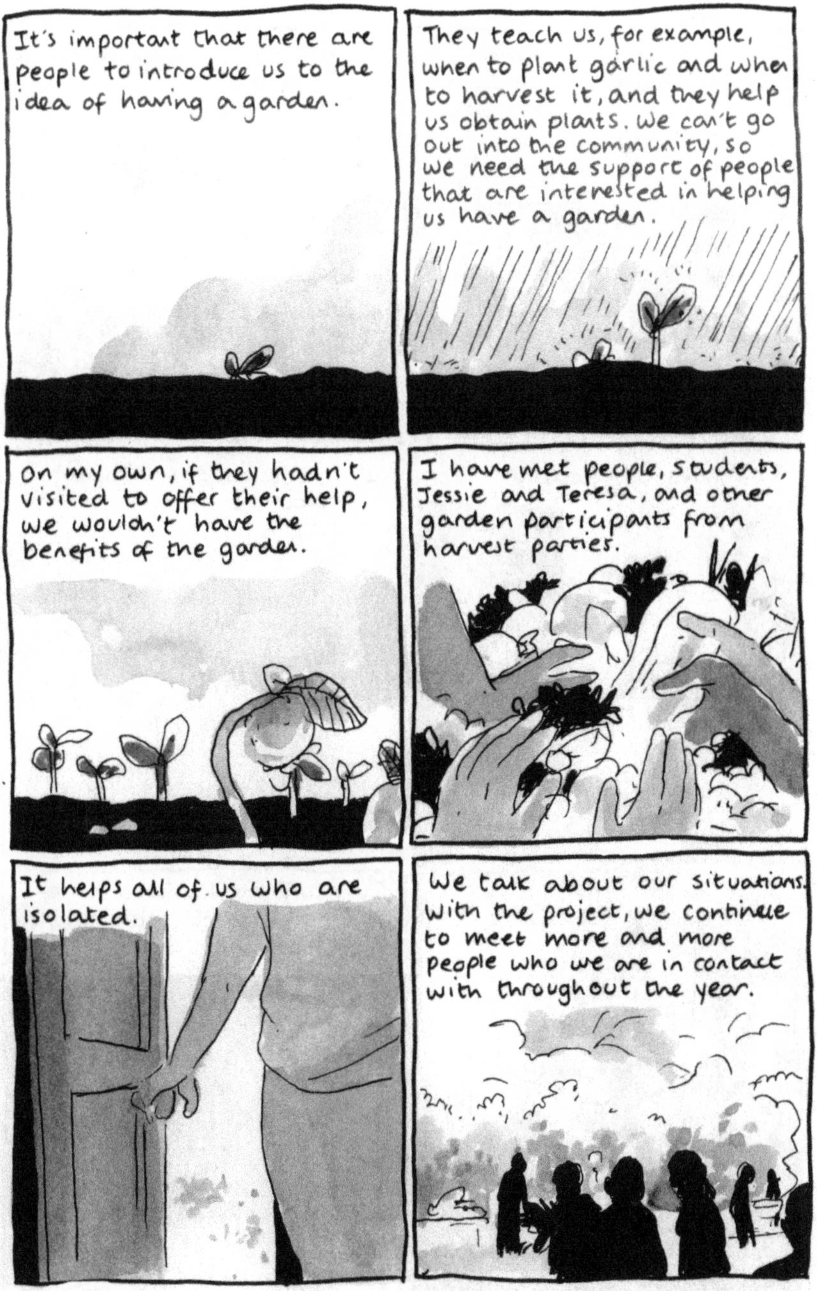
It's important that there are people to introduce us to the idea of having a garden.
They teach us, for example, when to plant garlic and when to harvest it, and they help us obtain plants. We can't go out into the community, so we need the support of people that are interested in helping us have a garden.
On my own, if they hadn't visited to offer their help, we wouldn't have the benefits of the garden.
I have met people, students, Jessie and Teresa, and other garden participants from harvest parties.
It helps all of us who are isolated.
We talk about our situations. With the project, we continue to meet more and more people who we are in contact with throughout the year.

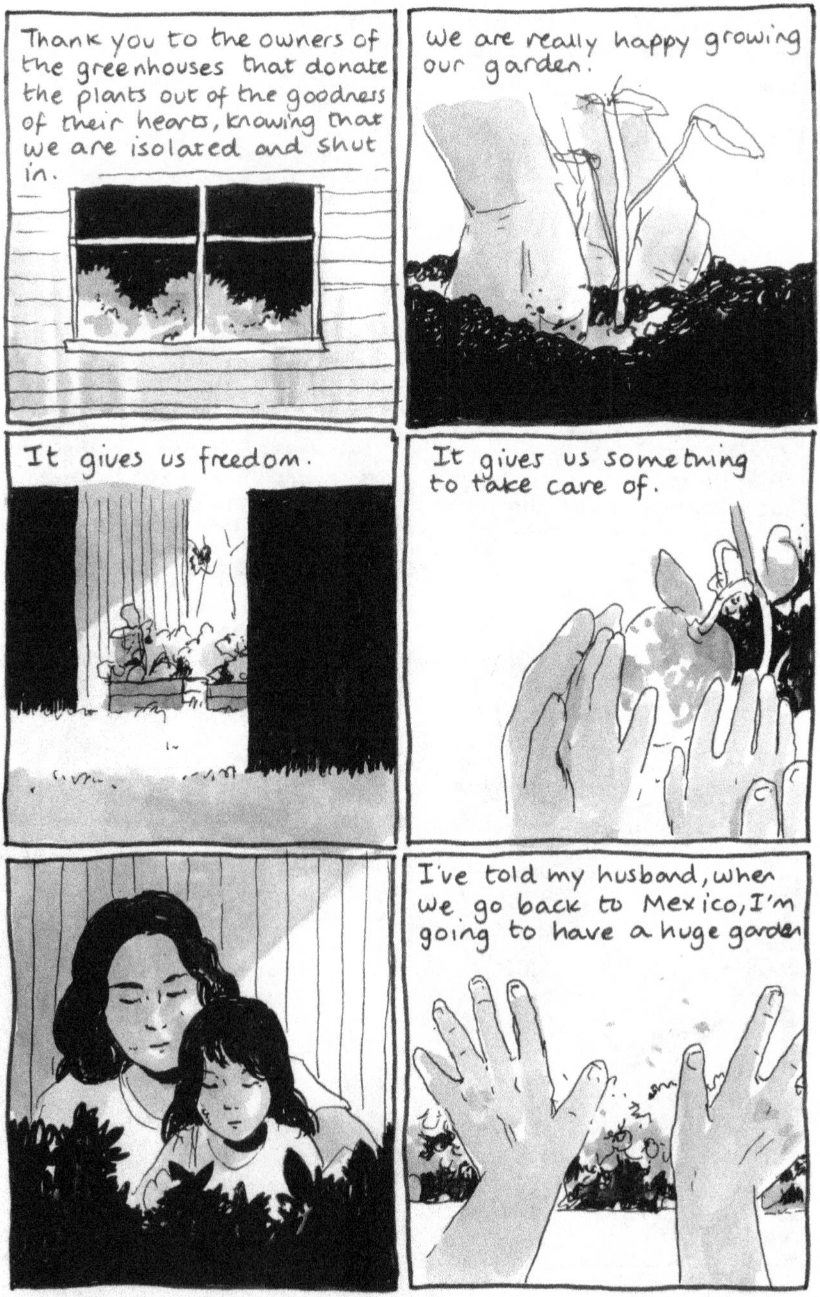
Thank you to the owners of the greenhouses that donate the plants out of the goodness of their hearts, knowing that we are isolated and shut in.
We are really happy growing our garden.
It gives us freedom.
It gives us something to take care of.
I've told my husband, when we go back to Mexico, I'm going to have a huge garden

He'll have to till the land and I'll plant what I've been growing here

and start a business selling vegetables.

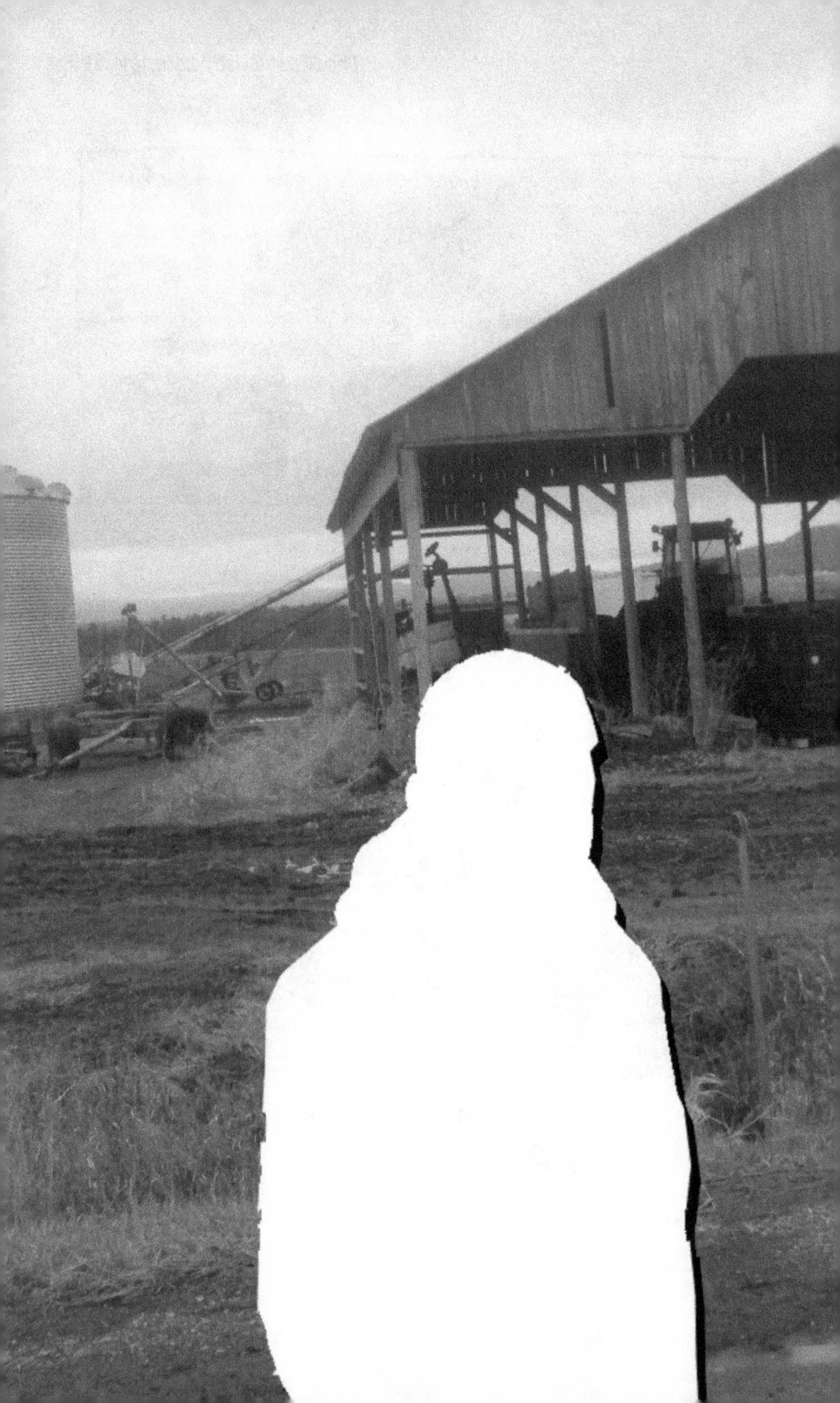

AFTERWORD

El Viaje Más Caro/The Most Costly Journey: Population & Process

Teresa Mares, PhD (University of Vermont)
Andy Kolovos, PhD (Vermont Folklife Center)

Milk, cheese, and ice cream have come to be synonymous with the Vermont brand and the state's working landscapes. Ben and Jerry themselves are perhaps the country's best-loved Vermonters, despite having been born in Brooklyn (no offense to Bernie Sanders, also from Brooklyn). Vermont is the U.S. state with the highest dependence upon a single commodity for agricultural revenue, that commodity being milk (Parsons 2010). According to the Vermont Dairy Promotion Council, Vermont currently sells more than 321 million gallons of milk each year, with 70% of agricultural sales coming from this single product. Approximately 80% of the state's farmland is dedicated to supporting dairy production, whether for dairy lots, for pasturing, or for growing feed crops. Dairy also accounts for 6000-7000 jobs (more than any of the state's key private employers), providing $360 million in wages and salaries (Vermont Dairy Promotion Council 2015).

While the Vermont brand continues to rely upon the image of the small-scale family farm, Vermont's dairy industry has been subjected to the same pressures of industrialization, consolidation, and concentration that we see in nearly all sectors of the U.S. food system. Over the past seventy-five years, Vermont has lost the vast majority of its dairy farms. In the 1940's there were approximately 11,000 dairy farms in the state, as of early 2020 there were only 677 farms remaining. Despite these devastating losses and the volatility of fluid milk prices, Vermont is currently producing milk at record levels (Parsons 2010). This increased production comes at significant ecological and social costs – water pollution, unjust working conditions, and corporate control, for instance -- and directly feeds into consumer trends such as the increased consumption of Greek style yogurt and whey protein, a byproduct that is often more profitable than the cheese and yogurt from which it comes.

Although a significant number of dairy farms (82%) have fewer than 200 cows, economic conditions have pushed Vermont's dairy farms to become larger with bigger herds to become more efficient and remain profitable. This efficiency and profitability depends upon intensive milking technologies and schedules, the latter being directly facilitated by Latino/a farmworkers who migrate in search of employment and the chance at a better life for themselves and their families. Since the late 1990s, Vermont has experienced significant shifts in the labor force that toils amidst the dairy farms that still dominate the pastoral working landscape. This shift parallels national and international trends in the food system where immigrant labor has become more central to production and profits, even if these workers are afforded little in the way of legal protections or the possibility of upward mobility. Increased migration from Latin America has entailed new considerations with respect to the programs, agencies, and retail outlets that provide food, healthcare, and other basic needs to Vermont's residents.

Between 1000-1200 immigrant workers from Latin America help to sustain Vermont's dairy industry. Given the few legal pathways for immigrant workers who are looking to work in this industry, it is estimated that more than 90% of these farmworkers are undocumented (Radel, Schmook, and McCandless 2010; Wolcott-MacCausland and Shea 2016). Nearly all of these workers come from the central and southern states of Mexico and northern Guatemala, and many have moved to Vermont after working other agricultural jobs across the country. Dairy workers encounter a number of emotional and psychosocial challenges as they migrate from their countries of origin, cross the U.S-Mexico border, and work in rural Vermont. These challenges result in significant and often severe mental health concerns, including anxiety, depression, and chronic stress. For those who find work in Vermont's border region, including the Northeast Kingdom and Franklin County, these mental health concerns are compounded by the active presence and surveillance of Border Patrol and Immigration and Customs Enforcement (ICE). Alongside these mental and emotional health challenges, these workers experience increased rates of physical illness and disease, including musculoskeletal pain, gastrointestinal issues, and diet-related disease. These physical and mental maladies stem from the systematic and structural forms of violence that are perpetuated both by the demands of the industrial food system but also by the criminalization and marginalization of immigrant workers.

Dairy farmworkers face significant challenges that are related to the rural nature of most dairy farms and the physical and social isolation they experience (Harrison, Lloyd, and O'Kane 2009). Farmworkers in this industry often work upwards of 70-80 hours per week year-round, and unlike many seasonal farmworkers who migrate multiple times throughout the year, migrant dairy workers in Vermont tend to stay on a dairy farm for an average of 12 months but often work within the industry for many years before returning home (Shea 2013). Farmworkers in Vermont experience additional barriers of living and working in a border state that is one of the least ethnically and racially diverse states of the nation. While many farmworkers are invisible in their places of work, the dominant whiteness of Vermont's rural landscape leaves them "hypervisible" when they are out in public places (Mares 2019). This leaves many farmworkers fearful of visiting grocery stores, health clinics, churches, or even their children's schools.

Most of the data on Vermont's farmworkers has been collected by health providers and community-based groups working to organize farmworkers. Based on the most recent data compiled by UVM Extension's Bridges to Health Program which connects farmworkers with health care and health services, for 489 individuals who enrolled in their services between 2012-2017, the two highest sending countries were Mexico (88%) and Guatemala (10%). The three most common sending states in Mexico were Chiapas (51%), Tabasco (23%) and Veracruz (9%). This group of patients was mostly male-identified (88%) and only 3% spoke English (with 5% speaking an indigenous language as their first language). The sample was mostly young (60% under the age of 30, with most between 20-29 years of age), and single (40%), and 49% had less than a ninth grade education. Only 3% of this group had health insurance, and only 4% had a driver's license (Wolcott-

MacCausland 2017). While this data represents only a subset of the total population of the state's migrant farmworkers, it provides a representative portrait of the demographic background of Latino farmworkers in the state.

While they encounter unique challenges in the dairy industry, Vermont's farmworkers experience a number of the same problems that confront Latino/a farmworkers across the food system. Latino farmworkers suffer from irregular and inconsistent work patterns, and experience unemployment at double the rate of all wage and salary workers (Kandel 2008). On both dairy farms and other types of farms, farmworkers encounter hazardous working conditions, which are often worsened by unsafe and unhealthy living conditions. Given the high percentage of farmworkers without documentation, these unsafe working conditions, combined with labor abuses and exploitation, leave few channels to seek redress. As of 2009, the occupational fatality rate for farmworkers was five times higher than the rate of any other worker.

Although farmworkers, including those working without documentation, pay billions into federal programs like Medicaid, Social Security, and unemployment, they are unable to access federal programs designed to help the poor (Southern Poverty Law Center 2010). Farmworkers also are unable to access SNAP benefits, unemployment insurance, worker's compensation or disability benefits. Farmworkers do not seek out the health care they need, because of barriers related to transportation, health insurance ineligibility, and poverty (Arcury and Quandt 2007; Kandel 2008; Villarejo et al. 2001; Villarejo 2003). It is estimated that only one-tenth of farmworkers have health insurance (Kandel 2008; Southern Poverty Law Center 2010). These barriers are particularly troubling given that a lack of adequate sanitation facilities, coupled with heavy exposure to pesticides and other agricultural chemicals, is a pressing and often deadly challenge confronting farmworkers.

Against this backdrop, *El Viaje Más Caro* represents a collaborative, community-based project to use the power of narrative and comics to address the mental health concerns of Vermont's farmworkers. By utilizing the complex alchemy of juxtaposed words and images, comics can serve as a powerful vehicle for the transmission of information and the sharing of experiences having to do with health and wellbeing. Through a structured collaboration with dedicated local comics artists who draw from this long history of applied visual narratives, *El Viaje Más Caro* empowers VT migrant farmworkers to share their personal stories with their community and beyond, in an accessible visual format that at once captivates, educates, and immerses readers in the everyday life and experiences of an under-represented and all-too-often invisible sector of the state's economy. While the project was not initially informed by the tenets and scope of graphic medicine, we have realized over the course of carrying out this project that this form of literature helps to provide a compelling framework for our project's objectives and aims.

Many Latin American dairy workers in the state experience a separation from family and community, and a loss of identity and support networks. Upon arriving to Vermont, they face isolated working and living conditions, language and cultural barriers, and a lack of mobility. Additionally, the economic motivations to migrate carry a sense of responsibility and associated pressures to meet the needs of those left behind. These challenges have been documented both by health providers in the state and by researchers working with this population who express concern about latent stress, anxiety, and depression. Having the opportunity to tell one's story, and hearing stories that reflect one's own experience, can be an important form of therapy and healing. At the same time, there is a stigma in many Latin American cultures surrounding acknowledging and accessing support services for mental health. For many Latino/a immigrants, close knit families, communities, and churches often help meet the support needs of those struggling with mental health issues. In Vermont, many farmworkers live far from their extended families, are not integrated into a community, and do not have access to churches with bilingual clergy. Furthermore, for those who do wish to seek out care there are limited bilingual and bicultural counselors and therapists in Vermont.

Julia Grand Doucet, the Outreach Nurse for Vermont's Open Door Clinic, and Naomi Wolcott-MacCausland, Director of UVM Extension's Bridges to Health Program, observed through their many years of working with the Latin American migrant farmworker community in Vermont that a number of mental and emotional health issues were going undiagnosed and untreated. Doucet and Wolcott-MacCausland were both aware of a culturally-grounded reluctance to discuss mental health concerns, but continued to search for non-threatening and culturally-appropriate ways to help their clients. After learning about the Center for Cartoon Studies in White River Junction, VT and a number of projects employing community-based applied cartooning, as well as the important role in popular education that comics have served in Latin America, Doucet wondered if this approach could be an appropriate means for addressing the mental health issues she witnessed through her work as a service provider. After meeting Teresa Mares through a separate research collaboration, Doucet realized that the power of telling one's—and hearing another's—story could be an incredibly effective form of mental health treatment for Latino/a migrant farmworkers. Doucet also believed that the graphic form could be particularly effective for a community that often has limited literacy abilities, in both Spanish and English.

Due to both the stigma around talking about mental health as well as the limited culturally appropriate resources in Vermont communities, those involved in migrant health in the state have struggled to find meaningful ways to engage farmworkers in reflecting on the impact their journey to Vermont and current linguistic, cultural, and geographic isolation has on their personal wellbeing. Moved by the power of patients' stories while acknowledging that "talk therapy" is not always culturally embraced, our project team was inspired to collect stories, hopeful that this innovative process of sharing these stories could alleviate some of the workers' pain, suffering, and isolation. Further, through reading these stories, we envisioned that other farmworkers could seek comfort in realizing that other members of their community were experiencing these forms of comfort, perhaps allowing for more open dialogue on mental health concerns. This project has served as a unique way to address mental health issues specific to this population in a non-judgmental and non-threatening way.

Together, Doucet, Mares, and Wolcott-MacCausland started collecting stories through in-person interviews with farmworkers, but they realized that they would also need a source of comic artists. They soon connected with Andy Kolovos, an archivist, ethnographer and self-professed comics nerd, and Marek Bennett, a New Hampshire-based cartoonist with experience working in Latin America. As a newly formed team, these five individuals, along with student research assistant Jessie Mazar and a number of Open Door Clinic volunteers, coordinated the collection and transcription of more than 20 interviews, with 20 resulting short-form graphic narratives, with the generous support of several local funders. These interviews covered a range of topics, from the trauma of crossing the U.S-Mexico border, to substance abuse, to domestic violence. Interviewers took an open-ended approach and allowed the storyteller to guide the direction of their narrative, however, we took care to ask about healthy coping mechanisms that could be shared with other farmworkers through the comics medium.

Participatory ethnographic methods and ethics formed the basis of the working methods of the project, including interviewing, analysis/editing of interview material, and comics production. Over the course of the project team members and several volunteers from the Open Door Clinic and Bridges to Health conducted multiple interviews in Spanish with a number of migrant dairy farm workers. These interviews were transcribed, condensed, and analyzed by project partners to highlight various themes within each interview and across the body of interviews. Transcripts were translated into English for use by non-Spanish speakers associated with the project, including cartoonists. The project developed two basic methods for the production of the comics—one where cartoonists met with and engaged directly with interviewees, and a second where cartoonists worked only from English versions of transcripts. In both cases cartoonists received feedback (directly or through project team members) from the interviewees and revised their work to address observations and concerns. Doucet and Kolovos provided editorial guidance to cartoonists and, with Bennett, created the final print volumes.

The primary deliverable of this project is a series of 20 short-format graphic narratives (and now, this collection) that integrates oral history interviews with migrant workers that focus on the experience of moving to and working in Vermont, including the stresses and mental health impacts of migration and working in some of the most dangerous occupations in the state's food system. The comics-based narratives have been illustrated by local and regional cartoonists, including independent artists and students associated with the Center for Cartoon Studies based in White River Junction, Vermont. The comics are now distributed by health promoters conducting site visits to farms in Addison and Franklin counties as well as to clients receiving care at the Open Door Clinic in Middlebury, Vermont. Under terms of a grant received by the Open Door Clinic in 2017, a team of health professionals are currently developing further curriculum and outreach materials based on the comics for use in outreach by health promoters and migrant education recruiters.

Throughout the project, the primary audience for these comics has been the farmworker community, and the funding solicitations and awards have reflected this orientation. However, our project team has found that the comics also serve an important secondary purpose, that of educating the broader public about the daily lives of farmworkers and structural violence and vulnerability that this population experiences.

This book represents our attempt to realize this second goal. All comics are available in both Spanish and English and are available for viewing both online through a site hosted by the Vermont Folklife Center and as hard-copy booklets. Both the online and print versions have been utilized in public school and university classrooms by teachers and professors who have chosen to include the comics as pedagogical tools for classes in Spanish, Geography, Food Systems, Anthropology, Literature, and Social Studies.

Ethnographic Cartooning

As noted above, ethnographic methods and ethics guided all aspects of the *El Viaje Más Caro* project, and the project drew heavily on D. Soyini Madison's, *Critical Ethnography: Method, Ethics, and Performance* (2019) for its theoretical and methodological framework. At its core, ethnographic work is bounded on one side by inquiry, the process of learning, and on the other by representation, the process of (re)presenting what one has learned. Through grounded inquiry ethnographers work to understand how someone other than themselves makes sense of the world. Through representation the ethnographer seeks to relay these perspectives using a variety of potential formats such as written text, images, film, audio and—as in our case—comics. Collaborative engagement with storytellers around the act of representation was a crucial part of our work. The inseparability of ethics and practice is a defining feature of the work of many contemporary ethnographers, and ethical considerations, rooted and collaborative methods as informed by the perspectives of critical ethnography, were central to how the *El Viaje Más Caro* engaged with our research partners and how we represented their stories in graphic form.

Critical ethnography encompasses a range of approaches that stress reflexive engagement with individuals and communities, the shared (dialogic) creation of meaning through ongoing interaction, and the transference of interpretive and representational authority away from the researcher and into the hands of the people with whom they work. In Madison's terms, critical ethnography "is always a meeting of multiple sides in an encounter with and among others, one in which there is negotiation and dialogue toward substantial and viable meanings that make a difference in others' worlds" (2019: 10). In this way the farmworkers, project interviewers, cartoonists, and editors were all partners in an unfolding, collaborative effort, one that sought to employ the sharing of stories as a therapeutic tool for the storytellers, the distribution of these stories in comic form in Spanish as a therapeutic tool both for storytellers and for others living in similar circumstances—and in English as a way to call broader attention to the lives of this group of people whose often unnoticed labor continues to make agriculture viable in Vermont.

For storytellers, the act of sharing their narratives and allowing them to be transformed into comics entailed risk—including a risk of social consequences for revealing sensitive personal experiences, as well as a legal risk of exposure and resulting deportation. From the side of *El Viaje Más Caro,* the project carried tremendous responsibility—foremost to limit risk—as well as to adhere to the project's mission, to engage sincerely with these people who trusted us, to respect their input on our efforts, and to represent fairly the experiences of a displaced population separated from our project team by language, culture, economic opportunity and legal standing. We did not—and do not—own the narratives shared with us. Rather we were given permission to make use of them for designated purposes. Furthermore, our obligations required that researchers, editors and cartoonists accept feedback from the storytellers and modify the final product to the storytellers' satisfaction. The interactive give-and-take of our process and the ceding of ultimate editorial control to the storytellers marks a core element of our critical ethnographic praxis, and is one of the key ways *El Viaje Más Caro* differs from many other non-fiction comics efforts to date. The collaborative processes employed by the project developed over time, and varied in response to the needs of different individual storytellers and the Spanish language skills of cartoonists.

These ethnographic underpinnings to our work inspired us to frame *El Viaje Más Caro* as an effort embedded in the emerging field of *ethnographic cartooning*—the use of comics as a vehicle for ethnographic representation. An aspect of the broader umbrella of graphic ethnography, ethnographic cartooning draws together the impulses and perspectives of the non-fiction cartoonist and invests them with the sensibilities of the ethnographer. As anthropologist Jay Ruby (2000) notes, "If Marx, Foucault, semiotics, and capitalism can be represented in a productive way in comic books, why not an ethnography?" (263). Comics offers ethnography distinctive benefits and possibilities, just as ethnography does for comics.

Some of the earliest self-consciously ethnographic comics were produced by anthropologist Gillian Crowther while a student at Cambridge University (1990, 2015). In recent years an increasing number of ethnographic and ethnographically framed comics have emerged (e.g. Atkins n.d., Bartoszko, Leseth and Ponomarew 2010; Galman 2007, 2017; Hamdy, Coleman, Bao and Brewer 2017; Theodossopoulos 2015; Venkataramani 2015; Walrath 2016; Wright 2018). As noted by Hannah Wadle (2012), to date visual anthropology has supplied the core theoretical grounding for ethnographic cartooning, with additional perspective taken from work by scholars such as Afonso and Ramos (2004), Causey (2015, 2019), Ingold (2011, 2012), Hoffmann-Dilloway (2016a, 2016b, 2016c), Taussig (2011) and others who explore the implications of drawing in the context of fieldwork. Scholarship outside ethnographic disciplines also informs the thinking on ethnographic cartooning, most notably Hilary Chute's concept of "witnessing" as articulated in her *Disaster Drawn* (2016). Works like Trevor Getz and Liz Clarke's graphic history, *Abina and the Important Men* (2015) provide important touch stones for comics as scholarly communication, and the classic works of graphic non-fiction themselves such as Bechdel (2007) , McCloud (1994), Sacco (2001), Satrapi (2003), Spiegelman (1973) and others provide broad context for the use of comics in non-fiction storytelling.

As the above suggests, ethnographic cartooning has only begun to emerge in earnest as a discrete form of practice, with scholars such as Kuttner, Sousanis and Weaver-Hightower (2018) discussing the emergence of comics a vehicle for scholarly research across multiple fields including of history, education, graphic medicine and anthropology, and others, in particular Wadle (2012) and Galman (2009), reflect on the intersection of comics and ethnography in relation to theory and practice. The implications of comics as a medium of ethnographic representation are truly just beginning to be articulated. Regarding *El viaje Más Caro,* the instinct to theorize practice centers on the following question: how does the medium of comics (inclusive of its structural elements and the formal conventions that shape how these elements manifest) both enrich ethnographic practice and representation and potentially limit them?

Cartooning in ethnographic practice represents a fusion of two distinct elements already widely employed by ethnographers in the field —drawing and writing. However, cartooning is more than just pictures fused with words—it is a union of sequential images and text with distinct narrative intent. Ethnographic cartooning extends the idea of visual representation in ethnography beyond the static roles it has historically held—for example a sketch made to preserve a memory of an object for future reference—and into the creation of dynamic representation that foregrounds the visual and invests it with narrative power. This process opens up whole new ways of thinking about the ethnographic text and the lives represented within it.

However, beyond just opening up new ways of representing ethnographic experience, cartooning offers ethnographers and their research partners practical and powerful approach to representation that dovetail with the methodological and ethical considerations that underpin critical ethnographic approaches. In the case of *El viaje Más Caro*, comics and ethnography came together concretely in two ways: through the ethnographically-informed development of collaborative working methods that brought migrant storytellers and cartoonists together as partners in representation, and through the ability of comics to present narrative in intimate, personal, and powerful ways while still providing anonymity and shielding individual members of a vulnerable population from excessive exposure to risk. Below we touch on these concepts in general terms as well as providing concrete examples that emerged in the execution of the *El Viaje Más Caro* project.

Ethnographic orientation toward collaboration is rooted in direct engagement with research partners around the interpretation and representation of their experiences. As noted above, collaboration and dialogue are earmarks of the critical ethnographic approaches that informed *El Viaje Más Caro*. Although collaborative working methods of these sorts were familiar to the ethnographers participating in the project, for many of the cartoonists the collaborative processes that emerged as *El Viaje Más Caro* unfolded marked a departure from other, more journalistically-framed, non-fiction comics projects they had worked on in the past. In the context of the *El Viaje*, collaboration took various forms along a continuum ranging from deeper reciprocal partnerships on one end to simple, mediated give-and-take on the other. At one extreme, cartoonists spent personal time with the storyteller—engaging with them directly and moving through their worlds as participant observers or communicating with them via telephone, as they worked together to revise the presentation of a story. At the other extreme, project partners shared drafts of comics with storytellers, and then relayed their comments back to cartoonists so they could make revisions and then resubmit their work. All storytellers had influence in shaping how their stories were represented, and in several cases cartoonists and storytellers engaged in direct partnership in revising and crafting the final comics.

An example of the unfolding of these collaborative working methods can be found in the revision process of *Un Recuerdo Doloroso/Painful to Remember* by José and Marek Bennett. *Un Recuerdo Doloroso* focuses on the trauma experienced by José during his travel from Guatemala to the United States. At one point in the journey through the desert of northern Mexico, a member of the group is bitten by a rattlesnake and abandoned. The story as told by José is extremely dramatic and Bennett, seeking to represent it accurately and thoroughly, and to capture its affective texture rendered it in comics form as follows:

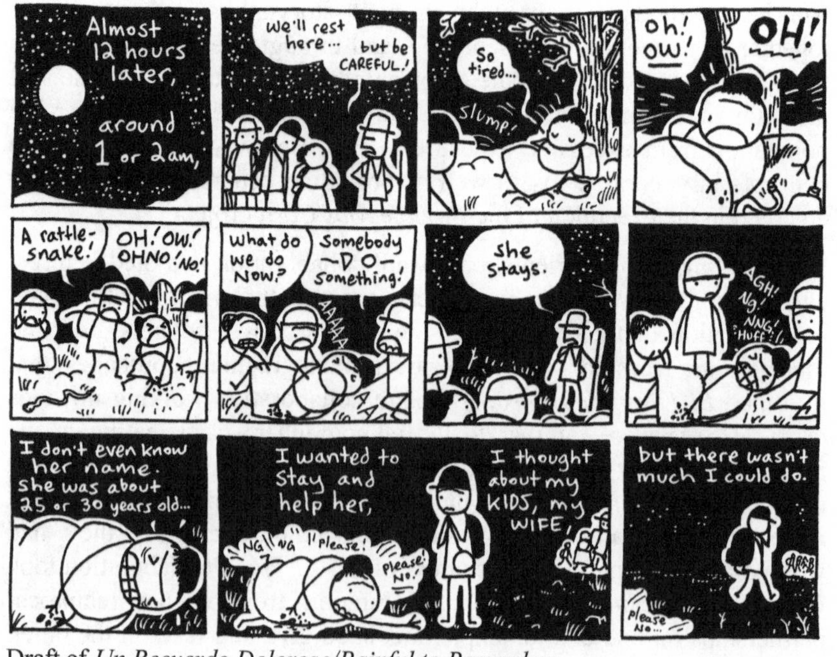
Almost 12 hours later, around 1 or 2am,
We'll rest here...
but be CAREFUL!
So tired...
SLUMP!
Oh! Ow!
OH!
A rattle-snake!
OH! OW! OHNO! NO!
What do we do NOW?
Somebody —DO— Something!
AAAAA
She stays.
AGH! NG! NNG! HUFF!
I don't even know her name. She was about 25 or 30 years old...
I wanted to stay and help her,
NG NG Please!
Please! NO!
I thought about my KIDS, my WIFE,
but there wasn't much I could do.
Please No...

Draft of *Un Recuerdo Doloroso/Painful to Remember*

When Bennett shared the story with José, the storyteller commented that the actual event happened extremely quickly, and that Bennett's representation—although not incorrect—failed to capture the suddenness of the actual experience and the rapidity with which it unfolded. In response to José's comments, Bennett returned to the

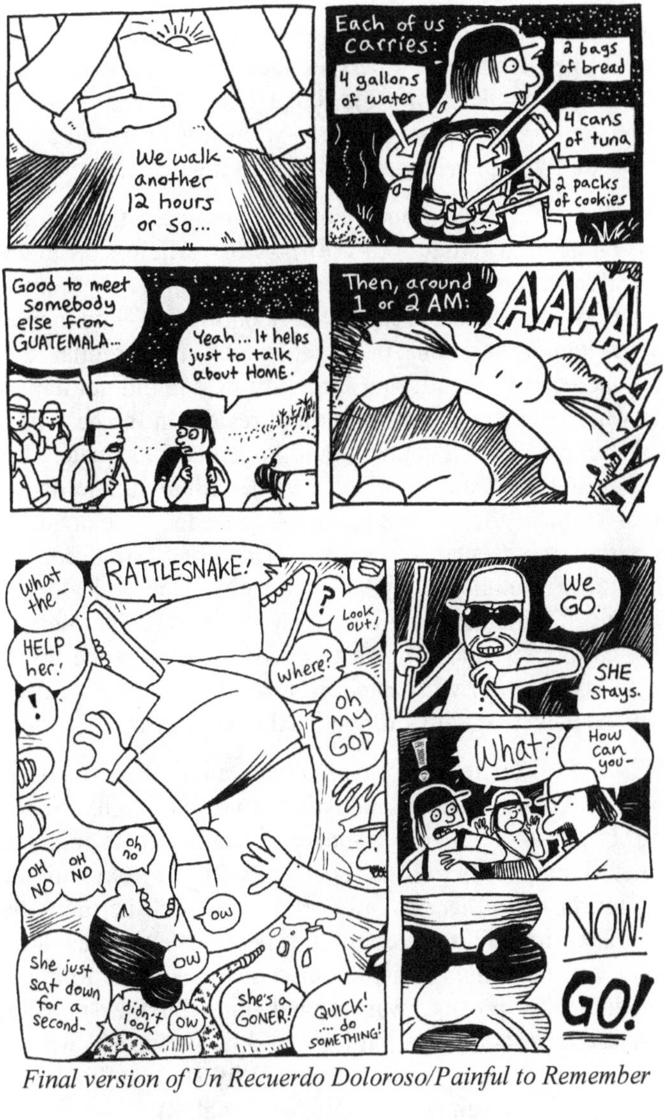
We walk another 12 hours or so...
Each of us carries:
4 gallons of water
2 bags of bread
4 cans of tuna
2 packs of cookies
Good to meet somebody else from GUATEMALA...
Yeah... It helps just to talk about HOME.
Then, around 1 or 2 AM:
AAAAAAAAA
What the-
RATTLESNAKE!
HELP her!
!
?
Look out!
where?
oh my GOD
OH NO
OH NO
oh no
ow
OW
she just sat down for a second-
didn't look
OW
she's a GONER!
QUICK! ... do SOMETHING!
We GO.
SHE stays.
!
What?
How can you-
NOW!
GO!

Final version of Un Recuerdo Doloroso/Painful to Remember

segment and reorganized it, reducing the snake bite itself from seven panels to two, and the entire incident from eleven panels to five.

Bennett then shared the revised version with José, who felt this new approach more accurately captured the experience. In this way, Bennett and José entered into dialogue about how José's story would be represented to the world—with José guiding and determining the direction of the work done by the cartoonist. Bennett ceded authorial control to José and then directed his efforts toward realizing, as best he could, José's story from José's perspective. While not every cartoonist engaged with storytellers on this level—due to language barriers, distance, availability and other factors—at the very least all storytellers had the opportunity to provide input on the completed comics.

Finally, over the course of the project, the coordinators maintained an acute awareness of the risks of participation in *El Viaje Más Caro* for farmworkers. Toward this end, as is common in ethnographic work, we obfuscated the identities of interviewees via pseudonyms, made alterations in the specifics of individual stories to remove any potentially identifying information, and did not name towns and farms where the storytellers work and reside. In the case of textual ethnographic narratives this alone would have been adequate. However, since *El Viaje* involved the creation of visual ethnographic narrative in the form of comics, these same principles needed to extend into the realm of visual representation as well. The use of traditional visual storytelling tools in ethnography—photographs, film, and video—often create challenges to maintaining anonymity of research partners. Unlike these tools, cartooning allows for a tailored visual presence that can be employed in conjunction with standard textual approaches, resulting in an anonymized narrative with strong visual components.

Wadle (2012) and two works she cites, Bartoszko, Leseth, Birgitte and Ponomarew (2010) and Atkins (n.d.) highlight the power of comics to bring anonymized visual representation to ethnography. Bartoszko et al. also reflect on the need to balance visual and narrative anonymization in ways that not only protect research partners, but also respect the integrity of their reported experience, "Just as in written ethnography, we have manipulated some situations so as to anonymize the informants. This process was carried out with the same level of precision and ethical consideration as would be performed with written ethnography. Our goal was to tell a trustworthy story and, thus, present trustworthy scientific result (sic)" (Bartoszko et al: 8).

In *El Viaje Más Caro* we addressed these factors as a facet of our larger collaborative praxis, inviting storytellers into the process of determining how they were visually represented as individuals, and how cartoonists rendered the places through which they moved. In the case of individual representation, cartoonists and project coordinators communicated with storytellers whenever possible to have them weigh in on how they would appear. While many storytellers did not have strong feelings on the matter, some did offer their perspectives ranging from general observations, "I look like a regular Mexican guy" to providing more specific direction to cartoonists about how they would prefer—or not prefer—to be represented. A point of consensus among storytellers was that they wanted to be represented as people rather than anthropomorphic animals or stick figures. Regarding anonymized environments, the project worked to set narratives in generic farmscapes that could not be tied to any particular location. Repeated across the stories are scenes featuring large industrial milking barns, fields of corn and hay, and scattered farm machinery whose renditions epitomize the power of cartooning to express the *sense* of something without needing to be specific in order to do so. Furthermore, these generic landscapes embody well the industrial nature of contemporary dairy farming in Vermont, and their facelessness is a reflection of the landscape in which these workers live and labor.

As noted above, these are just two aspects of the intersection of comics and ethnographic praxis that emerged through our work on *El Viaje Más Caro*, and as we plodded along in our efforts we stumbled over many other questions and challenges related to comics, health care and ethnography. One key consideration involved the ongoing need to balance the vital, applied health care goals of the project with the ethics and methods of ethnographic engagement. On one side we sought to create comics that addressed distinct categories of health care-related themes identified by the providers on the team—themes that emerged based on clinical interactions, and included topics such as loneliness, isolation, trauma, substance abuse among others. But what if the categories identified by our health care providers did not fully align with the data contained in the narratives recorded by the ethnographers? What if, through the process of ethnographic inquiry, we determined that the workers felt other issues related to their circumstances were more pressing? Whose perspectives do we privilege?

We also wrestled with the complexity of textual representation of oral speech, a challenge compounded by perceptions and biases in relation to regional and class-based variation in spoken Spanish, dialect, translation and re-translation. As noted above, the workers targeted by the project come from across Mexico and Central America and, for many, Spanish is a second language. Should we, as interlocutors, standardize the Spanish spoken by our research partners for the sake of a broader comprehensibility that might further our applied healthcare goals? Should we honor their individual ways of speaking at the risk of highlighting regional and class differences and potentially eliciting conscious and unconscious bias among Spanish-speaking readers? Furthermore, what constitutes "standard" Spanish and who is the arbiter of what makes it so? Add to this implications surrounding what it means to have non-Spanish speaking cartoonists work with translated text to begin with, and readers can develop a sense of some of the processes we worked through as the project unfolded.

Finally, what are the implications of drawing in relation to reflexivity and subjectivity? Due to the long-standing cultural perceptions of the subjectivity of visual art, is drawing *innately* reflexive in ways that differ from other modes of ethnographic representation— including text? And what more is there to learn? As Kuttner, Sousanis and Weaver-Hightower (2018) point out, comics represent an emerging medium for presenting scholarly research. Ethnographers are still at the very beginning of realizing the potentials and pitfalls of an ethnographic approach to cartooning, and we are happy that our efforts, in our own small way, can potentially contribute to the emerging discussion surrounding visual art and ethnographic narrative, particularly in how it intersects with graphic medicine.

Works Cited

Afonso, Isabel and M. J. Ramos. "New graphics for old stories. Representation of local memories through drawings." *Working Images: Visual Research and Representation in Ethnography*. Eds. Pink, L. Kürti, and A. I. Afonso, 72-90. London: Routledge, 2004.

Arcury, Thomas A., and Sara A. Quandt. "Delivery of Health Services to Migrant and Seasonal Farmworkers." *Annual Review of Public Health* 28 (1) (2007): 345–63. https://doi.org/10.1146/annurev.publhealth.27.021405.102106

Atkins, Michael. The Dark Side of the Village. Nd. https://comicsforum.files.wordpress.com/2012/02/dark-side-of-the-village.pdf (Accessed 2018-04-26)

Bartoszko, Aleksandra, Anne Birgitte Leseth and Marcin Ponomarew. "Public Space, Information Accessibility, Technology and Diversity at Oslo University College." 2010. https://anthrocomics.wordpress.com/ (Accessed 2019-09-19)

Bechdel, Alison. *Fun Home: A Family Tragicomic*. Mariner Books. NY, 2007.

Causey, Andrew. ""You've got to draw it if you want to see it": Drawing as an Ethnographic Method." Teaching Culture. 2015. http://www.utpteachingculture.com/youve-got-to-draw-it-if-you-want-to-see-it-drawingas-an-ethnographic-method/ (Accessed 2018-04-26)

Causey, Andrew. *Drawn to See: Drawing as an Ethnographic Method*. Toronto: University of Toronto Press, 2019.

Chute, Hilary. *Disaster Drawn: Visual Witness, Comics, and Documentary Form*. Harvard University Press, Cambridge, MA, 2016.

Crowther, Gillian. "Fieldwork Cartoons." *Cambridge Journal of Anthropology*. 14(2) (1990):57-68.

Crowther, Gillian. "Fieldwork Cartoons Revisited." Teaching Culture. 2015. http://www.utpteachingculture.com/fieldwork-cartoons-revisited/ (Accessed 2018-04-26)

Galman, Sally. *Shane, The Lone Ethnographer: A Beginner's Guide to Ethnography*. Lanham, MD: AltaMira Press, 2007.

Galman, Sally. "The truthful messenger: visual methods and representation in qualitative research in education." *Qualitative Research* 9 (2) (2009): 197-217.

Galman, Sally. *The Good, the Bad, and the Data: Shane the Lone Ethnographer's Basic Guide to Qualitative Data Analysis*. New York: Routledge, 2017.

Getz, Trevor R. and Liz Clarke. *Abina and the Important Men: A Graphic History*. New York: Oxford University Press, 2015.

Hamdy, Sherine, Coleman Nye, Sarula Bao and Caroline Brewer. *Lissa: A Story about Medical Promise, Friendship, and Revolution*. New York: University of Toronto Press, 2017.

Harrison, Jill, Sarah Lloyd, and Trish O'Kane. "Overview of Immigrant

Workers on Wisconsin Dairy Farms." *Changing Hands: Hired labor on Wisconsin Dairy Farms Briefing No. 1.* UW-Madison Program on Agricultural Technology Studies, 2009.

Hoffmann-Dilloway, Erika. 2016a. Chatting While Water Skiing, Pt. 1. Teaching Culture.
http://www.utpteachingculture.com/chatting-while-waterskiing-part-1/ (Accessed 2019-12-10)

Hoffmann-Dilloway, Erika. 2016b. Chatting While Water Skiing, Pt. 2. Teaching Culture.
http://www.utpteachingculture.com/chatting-while-waterskiing-part-2/ (Accessed 2019-12-10)

Hoffmann-Dilloway, Erika. 2016c. Chatting While Water Skiing, Pt. 3. Teaching Culture.
http://www.utpteachingculture.com/chatting-while-waterskiing-part-3/ (Accessed 2019-12-10)

Ingold, Tim. (Ed.). *Redrawing Anthropology*. London: Routledge, 2011.

Ingold, Tim. "Toward an Ecology of Materials." *Annual Review of Anthropology* 41 (1) (2012): 427–42.

Kandel, William. *Profile of Hired Farmworkers, a 2008 Update* Washington, DC Economic Service. 2008.
https://www.ers.usda.gov/publications/pub-details/?pubid=46041 (Accessed 2020-01-06)

Kuttner, Paul J., Nick Sousanis and Marcus B. Weaver-Hightower. "How to Draw Comics the Scholarly Way: Creating Comics-Based Research in the Academy." *Handbook of Arts-Based Research*. Ed. Leavy, Patricia, 396-422. New York: Guilford Press, 2018.

Madison, D. Soyini. *Critical Ethnography: Method, Ethics, and Performance*. Thousand Oaks, CA, 2019.

Mares, Teresa. *Life on the Other Border*. Oakland: University of California Press, 2019.

McCloud, Scott. *Understanding Comics: The Invisible Art*. William Morrow, NY, 1994.

Parsons, Bob. "Vermont's Dairy Sector: Is There a Sustainable Future for the 800 Lb. Gorilla?" Opportunities for Agriculture Working Paper Series, Vol. 1, No. 4. Burlington: University of Vermont

Center for Rural Studies, 2010.

Radel, Claudia, Birgit Schmook, and Susannah McCandless. . "Environment, Transnational Labor Migration, and Gender: Case Studies from Southern Yucatan, Mexico and Vermont, USA." *Population and Environment* 32, nos. 2–3 (2010): 177–97.

Ruby, Jay. *Picturing Culture: Explorations of Film and Anthropology.* 2000. University of Chicago Press, Chicago, 2000.

Sacco, Joe. *Palestine.* Fantagraphics, Seattle, W, 2001. http://www.fantagraphics.com/palestine/ (Accessed 2020-01-06)

Satrapi, Marjane. *Persepolis: The Story of a Childhood.* Pantheon, NY, 2003. (Translated edition)

Shea, Erin. Personal Communication. 2013.

Southern Poverty Law Center. "Injustice on Our Plates: Immigrant Women in the U.S. Food Industry." 2010. https://www.splcenter.org/sites/default/files/d6_legacy_files/do wnloads/publication/Injustice_on_Our_Plates.pdf

Spiegelman, Art. *Maus: A Survivor's Tale.* Pantheon, NY, 1986.

Taussig, Michael. *I Swear I Saw This.* University of Chicago Press, Chicago, 2011.

Theodossopoulos, Dimitrios. *Solidarity: a graphic ethnography.* 2015. https://imaginative-ethnography.com/solidarity-a-graphic-ethnography/ (Accessed 2020-01-06)

Venkataramani, Chitra. *Trachyte.* 2015. http://imaginativeethnography.org/imaginings/comics/trachyte/ (Accessed 2020-01-06)

Vermont Dairy Promotion Council. *Milk Matters: The Role of Dairy in Vermont.* 2015. http://vermontdairy.com/wp-content/uploads/2015/12/VTD_MilkMatters-Brochure_OUT-pages.pdf (Accessed 2020-01-06)

Villarejo, Don, David Lighthall, Daniel Williams III, Ann Souter, Richard Mines, Bonnie Bade, Steve Samuels, Stephen McCurdy. *Access to Heatlh Care for California's Hired Farm Workers: A Baseline Report.* California Program on Access to Care, University of California, 2001.

http://citeseerx.ist.psu.edu/viewdoc/download?
doi=10.1.1.452.89&rep=rep1&type=pdf

Villarejo, Don. "The Health of U.S. Hired Farm Workers." *Annual Review of Public Health* 24 (1) (2003): 175–93.
https://doi.org/10.1146/annurev.publhealth.24.100901.140901

Wadle, Hannah. "Anthropology goes Comics." Comics Forum. 2012.
https://comicsforum.org/2012/02/03/anthropology-goes-comics-by-hannah-wadle/ (Accessed 2020-01-06)

Walrath, Dana. *Aliceheimer's: Alzheimer's Through the Looking Glass.* Penn State University Press, 2016.

Wolcott-MacCausland, Naomi. *Vermont Dairy Farms and Bridges to Health.* Programmatic Report. Saint Albans: University of Vermont Extension, 2017.

———. "BTH Data." September 21, 2017.

Wolcott-MacCausland, Naomi and Erin Shea. Personal Communication. 2016

Wright, Lucy. "Ethnographics." 2018.
https://www.vermontfolklifecenter.org/fieldnotes/culture-through-comics-wright (Accessed 2020-01-07)

CREDITS

Our storytellers use pseudonyms to protect the privacy and security of people involved.

A New Kind of Work

Story by Delmar
Interview by Teresa Mares
Translated by Ammy Martinez
Artwork by Tillie Walden
Proofread by Sara Stowell

Painful to Remember

Story by José
Interview by Chris Kokubo
Translated by Chris Kokubo & Julia Grand Doucet
Artwork by Marek Bennett
Proofread by Magnolia O.

It's Worth It

Story by Gregorio
Interview by Julia Grand Doucet & Marie Vasitis
Translated by Marie Vasitis
Artwork by Kevin Kite

The Most Important Love of Every Woman...

Story by Guadalupe
Interview by Chris Kokubo & Julia Grand Doucet
Translated by Cooper Couch
Artwork by Iona Fox
Proofread by Diego Galan Donlo

Far From My Family

Story by Carlos
Interview by Teresa Mares & Julia Grand Doucet
Translated by Olivia Raggio
Artwork by Kane Lynch
Proofread by Roberto Veguez

Suffering to Come Here

Story by Rubén
Interview by Chris Kokubo & Julia Grand Doucet
Translated by Nathan Shepard
Artwork by Teppi Zuppo
Proofread by Roberto Veguez

Algo Adentro / Something Inside

Story by El Migrante de Hidalgo
Interview by Teresa Mares & Julia Grand Doucet
Translated by Susan Stone & Marek Bennett
Artwork by Marek Bennett (comics) &
            El Migrante de Hidalgo (paintings)

In Your Hands

Story by Jesús
Interview by Julia Grand Doucet & Josh Lanney
Translated by Marie Vasitis
Artwork by John Carvajal

You Will Be Accepted

Story by Daniel
Interview by Julia Grand Doucet & Raul Terrones
Translated by Raul Terrones
Artwork by Teppi Zuppo

A Heart Split in Two

Story by Juana
Interview by Estafania Puerta
Translated by Estafania Puerta
Artwork by Michael Tonn
Proofread by Roberto Veguez

The Best Thing

Story by Gustavo, Julia, & Alexis
Interview by Teresa Mares & Julia Grand Doucet
Translated by Susan Stone
Artwork by Angela Boyle
Proofread by Roberto Veguez

One Suffers to Provide for the Family

Story by Pablo & Riley
Interview by Naomi Wolcott-MacCausland
Translated by Naomi Wolcott-MacCausland
Artwork by Rick Veitch (a Eureka Comics Production)

It Wasn't Our Plan

Story by Ana
Interview by Jessie Mazar & Teresa Mares
Translated by GMR Transcription
Artwork by Glynnis Fawkes

Now That I Have My License

Stories by Piero, Saul, Olivia, & Paco
Interview by Naomi Wolcott-MacCausland
Translated by GMR Transcription & Marek Bennett & Julia Grand
Doucet & Naomi Wolcott-MacCausland
Artwork by Marek Bennett

The Two of Us Together (Mexican American)

Story by Felix & Alejandro
Interview by Naomi Wolcott-MacCausland
Translated by Naomi Wolcott-MacCausland, Sebastian Castro, &
Roberto Veguez
Script by William Woodcock, Jr.
Artwork by Greg Giordano
Proofread by Julia Grand Doucet & Roberto Veguez

Language Is Power

Story by Carlos & Bob
Interview by Julia Grand Doucet
Translated by GMR Transcription
Artwork by Ezra Veitch
Proofread by Julia Grand Doucet

How Do You Explain This?

Story by Ana Teresa
Interview by Julia Grand Doucet
Translated by C. Alicia Rodriguez
Artwork by Sashwat Mishra
Proofread by C. Alicia Rodriguez

School of Life

Story by Ponciano
Interview by Teresa Mares & Jessie Mazar
Translated by Jessie Mazar
Artwork by Michelle Sayles
Proofread by Naomi Wolcott-MacCausland & Marita Canedo

What I've Planted Here

Story by Lara
Interview by Naomi Wolcott-MacCausland
Translated by Naomi Wolcott-MacCausland
Artwork by Tillie Walden

Special thanks to:

MK Czerwiec

Christopher Kaufman Ilstrup

Ximena Mejia

Kaitlin Thomas

University of Vermont Humanities Center

Vermont Community Foundation

Vermont Farm Health Task Force

Vermont Humanities Council

All the backers of this edition's Kickstarter

& especially

All the immigrant farmworkers
who help produce the food we eat.

CPSIA information can be obtained
at www.ICGtesting.com
Printed in the USA
FSHW010719150521